THE HISTORY OF CALIFORNIA COMMUNITY COLLEGE WRESTLING

1957-2024

Compiled and Edited by
MIKE STRICKER

JANAWAY PUBLISHING
Santa Maria, California

The History of California Community College Wrestling
1957-2024

Copyright © 2025 by Mike Stricker

ALL RIGHTS RESERVED.
No part of this publication may be reproduced, stored in a retrieval
system, or transmitted in any form or by any
means whatsoever, whether electronic, mechanical,
magnetic recording, or photocopying, without the
prior written approval of the Copyright holder
or Publisher, excepting brief quotations
for inclusion in book reviews.

Published by:

Janaway Publishing, Inc.
Santa Maria, California 93454
www.janawaypublishing.com
(805) 925-1952

2025

ISBN: 978-1-59641-488-4

Cover Photo: Bruce Burnett, with his back to the camera, with Joe Nigos and Coach Bruce Pfutzenreuter of Bakersfield College receiving the 1969 State Championship Trophy – Burnett and Nigos were two-time State Champions.

Made in the United States of America

Table of Contents

Dedication I
Introduction II

Section I: CCCAA State Wrestling Championships

State 1957-2024 (Organized by Year and Date of Tournament) 1
    Photo – 1980 & 1981 State Champions 27
    Photo – 1990 State Champion 39
    Photo – 1992 & 1993 State Champions 42
    Photo – 1995 & 1996 State Champions 46
    Photo – 1998 & 1999 State Champions 51
    Photo – 2004 (various weight categories, BC Champions) 58
    Photo – 2008 – 2009 Individual Champions 65
    Photo – 2010 – 2011 Individual Champions 68
    Photo - 2022 State Champions (Fresno City) 80

Section II: CCCAA Regional Wrestling Championships

Regional 1962-2024 (Organized by Year and Date of Tournament) 83
    Photo - 1963 North Central Regional Championship 86

Credits 243

DEDICATION

This book is dedicated to a man who not only was an outstanding coach but an outstanding educator, spending a large part of his life supporting and helping student-athletes. Hall of Fame Wrestling Coach Bruce Pfutzenreuter - South Bakersfield High School and Bakersfield College

Bruce Pfutzenreuter started the wrestling program at South Bakersfield High School. From 1957 to 1964, he had an outstanding record of 74 and 14 dual record and coached seven CIF "Valley" Champions. While at South he was an Assistant Football Coach, Head Wrestling Coach, Head Track Coach, Department Chair and Counselor.

He coached Bakersfield College from 1964 to 1985 with a dual meet record of 264 and 81 with 2 ties - 3 undefeated dual meet seasons. Coached 30 Tournament Championships Teams, 1969 State Champions, 3 seconds, 3 thirds and his teams placed in top 10 of the state 15 times - 18 individual state champions, 67 state place winners, coached 199 individual tournament champions, 7 Regional Tournament Championships, 7 seconds, 4 thirds, with 41 individual Champions, 7 Conference Tournament Championships, 9 seconds, with 61 individual champions. He coached 3 World Team Members, 1 National AAU Champion, 4 Division II Champions, 22 Division II place winners, 5 Division l place winners and 1 alternate US Olympic Team.

In Coach Pfutzenreuter years at Bakersfield College he was an Assistant Football Coach, Head Wrestling Coach, Department Chair and Athletic Academic Counselor.

Recognition:

1969 Community College Coach of the Year - nominated 14 times
President of the Community College Coaches 3 years
Inducted into the California Wrestling Hall of Fame 2000
Inducted into the National Wrestling Hall of Fame California Chapter 2002
Inducted into the Bob Elias Kern County Sports Hall of Fame 2005
Inducted into the South Bakersfield High School Hall of Fame 2015

INTRODUCTION

Over the last three years, I have spent countless hours researching the rich history of California Community College Wrestling-Junior College Wrestling. In this book I have compiled the results of the four regional state qualifiers; North Regional, North Central Regional, South Regional and South Central Regional.

In 1992, The California Community College Athletic Association (governing body) reduced the state qualifiers down to North Regional and South Regional. Along with compiling a large part of the qualifiers, I have compiled the California State Championships from 1957 to 2024.

My research of the CCCAA or Junior College Wrestling has allowed me to share the rich wrestling history and bring forth the proud tradition of California wrestling. It has produced NCAA wrestling champions and numerous wrestlers who have competed and captured victories at the highest level of competition.

Mike Stricker
Bakersfield, CA
2025

ABOUT THE AUTHOR

Mike Stricker has made numerous contributions to the sport of Wrestling through his life. As a founding executive board member and CEO of the Coyote Club, an amateur wrestling support group established in 1986, Stricker has led the organization in raising over $4 million in the last 39 years to support the "the world's oldest sport." In addition, he serves on various committees and associations, including the committees responsible for having his hometown of Bakersfield the home of state wrestling championships. Stricker was a founding member and officer of Kern County Wrestling Association from 1974 to 1984. He is an inductee of the California Wrestling Hall of Fame, the California Chapter of the National Wrestling Hall of Fame, and the South Bakersfield High Hall of Fame.

Stricker has been a competitor as a youth in high school and college, a wrestling referee, and a youth high school and college coach, and continues to support the sport as a fan, booster and fundraiser. In 2000, Stricker was honored with the prestigious Irv Olinger Award by the California Wrestling Coaches Association at the state wrestling championships in Stockton. In 2024 at the 23rd Annual California Wrestling Hall of Fame banquet, he was honored by being presented with the Lynn Dyche Legacy Award.

His 30-year career began at Chico State under coaching legend Dick Trimmer. Stricker went on to coach with some of the finest coaches in the history of the Central Section, including Joe Seay, Art Chavez, Bob Lathrop and Eugene Walker.

Stricker resides in Bakersfield with his wife Lynn. He has two sons, who he is immensely proud of. Ty, who wrestled at South High and Bakersfield College and was the Head Coach for West High and North High, and Tad, who wrestled at South High and Oklahoma State University and was the Head Coach at Loara High in Anaheim and Assistant Coach at Servite High School. Stricker is a board member of the California Hall of Fame, an Ad Hoc committee member of the California Chapter of the National Hall of Fame and on the Board of Directors of the Bakersfield Jockey Club.

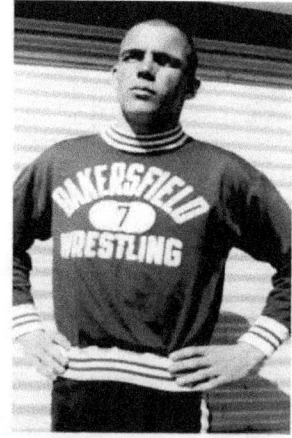

Mike Stricker – Bakersfield College 1963

SECTION I

*CCCAA STATE
WRESTLING CHAMPIONSHIPS*

1957 CCCAA State Wrestling Championships
El Camino College

118

123

Richard Fernandez-Modesto

130

137

147

157

167
G W Wingo-Modesto
　　Moore-Fresno

177

190

Heavyweight

Most Outstanding Wrestler
G W Wingo-Modesto
Coach of the Year
Bob Smith-San Bernadino

Team Scores
1 San Bernadino
　El Camino
　Fresno
4 Modesto
　Sequoias

GW Wingo Fall :05 Ray Lombari

Results from the Modesto Bee

1958-59 CCCAA State Wrestling Championships
March 13-14, 1959 Santa Ana College

115
Don Clark-San Bernardino
Dale Deffner-El Camino
Larry Nehring-Fresno
    Daly-Chaffey

123
Frank Rodriguez-Fresno
Neil Yoshida-Reedley
Claude Burnett-LA City
    Richardson- Modesto

130
Foster Johns-El Camino
    Keith-Santa Ana
Harold Des Jardins-Modesto
    Steiner-LA City

137
Jim Moore-Fresno
Jerry Pamp-San Bernardino
    Wright-Modesto
    Mossinger-Mt. SAC

147
Hank Lomax-Chaffey
Frank Addleman-El Camino
    Cook-San Diego
    Hemphill-San Bernardino

157
Jerry Kirkhart-Fresno
Kroecker-Mt. SAC
    Miller-San Bernardino
    Walltower-San Diego

167
Bob Moore-Fresno*
    Reynolds- Mt. SAC
    Easley-LA City
    Overman-Chaffey

177
John Standich San Bernard
    Rebeck-Orange Coast
    Strasngio-Modesto
    Wamhof-Fresno

191
Ken Roberts-Modesto
Wayne Adkins-El Camino
Aaron Oliverson-San Bernar
    White-Chaffey

Heavyweight
Warren Roberts-Modesto
Lori Belger-El Camino
    Oliverson-San Bernard
    Luiz-Mt. SAC

Most Outstanding Wrestler
Bill Moore-Fresno

Coach of the year
1957-58 Bob Smith-San Bernadino
1958-59 Hans Wiedenhoefer Fresno

Team Scores
1	San Bernardino	62
1	Fresno	62
3	El Camino	43
4	Modesto	36
5	Mt. San Antonio	35
6	Chaffey	26
7	Orange Coast	25
8	LA City	17
9	San Diego	10
9	Santa Ana	10
11	Reedley	8

92 Wrestlers, 15 schools

1959-1960 CCCAA State Wrestling Championships

118
Dale Deffner El Camino

123
Cisco Andrade Cerritos *

130
Bob Combs San Bernadino

137
Jim Moore Fresno

147
Chuck Booth Cerritos

157
Jerry Pamp San Bernadino

167
John Bell LA City

177
Paul Sallinger Cerritos

191
Allan Elliot Modesto

Heavyweight
Aaron Oliverson San Bernadi

Most Outstanding Wrestler
Cisco Andrade Cerritos

Team Results
1 San Bernadino
2
3

Results from the CCCAA Web Site

1960-61 CCCAA State Wrestling Championships
March 10-11, 1961 El Camino College

115
Roy Stucky-Fresno
    Davies-San Bernardino
    Watanable-El Camino
    Dan Ruiz-Bakersfield

123
Larry Nehring-Fresno
    Richard-San Bernardino
    Skow-Cerritos
    Harris-El Camino

130
Eddie Davies-Fresno
    Lucas-San Bernardino
    Arnold-El Camino
    Lewis-Mt. San Antonio

137
Sam Huerta-Modesto 6-3
    Horan-Orange Coast
    Payne-San Bernardino
    Michael-Citrus

147
Dennis O'Connell-Modest 6-4
    Becker-Santa Ana
    Snyder-San Bernardino
    Booth-Cerritos

157
Gary Scrivens-LA City
Dave Stitt-Modesto
    Pollack-San Bernardino
    Jones-Riverside

167
Errol Johansen-Fresno
    Goedker-San Bernardino
    Bressler-Sequoias
Larry Carpenter-Bakersfield

177
Charles Tribble-S Bernardin*
Don Nelson-Fresno
Roy Rea-Modesto
Willard Roberson-Bakersfield

191
Allan Elliot-Modesto 5-3
    Johnson-LA City
    Christian-San Bernardino
    Maus-El Camino

Heavyweight
Earl Corley-Bakersfield F 1:05
Doug Stiles-Modesto
    Sagouspe-Chaffey
    Royer-El Camino

Most Outstanding Wrestler
Charles Tribble-San Bernardino

Coach of the Year
Bob Smith-San Bernadino

Team Scores

1	San Bernardino	87
2	Modesto	68
3	Fresno	65
4	El Camino	36
5	Bakersfield	24
5	LA CITY	24
7	Chaffey	15
8	Cerritos	12
9	Orange Coast	10
10	Sequoias	9
11	Riverside	8
12	Mt. SAC	7
13	Citrus	3
14	Palomar	1

Career record
Earl Corley 20-0

Bob Smith- San Bernardino
1953-1975, His first team was 1955-56, Coached 7 State Championships Teams, 7 Regional, 14 Conference Championships Teams were 96-0, Coaching Record 183-18-3, Named Coach of the Year 6 Times, Coached 22 Induvial State Champions, 5 All-Americans, One of the Founding Fathers of the State Championships.

1961-62 CCCAA State Wrestling Championships
March 9-10, 1962 Cerritos College

115
Jess Cuevas-S Mateo Dec
Jim DeMille-Mt. SAC

123
Larry Nissen-O Coast Default

130
Aurelio Andrade-Cerritos*
Rich Garcia Phoenix

137
Mike Ruiz-S Mateo Decision
John Arnold-El Camino

147
Don Holt-El Camino
Don Matson
Drew Washington-Bakfld
Paul Flimidc-Phoenix

157
Bill Lung-Fresno
Rahim Jabawnwid Fullerton

Jim Bridger-Bakersfield

167
Don Nelson-Fresno
Jim Sparks Mt. SAC

177
Claude Potts-San Bernardino
Sheldon Bromberg-LA City

191
Willard Roberson-Bakfld 3-2
Jay Johnson-LA City

Heavyweight
Joe Aquino-Fresno Fall
Carl Schroeder San Bernadin

Dean Sensenbaugh Modesto, One of the founding fathers of California State Junior College Wrestling Championships, 1957-1985, 374-78-2, Northern California Coach of the Year 12 Times.

Career Records
Drew Washington 26-8
Willard Roberson 20-4
Season Record
Mike Ruiz 17-5
Aurelio Andrade Cerritos undefeated in five years of wrestling

Most Outstanding Wrestler
Aurelio Andrade-Cerritos
Coach of the Year
Han Wiedenhoefer-Fresno

Team Scores
1	Fresno	82
2	San Bernardino	46
3	El Camino	40
4	Phoenix College	28
5	Orange Coast	33
6	Bakersfield	32
7	San Mateo	31
8	Cerritos	28
9	Mt. San Antonio	22
10	Fullerton	20
11	Modesto	16
12	Cabrillo	13
13	College of Sequoias	12
14	LA City	10
15	Pierce	6
15	San Jose	6
17	San Diego	4
18	Chaffey	3
18	Palomar	3
20	Imperial	2
21	Antelope Valley	0
21	Citrus	0
21	Riverside	0

22 Teams – 144 Wrestlers

1962-63 CCCAA State Wrestling Championships
December 8-9, 1963 Bakersfield College

115
Mike Remer-Chabot
Jess Cuevas-San Mateo
Steve Calhoun-S Western 3-0
George Lopez-San Berdo

123
Dave Hollinger-Fullerton 11-2
Bob Janko-San Berdo
Mario Marquez-Hartnell 6-2
Marshall Alcarez-Fresno

130
Larry Nissen-Orange Coas 7-2
Sam Garcia-El Camino
Lennis Cowell-Diablo Vall 6-1
Tom Warner-San Diego

137
Mike Ruiz-San Mateo 6-3
Chuck Fenton-Bakersfield
Ron Von Kaenel-Riverside
Dave Hernandez-San Berdo

147
Don Holt-El Camino 2-1
Steve Carranza-San Jose
Cy Lucas-Foothill 11-4
George Taylor-San Berndo

157
John Sowden-El Camino 4-2
Laverne Carradine-Laney
Sam Cerecres-San Bernadino
Pete Delis-Bakersfield

167
Bob Anderson-El Camino 5-2
Jim Wilson-Fullerton
Terry Wigglesworth-Dieblo*
Joe Giulian-San Jose

177
Claude Potts-San Berd F3:50
Sheldon Bromberg-Cerritos
Fred Aiken-San Diego*
Ray Delgado-San Jose

191
Charles Tribble-S Berd F6 :56
Bill Fife-San Mateo
Ned Murphy-Citrus
Dennis Albright-El Camino

Heavyweight
Walt Wenger-S Mateo F 4:32
Bernie Christian-San Bernardi
Roland Fox-Antel Vall Forfeit
Richard Glazer-LA City

Officials
Head Official Stan Panko
Leon Tedder, Joe Incorvaia,
Ray Daugherty, Martin Olavarri

Hans Wiedenhofer- Fresno
City College His teams won two State Championships, 12 individual State Champions, named Coach of the Year in 1959 and 1962, Coach FCC Wrestling for 9 years also coach Football, Track and Golf and served as Athletic Director for a number of years

Most Outstanding Wrestler
Claude Potts-San Bernardino
Coach of the Year
Bob Smith-San Bernadino

Team Scores
1 San Bernardino 79
2 El Comino 60
3 San Mateo 58
4 Fullerton 26
5 Bakersfield 25
6 Orange Coast 22
7 San Diego 20
7 San Jose 20
9 Diablo Valley 18
10 Fresno 17
11 Oakland 14
12 Chabot 13
13 Cerritos 12
13 Antelope Valley 12
15 Foothill 11
16 Modesto 9
17 Citrus 8
17 Hartnell 8
17 LA City 8
17 Southwestern 8
21 Riverside 7
22 Cabrillo 5
23 Grossmont 4
23 Pierce 4
25 Imperial Valley 3
26 Mt. San Antonio 2
27 College of Sequoias 0
27 LA Valley 0
27 Victor Valley 0

Claude Potts 4 Falls
Walt Wenger 4 Falls
Career Record
Pete Delis 36-8
*= Referee Decision

1963-64 CCCAA State Wrestling Championships
March 13-14, 1964 Diablo Valley College

115
Mike Remer-Chabot 6-3
Ron Marquez-Fresno
Rich Tamble-El Camino 5-3
George Lopez-San Berdo
123
Tom McCann-El Camn F 1:14
Dave Bruce-Diablo Valley
Wayne Lenhares-Chab F 5:12
Gene Hess-Bakersfield
130
George Schaefer-Grossm 9-2
Sam Garcia-El Camino
Gabe Rocha-Fresno 7-1
Richard Paramo-San Berdo
137
Paul Stienel-El Camino 2-0
Bob Munger-Imperial Valley
Roger Pickens-Grossmont
Jim Norsworthy-Bakersfield
147
George Taylor-San Berdo 6-3
Dennis Downing-Cerritos
Armando Jacobo-Fresno 5-2
Jack Catton-Riverside
158
Dennis Albright-El Camin 2-0
Pete Delis-Bakersfield
Irv Rosenberg-San Jose 5-2
Laverne Carradine-Oakl City
167
Bob Anderson-El Camino 6-4
Frank Kerby-Fresno
Richard Wittington- Ber 4-3
George Shaner-Imperial Vall

177
Jim Wilson-Fullerton Fall 3:15
Roy Williams-San Bernardino
Larry Wolfe-El Camino 7-4
Fred Aiken-San Diego City
191
Bob Braham-Fullerton 8-7
Woody Knott-Fresno
Tony Costello-Southws F 5:40
Ron Boeger-Diablo Valley
Heavyweight
Walt Wenger-San Mate 13-5
Jim Porter-Oakland City
Buck Deadrich-Chabot 7-4
Bob Hammas-San Diego

Most Outstanding Wrestler
Bob Anderson El Camino
Coach of the Year
Dave Hengsteler El Camino

Team Scores
1 El Camino   88
2 Fresno   54
3 San Bernardino   484
4 Fullerton   33
5 Chabot   32
6 Grossmont   31
7 Bakersfield   25
8 Diablo Valley   21
8 San Mateo   21
10 Oakland City   20
11 San Diego   17
12 Imperial Valley 16
13 Cerritos   15
14 Southwestern   8
15 San Jose   7
16 Riverside   5
16 Hartnell   5
16 Foothill   5
19 Modesto   4
20 Cabrillo   3
21 LA City   2
22 Chaffey   1
22 Santa Ana   1
22 Sequoia   1
22 S J Delta   1
San Francisco, Sierra, Merced, Orange Coast, LA Valley, Victor Valley Victor Valley, All 0

Walt Wenger San Mateo 2 years 7 of 8 matches end in falls

1964-65 CCCAA State Wrestling Championships
March 12-13, 1965 Orange Coast College

115
Rich Tamble-El Camino
Dick Vaughn-San Jose
John Yasuda-Diablo Valley
Ron Marques-Fresno
Shouse San-Mateo
Perales-Chabot

123
Tom McCann-El Camion
Wayne Lenhares-Chabot
Tim Phillips-Orange Coast
Dave Bruce-Diablo Valley
Manuel Villarreal-Bakersfield
   Lawson-Fullerton

130
Norm Dean-El Camino*
John Geyer-Orange Coast
Art Silva-San Jose
Ron Matheson-Diablo Valley
   Trujillo-Mt. SAC
   Cano San-Mateo

137
Tom Hook-Diablo Valley
Gary Loreng-Foothill
Jim Norsworthy-Bakersfield
Ezel Culver-Antelope Valley
Dennis Deliddo-Fresno
Steve Johnson-Cerritos

147
Kent Wyatt-El Camino
Dennis Downing-Cerritos
Robert Hicks-West Valley
Eugene Teasley-Merritt
   Cook-Grossmont
Terry Moreland-Bakersfield

157
Lee Elder-Modesto
Don Apodaca-El Camino
Sylvester Hodges-Merrit Def
Bill Kinnett-Bakersfield
   Powell-Fullerton
   Weathers-Foothill

167
Cy Lucas-Foothill
Joe Widner-S J Delta
Tim Young-Southwestern
Paul Hooper-El Camino
Butler-San Bernardino
Maxwell-Orange Coast

177
Ralph Orr-Chaffey Fall
Rich Whittington-S Borodino
Wayne Partee-Cerritos
Bob Buehler-Foothill
   Fritz-El Camino
   Blickfelt-Chabot

191
Bob Braham-Fullerton
Dan Johnson-Riverside
Jim Palmer-Southwestern
Ron Boeger-Diablo Valley
Tim Cotton-Bakersfield
Buck Deadrich-Chabot

Heavyweight
Nick Carollo-El Camino
Dave Cranford-San Bernardo
Booker Williams-S Diego City
Ben Brase-Fresno
   Stiger-COS
   Shuford-West Valley

Most Outstanding Wrestler
Norm Dean-El Camino
Coach of the Year
Dave Hengsteler-El Camino

Team Scores
1	El Camino	94
2	Diablo Valley	44
3	Foothill	37
4	Bakersfield	27
5	Fresno	26
6	Orange Coast	25
7	Fullerton	24
8	San Bernardino	23
9	Cerritos	22
10	Chabot	20
10	San Jose	20
12	Southwestern	17
13	Merritt	16
14	Chaffey	15
14	West Valley	15
16	Modesto	14
17	Riverside	11

S Diego 10, Delta 10, S Mateo 9, Mt. SAC 9 COS 8, Antelope Valley 6, Grossmont 6, American River 2 Sacramento 2, Merced 1, Victor Valley 1

38 Teams, 173 Wrestlers

1965-66 CCCAA State Wrestling Championships
March 11-12, 1966 Fresno City

115
Roland Garza-Cerritos
Paul Duarte-Orange Coast
Dan Guevara-El Camino
Ruben Ruiz-San Bernardino
John Shinault-Diablo Valley
Fred Contreras-Fresno

123
Robert Hernandez- Sequ 4-3
Art Chavez-Bakersfield
Tim Phillips-Orange Coast
Floyd Davis-San Bernardino
Mike Rizzo- Chabot
Gary Lopez-Diablo Valley

130
Steve Niles-Sacramento
Ed Acosta-El Camino
Al Navarro-S J Delta
Art Silva-San Jose
Richard Neal San Bernardino
Mike McMahon Chabot

137
Mike Brown-Bakersfield
Glen Stenstrom-San Mateo
Carlos Gayton-Fresno
Kirk Alder-El Camino
Gary Lopez-Foothill
John Chuckta-S D Mesa

147
Kent Wyatt-El Camino
Jim Goddard-American River
Steve Johnson-Cerritos
Mike Frazer-Foothill
Rick Alle-Apple-Valley
Harold Dugger-Grossmont

152
Fern Arsenault-Cerritos
Ken Cook-Grossmont
Al Katuin-Fresno
Ted Job-Merced
Roger Drew-San Jose
Bill McMillian-Orange Coast

160
Jim Hodge-Orange Coast
Bob Powell-Orange Coast
Monty Muller-America River
Larry Brewer-Bakersfield
Charles Hovartos-El Camino
Tom Opperman-Fresno

167
Ben Welch-Bakersfield
Rich Davis-Chaffey
Neil Posson-Sequoias
Charles Bishop-Cerritos
Tim Pitman-Grossmont
Greg Hobson-Merced

177
Wayne Partee-Cerritos
Dwight Fritz-El Camino
Joe Barton-Bakersfield
Ray Macedo-Modesto
Joe Hollins-San Bernardino
Don Guinn-Riverside

191
Stan Hackett-Foothill
Steve Nicholas-Fullerton
Glen Engle-El Camino
Art Haskins-Sequoias
Jim Palmer-Southwestern
Barry Schneider-Cerritos

Heavyweight
Nick Carollo-El Camino*
John Sachs-San Bernardino
Rocky Rasley-Bakersfield
John Perez-Merced
Joe Spencer-Gavilan
Steve Hanrahan-Chabot

Career Record
Steve Niles 69-?

Most Outstanding Wrestler
Nick Carollo-El Camino
3 Falls in 4 Matches

Coach of the Year
Dave Hengsteler-El Camino

Team Scores
1	El Camino	78
2	Bakersfield	68
3	Cerritos	59
4	San Bernadino	38
4	Orange Coast	38
6	Sequoias	31
7	Foothill	25
8	Fresno	24
9	Fullerton	23
10	American River	22
11	Chaffey	18
12	Grossmont	14
12	Merced	14
14	San Mateo	13
15	Diablo Valley	11
15	Chabot	11
15	Sacramento	11
18	San Jose	10
19	S J Delta	9
20	Southwestern	8
20	Modesto	8
22	Oakland	6
22	Gavilan	6
22	Merritt	6
25	S D Mesa	5
26	Antelope Valley	4
27	Riverside	2
28	Mira Costa	1
28	LA Valley	1

Laney, Mt. SAC, Pierce, San Diego, Santa Ana, Sierra, West Valley All 0

1966-67 CCCAA State Wrestling Championships
March 10-11, 1967 Southwestern College

115
Terry Hall-San Bernard F 1:01
Ed Moraga-Fresno
Jim Finster-S Diego Mesa 3-1
Jack Serros-Bakersfield
Art Stone-Southwestern 5-4
Alex Docharty-Sacramento

123
Jim Galvan-Rio Hondo Deft
Shep Bloom-Cerritos
Roger LaPointe-San Bern 4-2
Mike Rizzo-Chabot
Richard Ruz-G West Default
Don Ellison-Diablo Valley

130
Chuck Newman-San Bern 6-0
Art Olmos-Foothill
Dan Dean-Santa Ana 2-0
Bob Hall-Cerritos
Katsuji Nerio-Gl West Default
Joe Marquez-Fresno

137
Steve Warren-El Camino 8-4
Bob Richard-Pierce
Russ Simpson-Fresno 5-2
Al Rivera-Santa Ana
Ron Baldwin-Sacrament Deft
Bill Nelson-S D Mesa

145
Gordon Levy-Fullerton Deft
Richard Dees-San Bernardino
Mike Collier-Bakersfield
Mark Racousky Pierce
Pedro Rios-Fresno 5-4
Gary De Baueien-El Camino

152
Curtis Alder-El Camino 3-2
Fern Arsenault-Rio Hondo
Steve Moran San Bernard 7-3
Tom Moule-Sierra
Oliver Wesson-San Mate 5-2
Scott Rehm-Foothill

160
Bob Hicks-Foothill 2-1
Dan Churchill-San Bernardino
Jim West-Cerritos 5-0
Tom Opperman-Fresno
Saul Nava-Chabot 3-2
Bill Kinnett-Bakersfield

167
Pat Farmer-Palomar Fall 7:28
Don Sheldon-San Mateo
Greg Tribble-San Bernadi 4-3
John Hall-Cerritos
Ron Taylor-West Valley 4-0
Walter Thatcher-Southwest

177
Bill Halsey-Cerritos 3-0
Phil Baylis-Chabot
Rich Davis-Chaffey 7-3
Don Lundgrun-Bakersfield
Randy Straphman-S Bern Def
Glen Engle-El Camino

191
Stan Hackett-Foothill* 9-1
Joe Barton-Bakersfield
Paul Weston-Chabot 7-0
John Mendaris-Fresno
Gene Bernard-Cerritos 3-0
Ken Morris-Pierce

Heavyweight
Jeff Smith-Cerritos 4-1
Rocky Rasley-Bakersfield
Ken Oyer-San Bernardin F :52
John Perez-Merced
Dennis Petracer-Amer Riv 5-0
Ric Rosenquist-Foothill

Most Outstanding Wrestlers
Stan Hackett-Foothill and
Terry Hall-San Bernardino

Coach of the Year
Bob Smith-San Bernardino

Team Scores
1 San Bernardino 89
2 Cerritos 67
3 Bakersfield 51
4 Foothill 46
5 Fresno 42
6 El Camino 38
7 Chabot 32
8 Rio Hondo 24
9 Pierce 20
10 San Mateo 19
11 Fullerton 18
12 Golden West 15
13 Santa Ana 14
14 Golden West 13
14 San Diego Mesa 13
16 Merced 9
17 Chaffey 8
17 Sierra 8
19 Sacramento 7
20 Southwestern 6
21 American River 5
21 Diablo Valley 5
23 West Valley 4
24 Modesto 2
24 Mt. SAC 2
24 Cuesta 2
24 Imperial Valley 2
28 Grossmont, Meritt, Orange Coast, Riverside, S J Delta, Sequoias All 1

Career Record
Rocky Rasley 36-11, Bakersfield, Mike Collier 34-9 Bakersfield
Stan Hack

1967-68 CCCAA State Wrestling Championships
March 8-9, 1968 Chabot College

115
Vic Gonzales Sequoias*Fall
Bernie Olmos Foothill
Armand Brett San Mateo 6-4
 Ed Moraga Fresno
Herb Cosme Bakersfield 6-4
Dan Martinez Cypress

123
Terry Hall San Bernardino 4-1
Ray Contreras Fresno
Jim Galvin Rio Hondo 5-2
Karl Herrera Bakersfield
Nash Martinez Riverside
Dave Raptis Cerritos

130
Dan Dean Santa Ana 5-3
Wendell Jefferson Laney
 Verduzco El Camino 9-0
Tony Searing Cerritos
5
6

137
Chuck Newman San Berd 7-1
Jeff Fern Chabot
Bob Richard Pierce 2-1
Brad Druktenis A Hancock
5
6

145
Ron Kenworthy Cerritos 8-5
Rich Slack Foothill
Marty Harris El Camino 5-0
Mike Taylor Diablo Valley
5
6

152
Lee Torres Fresno 5-3
John Norfleet Cerritos
Ray Kaiser Santa Ana
 Wallace Shasta
Ken Wilson Yuba 4-0
Dan McGee Diablo Valley

160
Dan Churchill San Bernad 8-6
Pat McCormick Orange Coast
John Hall Cerritos 8-2
 Miller San Diego Masa
5
6

167
Joe Nigos Bakersfield 7-3
Saul Nava Chabot
Steve Pearson Fullerton 6-4
Dave Brigham De Anza
5
6

177
Dave Reed Pierce 9-1
Jim Shields Cypress
Victor Holloway S Bernar 3-2
 Lucio Redwoods
Charles O'Brian Modesto Fall
Gene Bernard Cerritos

191
Paul Weston Chabot 5-2
Bob Garcia De Anza
Art Haskins Sequoias 14-1
Art Osborn Redwoods
5
6

Heavyweight
Dan Felix El Camino 3-2 OT
Bill Struve Cerritos
Ken Oyer San Bernardino 8-0
Tim Kopitar Diablo Valley
5
6

College of the Redwoods were the Small-College State Champions. To qualify as a Small-College the fulltime enrollment less 2000 Students

Most Outstanding Wrestler
Vic Gonzales Sequoias
Coach of the Year
Bob Smith San Bernardino

Team Scores

1	San Bernardino	80
2	Cerritos	66
3	Fresno	53
4	El Comino	52
5	Chabot	42
6	Bakersfield	33
7	Foothill	31
7	Diablo Valley	31
7	Santa Ana	31
10	Pierce	27
10	Sequoias	27
18	Redwoods	
20	Modesto	9

Others – Cypress, De Anza, Fullerton, Allan Hancock, Laney, Orange Coast, Redwoods, Rio Hondo, S D Mesa, San Mateo, Shasta.

Records
Joe Nigos Bakersfield 34-1
Ken Wilson Yuba 25-7
Dave Reed Pierce 38-1

51 Total Teams in the State Championships.
Over 90 JC Wrestling Teams in California.

1968-1969 CCCAA State Wrestling Championships
March 7-8, 1969 San Bernardino Valley College

115
Ed Oquendo-San Berd 8-3OT
Bernie Olmos-Foothill
Armand Brett-San Mateo 5-3
Herb Cosme-Bakersfield
Dave Raptis-Cerritos
Terry Tamble-El Camino

123
Ray Contreras-Fresno 5-2
Vic Gonzales-Sequoias
Al Gonzales-El Camino 7-1
Bill Harris-Golden West
David Tormori-Diablo Valley
Ken Turner-Cerritos

130
John Norris-El Camino 12-3
Gary Wolt-Butte
Eugene Walker-Bakfld 11-4
George Bigelow-Sacramento
Glenn Warner-Cuesta
Ken Wright-San Mateo

137
Bruce Burnett-Bakfld 6-1
Grant Connell San Mateo
John Zenith-Lassen 4-1
Gabe Rulz-Santa Ana
Ron McCormick-Cerritos
Katsuji Nerio-Golden West

145
Ron Kenworthy-Cerritos 2-1
Brad Duruktenis-A Hancock
Marty Harris-El Camino 4-1
Rich Slack-Foothill
Roger Thomas-LA City Norm
Hale Diablo-Valley

152
Joe Smart-Bakersfield 3-2
Lee Torres-Fresno
Steve Sanchez-Diablo Val 6-0
Al Price-Santa Ana
John Norfleet-Cerritos F 5:07
Don Loflin-Lassen

160
Steve Dildine-San Berdo 13-8
Joe Hall-Pierce
Gordon George-W Valley 2-1
W D Martin-Santa Ana
Wes Williams-Sequoias
Corky Napier-Fresno

167
Joe Nigos-Bakersfield 3-1
Bill Bolar-Chabot
Stock Schleuter-Redwood 8-4
Gorge Maddox-Cerritos
Chancey Turnbow-Con Costa
Ernell Smith San-Bernardino

177
Jim Shields-Cypress* F 6:30
Vic Holloway-San Bernardino
Tom Giempietro-Sequoias
Semas Owen-Merritt 4-2
Charles O'Brien-Modesto
Dave Alexander-Santa Ana

191
Pete Lutz-San Bernardino 6-5
Gary Maiolfi-Cerritos
Frank Lucio-El Camino 3-1
Gene Hansen-Diablo Valley
Jim Schlueter-Redwoods
John Miller-Bakersfield

Heavyweight
Dan Felix-El Camino F 6:03
Jim Robesky-Bakersfield
Ed Galigher-Chabot OT RD
   Bill Trippett
John Johnson-Redwoods
Ernie Pilar-Mt. SAC

College of the Redwoods
Small College Champions

Most Outstanding Wrestler
Jim Shields-Cypress
Coach of the Year
Bruce Pfutzenreuter-Bakersfield

Team Scores
1 Bakersfield	83
2 San Bernadino	67
2 El Camino	67
4 Cerritos	60
5 Fresno	36
5 Sequoias	36
7 Chabot	22
7 Foothill	22
9 Cypress	19
10 Lassen	14
11 Butte	13
11 Pierce	13
13 Hancock	12
13 West Valley	12
15 Golden West	11
16 Cuesta	3

39 Teams

Career Record
Joe Nigos-Bakersfield Season 31-0 Career 52-1
Herb Cosme-Bakersfield 48-16
Lee Torres-Fresno 61-1

Coach Bob Thomson Chabot
1962-69 coached 17 state placers, 14 All-Americans, 4 regionals, 4 conference, championship teams and 3 State Champions, teams won 48 consecutive duals

1969-1970 CCCAA State Wrestling Championships
March 12-13, 1970 Bakersfield College

115
Ed Oquendo-San Berdo 4-3
Danny Kida-Grossmont
Stacy Cody-Cerritos
Terry Purnty-Lassen
Ray Hernandez-Sequoias
Pat Wheeler-West Valley

126
Larry Watanabe-Mt SAC Deft
Antonio Rodriguez-Riverside
Larry Little-Bakersfield
Dave Brunner-Diablo Valley
Harold Jordan-Cerritos
Mike Jauregui-Canada

134
Jim Rivera-Allan Hanc 7-6
Ken Turner-Cerritos
Eugene Walker-Bakersfield
Tom Eckes- Solano
Gary Garcia-Chabot
Pete Gomez-Sequoias

142
Bruce Burnett-Bakfld Fall
Jarrett Williams-Cerritos
Joe Tice-San Diego Mesa
Derry Converse-Santa Jose
Mitch Anderson-So-westrn
Bruce Blanchard-Foothill
Wayne Branstetter-Ventura

150
Pat Burris-Santa Anna 4-3OT
John Hardy-Southwestern
Bob Greco-Fresno
Joe Smart-Bakersfield
Werner Haase-West Valley
Henry MacErnie-El Camino

158
W.D. Martin-Santa Ana 7-5
Norman Hale-Diablo Valley
Bill Drennan-Bakersfield
Greg Mason Redwoods
Mike MacIntyre-El Camino
Ken Berribge-De Anza

167
Lancer Smith-Diablo Vall 8-2
Bill Bolar-Chabot
David Starr-El Camino
Mike Mendez-Fresno
Tom Wenbourne-Grossmont
Larry Miller-San Diego Masa

177
Dave Alexander-Santa An 6-2
Mike O'Brian-Modesto
Ken King-Diablo Valley
Tim Del Toro-Fresno
Wayne Cagle-Bakersfield
Ricard Bacciarini- Al Hancock

191
Jim Schluter-Redwoods Fall
Ben Ohai-Cerritos
John Ming-Sacramento
Doyle Nelms-Porterville
Jim Bishop-Fullerton
Frank Barnhart-Palomar

Heavyweight
Tim Kopitar-Diablo Valley Fall
John Johnson-Redwoods
Dan Graham-Modesto
John Stahl-Riverside
Larry Ramos-Cuesta
Bob Raymond-Golden West

41 Chaffey, Laney, Pierce, Skyline, Ventura all 1

Career Records
Larry Little 51-5 & 28 Falls
Eugene Walker 58-9
Bruce Burnett 55-3
Joe Smart 32-8
Bill Drennan 32-7
All of Bakersfield
Mike O'Brian Modesto 41-3

Season Record
Pat Burris Sata Ana 32-1

Most Outstanding Wrestler
Bruce Burnett-Bakersfield
Coach of the Year
Bob Ericson-Diablo Valley
Team Scores
1 Diablo Valley 70
2 Bakersfield 68
3 Cerritos 54
4 Santa Ana 45
5 Redwoods ** 40
6 Fresno 29
7 Modesto 24
8 Riverside 22
9 El Camino 20
9 Southwestern 20
11 Chabot 18
11 Grossmont 18
11 San Bernardino 18
11 Allan Hancock 18
22 Mt. SAC 15
23 Sacramento 14
24 SD Mesa 12
25 Solano 11
26 Victor Valley 10
27 San Jose 9
27 Porterville 9
29 Lassen 7
29 Sequoias 7
31 Fullerton 5
31 Canada 5
31 Cuesta 5
34 DeAnza 4
35 Palomar 3
35 Foothill 3
37 East LA 2
37 Hartnell 2
37 Golden West 2
37 Santa Monica 2
Total of 51 teams **
** Small-College Champions

1970-71 CCCAA State Wrestling Championships
March 12-13, 1971 El Camino College

115
Stacy Cody-Cerritos 9-4
Allen Gonzalez-El Comino
Glen Maxon-Redwoods 10-9
Eddie Lee Mt. San Antonio
Robert Vargas-San Berdo 5-3
Maurice Howard-Riverside

126
Robert Arballo-Fresno 8-2
Dave Bruner-Diablo Valley
Robert Leininger-Cypress 5-2
David Womack-Golden West
Vic Oquendo-San Berdo 9-2
Marshall Thompson-Mt. SAC

134
Harold Jordan-Cerritos 8-4
Rob Manley-Mt. San Antonio
Dave Giggy-Bakersfield 6-2
Derry Converse-San Jose
Mitch Finney-De Anza F 5:25
Ivan Meadows-Santa Ana

142
Harold Blanchard-Foothill 7-1
Don Wright-Skyline
Burni Molony-Cypress 4-3
Charles Freeman-Fresno
Chris Louisell-Pierce Forfeit
Guy Morrison-Orange Coast

150
Bruno Bicocca-W Valley 5-2
Roger Warner-Diablo Valley
Gary Garcia-Chabot 3-1
Bob Marsella-De Anza
Lonnie Patterson Fresno 10-3
Keith Wecker-American River

158
Bill Long-Mt S Antonio F 3:47
Cliff Hatch-Diablo Valley
John Hardy-Southwester 3-2
Doug Stone-Bakersfield
Bob Curry-Orange Coast 6-5
Tracy Mitchell-Pierce

167
Bert Dalton-Chabot 2-1
Chris Hurchanik-Canada
Malcom Poemoceah-Ful 10-4
Mat Harris-Sacramento
David Starr-El Camino 4-2
Bob Herndon-Bakersfield

177
Dave Osterkamp Solano F :41
Jerry Greer-Bakersfield
Mike Mendez-Fresno 8-3
John Needham-Chabot
Jim Smith-Skyline F 5:10
Jim Bishop-Fullerton

190
Ben Ohai-Cerritos*F :36
Tim Del Toro-Fresno
Keith Smith-Imperial Vall 2-0
Mark Padilla-Bakersfield
Harold Morris-Canada F 5:37
Al Otterman-Santa Ana

Heavyweight
Dave Campbell-Cerritos 3-1
Tom Hazell-El Camino
John Stahl-Riverside 3-0
Dan Hart-American River
Terry Gorman-Chabot 4-2
Alvin Davis-Diablo Valley

Bill Kalivas-Bakersfield College 27-year Coaching Record 208-72-2, Coached 22 Academic All-Americans, 15 State Champions, 38 State Finalist, 75 All-Americans, 122 State Place Winners, 69 Western State Conference Champions, 5 Time Western State Conference Coach of the Year, Team State Champions 2002 Third, 2003 and 2004 Champions, 2005 Second, Nominated 10 Times for Coach of the Year, Honored as Coach of the Year 2003 and 2004.

Most Outstanding Wrestler
Ben Ohai-Cerritos
Coach of the Year
Hal Simonek-Cerritos

Team Scores

1	Cerritos	61
2	Fresno	56
3	Bakersfield	42
3	Chabot	42
5	Mt. San Antonio	41
6	Diablo Valley	40
7	El Camino	32
8	Cypress	21
9	Canada	20
9	Fullerton	20
11	Skyline	18
12	De Anza	17
12	Solano	17
14	Foothill	15
14	Riverside	15
14	West Valley	15
17	American River	13
18	Redwoods	12
19	Imperial Valley	10
19	Southwestern	10
19	Pierce	10
22	Sacramento	9
22	San Bernardino	9
24	San Jose	8
24	Orange Coast	8
26	Santa Ana	6

Hal Simonek – Cerritos
Coached State Championship Team in 1971, Coached 19 individual State Champions, and 55 All-Americans

Career Record
Jerry Greer Bakersfield 49-4
Bert Dalton Chabot 38-5
Chris Hurchanik Canada 47-1

1971-72 CCCAA State Wrestling Championships
March 3-4, 1972 Skyline College

115
Ed Lee-Mt. San Antonio 2-1
Jerry Munoz-San Bernardino
Steve Siroy-Chabot 4-3
Gene Hughes-Fresno
Mitch Steinauer-Grossmo 7-6
Jim Hamada-Palomar

126
George Palmer-Cuesta 4-0
Dave Gonzales-San Jose
Gary Tacket-Imperial Vall 6-0
Alex Gonzales-Solano
Conrad Kauble-El Camino 6-3
Victor Oquendo-San Berdo

134
Paul Strait- Cerritos 6-2
Mike Flook-Cypress
Victor Vorobieff-Mt. SAC 4-3
Simon Flores-Chabot
Eldon Ross-Bakersfield 5-1
Ed Bournaccorsi-Santa Rosa

142
Charles Freeman-Fresn 11-10
Dan MacErnie-El Camino
Brent Jacinto-Chabot 4-2
Bill Amadon-Cerritos
Bob Loflin-Lassen 13-2
Pete Araujo-De Anza

150
Rodger Warner-Diablo Va 6-4
Larry Willeman-El Camino
Spencer Call-Cerritos 5-4
Steve Tirapelle-Am River
Greg Anderson-S J Delta 8-1
Larry Shubat-Yuba

158
Cliff Hatch-Diablo Valley 7-6
Bob Marsella-De Anza
Leif Grunseth Contra Cost 3-1
Doug Porter-Santa Ana
Bill Long Mt. S Antonio F 3:30
Julian Fernandez-Cerritos

167
Brady Hall-Modesto 7-5
Andy Soares-West Valley
Dan Lewis-Orange Coast 3-1
Jay Lawson-De Anza
Ken Kalcevich-Cypress 6-0
Bill Kalivas-Pierce

177
John Needham-Chabt Forfeit
Bret Noon-Foothill
Rich Caldron-San Jose 9-5
Brent Wissenback-Sierra
Tim Bandel-Orange Coast 4-0
Rick Lewis-De Anza

190
Mal Alexander-San Jose 8-2
Doug Holt-De Anza
Harold Morris-Canada 8-2
Gary Ramos-American River
Paul Fritz-Foothill 2-0
Steve Fisher-Riverside

Heavyweight
Tom Hazell-El Camino* 10-2
Bill Van Worth-Bakersfield
Rudy Huerta-Imperial F 3:43
Ron Tate-Hartnell
Jim Kish-Antelope Vly F 3:26
Dan Hart-American River

Records
Mal Alexander 34-8, Tom Hazell 38-2, Steve Siroy 39-3-1, Simon Flores 31-9, Bob Marsella 64-10, John Needham 66-13, Ed Lee 78-6-2, Jerry Munoz 40-2-1, George Palmer 73-7. Dave Gonzales 36-4, Roger Warner 51-0, Larry Willeman 37-3, Cliff Hatch 48-1
Bill Van Worth 47-5 & 37 Falls

Most Outstanding Wrestler
Tom Hazell-El Camino
Coach of the Year
Zack Papachristos-Chabot

Team Scores
1	Chabot	52
2	El Camino	48
3	De Anza	41.5
4	Cerritos	39.5
5	San Jose	39
6	Mt. San Antonio	36
7	Diablo Valley	26
8	Imperial Valley	35.5
9	American River	25.5
10	Fresno	24.5
10	Imperial Valley	25
12	Golden West	24
13	Modesto	23
14	Bakersfield	18.5
15	Orange Coast	18
15	Foothill	18
17	Cuesta	16.5
18	San Bernadino	16
19	Yuba	15.5
19	S D Mesa	15.5
19	West Valley	15.5
22	Canada	11.5
23	Sierra	11
23	Solano	11
25	Antelope Valley	9
26	Palomar	6
26	Lassen	6
28	Grossmont	3
29	Long Beach	2
30	Golden West	1

College of the Redwoods won 47 straight Golden Valley Conference Duals in a row

1972-73 CCCAA State Wrestling Championships
March 2-3, 1973 Fullerton College

118
Steve-Siroy Chabot
Mitch-Steinhauer Grossmont
Jack Serros-Bakersfield 5-3
Bert Gonzales-San Jose
Ken Crumley-Redwoods
Robert Martinez-Antel Valley

126
Robert Arballo-Fresno F 3:35
David Gonzales-San Jose
Carl Slocum-Santa Ana
John Shea-Cerritos
Alex Gonzales-Solano
John Martin-Consumer River

134
Juan Pichardo-Diablo Valley
Ted Wilton-Cypress
Gary Tackett-Imperial Valley
Mike Bertetto-Long Beach
Jeff Ortiz Allan-Hancock
Tom Zehnder-Sacramento

142
Grant Arnold-Modesto
David East-Bakersfield
Brent Jacinto-Chabot
Richard Zarp-Cerritos
Pete Buono-Golden West
Paul LeBlanc-Orange Coast

150
Dennis Bardsley-Santa Rosa*
Ivan Meadows-Santa Ana
Larry Willeman-El Camino
John Noon-Orange Coast
Logan Cox-Redwoods
Tom Rosenthal-Chabot

158
Dan Houchins-Modesto
Leif Grunsetta-Contra Costa
Bob Snowen-San Diego Mesa
R. Johns-Riverside
Jon Leifer-Long Beach
Eusebo Sams-El Camino

167
Chris Anaya-Chabot
Dan Lewis-Orange Coast
Ken Lalcevich-Cypress 5-3
Tony Alvarez-Bakersfield
Dan Buetschi-Modesto
Ken Meffan-El Camino

177
Don Wakefield-Cerritos
Bob Loyst-San Jose City
Ed Spann-Santa Ana
Rick Hale-Diablo Valley
G. Casey-Orange Coast
Gary Allen-Palomar

191
Rich Calderon-San Jose
Paul Schantz-Chabot
Greg Gibson-Shasta
Tim Bandel-Orange Coast
S. Stone-Southwestern
Steve Fisher-Riverside

Heavyweight
Rudy Huerta-Imperial Valley
Mike Henry-Cypress
Randy Hodson-Chabot
Bill Van Worth-Bakersfield
Don Watson-Fresno 4-2
John Sawyer-Cerritos

Career Records
Dennis Bardsley Santa Rosa
59-1 & 40 Falls
Bill Van Worth Bakersfield
41-5 & 37 Falls

Season Records
Jack Serros 22-5, Steve Siroy 32-4, Brent Jacinto 31-2
Chris Anaya 38-4, Tom Rosenthal 40-4-1
College of the Redwoods second in the Small College State Championships

Most Outstanding Wrestler
Dennis Bardsley-Santa Rosa
Coach of the Year
Sam Huerta-San Jose
Team Scores
1 Chabot 73
2 San Jose 53
3 Bakersfield 45
4 Cerritos 43
5 Santa Ana 42
6 Orange Coast 41.5
6 Modesto 41.5
8 Cypress 34
9 Imperial Valley 31
9 Fresno 31
11 Diablo Valley 30
12 Santa Rosa 17.5
13 El Camino 17
14 Shasta 14
16 Long Beach 13
16 Riverside 13
16 Redwoods ** 13
19 Contra Costa 12.5
20 San Diego Mesa 11
21 Golden West 8.5
22 Solano 7
22 Moorpark 7
24 Hancock 5
24 Southwestern 5
26 Palomar 4
26 Consumnes River 4
28 Sacramento 3
28 Antelope Valley 3
30 West Valley 2.5
31 Skyline 2.5
32 Hartnell, SJ Delta, Gavilan, Chaffey, Sierra 2, American River, Butte, Canyons 1

1973-74 CCCAA State Wrestling Championships
March 1-2, 1974 American River College

118
Steve Pivac-Mt SAC 5-2*
Alex Hernandez-Sequoias
Ernest Flores-Fresno
Mike Fleming-Fullerton
Roger Flook-Gavilan
Bob Martinez-Antel Valley

126
Mike Salcido-Cerritos 5-3
Ed Alves-Modesto
Manuel Ibarra-Bakersfield
Ray Yocum-Antelope Valley
John Phillips-Pierce
Mario Lacasse-East LA

134
Frank Gonzales-Santa An 7-6
Terry Martin Mt. San Antonio
Joe Zeller-El Camino
Jerry Tingle-Southwestern
Artemio Flores-Chabot
Greg Hill-De Anza

142
Jim Wood-Santa Ana 13-8
Rich Walke-Modesto
Tom Flores-San Bernardino
Guy Martin-Cuesta
Kenny Lewis-Diablo Valley
Mike Gerton-Chabot

150
Jeff Noon-Orange Coast 6-4
Tom Tice-San Diego Mesa
Kirk McConcie-Santa Ana
Kevin Clark-Grossmont
John Correa-Cypress
Larry Correia-Fresno

158
Brad Johnson Chabot 6-3
Jon Leifer-Long-Beach
Tom Knoblock-Diablo Valley
Chuck Mackey-Cypress
Mike Anderson-Bakersfield
Jeff Jaquot-Santa Ans

Season Records
Ed Alves 29-1
Rudy Burtschi 33-3-1
Rich Walke 33-3

167
Florencio Rocha-Bakfld 5-4
Don Shuler-Santa Ana
Jerry Hoffman-Chabot
Kenny Heidenberger-S Berdo
Dan Burtschi-Modesto
Skip Davies-Solano

177
Rick Hale-Diablo Valley 4-1
Don Wakefield-Cerritos
Jeff Ramona-San Jose City
Dave Hill-El Camino
Chris Anaya-Chabot
Dennis Zabinski-Palomar

191
Mike Bull-Bakersfield 5-1
John Plant-Chabot
Dave Duke-Fullerton
Ed Acosta-Mira Costa
Marty Rodriguez-Dialo Valley
Jim Brazil-Sierra

Heavyweight
Bob Green-Diablo Valley 2-1
Fran Fredette-Moorpark
Tom McClure-S J Delta
Bob Anderson-Shasta
Duane Williams-Bakersfield
Todd Starr-Modesto

Small School Champion
Antelope Valley

Fastest Fall :20
Jerry Stanges-San Jose

Redwoods, Sacramento, Santa Monica, Foothill, Lassen, Merced, Butte, Canada, Chaffey All 0

Career Records
Manuel Ibarra 52-6
Mike Anderson 51-15
Mike Bull 30-2
Season Record
Frank Gonzales 34-0

Most Outstanding Wrestler
Steve Pivar-Mt. San Antonio
Coach of the Year
Frank Addleman-Santa Ana

Team Scores
1	Santa Ana	78.5
2	Bakersfield	70.5
3	Chabot	68
4	Diablo Valley	67
5	Modesto	49.5
6	Mt. San Antonio	38.75
7	Cerritos	33
8	El Camino	25
9	Fullerton	23.5
10	San Bernardino	23
11	Cypress	21.5
12	Orange Coast	19.5
13	Fresno	19
14	Moorpark	18.5
15	Long Beach	15.5
16	San Diego Mesa	15
16	Sequoias	15
16	San Jose	15
19	Antelope Valley	14.5
20	Cuesta	12.5
21	Shasta	11.5
22	Grossmont	11
22	Mira Costa	11
24	Gavilan	8
24	Pierce	8
26	S J Delta	7.5
27	East LA	7
27	Sierra	7
29	DeAnza	6.5
30	Skyline	6
31	Solano	4
31	Palomar	4
33	Santa Barbra	2
33	American River	2
33	West Valley	2
33	Imperial Valley	2
37	Contra Costa	1.5
37	Golden West	1.5
39	Rio Hondo	1
39	Ventura	1
41	Cabrillo	.5

1974-75 CCCAA State Wrestling Championships
March 7-8, 1975 Cerritos College

118
Mike Fleming Fullerton 10-3
Mark Baker Cerritos
Curt Kawabata Chabot 8-3
Brand Wendt Cypress
Ernie Flores Fresno 4-1
Andrew Gonzales San Jose

126
Butch Escalante Vent 4-0 OT
Mike Salcido Cerritos
Ray Yocum Antelope Vall 6-2
Guy Reilly Lassen
Joe Stallworth Chabot 9-3
Frank Sabala Grossmont

134
Frank Gonzales Santa An 7-6
Carlos Rodriguez San Jose
Franc Affentranger Bakfld 7-2
Reynolds Capps Sierra
Tom Gongora Fresno 5-1
Dan Field Palomar

142
Rod Balch Fresno 12-5
Terry Bautista Chabot
Jerry Nobles San Jose 12-8
Steve Thomson Cypress
Mike Harr De Anza 8-2
Spencer Call Cerritos

150
Gordon Cox El Camino 4-3
Bob Rinehart Moorpark
Glen Arenas Mt. SAC F 1:16
Kevin Clark Grossmont
Jim Wood Grossmont 4-3
Dave Edgeworth Antel Valley

158
Dan Rutschke Cypress 2-1 OT
Dusty Clark Butte
Steve Clark Skyline 5-2
Dana Smith De Anza
Randy Lopez Fresno 17-3
Pete Grisali Grossmont

167
Dan Shuler Sant Ana* 6-0
Florencio Rocha Bakfld
Henry Heidbreder S Ber 10-4
Eusebio Sams El Camino
Eddie Lopez Moorpark 2-1
Joe Bracmonte Fresno

177
Jeff Ramona San Jose 7-5
Tony Manning Fresno
Dave Hill El Camino 3-2
Ricard Rose Moorpark
Charles Cacciata Cypres 10-6
Dave Rottenberg Diego Mesa

190
Warren Nikulus Palom F 7:29
Lee Austin Golden Valley
Eric Woosley Redwoods 4-1
Jim Ainlay Cabrillo
Kevin Hustad Cuesta Default
Stuart Felker El Camino

Heavyweight
Chris Wernicke Rio Hond 4-3
Ralph Kuehn Foothill
Wayne Nickerson Paloma 2-0
Greg Metcalf Santa Barbara
Terry Watson Yuba 6-0
Andy Guthrie Cypress

Jim Sylvia College of the Redwoods Coached 7 North Regional Championship Teams, 5 Second place Teams 2 State Champions, 6 All-Americans, Golden Valley Conference Dual Record 95-15, Coaching Record 114-42-2, Coached 23 All-Americans, Coached 4 State Small College Championship Teams.

Career Record
Florencio Rocha 63-4
El Camino 23-3 in Dual Meets

Most Outstanding Wrestler
Dan Shuler Santa Ana
Coach of the Year
Bill Musick Fresno
San Bernardino College
Coach Bob Smith 1955-1975
CCCAA Titles 59,60,61,63,67
14 Conference Titles,
90-0 in Conference Duals,
6 Coach of the Year Awards,
22 State Champions,
53 State Placers,
181-18-3

Team Scores
1 Fresno	63
2 San Jose	56.5
3 Cypress	54
4 El Camino	52
5 Santa Ana	48
6 Palomar	43
7 Moorpark	38
8 Cerritos	34.5
9 Bakersfield	30
10 Grossmont	22.5
11 Ventura	21.5
12 Fullerton	20.5
12 Rio Hondo	20.5
14 Chabot	20
15 Golden West	18
16 Antelope Valley	16.5
16 Foothill	16.5
18 Mt. SAC	15.5
19 Butte	19
20 Redwoods	14
20 Skyline	14

San Bernardino 12, Cabrillo 11.5, Lassen 10.5, Santa Barbra 10.5, S D Mesa 9.5, Cuesta 8.5, Yuba 7, Sequoia 3, Merced 2.5, Santa Rosa 1.5, Diablo Valley 1.5 Orange Coast 1, West Valley 1

1975-76 CCCAA State Wrestling Championships
March 5-6, 1976 West Valley College

118
Joe Gonzales-East LA 5-2
Andy Gonzales-San Jose
Brad Morton-El Camino 7-1
Kevin Smith-Golden West
Jim Hamada-Palomar 13-2
Jim Platts-Antelope Valley

126
Butch Escalante-Vent*F 1:43
Sherwood Miller-Cuesta
Dwight Miller-Foothill 8-1
Vic Yslas-Cypress
Ben Martinez El Camino 11-1
Tad Overmire-Palomar

134
Franc Affentranger Bakfl 14-1
Allen Willeman-El Camino
Reynold Capps-Sierra 7-2
Mark Okoorian-Cypress
Jim Nelson-Solano 9-4
Jack Scruggs-Santa Ana

142
Tom Gongora-Fresn 13-3OT
Joe Lopez-Bakersfield
Leonard-Jacobson Gro F 2:15
Greg-Okoorian Cypress
Tony Gonella-Mt. SAC
Jon Blazei-Moorpark

150
Bill Cripps-El Camino F 4:21
Jon Parreira-Modesto
Jim Matthie-Grossmont 5-3
Don Barrios-Palomar
Jeff Wilton-Cypress 5-3
Robert Clair-San Diego Masa

158
Mike Burgher-Palomar 8-3
Ted Kelly-El Camino
Kevin Hejnal-West Valley 5-4
Ron Shilliday-Orange Coast
Dean Reichenberg-A R13-6
Ken Clark-Grossmont

167
Pete Grisafi-Grossmont 7-1
Tony Fuertsch-Cerritos
Joe Bracamonte-Fresno 3-1
Eddie Lopez-Moorpark
Kirk Poppay-West Valley 7-1
Bill Merriott-San Jose

177
Craig Foster-Cypress 7-6
Rich Blanton-Chabot
Mike Diaz-Modesto 9-1
John Parrish-American River
Frank Lockett-Contra Costa
Andy Huyck-Allan Hancock

190
Eric Woolsey-Redwoods 3-1
Curtis Bledsoe-Chabot
Roy Austin-Cypress 3-1
Andy Lassak-Orange Coast
Kevin Hunstad-Cuesta 10-2
Brent Causey American River

Heavyweight
Dave Shaw-Chabot 7-3
Gene Gonzales-Merced
Scott Moore-Grossmont Fall
Joe De Rosa-Cabrilla
Mike Fox-Redwoods Forfeit
Gary Krigbaum-Modesto

38 Santa Rosa .5
Long Beach, Hartnell, Gavilan, Chaffey, Delta, San Bernardino, Shasta, Sequoias, Yuba, Victor Valley, Butte ALL 0

Small College Champions
Redwoods

Career Records
Franc Affentranger Bakersfield 67-7 & 20 Falls
Butch Escalante Ventura 74-4
Joe Gonzales East LA 48-1

Most Outstanding Wrestler
Butch Escalante-Ventura
Coach of the Year
Dave Hengsteler-El Camino

Team Scores
1	El Camino	76.25
2	Cypress	71
3	Grossmont	63.5
4	Chabot	56
5	Palomar	48.25
6	Modesto	42.5
7	Bakersfield	38.75
8	Fresno	33.5
9	Redwoods	31
10	Cuesta	27.25
11	Amer River	24.25
12	San Jose	24.25
13	Ventura	24
14	West Valley	22.5
15	Orange Coast	20.5
16	East LA	20.25
17	Cerritos	18
18	Merced	17
19	Moorpark	16.5
20	Foothill	14.5
21	Cabrillo	11.5
21	Sierra	11.5
23	Mt. SAC	11
24	Solano	9.5
25	Golden West	8.5
26	Santa Ana	7.5
27	Antelope Valley	6
28	Contra Costa	5.5
29	Allan Hancock	4
29	S D Mesa	4
31	Southwestern	3
31	Diablo Valley	3
33	Ohlone	2.5
34	Canyons	2
34	Sacramento	2
36	Rio Hondo	1.5
37	Skyline	1.25

1976 CCCAA Small College Wrestling Championships
February 21, 1976 Antelope Valley College

118
Ruben Rios-Merced 8-2
Brad Fuller-Sierra

126
Sherwood Miller-Cuesta 8-1
Joe Montes-Sierra

134
Reynold Capps-Sierra 10-2
Greg Chappel-Hartnell

142
Greg Pollard-Victor Valley 6-2
Rick Bredgerd-Skyline

150
Ken Cushman-Redwoods 9-4
Jeff Williams-Butte

158
Richard Ramirez-V Valley 5-3
Matt Keeler-Merced

167
Mike DeArmon-Ohlone 4-3
Ed Scantling-Sierra

177
Mark Martinez-Redwood 7-3
John Sallenberger-Merced

190
Kevin Hunstad-Cuesta 6-3
Eric Woolsey-Redwoods

Heavyweight
Geno Gonzales-Merced Fall
Mike Fox-Redwoods

Most Outstanding Wrestler
Kevin Hunstad-Cuesta
Coach of the Year
John Horrillo-Sierra

Team Scores
1	Sierra	106.5
2	Redwoods	96.25
3	Merced	90.75
4	Ohlone	61.5
5	Victor Valley	61
6	Cuesta	60.25
7	Skyline	51.25
8	Imperial Valley	35
9	Butte	34
10	Hartnell	33.5

1976-77 CCCAA Small College Wrestling Championships
February 18, 1977 Sierra College

118
Javier Lopez-Butte
Mark Matthews-Lassen

126
Guy Reilly-Lassen
Collin Kinser Redwoods

134
Sherwood Miller-Cuesta
Burt Van Duzer-Redwoods

142
Greg Young-Sierra
Sam George-Yuba

150
John Silva-Redwoods
Mario Lomas-Ohlone

158
Bob Roberts-Cuesta
Bill Baker-Ohlone

167
Wayne Christian-Ohlone
Rocky Harris-Redwoods

177
Gene Wais-Cuesta
Jesus Aboytes-Cabrillo

190
Mike Wilson-Cuesta
Nel McClellan-Lassen

Heavyweight
Tom Martin-Merced
Vern Hart-Shasta

Most Outstanding Wrestler
Greg Young-Sierra

Sherwood Miller and Greg Young were repeat winners from last year

Team Scores
1 Cuesta   101.25
2 Redwoods   71
3 Sierra   68
3 Lassen   62
5 Skyline   57.5
6 Ohlone   53
7 Yuba   45.5
8 Merced   42.25
9 Cabrillo   39.25
9 Butte   25.5

1977 CCCAA State Wrestling Championships
March 4-5, 1977 Cypress College

118
David Cotti-San Jose 7-5
Dave Suarez-Cerritos
Dan Hillinan-Grossmont 7-4
Mark Matthews Lassen
Robert Wurm-Yuba
Edwin Dilbeck-Palomar

126
Ben Martinez-El Camino 8-1
Dean Busk-Rio Hondo
Mike Engle-Cypress
Joaquin Maldonado-Cerritos
Guy Reilly-Lassen
Joel Chavez-San Jose

134
Tyrone Rose-Diablo Valle 8-6
Mike Needham-Chabot
Aaron Thomas-Santa Ana 8-7
Hal Delashaw-S J Delta
Al Morita-Cerritos
None Awarded

142
Joe Lopez-Bakersfield 10-7
Greg Okoorian-Cypress
John Blazej-Moorpark
Marty Maciel-Cerritos
Jim Gagliardi-Modesto
Phil Brewer-Cabrillo

150
Bill Cripps-El Camino Fall 1:56
Mike Burger-Palomar
John Parreira-Modesto
Mario Betti-Sacramento
Andy Wilson-American River
Gary Murphy-Moorpark

158
Rick Worel-Palomar 5-3
Kevin Dugan-Chabot
Pinto Para-El Camino
Greg Johnson-Cypress
Bob Roberts-Cuesta
Bill Baker-Ohlone

167
Tony Brewer-Foothill 5-1
Tom Pender-San Jose
Mark Hall-Moorpark
Dave Pacheco-Sacramento
Don Zeller-El Camino
Glenn Thoreson-Palomar

177
Steve Draper-Santa Ana 4-1
Rudi Burtscei-Modesto
Roy Austin-Cypress 4-2
Mark Vick-Golden West
Eugene Wais-Cuesta
Curt Wiedenhoefer-Fresno

190
Curtis Bledsoe-Chabot 4-3
Amas Scott-Fresno
Don Hill Santa-Ana 3-1
Cam Herrick-Grossmont
Cedric Grham-El Camino
John Parrish-American River

Heavyweight
Ken Harbuck-Ame River 8-3
Craig Schoene-Skyline
David Shaw-Chabot 4-3
Bob Woy-Moorpark
Allan Tanner-Palomar
George-Boeger

39 Antelope Valley .5
39 Ventura .5
41 Chaffey, DeAnza, Hartnell, Riverside, San Mateo, Solano West Valley All 0

Small College Champion
Cuesta

Steve Drapper-Santa Ana
39-0

Career Record
Joe Lopez-Bakersfield
61-12

Most Outstanding Wrestler
Bill Cripps-El Camino
Coach of the Year
Don Conway-El Camino

Team Scores
1 El Camino 74.75
2 Chabot 67.25
3 Palomar 56.75
4 Cypress 50
5 Santa Ana 45.75
6 Cerritos 45.5
7 San Jose 39.5
8 Modesto 37.5
9 American River 32.25
10 Moorpark 31.5
11 Diablo Valley 27.5
12 Fresno 22
13 Grossmont 21.5
14 Bakersfield 20
15 Foothill 19.5
16 Lassen 19
17 Sacramento 18.5
18 Rio Hondo 17.75
19 Cuesta 17.5
20 Skyline 15
21 Hancock 12.5
22 S J Delta 9.5
22 Golden West 9.5
24 Mt. SAC 8.5
25 Yuba 7.5
26 Cabrillo 6.5
26 Ohlone 6.5
28 Redwoods 3
29 Long Beach 2.5
30 S D Mesa 2
30 Imperial Valley 2
30 Orange Coast 2
33 Sierra 1.25
34 Pierce 1
34 Fullerton 1
34 Sequoias 1
34 Santa Rosa 1
34 Southwestern 1

1977-78 CCCAA State Wrestling Championships
February 10-11, 1978 Bakersfield College

118
Ed Dibeck-Palomar 6-5
Dave Suarez-Cerritos
Pete Gonzalez-Bakersfield 5-2
Everett Winters-Santa Ans
Ricky Gillyard-Pierce 4-2
Bruce Kawabata-Chabot

126
William Gonzales-Bakfld 9-6
Dean Busk-Rio Hondo
Don Le Melle-M SA R Dec OT
Charlie Cheney-A Hancock
Dave Robison-Diab Valley 4-3
Jess Bails-Chabot

134
Chris Cane-Palomar 5-2
Dave Cortier-Cabrillo
Nick Restivo-Rio Hondo 4-2
Rick Bracamonte-San Jose
Jim Dolan-Chaffey 3-1
Ed Delgado-Cerritos

142
Greg Porter-Moorpar*F 1:35
Brad Vadnals-Chabot
Mike Frendenburg-W Val 6-5
Marlin Royal-Fresno
Glenn Oltmans-Cypress 5-2
Dan Mills-Modesto

150
Mario Lomas-Ohlone 12-5
Les Santos-Chabot
Bob Soul Rio-Hondo 4-0
Jim Porter-Moorpark
Craig Vejvoda-Sequoias 4-2
John Davis-Palomar

158
Pinito Para-El Camino 7-0
Doug Johnson-Foothill
Kevin Dugan-Chabot 6-1
Steve Holt-De Anza
George Vega-Santa Ana 4-2
Ron Garcia-Diablo Valley

167
Bill Choate-Chabot 5-2
Jim Thornton-El Camino
Jeff Gianni-Palomar F 1:52
Ron Packer-Solano
Rocky Harrison-Redw Forfeit
Mike Couch-Cerritos

177
Wayne Christian-Ohlone 8-4
Rick Worel-Palomar
Bob Grimes-Fresno 13-9
Rich Syles-De Anza
Bob Prince-Cypress 7-3
Jarl Grunseth-Diablo Valley

190
John Diaz-Fresno 10-4
Cedric Graham-El Camino
Scott Speck-Cypress 4-3
Gaylord Lane-West Valley
Mike Haschak-Cabrillo Forfeit
John Inli-Cerritos

Heavyweight
Doug Severe-Modesto F 1:02
Allan Tanner-Palomar
Craig Schoene-Skyline F 1:38
Scott Moore-Grossmont
Tom Van Arkel-Bakfld 4-3
Casey Delliford-Shasta

East LA 0
Golden West 0
Long Beach 0
Mendocino 0
Merced 0
Orange Coast 0
Santa Rosa 0
Ventura 0

Most Outstanding Wrestler
Greg Porter-Moorpark
Coach of the Year
John Woods-Palomar

Team Scores
1 Palomar   89.25
2 Chabot   74.75
3 El Camino   54.75
4 Fresno   46.5
5 Rio Hondo   46
6 Bakersfield   41.75
6 Ohlone   41.75
8 Cerritos   38.5
9 Moorpark   34.75
10 Cypress   28.5
11 Modesto   27.5
12 Cabrillo   26.5
13 De Anza   23
14 West Hills   20.5
15 Santa Ana   18.34
16 Diablo Valley 17.5
17 Mt. SAC   15.5
18 Foothill   15
19 Grossmont   13.5
20 Skyline   13.25
21 San Jose   12.75
22 Allen Hancock 12.5
23 Pierce   9
23 Shasta   9
25 Chaffey   8.5
Solano 8.5, Redwoods 8, Sequoias 7, Lassen 5, Imperial Valley 2.5, Yuba 2.5, Cuesta 2.25, Sierra 1.5, Antelope Valley 1, Porterville 1, Canada 1, Sacramento .5

Career Record
Pete Gonzalez 58-17
Willie Gonzales 44-15
Greg Porter 58-4, 29 Falls
Season Record
Greg Porter 30-2

1978-79 CCCAA State Wrestling Championships
February 9-10, 1979 El Camino College

118
Karl Glover-Rio Hondo 13-10
Paul Bolanos-Fresno
Victor Duarte-Santa Ana
Steve Lutz-Ohlone
Fred Gonzalez-Bakersfield
Herb Kaichi-El Camino

126
Jim Hamilton-Palomar 10-7
Keith Azevado-Yuba
Paul Tucker-Rio Hondo
Mike Powell-Sequoias
Larry Kaprielian-Fresno
Terry Burton-Chabot

134
Chris Cain-Palomar 5-0
Jim Dolan-Chaffey
Mike Matsuoka-El Camino
Van Hollaway-Cypress
Coty Tanner-Diablo Valley
Disqualified

142
Greg Porter-Moorpark 8-
George Crower-San Jose
Robert Sole-Chaffey
Bob Legaspi-Cerritos
Steve Nickell-Bakersfield
Carlos Santanmaria-El Cam

150
Perry Shea-Cerritos 11-9
Lee Noble-West Valley
Nelson Imamura-El Camino
Marlin Royal-Fresno
Glenn Kuhn-Modesto
N/A

158
Dan Mather-Rio Hondo* Fall
Eddie Carver-Chabot
Chris Fuertsch-Cerritos
Joey Guillroy-San Jose
Phil Reed-Mt. San Antonio
Vertis Elmore-Lassen

167
Jim Thornton-El Camino 11-
Tim Vaughn-Ventura
Mike Roberson-Chabot
Vic Rendon-Sierra
Ron Garcia-Diablo Valley
Frankie Scott-Fresno

177
Mark Hall Allan Hancock 11-4
Tony De Paoli-Imperial Valley
Dave Deal-Cerritos
Rich Sykers-Diablo Valley
Marty Jones-Bakersfield
Roy Coudright-Chabot

190
Scott Speck-Cypress 7-6
Bruce Kopitar-Diablo Valley
Ron Freeman-Chabot
Jim Batson-Rio Hondo
John Webb-Pierce
Chris Roll-Santa Ana

Heavyweight
Ernie Velton-Palomar 8-3 OT
Matt Clark-Cypress
Manny Estrada-Santa Ana
Casey Guillford-Shasta
Tom Thomsen-Chabot
Mike Malkovich-Diabl Valley

Most Outstanding Wrestler
Dan Mather-Rio Hondo

Coach of the Year
Ken Bos-Rio Hondo

Team Scores
1 Rio Hondo   70
2 Palomar   67.25
3 Cerritos   62.25
4 Chabot   61
5 El Camino   57.25
6 Diablo Valley   51.5
7 Cypress   47.5
8 Fresno   44
9 Santa Ana   31.5
10 San Jose   29.5
11 Chaffey   29
12 Moorpark   26
13 Bakersfield   25.5
14 Allan Hancock   22.5
15 Shasta   17.5
16 West Valley   16.5
17 Yuba   16
16 Ventura   16
16 Imperial Valley 16
18 Sequoias   13
19 Ohlone   12.5
20 Sierra   12.25
21 Mt. SAC   9.5
21 Modesto   9.5
23 Pierce   7
24 Lassen   6
25 Fullerton   4.25
SD Mesa 1.5, Cuesta 1.5, Sacramento 1.5, Canada 1, San Mateo .5, Santa Rosa .5

Career Record
Fred Gonzalez 50-17

1979-80 CCCAA State Wrestling Championships
February 8-9, 1980 Chabot College

118
Al Gutierrez-Sequoias 10-5
Ferando Venegas-Cypress
Bill Brookens-Gold West 7-6
John Lawrence-San Jose
Jorge Acosta-El Camino
Fred Gonzalez-Bakersfield

126
Tony Ovalle-R Hond Fall 3:55
Don Evans-West Valley
Mike Powell-Sequoias 4-3
Kurt Wardley-Ohlone
Adley Parker-Ventura
Brett Nadeau-Chabot

134
Mike Matsuoka-El Cami 8-4
Bob Wellander-Cerritos
Jerry Niewoehner-S Jose 13-1
Brian Brown-Moorpark
Dan Parker-Ventura
Randy Ashenbrenner-Mt SAC

142
Steve Nickell-Bakersfield 9-8
Charlie Cheney-A Hancock
Cory Salmon-Diablo Vall 6-3
Steve Ellsworth-West Valley
Steve Markey-Chabot
Jim Valentine-Sequoias

150
Bill Wieskopf-Cypress 4-3
Mike Mills-Cuesta
Mitch Heredia-Chabot 9-5
Tim Santos-Modesto
Glade Bacon-Grossmont
Alvaro Cano-Sequoias

158
Dan Mather-Rio Hondo 25-4
Dave Bridgewater-Moorpark
Allan Thacker-Sierra 4-3
Scott Teuscher-Sacramento
Frank Bitetto-Cypress
Kelly Boyd-Cuesta

167
Chris Fuertsch-Cerritos 5-4
Tim Vaughn-Ventura
Eddie Carver- Chabot 6-1
Tim Johnson-Diablo Valley
John Bufford-Fresno
Ted Martinez-Orange Coast

177
Mike Robinson-Chabot 14-8
Marty Jones-Bakersfield
Luis Garcia-Chaffey 5-2
Dave Deal-Cerritos
David Ernaga-Lassen
Chris Vaughn-Ventura

190
Mark Loomis-Sacra*Fall :57
Jim Batson-Rio Hondo
Brian Ward-Foothill 5-0
Bill Kropos-Sequoias
Mark Surdyka-San Diego
Rick Boyer-Orange Coast

Heavyweight
Matt Clark-Cypress 8-6
Joshua Washington-Sequoias
Roger Herrera-Chabot F 2:46
Joe Kaminski-Ventura
Doug Harrell-Modesto
Dan Barrios

John Woods - Palomar
179-19-3, Coached 4 State Championship Teams, 11 State Individual Champions, 51 All-Americans.

Dave Hengsteler-El Camino
1953-1975, Coached 5 State Championship Teams, Coaching Record 104-15

Division II Team Champion
Cuesta

Most Outstanding Wrestler
Mark Loomis-Sacramento

Coach of the Year
Zach Papachristos-Chabot

Team Scores
1 Chabot	78.25
2 Sequoias	67
3 Cypress	66.5
4 Rio Hondo	58.25
5 Ventura	49
6 Cerritos	46.5
7 Bakersfield	44
8 El Camino	36
9 Sacramento	35.5
10 West Valley	29
10 Chaffey	29
11 Moorpark	28
12 Diablo Valley	24
13 San Jose	22.5
14 Modesto	19.5
15 Allan Hancock	15.5
16 Foothill	13.5
16 Orange Coast	13.5
18 Sierra	12.5
19 Chaffy	12.5
20 Ohlone	11.5
20 Lassen	11.5
22 Golden West	11
23 Fresno	8.5
24 San Diego	8
25 Grossmont	7
26 Mt. SAC	6
27 Santa Rosa	4.5
28 SJ Delta	3
29 Pierce	2
30 Butte	1.5
31 Redwoods	1
32 Long Beach	1

Career Records
Fred Gonzalez 50-17
Steve Nickell 54-13
Marty Jones 60-11

1980 CCCAA State Champions

Front Row L-R 150-Bill Wieskoff-Cypress, 142-Steve Nickell-Bakersfield, 134-Mike Matsuoka-El Camino, 126-Tony Ovalle-Rio Hondo, 118-Al Gutierrez-Sequoias. **Back Row L-R** Heavyweight-Matt Clark-Cypress, 190-Most Outstanding Wrestler-Mark Loomis-Sacramento, 177-Mike Robinson-Chabot, 167-Chris Fuertsch-Cerritos, 158-Dan Mather-Rio Hondo

1981 CCCAA State Champions

Front Row L-R: 118-Al Gutierrez-Sequioas; 126-Keith Jardine-Diablo Valley; 134-Victor Lizama-Mt. San Antonio; 142-Steve Markey-Chabot; 150-Ray Hammond-Rio Hondo. **Back Row:** 158-Lance Anzivine-Diablo Valley; 167-Scott Teuscher-Sacramento City; 177-Steve Bailey-San Jose; 190-Mike Porcelli-San Diego City; Heavyweight-Joshua Washington-Sequoias.

1980-81 CCCAA State Wrestling Championships
February 1981, Rio Hondo College

118
Al Gutierrez-Sequoias*
Victor Tanksley-Lassen
Joe Castorena-Mt. SAC
Brian Heinselman-Moorpark
Leonard Munoz-San Jose
William Taylor-Golden West
Darrian Guilford-Ohlone
Robert Simpson-Sacramento

126
Keith Jardine-Diablo Valley
Benjie Gutierrez-Sequoias
Tom Haratuneian-Fresno
Cliff Gosse-Chabot
Jose Martinez-Mt. SAC
Dave Orani-S J Delta
Mike Saucedo-Cypress
James Cortes-Pierce

134
Victor Lizama-Mt. SAC
Dave Barona-Moorpark
Brian Miller-Modesto
Glenn Evans-Cypress
Rod Lemos-Lassen
Scott Housel-Golden West
Roger Blackshear-El Camino
Vince Fierro-Chaffey

142
Steve Markey-Chabot
Eric Lessley-Santa Rosa
Cory Salmon-Diablo Valley
Tony Coppinger-Santa Ana
Ken Jenkins-Palomar
Bernardo Miranda-Mt. SAC
Brian Smith-Sierra
Pat Welch-Cerritos

150
Ray Hammond-Rio Hondo
Clark Cavanaugh-Cerritos
Tim Santos-Modesto
Alan Thacker-Sierra
Gregg Olson-Mt. San Antonio
Chris Cordova-Moorpark
Mike Chumpitazi-Cypress
Ken Hindmarch-San Mateo

158
Lance Anzivine-Diablo Valley
Sylvester Carver-Chabot
John Holbrook-Palomar
Randy Roberts-Cerritos
Gene Allison-Sequoias
Art Straus-Long-Beach
Rex Davis-Moorpark
Wade Workman-Lassen

167
Scott Teuscher-Sacramento
Kerry Hiatt-Palomar
Phil Welch-Sequoias
Mark Ballard-El Camino
Tom Mikalson-Santa Rosa
Mike Hairston-Ohlone
Robert Ruiz-Mt. San Antonio
Brett Hall-Santa Ana

177
Steve Bailey-San Jose City
Rob Mella-Orange Coast
Luis Garcia-Chaffy
Dennis Townsend-Sequoias
Carl Newman-Skyline
John Taylor-Skyline
Phil Dunford-Cerritos
Ray Mann-Diablo Valley

190
Mike Porccelli-San Diego
Ali Nazari-Skyline
Jeff Steward-Ventura
Garen McDonald-Chabot
Mitch Finklea-Orange Coast
Olivio Salazar-Modesto
Mitch Babcock-Diablo Valley
Paul White-San Mateo

Heavyweight
Joshua Washington-Sequoias
Roger Herrera-Chabot
Dennis Martin-Bakersfield
Terry Fredette-Moorpark
Joe Kaminski-Ventura
Craig Broderick-Rio Hono
Daniel Soden-S J Delta
Steve Catafamo-Cerritos

Most Outstanding Wrestler
Al Gutierrez-Sequoias
Coach of the Year
Dave Adams-Sequoias

Team Scores
1 Sequoias 95.25
2 Chabot 92.75
3 Mt. SAC 61.25
4 Diablo Valley 60.5
5 Moorpark 46.25
6 Palomar 40.75
7 Modesto 32.25
8 San Jose 30
9 Lassen 28.25
9 Rio Hondo 28.5
11
12
13
14
15
16
17
18
19
20
21
22 Bakersfield 14

Career Record
Scott Teuscher 71-?
Dennis Martin 46-10

1981-82 CCCAA State Wrestling Championships
February 5-6, 1982 San Joaquin Delta College

118
Jeff Chedester-Sequoias 11-7
Jose Martinez-Mt. S Antonio
Chris Hartley-Diablo Valle 7-6
Alex Duarte-Golden West
Rick Palomino-San Jose 4-0
Scott Schneider-Cerritos
Chris Laudise-Palomar 8-1OT
Greg Gutierrez-Shasta

126
Dan Hopkins-Santa Ana 4-1
Cliff Gosse-Chabot
Steve Slade-Diablo Vall 8-1OT
Joe Ismay-Palomar
Dan Duncan-Cypress 19-5
Alfred Padilla-Modesto
Brian Heinselman-Moorp 6-5
Ron Anaya-Cerritos

134
John Vega-Cerritos 12-5
Joe Guerrero-S J Delta
Joe Triggs-Chabot 9-1
Roger Blackshear-El Camino
Dondi Teran-Rio Hondo 9-2
Ram Bryant-Cypress
James Cortez-Pierce 3-2
David Avina-Palomar

142
Dave Wood-Chabot Fall 4:14
George Ishak-Rio Hondo
    Jenkins- Palomar 9-5
Dan Hartano-El Camino
Matt Vanni-West Valley 7-6
Doug Ruiz-Cerritos
Lee Patrick-Bakersfield 4-1OT
Frank Torres Mt. San Antonio

150
Chuck Justice-Chabot 28-15
Clark Cavanaugh-Cerritos
Hector Vargas Skyline 17-5
Larry Tevis-Ventura
Don Reppond-Sacramento 6-
Barry Cole-Modesto
Kief Fortier-Pierce 13-9
Jeff Boyko-Sequoia

158
Don Dobbs-West Valley 10-6
Ky Fugosh-El Camino
Ty McGuire-Sequoias 8-7
Doug Carnation-Chabot
Mitch Pagnao-Rio Hondo 9-7
Steve Haxby-Butte
Dave Nahay-Cypress 4-2
Chris Cordova-Moorpark

167
Sylvester Carver-Chabot 12-4
Gene Allison-Sequoia
Todd Stragler-Mt SAC 5-2
Ted Keyes-Santa Rosa
Jack Norton-Redwoods
Matt Kirk-West Valley
Ray Cox-Bakersfield 8-1
Bob Campuzano-Cypress

177
Phil Dunford-Cerritos 20-6
Dale Delaney-Redwoods
Bill Elbin-Sequoias 6-3
Russ Jones-Sierra
Herb Weller-Skyline 9-3
Jon Head Palomar
Jim Hull-Sacramento 13-6
Tim Olson-Mt. San Antonio

190
Garen-McDonald Chabot
Ali Nazaei-Skyline
Jeff Young-Palomar 3-2
Joey Sansinena-Sequoias
Tom Kelly-Porterville Forfeit
Steve McGee-San Diego
Brlan Hyder-Redwood Deft
Rod Prnjak-Cabrillo

Heavyweight
Tim Reilly Golden-West 5-2
Steven Ramirez-Butte
Craig Broderick Rio Hondo17-
Joe Quinn-Santa Rosa
Marcus Johnson-Santa Ana
Frank Easter-Cabrillo
Alonso West-Chabot Default
Bill Pierce-Bakersfield

Most Outstanding Wrestler
Dave Wood-Chabot

Coach of the Year
Zack Papachristos-
Diablo Valley

Team Scores
1	Chabot	127.75
2	Sequoias	74
3	Cerritos	72.25
4	Palomar	52.5
5	Rio Hondo	48.5
6	Skyline	39
7	El Camino	38.5
8	Santa Ana	34.25
9	Mt. SAC	33.5
10	West Valley	33
11	Golden West	30.5
11	Redwoods	30.5
13	Diablo Valley	27.5
14	Cypress	20.5
15	Butte	20
16	Santa Rosa	16.5
17	S J Delta	15.5
17	Sacramento	15.5
19	Bakersfield	14
20	Sierra	12.5
21	Modesto	12.5
22	Porterville	11
23	San Jose	8.75
24	Ventura	8.5
25	Cabrillo	8.25
26	Pierce	8
27	Moorpark	6.5
28	San Diego	6
29	Shasta	2.5

The CCCAA held two State Championships in 1981-1982 the same season

1982 CCCAA State Wrestling Championships
December 17-18, 1982 Cerritos College

118
Steve Martinez Cypress 12-3
Tony Trabucco El Camino
Brent McNamara Dialo Valley
Mike McHugh Sierra
Jimmy Estrella Rio Hondo
Wes Gaston Sacramento
Jon Ball Moorpark
Alfred Padilla Modesto

126
Ram Bryant Cypress F 6:13
Marty Gonzales Sequoias
John Leandro Chabot
Jon Love Santa Ana
Ron Sigler Palomar
Jack Mejazi El Camino
Brian Mills Rio Hondo
John Contreras Skyline

134
Dondi Teran Rio Hond 19-13*
Joe Ismay Palomar
Joe Triggs Chabot
Tim Mattos Butte
Ernie Geronimo Bakersfield
Ron Atwell Modesto
Danny Nunez Cuesta
Tom Ketelle Sierra

142
Dave Wood Chabot 18-9
Cesar Escudero Cuesta
Glenn Evans Cypress
Todd Giurlani Bakersfield
Jim Scarr Sacramento
Dan Casey Modesto
Rich Rodgers Diablo Valley
Tom Valentine Palomar

150
Mitch Pagano Rio Hondo13-3
Les Lewis El Camion
Chuck Justice Chabot
Richie Sinnott Bakersfield
Dave Nahay Cypress
Barry LaBass Modesto
Tim Coykendall S J Delta
Gary Williams Cerritos

158
Fred Little Bakersfield 7-1
Tony Porcelli San Diego
Doug Carnation Chabot
Jack Ward Cypress
Barry Cole Cypress
Frank Torres Mt. San Antonio
Scott Bilyeu Sequoias
Robert Connelly Moorpark

167
Chris Duran Cerritos 5-1
Steve Haxby Butte
Mike Andrews Diablo Valley
James Cook Porterville
Steve Glore Golden West
Kent Davis Mt. San Antonio
Jim Matire Skyline
Steve Aguiar Chabot

177
Todd Stragier Mt. SAC F 2:16
Vic Ceja Chabot
Craig Bogard Cypress
Bill Blbin Sequoias
Dave Virik Palomar
Dan Castaneda Bakersfield
Tony Garcia S J Delta
Clayton Ray Sierra

190
Tim Boyd Chabot 10-9
Jeff Young Palomar
Troy Ulmer S J Delta
Dana Ott Mt. San Antonio
Scot Crow Rio Hondo
Ed Duggan Sierra
Joey Sansinera Sequoias
Chris Roll Santa Ana

Heavyweight
Alonzo West Chabot 5-2
John Smith Cerritos
Flip Levender Sequoias
Craig Edling Modesto
Ron Prnjak Sequoias
Ernie Ortega Palomar
Jim Traffenstedt Bakfld
Ed Gonsell Redwoods

Most Outstanding Wrestler
Dondi Teran Rio Hondo

Coach of the Year
Zack Papachristos Chabot

Team Scores
1 Chabot 121.75
2 Cypress 79.75
3 Rio Hondo 63.5
4 Bakersfield 59.75
5 Palomar 53.75
6 Sequoias 45.75
7 Mt SAC 42
8 Cerritos 39.25
9 Modesto 37.75
10 El Camino 36.5
11
12
13
14 Cuesta

Small College Champion
Butte

Career Record
Fred Little 34-1-1

Zack Papachristos Chabot
1969-1982 Coached 77 state placers, 56 All-Americans, 17 state champions, 11 regional, 12 conferences, 5 State Championship Teams, 152-6-2 dual meet record

CCCAA had 2 state tournaments in 1981-1982 and the state CCCAA Wrestling became a fall sport in 1992

1983 CCCAA State Wrestling Championships
February West Valley College

118
Ernie Neri Moorpark 8-7
Alan Paradise Sequoias
Greg Gascon Cypress 5-1
Moses Martin Rio Hondo
Tony Ramirez Bakersfield
Tony Tubucco El Camino
Art Taylor Diablo Valley
Jose Nunez Chabot

126
Dan Thomas Cypress 8-3
Luis Loya Palomar
Aaron Jackson Moorpar 15-6
Walt Keller Sequoias
John Ybarra San Jose
Rick Evens Modesto
Zalen Liley Rio Hondo
Mick Perez San Diego

134
Ernie Geronimo Bakfld 14-9
Derrick Adams Chabot
Walter Ulrich Butte 8-5
Gus Paz West Valley
Ron Singler Palomar
Ron Hughes San Jose
Kurt Hand Cuesta
Brian Ransom Cypress

142
Dan Hartano El Cami F 2:40*
Ron Atwell Modesto
Scott Palmer Rio Hondo 5-0
Jerry Ford Diablo Valley
Tom Brekke Moorpark
Dave Love San Jose
Brian Acosta Mt. San Antonio
Derek Kartchner Cerritos

150
Pat Glynn San Diego 3-1
Jack Duby Palomar
Barry La Bass Modesto 14-3
Leonard Branzuela Skyline
Shannon Felix Diablo Valley
Todd Meulman West Valley
Jeff La Fleur Sequoias
Luis Demas Sacramento

158
Brian Folsom Cypress Default
Vince Gonsalves Diablo Valle
Steve Bowden Palom F 1:58
Dave Williams Sacramento
Ruben Martinez Modesto
Anthony Holmes Cerritos
Dan Vasquez Bakersfield
Jerry Johnson Sierra

167
Jon Head Cuesta 5-3
Anthony Porcelli San Diego
Bill Merrell Diablo Valle 10-2
Steve Agular Chabot
Frank Barajas Moorpark
Mike Rowden Palomar
Terry Ray Thompson Sequoia
Dan Rodriguez Rio Hondo

177
Scott Bilyeu Sequoias F 2:27
Victor Ceja Chabot
Craig Bogard Cypress 15-6
Dave Vurik Palomar
Jason Greemore Bakersfield
Bruce Irwin West Valley
Ron Sturges Cerritos
Kelly St. John Diablo Valley

190
Mark James Palomar 11-2
Dave Williams Porterville
Dan Dobbs West Valley 6-0
Dana Ott Mt. San Antonio
Krieg Davis San Diego
Dave Abbott Cypress
Rob Watkins Chabot
Tim Hausler Diablo Valley

Heavyweight
Mark Manning Chabot F 1:35
Mike Roberts Sequoias
Greg Wallace Mt. SAC 11-1
Robert Leff El Camino
Jamie Martinez Palomar
John Gonzales Cypress
Jim Traffenstedt Bakfld
Allen Paicius Moorpark

Most Outstanding Wrestler
Dan Hatano El Camino
Coach of the Year
John Woods Palomar

Team Scores
1	Palomar	92.5
2	Cypress	73.75
3	Sequoias	69.75
4	Chabot	68.25
5	Diablo Valley	51.75
6	Moorpark	49.25
7	San Diego	44.5
8	Modesto	41.75
9	Bakersfield	41
10	El Camino	37.5
11	West Valley	34.5
12	Rio Hondo	27.25
13	Mt. SAC	25.25
14	Cuesta	22
15	San Jose	20.75
16	Porterville	14
17	Butte	11.5
17	Cerritos	11-5
19	Sacramento	11
20	Skyline	8.5
21	Sierra	2
22	American River	
	S J Delta	0

Career Record
Ernie Geronimo 58-12

1984 CCCAA State Wrestling Championships

118
Greg Gascon-Cypress
Jesse Orduno-Butte
Walt Keller-Sequoias
Dave Hartley-Diablo Valley
Tim Atkinson-Moorpark
Scott Nelson-West Valley
Frank Bettencourt-Modesto
Dave Montano-Santa Rosa

126
Alan Paradise-Sequoias
Harold Coleman-Palomar
Rick Evans-Modesto
Deets Winslow-Diablo Valley
Tony Leanos-San Jose
Ernie Garcia-Cuesta
Tony Ramirez-Bakersfield
Pete Clemente-Moorpark

134
Dan Thomas-Cypress
Derrek Adams-Chabot
Shane Desjardins-Sequoias
Walter Ulrich-Butte
Shawn Jorgenson-Palomar
Ken Wharry-Sacramento
Dan Nunez-Cuesta
Mike Longshaw-Cerritos

142
Jeff Tripp-Mt. San Antonio
Richard Martinez-Palomar
Dave Love-San Jose
Scott Palmer-Rio Hondo
Brett Davis-Porterville
Mike Box-Butte
Jeff Hockaday-Palomar
Fernando Zubia-Cuesta

150
Jack Duby-Palomar
Rob Helm-Porterville
Rodney Zeisse-Chabot
Tim Coyendall-S J Delta
Tim Monohan-Lassen
Paul Arlon-Moorpark
Ben Mills-West Valley
Shane Blanton-Modesto

158
Bill Merrell-Diablo Valley
Brian Folsom-Cypress
Steve Bowden-Palomar
Marty Mitchell-Sequoias
Joe Dragseth-Santa Rosa
Dean Pfutzenreuter-Bakfld
Steve Blickenstaff-Modesto
Edwin Van-Cerritos

167
Jose Reyes-Sacramento
Ernie Aguiar-Modesto
Richard Riley-Porterville
Mike Rowden-Palomar
Dan Espareza-Chabot
Jeff Tice-Cuesta
Mike Scarminach-Sequoias
Bill Estenson-Diablo Valley

177
Robert Watkins-Chabot
Frank Barajas-Moorpark
Krief Davis-San Diego
Anthony Belew-Modesto
Tom Spaulding-Cypress
Terry Ray Thompson-Sequoia
Tim Greenwood-El Camino
Dan DeWater-Sacramento

190
Dan Dobbs-West Valley
David Lanham-Sequoias
John Moses-Mt. San Antonio
Vince Aguilar-Moorpark
Phil Scott-Sacramento
Jeff Murchand-Chabot
Mike Williams-Diablo Valley
Tom Howe-Cerritos

Heavyweight
Ricky Salas-Sequoias
Dave Williams-Porterville
Russ Stringer-Napa Valley
John Haupt-Cerritos
Mark Moreno-Cuesta
Frank Rutledge-Butte
Mike Malloy-Skyline
Al Akins-Modesto

Most Outstanding Wrestling
Dan Thomas-Cypress

Coach of the Year
Steve Hitchcock-Sequoias

Team Scores

1	Sequoias	104.25
2	Cypress	79.25
3	Palomar	71.25
4	Chabot	59.25
5	Porterville	52.75
6	Diablo Valley	48.50
6	Modesto	48.50
8	Moorpark	41.50
9	Sacramento	36.25
10	Butte	35.75
11	Mt. San Antonio	32.50
12	West Valley	29.25
13	Cuesta	25.50
14	San Jose	20
15	Cerritos	17
16	Napa Valley	11.50
17	Rio Hondo	11
18	Santa Rosa	10.50
19	S J Delta	10
20	Lassen	9

1985 CCCAA State Wrestling Championships

118
George Williams-Cerritos
Victor Coboas-Sierra
Dave Montano-Santa Rosa
Than Tran Rancho-Santiago
John Esquivel-Rio Hondo
Ray Esparza-Moorpark
Jeff Ogata-El Camino
Pere Ramirez-Bakersfield

126
Mel East-Bakersfield
Deets Winslow-Diablo Valley
Rafik Tadros-Mt. San Antonio
Jim Walker-West Valley
Bill Nickerson-Lassen
Arnie Bautista-Moorpark
Vincent Cobos-Sierra
Tom Lazano-El Camino

134
Darryl Terukins-Skyline
Shawn Jorgenson-Palomar
Brian Ranson-Cypress
Brett Verch-El Camino
Mark Mansfield-Lassen
Marco Orozco-
Mike Dallas-Bakersfield
David Lincoln-Sierra

142
Jeff Hockaday-Palomar
Gus Paz West-Valley
Jay Wilkins-Chabot
Trent Kenney Golden West
David Crisp Lassen
Jim Hembree-Bakersfield
Doug Losak-Cerritos
David Burch-Modesto

150
Rodney Zeisse-Chabot
Greg L'Amoreaux-Diablo Vall
David Watts-Palomar
Alford Martinez-Rio Hondo
Kerry Collins-Cuesta
Chris Schulz-Golden West
Tim Monahan-Lassen
Eric Cortez-Moorpark

158
Edwin Van-Cerritos*
David Rosario-Cuesta
Joe Dragseth-Santa Rosa
Kip Magnussen-Modesto
Dale Kendall-Sierra
Elvin Jones-Lassen
Sam Mason-Palomar
Bill Weatherill-Cypress

167
Danny Esparza-Chabot
Rob Alleman-Pierce
Eddie Shelton-Diablo Valley
Rick Lambert-Palomar
Brian Bennett-Moorpark
Cy Cole-Modesto
Dean Heath-S J Delta
Robert Rico-Rio Hondo

177
Kelvin Colvin-El Camino
Reid O'Connor-Diablo Valley
Dan DeWater-Sacramento
Joe Riedell-Skyline
Mike Whitfield-Lassen
Mark Cavassa-Palomar
Dale Fowler-Bakersfield
Dave Stidham-Cerritos

190
Rich Brenton-Golden West
Tim Hess-Chabot
John Moses-Palomar
Tom Mejia-Palomar
Sean Hannigan-Santa Rosa
Tom Howe-Cerritos
Sean Goodwin-Cypress
Mike Gamberg-Butte

Heavyweight
Matt Blevin-West Valley
Ricky Salas-Cuesta
Greg Wallace-Mt. SAc
Paul Miramingos-Palomar
Bill Flores-Cypress
Nick Skourtas-Cerritos
Tim Richards-Sierra
Russell Stringer-Napa Valley

Most Outstanding Wrestler
Edwin Van-Cerritos

Coach of the Year
John Woods-Palomar

Team Scores
1	Palomar	88.5
2	Chabot	71.75
3	Diablo Valley	59.75
4	Cerritos	59
5	West Valley	50.5
6	Lassen	45
7	El Camino	41
8	Mt. SAC	40.5
9	Bakersfield	40.25
10	Cuesta	39
11	Golden West	35.5
12	Sierra	33
13	Skyline	30.5
14	Santa Rosa	29.75
15	Cypress	29.25
16	Moorpark	20.5
17	Rio Hondo	20.5
18	Modesto	19
19	Pierce	15
20	Sacramento	13
21	R Santiago	11.5
22	Napa Valley	6.5
23	S J Delta	3
24	Butte	2

Bruce Pfutzenreuter
Bakersfield College
1964-1985 – 264-81-2
Tournament Championship Teams 30, Conference Championship Teams 8. Individual Champions 63, Regional Championship Teams 7, Individual Champions 44, State Championship Teams 2, Individual Champions 18, All-Americans 47, 42 duals in a row without a loss

1986 CCCAA State Wrestling Championships
December 12-13, 1986 Bakersfield College

118
Victor Cobos-Galvin 3-0
Kyle O'Naga-El Camino
Keith Hernandez-Moorpark
Rick Fehr-Lassen
Eric Milsap-Mt. San Antonio
Casey Hankin-Palomar
Gus Gutierrez-Rio Hondo
David Rowan-Diablo Valley

126
West Fehr-Lassen 13-0
Mike Field-Gavilan
Brian Buffone-Palomar
Don Garriott-El Camino
Greg Bragg-Cuesta
Ray Esparza-Moorpark
Dennis Rulli-Pierce
Dan Freund-Cerritos

134
Albert Alpert-R Santi Crit. OT
Bill Nickerson-Lassen
Brent Verch-El Camino
Ken Stankevitz-Mt. SAC
Levi Chin-Cerritos
John Carroll-Skyline
Greg Gavino-Palomar
Julian Herrera-Chabot

147
Rodney Ford-Lassen 5-0
Scott Maulton-Diablo Valley
Ben Terukina-Skyline
Steve Harris-Mt. San Antonio
Adam Banks-Palomar
Steve Fuess-Moorpark
Scott Stacer-Cerritos
David Burch-Modesto

150
Paul Herrera-Go West 9-5*
Gregg L'Amoreaux-Diablo Val
Ross Meier-Sacramento
Monty Ventura-Chatbot
Jeff Hernandez-Lassen
John Tasabia-Mt. SAC
Joe Powers-Cerritos
Eric Jackson-Santa Rosa

158
David Rumfield-Lassen 7-6
Bill Weatherill-Cypress
Sidney Ahn-Chabot
Lenny Pazik-Palomar
Scott Horrillo-Sierra
Tim Murphy-Napa Valley
Kraig Magnussen-Modesto
Kurt Mathey-Moorpark

167
Tony Darone-Diablo Valle 4-2
Joey Gillis-Cypress
Brent Krang-Sacramento
Rick Lambert-Palomar
Eric Espinal-Rio Hondo
Greg Parvin-Lassen
Devin Cole-Modesto
Tom Blair-Gavilan

177
Tom Rodgers-Lassen 6-3
John Schneider-Cerritos
Bob Kocev-Diablo Valley
Henry Alsept-Mt. SAC
John Geanakos-Rio Hondo
Pete Scibitzski-Sierra
Averel Morales-Bakersfield
Mike Camacho-Gavilan

190
John McIntyre Diablo Vly 4-2
Adam Cole-Palomar
Ross Boomhower-Moorpark
Leo Woodfork-Sacramento
Sean Goodwin-Cypress
Ciro Martinez-Skyline
Dino Markette-Chabot
Brent Bartlett-Mt. SAC

275
Bill Flores-Cypress 5-3
Paul Miramingos-Palomar
Leo Guzman-Gavilan
Nick Skourtas-Cerritos
Luis Flores-Lassen
James Varnum-Rio Hondo
Frank Caruso-Skyline
Steve Hinkson-Diablo Valley

Outstanding Wrestler
Paul Herrera-Golden Valley

Coach of the Year
Dave Foster-Lassen

Team Scores
1 Lassen   125.5
2 Diablo Vly   86.5
3 Palomar   79.5
4 Cypress   62.5
5 Gavilan   56.5
6 Mt. SAC   44
7 Cerritos   43.5
8 Moorpark   42.5
9 El Camino   39
10 Sacramento   36.5

1987 CCCAA State Wrestling Championships

118
Darren Uyematsu-El Camino
Brett Southwick-Butte
Andre Bartlett-Palomar
Luis Nebel-Rio Hondo
Saul Maes-Mt. SAC
Jacob Perez-Chabot
Ron Barta-Lassen
Terry Walden-Sierra

126
Frank Trujillo-Cypress
Es Fehr-Lassen
Keith Hernandez-Moorpark
Bo-Bo Leyva Rancho Santiago
Greg Bragg-Cuesta
Dean Yoshizumi-Mt. SAC
Julian Herrera-Chabot
Bret Ugalde-Modesto

134
Eddie Ruiz-Golden West
Morteza Abedi-Cerritos
Bill Montgomery-Cypress
Dennis Rulli-Pierce
Dave Rowan-Diablo Valley
Victor Saucedo-Cuesta
Junior Andrade-Moorpark
Steve Gordon-Sierra

142
Gordon Stacer-Cerritos
Mike Taylor-Lassen
Scott Perry-Mt. SAC
Dwayne Denolf-Cypress
Monty Ventura-Chabot
Steve Toves-West Valley
Dan Hall-Sierra
Steve Freund-Cuesta

150
Paul Herrera-Golden West
Jeff Hernandez-Lassen
Marty Koujoumtjian-R Hondo
Mac Fredrick-Palomar
Jeff Buckalou- Diablo Valley
Dean Henderson-Cuesta
Leon Kuhn-Delta
Art Orozco-Cypress

158
Scott Schumm-Rio Hondo*
Blu Taylor-Sacramento
Ralph Rucker-Cypress
Denny Furnish-R Santiago
George Oakley-Palomar
Steve Ball-West Velley
Larry Nash-Cuesta
Joe Rubino-Butte

167
Pete Skibitzki-Sierra
Glenn Clutter-Palomar
Matt Fletcher-R Santiago
Joe Orozco-Cypress
Dale Fowler-Bakersfield
Adrian Burley-Sacramento
Bill Peterson-Santa Rosa
Chres Feree-Cuesta

177
Henry Alsept-Mt. SAC
Jay Martinez-Rio Hondo
Greg Parvin-Lassen
John Schneider-Cerritos
Dean Heath-S J Delta
Jesse Tautalatasi-Chabot
Brian Millum-Palomar
Gary Dickerson-Pierce

190
Leo Woodfolk-Sacramento
Mark Reimers-Rio Hondo
Richard Brenton-Go West
Sean Hannigan-Santa Rosa
Fernando Rodriquez-Lassen
Raybon Johnson-West Valley
Joey Gillis-Cypress
John Rydeen-Palomar

Heavyweight
Vince Plymire-Moorpark
Dave Warner-Sierra
Chuck Guptill-Lassen
Mike Tellez-Rio Hondo
Osiel Salinas-Cerritos
Rudy Gonzales-Cypress
Mike Galindo-El Camino
Scott Thompson-Diabo Valley

Most Outstanding Wrestler
Scott Schumm-Rio Hondo
Coach of the Year
Ken Bos-Rio Hondo

Team Scores
1 Rio Hondo   86.25
2 Lassen   86
3 Cypress   78.25
4 Golden West   52.5
5 Palomar   49.25
6 Cerritos   48.5
7 Mt. SAC   42.5
8 Sacramento   42.5
9 Sierra   41.5
10 Moorpark   37.5
11 R Santiago   30.5
12 Cuesta   25.75
13 Chabot   22
14 El Camino   21.5
15 S J Delta   20.75
16 Butte   18.75
17 West Valley   17
18 Santa Rosa   15
19 Diablo Valley 14.5
20 Pierce   13.5
21 Bakersfield   11
22 Modesto   1
23 Napa   0
23 S Bernadino   0
23 Skyline   0

Ken Bos-Rio Hondo 1972-1989, Coach of the Year 1979 and 1988, 2 State Championship Teams, 9 State Champions, 34 All-Americans, 10 Conference and Regional Championship Teams.

Season Record
Vince Plymire 31-3

1988 CCCAA State Wrestling Championships
December 9-10, 1988 El Camino College

118
Eric Millsap-Moorpark 3-2OT
Robert Kawamura-Rio Hondo
Casey Hankin-Palomar 4-3
Jim Feckner-Sierra
Gary Olivera-Chabot 9-7
Hugh Northington-Bakfld
Manuel Bettencourt-M 12-2
Raymond Parker-Lassen

126
Dave Singletary-Lassen 7-6
Tom Goodman-Bakersfield
Bill Montgomery-Cypress 7-3
Don Garriott-El Camino
Lee Soto-Sacramento 2-1
Don Fontana-Modesto
Fred Mora-R Santiago 7-2
Brad East-Fresno

134
Armando Morales Cerrito 8-0
Shawn Gilbert-West Valley
Bret Fry-Ranch Santiago 9-2
Doug Haring-Cypress
Martin Cisneros-SAC Forfeit
Bill Kopp-Lassen
Lewis Nebel-Rio Hondo Fall
Arron McDaniel Diablo Valley

142
Antonio McKee-Cerritos 6-4
Serg Mezheritsky-Moorpark
Chris Lovato-W Valley 11-5
Mokie McGee-Bakersfield
Billy Reid-Lassen Forfeit
Aaron Fontes-Chabot 7-2
Mike Saletta-Palomar

150
Jeff Buckalew-Diablo V 3-2OT
Ralph Rucker-Cypress
Gordon Stacer-Cerritos 7-3
Robert Nieto-West Valley
Trent Kenney-Golden V 6-1
Augie Senquiz-Lassen
R J Fairless-Palomar 9-1
Bret Harvey-Modesto

158
Aaron Gaier-Palomar 15-4
Blu Taylor-Sacramento
Art Orozco-Cypress 5-1
Scott Horrillo-Sierra
Ociel Zarate-Fresno 13-7
Manuel Gallego-Moorpark
David Gyorfi-Lassen 8-6
Casey Rhyan-Diablo Valley

167
Scott Boness-Lassen 24-10
Adrian Burley-Sacramento
Brian Millum-Palomar 5-4
Carl Pierce-El Camino
Pat Laeng-Modesto 11-8
Polo Ornelas-Rio Hondo
John Wallace-Butte Fall 3:49
Chad Sessons-R Santiago

177
Robert Zapata-Fresno 24-8
Paul House-Modesto
Billy Bennett-Lassen 6-4OT
Matt Hoffman-Golden Valley
Veto Becerra-Cypress 4-0
Chuck Leptich-Palomar
Clint Burch-Sacramento 11-7
Luis Castro-Bakersfield

190
Raab Rydeen-Palomar 16-7
Tedd Williams-Cerritos
Leo Garand-Cypress 4-2
Carsen Wollert Moorpark
Glenn Nye-Butte 8-4
Ken Cominsky-R Santiago
Brian Ormson-Sacram Forfeit
Marty Norris-Sierra

Heavyweight
Vince Plymire-Moorpk 9-1OT
Randy Gonzales-Cypress
Chuck Guptill Lassen Fall 2:30
Nick Barrios-Palomar
Osiel Salinas-Cerritos Forfeit
Hossein Kalabi-R Santiago
Derrick Cooper-Mt SAC 6-1
Adam Aikman-Santa Rosa

Most Outstanding Wrestler
Scott Boness-Lassen
Coach of the Year
Roye Oliver-Palomar

Team Score
1	Palomar	88
2	Lassen	87.75
3	Cypress	85
4	Cerritos	77
5	Moorpark	72.75
6	Sacramento	44
7	West Valley	39.25
8	Modesto	39
9	Bakersfield	32.5
10	Fresno	31.75
11	R Santiago	30.25
12	Rio Hondo	28.25
13	Sierra	25.5
14	Diablo Valley	23
15	El Camino	20.75
16	Golden West	17.5
17	Mt. SAC	12.5
18	Butte	11
18	Chabot	11
20	Santa Ana	2.5
21	San Bernadino	1
22	Cuesta	0
22	San Diego	0

Fred Burri Mt. SAC 34 years
157-92, 9 State Champions,
60 State Placers,
15 All-Americans

1989 CCCAA State Wrestling Championships
December 8-9, 1989 Fresno City College

118
Delfino Ochoa-Moor 4-1
Brian Ramirez-Fresno
Sam Lopez-Cypress 5-2
Pedro Fambona-Bakersfield
Albert Lalonde-Lassen 9-3
Jim Feekner-Sierra
Eric LeGarreta-G Valley 10-4
Steve Munson-Modesto

126
Orlando Montero-Cerris 21-6
Sam Bailey-Palomar
Maurice Hernandez Lasse 6-3
Pat Kinney-Rancho Santiago
Brad East-Fresno 6-2
Hugh Culebro-Modesto
Juan Padilla-West Valley 10-6
Brian Bertrand-Cypress

134
Shawn McGee-Lassen 8-4
Robby Cook-Moorpark
Chris Winkler-Palomar 4-3
John Petty-Fresno
Steve Hiller-Butte 14-4
Ben Mauriello-Bakersfield
John Peavier-Skyline 16-6
Shaune Silva-Sacramento

142
Antonio McGee-Cerritos*2-2
Serge Mezhertsky-Moorpark
Ray Rangel-Fresno-14-4
Doug Haring-Cypress
Chris Lovato-West Valle 14-4
Jose Juarez-Modesto
Efrain Gonzales-Mt. SAC 13-4
Donny Merlino-Golden Valley

150
Darren Status-Sierra 12-6
Scott Saltz-Sacramento
Robert Nieto-West Valley 2-1
Kevin Olivas-Fresno
Ron Fairness-Palomar Forfeit
Derek Patton-Bakersfield
Casey Rhyan-Diablo Valley
Craig Garriott-El Camino

158
Aaron Gaier-Palomar 11-10
Tom Henderson-Cerritos
Ociel Zarate-Fresno 12-6
Ryan Owings-R Santiago
Mokie McGee-Bakld Fall 2nd
Jim Grundler-Cuesta
Todd Burk-Lassen 10-3
Brian Swisher-Diablo Valley

167
Matt Davis-Lassen 9-4
Kevin Ivie-Cuesta
Carl Pierce-Cerritos Default
Greg Monteith-Cypress
Ty Stricker-Bakersfield 10-9
Chris Shaul-Golden West
Pat Laeng-Modesto 7-2
John Prefontaine-El Camino

177
Robert Zapata-Fresno 20-9
Tony Forres-Moorpark
Steve Clemmer-Pal Fall 2ND
Robert Hogue-Cuesta
Keith Spataro-Skyline 10-1
Vance Rea-Modesto
Mike Robles-Cypress 4-3
Jim Frohich-Bakersfield

190
Glenn Nye-Butte 5-2
Carson Wollert-Moorpark
Jack Sperry-Modesto 11-6
Mike Morin-Fresno
Ben Rice-El Camino 9-6
Tedd Williams-Cypress
Phil Myer-Golden West 12-0
Kirk Walukiewicz-West Valley

Heavyweight
George Anderson-Bakfld 5-2
Ken Fontes-Fresno
Robert Avila-El Cami Fall
Mike Rodgers-Butte
Brian Ormson-Sacrament 6-0
Phil Jones-Palomar
Trever Hargrave-Cyp Fall 2ND
Abran Salazar-Lassen

Most Outstanding Wrestler
Antonio McGee-Cerritos
Coach of the Year
Bill Musick-Fresno

Team Scores
1 Fresno   120.75
2 Moorpark   79
2 Cerritos   79
4 Palomar   76.5
5 Lassen   63.5
6 Bakersfield   60
7 Cypress   40.5
8 Butte   39.75
9 Cuesta   40.5
10 Modesto   33.25
11 West Valley   26.5
12 Sacramento   26.25
13 Sierra   25
14 Rancho Santiago 24.5
15 El Camino   24
16 Golden Valley 16
17 Skyline   9.5
18 Diablo Valley 7
19 Mt. San Antonio 4
20 Rio Hondo   1
21 Chabot   0
21 S J Delta   0
21 San Bernadino 0
21 San Diego   0
21 Santa Rosa   0

Career Record
Antonio McKee 61-1
Robert Zapata 71-2
Mokie McGhee 45-16
Ty Stricker 40-18
Derek Patton 43-18
Serge Mezhertsky 65-6
Season Record
Serge Mezhertsky 33-3

1990 CCCAA State Wrestling Championships
December 7-8, 1990 Cypress College

118
Sam Lopez-Cypress
Brian Ramirez-Fresno
Bill Scannell-Moorpark 20-4
Clint Hunter-Santa Rosa
Leroy Rivers-Diablo Valle 4-0
David Dawal-Chabot
Jason Booth-R Santigo Forfeit
Tom Gallegos-San Bernadino

126
Delfino Ochoa-Moorpark
Orlando Montero-Cerritos
Pat Kinney-Rancho Santa 7-6
Darren Uyematsu-El Camino
Al Reyes-West Valley 3-2
Brandon Keosky-Cuesta
Donnie Fontana-Modesto 6-2
Anthony Hamlett-San Berdn

134
Shawn McGee-Lassen
Angelo Gama-Modesto
Carlos Padilla-W Vall Fall 2:30
Mike Ortega-Fresno
Bo Leyva Rancho-Santiag 9-7
Ben Mauriello-Bakersfield
Abraham Sanchez-Paloma 5-2
Gustavo Ceja-Skyline

142
Robby Cook-Moorpark
B. Fortunbaugh-Cuesta
Ralph Olivas-Fresno 9-5
Dusty Harless-Palomar
Greg Valencia-East LA Defaut
Tim Lewis-Modesto
Pete Hedrick-West Valley
Howie Blair-Sierra

150
Country Taylor-Lessen
Scott Herndon-Bakersfield
Ismael Quintana-Fresno 13-1
Tyler Burbank-Cuesta
Rex Rabine-Modesto 5-1
Craig Sweeny-Sierra
John Luksa San Bernardin 5-3
Daryl Brenner-Palomar

158
Craig Le-West Valley
Clark Conover-Chabot
Marcus Boness-East LA 2-1
Ryan Owings-R Santiago
Neal Mason-Moorpark 13-1
Ian Swisher-Diablo Valley
Heath Haupt-Fresno
Not Given

167
Craig Doerfert-Diablo Valley
Polo Ornelas-Cerritos
Ed Luna-Palomar-Fall 5:38
Todd Burk-East LA
Kevin Ivie-Cuesta Fall 2:59
Deron Knarr-Sierra
Joe Ciprian-West Valley 18-3
Brandon Procter-Mt SAC

177
Luis Castro-Bakersfield
Phil Guerrero-Moorpark
Monday Eguabar-E LA 10-1
Scott Sperry-Modesto
Leo Perez-R Hondo Fall 1:10
Richard Estrada-Fresno
Dan Corah-West Valley 6-3
Shawn Slaven-Cuesta

190
Ken Stegall-Cypress
Tony Flores-Moorpark
Keith Spataro-Skyline 15-4
Steve Bach-Chabot
Mike Morin-Fresno 4-3
Eric Johnson-Palomar
Rick Herman-El Camino 9-0
Matt Scanavino-Sacramento

Heavyweight
Lamar Washington-East LA
Fred Ruiz-Mt San Antonio
Mike Rodgers-Butte 11-0
Tyron Smith-Santa Rosa 5-2
John Woltz-Bakersfield 9-1
Phil Davis-West Valley
Jesse Frost-Modesto Default
Joe Islas-Gavilan

Most Outstanding Wrestler
Delfino Ochoa-Moorpark

Coach of the Year
John Keever-Moorpark

Team Scores
1 Moorpark   96.25
2 Lassen   88
3 Fresno   77.5
4 West Valley   64.5
5 Modesto   53.75
6 Cuesta   46.5
7 Bakersfield   46
8 Cypress   43.75
9 Palomar   41.5
10 R Santiago   36.5
10 Cerritos   36.5
12 Diablo Valley 34.25
13 Chabot   32.5
14 Santa Rosa   20
15 Mt. SAC   17.5
15 Skyline   17.5
17 East LA   17
18 Sierra   16.5
19 El Camino   15.5
20 Butte   15
21 Rio Hondo   11.75
22 S Bernardino   9
23 Golden West   5
23 Gavilan   5
25 Sacramento   4
26 S J Delta   0
26 San Diego   0

Season Records
Sam Lopez 34-0
Brian Ramirez 38-5
Neal Mason 31-3

Career Records
Luis Castro 52-20-1

1990 CCCAA Champions

Front Row L-R: 150-Country Taylor-Lassen; 142-Robby Cook-Moorpark; 134-Shawn McGhee-Lassen; 125-Delfino Ochoa-Moorpark; 118-Sam Lopez-Cypress. **Back Row:** 275-Lamar Washington-Lassen; 190-Ken Stegall-Cypress; 177-Luis Castro-Bakersfield; 167-Craig Doerfert-Diablo Valley; 158-Chung Le-West Valley.   Photo by Irvin Oliner

1991 CCCAA State Wrestling Championships
December 13-14, 1991 West Valley College

118
Valo Barajas-Moorpark
Tom Gallegos-San Bernadino
Jason Booth-Rancho Santiago
Steve Ward-Bakersfield
Fernando Garcia-Cuesta
Mike Fore-Santa Rosa
Lkaika Molina-Palomar
Paul Gilman-West Valley

126
Jeff Hobart-Sacramento
Steve Morales-S Bernardino
Andy Norden-West Valley
Brad Miya-Moorpark
Anthony Hamlett-Cerritos
Mike Wilkey-Palomar
Eric La Garreta-Fresno
Dave Dawal-Chabot

134
Ben Ervin-Fresno
Richard Gutierrez-W Valley
Richard DelLaSelva-Moorprk
Gus Ceja-Skyline
Chris Pena-Cuesta
Angelo Gama-Modesto
Albert Morales-Cerritos
Jon Peterson-Santa Rosa

142
Dustin Riley-Fresno
Troy Monge-Cerritos
Raul Huerta-Palomar
Chad Lavezzo-Sacramento
Lee Heigi-Golden West
Chris Camarena-Moorpark
Marcial Cruz-West Valley
Geof Hayden-Diablo Valley

150
Dusty Harless-Palomar
Tim Louis-Modesto
Randy Moti-Fresno
Homer Ruiz-Cerritos
Kenny Richards-Golden West
Vance Wheatly-Sacramento
Wayne Blasingame El Camino
Kyle Behmlander Diablo Valle

158
Kent Davis-Mt. San Antonio
Neal Mason-Moorpark
Cung Lee -West Valley
LeMans Wells-Cerritos
Heath Haupt-Fresno
Demian Botero-El Camino
Chris Anderson-Modesto
Wendell Jefferson-Chabot

167
Clark Conover-Chabot
Erick Gaunt-El Camino
Luke Corona-Gavilan
Josh Gale-Cypress
Dan Kriger-Golden West
Lance Thurman-Sacramento
Ben VanStaavern-Modesto
Walter Muirhead-Moorpark

177
Monday Eguabor-East LA
Trent Williams-Cuesta
Todd Falk-Palomar
Dan Corah-West Valley
Ryan Miller-Sacramento
Richard Aguila-Rio Hondo
Todd Hoult-Moorpark
Mike Parcells-Cypress

190
Todd Parham- Sacramento
Phil Guerrero-Moorpark
Dan Stonebarger Diablo Valle
Pat King-San Joaquin Delta
Clint Madden-Sierra
Eric Johnson-Palomar
Leo Perez-East LA
Richard Garcia-West Valley

Heavyweight
Ed Neal-Fresno
Josh Gormley-El Camino
Adam Flores-Moorpark
Brian Tomazic-R Santiago
Bob Odiorne-Santa Rosa
Phil Martinez-Palomar
Tom Beavers-Bakersfield
John Meade-Modesto

Most Outstanding Wrestler
Monday Eguabor-East LA
Coach of the Year
John Keever-Palomar
Assistant Coach of the Year
Dan Martin-Moorpark

Team Scores
1 Moorpark   101.25
2 Fresno   86.5
3 Palomar   73.25
4 Sacramento   69.5
5 West Valley   63.5
6 Cerritos   50.5
7 El Camino   41.5
8 Modesto   36.25
9 Cuesta   35.5
10 S Bernadino   33
11 Chabot   31.5
12 East LA   26.75
13 R Santiago   24.75
14 Golden West   24
15 Mt. SAC   22.5
16 Diablo Valley   21.5
17 Santa Rosa   18.75
18 Cypress   17.5
19 Bakersfield   16.5
20 Gavilan   13.5
21 S J Delta   12.5
22 Skyline   12
23 Rio Hondo   9
24 Sierra   8.5

1992 CCCAA State Wrestling Championships
December 11-12, 1992 Cerritos College

118
Jesse Espinoza-Cerritos Fall*
Lkaika Molino-Palomar
Valo Barajas-Moorpark 10-9
Charles Valencia-East LA
Mike Evans-Cypress 3-0
Richard Morales-Bakersfield
Dan Palmar-Mt. SAC 11-6
Minh Pham-Golden West

126
Jeff Hobert-Sacramento 9-3
David Niedringhaus R Sntiago
Mike Wilkey-Palomr Fall 5:57
John Jimenez-Moorpark
Andy Nordeen-W Vall Forfeit
Alex Solano-Fresno
James Lopez-Cypress 3-2
Gilbert Silva-East LA

134
Ben Ervin-Fresno
Joey Solis-Rio Hondo
Jorge Ruiz-Moorpark 9-2
Chris Hofer-Palomar
Brian Burgess-R Santiago 2-1
Mark Cody-Cerritos
Aaron Reeves-Sacramen 10-7
Mario Barona-Diablo Valley

142
Marcial Cruz-West Valley
Kenny Williams-Cuesta
Dustin Riley-Fresno 7-1
Randy Wings-San Bernadino
Tony Okada-Cypress 9-2
Don Riddle-Modesto
Salvador Razo-Cerritos 7-4
Chris Camorena-Moorpark

150
Byron Campbell-Palomar
Alfonzo Tucker-Fresno
Kevin Burgess-R Santiago 7-5
Homer Ruiz-Cerritos
Ed Solis-Rio Hondo 15-4
Jim Casey-Cypress
Justin Schneider-Sac 2-0
Robert Favre-Moorpark

158
Rod Ludington-Cerritos
Gabe Estrada-Sacramento
Jason Pratt-Moorpark 6-1
Matt Wallace-Palomar
James Froelich-Modesto 7-1
Jeff Bronson-Sierra
Jimmie Bowers-R Hon Forfeit
Gabe Blanco-Diablo Valley

167
Eddie Luna-Palomar
Ben VanStaaveren-Modesto
Josh Gale-Cypress 7-5 OT
Ron Davis-Bakersfield
Jesse Bueno-Cerritos 9-1
Wade Caddin-Moorpark
Dave Crumpler-W Vall Forfeit
Rodger Norred-Fresno

177
Vahan Adzernyan-East LA
Jason Hendrick-Palomar
Doug Reisz-Modesto 9-2
Dave Franks-Bakersfield
Dave Umeda-Fresno 11-7
Xavier Flores-West Valley
Walter Muirhead-Moorp 8-2
James Enos-Chabot

190
Brian Tomasic-R Santiago
Ricardo Garcia-West Valley
Pat King-S J Delta 8-6
Todd Parham-Sacramento
Aaron Hayes-San Berdo 7-6
Phil Martinez-Palomar
Nicham Seamaan Cerri F 3:20
Tony Dorado-Sierra

275
Mike Carolan-Diablo Valley
Mike Bolster-Golden Valley
Ed Neal-Fresno 3-0
Matt Dellar-Sacramento
T C Gholar-Sacramento 15-4
Frank Blessing-Moorpark
William Green-Cypress Forfei
Chris Wenzler-Chabot

Most Outstanding Wrestler
Jesse Espinoza-Cerritos
Coach of the Year
Joe Ismay-Palomar
Assistant Coach of the Year
Steve Glassey-Cerritos

Team Scores
#	Team	Score
1	Palomar	116
2	Cerritos	86.75
3	Fresno	82
4	Moorpark	74.75
5	Sacramento	63
6	West Valley	58
7	R Santiago	57
8	Cypress	43.5
9	Modesto	41.5
10	East LA	34
11	Rio Hondo	33
12	Diablo Valley	30
13	Bakersfield	25
14	S Bernadino	18
15	Cuesta	17
16	Golden West	16.5
17	S J Delta	13.5
18	Sierra	11.75
19	Chabot	10
20	Mt. SAC	6.5
21	Santa Rosa	1
21	Gavilan	1
23	Skyline	.5

Record
Eddie Luna 40-2

Coaches
Palomar Joe Ismay
Cerritos-Jeff Smith
Fresno-Bill Musick
Moorpark-John Keever
Sacramento-Dave Pacheco
West Valley-Jim Root

1992 CCCAA CHAMPIONS Front Row L-R: 118-Jesse Espinosa-Cerritos; 126-Jeff Hobart-Sacramento; 134-Ben Ervin-Fresno; 142-Marcial Cruz-West Valley; 150-Byron Campbell-Palomar. **Back Row L-R:** 275-Mike Carolan-Diablo Valley; 190-Brian Tomazic-Rancho Santiago; 167-Eddie Luna-Palomar; 158-Rod Ludington-Cerritos; 177-Vagan Adzhemyan-East LA (not pictured)

1993 CCCAA CHAMPIONS Front Row L-R: 118-Charlie Valencia-East LA; 126-Gus Banuelos-West Valley; 134-Detren Gant-Fresno; 142-Pat Coffing-Sacramento City; 150-Tony Cooper-Sacramento City. **Back Row:** 275-Mike Carolan-Diablo Valley; 190-Brian Campbell-Modesto; 177-Vagan Adzhenyan-East LA; 167-Matt Padgett-Rancho Santiago; 158-Alfonzo Tucker-Fresno. Photo by Irvin Oliner

1993 CCCAA State Wrestling Championships
December 10-11, 1993 Santa Rosa College

118
Charlie-Valencia East LA
Victor Delacruz-Fresno
Orlano DeCastroverde-Cuest
Matt Jackson-Bakersfield
Louie Alejo-Gavilan
Stanley Parker-Palomar
Kelly Martinez-Cerritos
Phat Hoang-Rio Hondo

126
Gus Banuelos-West Valley
Yero Washington-Fresno
Rudy Garcia-Cerritos
Danny Hernandez-Cuesta
Ty Jacob-Palomar
Ruben Loera-Rio Hondo
Jerry Goodspeed-Cypress
Lance Wage-Santa Rosa

134
Detran Gant-Fresno
Dave Niedringhaus-R Sntia
Mark Cody-Cerritos
Saul Gomez-West Valley
Vance Elliott-Modesto
Aaron Rives-Sacramento
Sergio Mar-Gavilan
Chris Pena-Cuesta

142
Pat Coffing-Sacramento
Eddie Ramos-Fresno
Jason Gear-Bakersfield
Pete Hendrick-West Valley
Jorge Ruiz-Moorpark
Craig Welk-Palomar
Joe Lesage-Skyline
Shane Roberts-Santa Rosa

150
Terry Cooper-Sacramento
Emilio Vadnais-Diablo Valley
Dan Santana-Cerritos
Chris Hefar-Palomar
Doug Gaines-Santa Rosa
Ryan Johnson-Fresno
Mike Prefontaine-Mt. SAC
Josh Bankman-Chabot

158
Alfonzo Tucker-Fresno
Jason Pratt-Moorpark
Rick Carson-Cerritos
Ron Davis-Bakersfield
Todd Oliver-Sacramento
Joe Totsis Rio Hondo
Clayton Schneider-Cuesta
Mike Perez-West Valley

167
Matt Padgett-R Santiago*
Brian Haupt-Fresno
Trent Williams-Cuesta
Jesse Bueno-Cerritos
Mario Varela-Moorpark
Rich Peterson-Santa Rosa
Atti Toth-Palomar
Oscar Balderrama-Mt. SAC

177
Vahan Adzhernyan-East LA
Eric Gaunt-Golden West
Bislot Detsiev-Cerritos
Dave Crumpler-West Valley
Nayif Abudullah-R Santiago
Don Burdis-Mt. SAC
Johann Gerlach-Santa Rosa
Tim Bruce-Diablo Valley

190
Brian Campbell-Modesto
Todd Hoult-Moorpark
James Hill-Cerritos
Brandon Burks-Sacramento
Elliot Booker-West Valley
Joe Lipps-Rancho Santiago
Amilcar Choeun-Skyline
Kory Westbury-Fresno

275
Mike Carolan-Diablo
Mike Balster-Golden West
Jeff Wara-Cerritos
Mike Gamble-Palomar
Chris Wellisch-West Valley
Dan Jones-Sacramento
Joe Demirjian-East LA
Jack Kearnat-Gavilan

Most Outstanding Wrestler
Matt Padgett-Rancho Santiago

Coach of the Year
Bill Musick-Fresno

Assistant Coach of the Year
Robert Arbalo-Fresno

Team Scores
1 Fresno   116.5
2 Cerritos   104.25
3 West Valley   74.25
4 Sacramento   72
5 Moorpark   55.75
6 East LA   49.25
7 Palomar   48
8 R Santiago   47.75
9 Cuesta   43
10 Diablo Valley   42
11 Bakersfield   34.25
12 Golden West   33.5
13 Modesto   32
14 Santa Rosa   25
15 Rio Hondo   16.25
16 Gavilan   15.75
17 Skyline   11.5
18 Cypress   7.5
19 Mt. SAC   6.25
20 Chabot   3.5

Record
Alfonzo Tucker 37-0
Career record
Alfonzo Tucker 70-4

1994 CCCAA State Wrestling Championships
December 2-3, 1994 Rio Hondo College

118
Jake Roberts-Palomar F 2:27
Isaac Pumarejo-Fresno
Aaron Radman-Bakfld 4-2
Brian Gilliland-Cerrito
Lam Duong-Victor Valley 9-3
Eric Moellar-West Valley
David Rivas-East LA Fall :37
Tom Manibusian-Diab Valley

126
Gus Banuelos-West Vall 11-2
Vic Delacruz-Fresno
Manuel Tabarez-Cuesta 6-5
Chris Wright-Palomar
Phat Hoang-Rio Hondo 10-8
Tyson Escobar-Sierra
Ahid Diab-Cerritos 12-7
Frankie Norton-Chabot

134
Yero Washington Freso* 25-6
David Gayer-Cerritos
Shane Holloway-R Santia 8-1
John Jimenez-Moorpark
Sergia Mar-Gavilan 1-0
Javier Delgado-Golden West
Brad Curry-Cypress 4-3
Jesse Mindlin-Palomar

142
Eddie Ramos-Fresno 23-7
Ray Fonseca-Sierra
Dennis Cummings-Cuesta 7-2
Johnny Torres-R Santiago
Juan Alvarez-Cerritos 6-5
Tim Bonebright-Moorpark
Robert North-Palomar 10-5
Ignacio Franco-Santa Rosa

150
Ernesto Espinoza-Paloma 6-1
Rudolph James-Cerritos
Donald Riddle-Modesto 11-1
Mike Williams-Bakersfield
Raul Tapia-Mt. SAC 17-4
Jack Crosby-Santa Rosa
Ray Benavides-Fresno 5-4
Mark Burnes-Sacramento

158
Doug Blake Mt San Anton 7-2
Mark Shin-Skyline
Craig Welk-Palomar 5-4
Doug Miller-Fresno
Josh Nogarr Diablo Valley 5-0
Kyle Plummer-Moorpark
Mario Moreno-Cerritos 8-0
Cliff Randolph-S J Delta

167
Shawn Dawley-Sierra Fal 1:31
Nick Spataro-Skyline
Warren Newsome-W Vall 3-2
Enrique Carreon-Cerritos
Doug Gaines-Santa Rosa 4-1
Chris Delgado-Gavilan
Derek Nendel-Sac Forfeit
Jeremy Pratt-Moorpark

177
Brain Bowley-Santa Rosa 8-6
Terry Tuzzolino-R Santiago
Jacob Harman-Cerritos 3-2
Elias Zamorano-Fresno
Dustin Lewis Diablo V Default
Eric Parham-Sierra
Ben Spencer-Cuesta 13-5
Darren Hill-Mt San Antonio

190
Adimu Madyum-Cerritos DQ
2 no place
Nayif Abudullah-R Santia 9-8
Mike Barns-Gavilan
Johann Geriach-Santa Ra Def
Brian Campbell-Modesto
Joey Oliveira-West Valley
8 didn't make weight

275
Chad Mast-Fresno 6-4OT
Dan Jones-Sacramento
Willie Green-Cypress Fal 1:04
Dan Bracamonte-Cerritos
Diggory Williams-Santa R12-4
Chris Wellisch-West Valley
Robert Vasquez-G West 9-2
Jason Sparks Ranch-Santiago

Most Outstanding Wrestler
Yero Washington-Fresno
Coach of the Year
Bill Musick-Fresno
Assistant Coach of the Year
Keith Spataro-Skyline

Team Scores
1	Fresno	130.5
2	Cerritos	109.5
3	Palomar	81.5
4	R Santiago	69
5	Santa Rosa	64
6	Sierra	57
7	West Valley	50.5
8	Moorpark	38
9	Skyline	37
10	Mt. SAC	36.5
11	Bakersfield	34.5
12	Cuesta	34
13	Sacramento	30
14	Gavilan	29.5
15	Modesto	28.5
16	Diablo Valley	26.5
17	Cypress	24.5
18	Rio Hondo	16
19	Golden West	14
20	Victor Valley	9.5
21	Chabot	6.5
22	East LA	6.0
23	San Bernadino	1
24	S J Delta	0

1995 CCCAA State Wrestling Championships
December 1-2, 1995 Chabot College

118
David Rivas-East LA
Jake Roberts-Palomar
Damon Broadbent Rio Hondo
Julio Garcia-Skyline
Norman Abas-Fresno
Kelly Martinez-Cerritos
Miguel Iniguez-Mt. SAC
Thoumes Vesapralich Modes

126
Joe Estrada-San Bernadino
Ed Morton-Cuesta
Randy Bowers-Cerritos
Jason Allen-Mt. San Antonio
Leonard Caniamilla-Diablo Va
Sid Garcia-Bakersfield
Jimmy Gonzalez-Golden Wes
Wes Barone-West Valley

134
Omar Diaz-Mt. San Antonio
Geovanny Aquilar-Rio Hondo
Patrick Hammond-Fresno
Dave Gayer-Cerritos
Chris Wright-Palomar
David Lupinsky Diablo Valley
Jason Merrell-Bakersfield
Nate Harrison-Santa Rosa

142
Alfred Frausto-R Santiago
Fred Leavy-Cerritos
Randy Velarde-Mt. SAC
Ken Alexander-West Valley
Ernesto Espinoza-Palomar
Jesse Kuntz-Fresno
Jose Ramirez-Rio Hondo
Dylan Burgess-Modesto

150
Anthony Valencia-East LA
Marino Castillo-West Valley
Eric Vera-Cerritos
Marino Moreno-Cerritos
James Smithson-Fresno
David Afoa-Golden West
Ricco Morel-Palomar
Carlos Gonzales-Sierra

158
Phil Holmgren-Mt SAC
Rudolph James-Cerritos
Brandon Rush-Sacramento
Ryan Williams-Bakersfield
Brian Samhammer-Palomar
Beto Medrano-Fresno
Carlos Castellanos-Rio Hondo
Jerry Sutherland-West Valley

167
Greg Jackson-Cerritos
Paul Healy-Rio Hondo
Albery Romero-Palomar
Doug Miller-Fresno
Ismael Abdullah-R Santiago
Nick Spataro-Skyline
Chris Edwards-Golden West
Davey Bowles-Santa Rosa

177
Brian Bowles-Santa Rosa
Terry Tuzzolino-R Santiago
Raphael Davis-Golden West
Chris Cabrera-Victor Valley
Eric Magana-Rio Hondo
Derek Stonebarger-Cypress
Lawrence Saenz-Sacramento
David Serrano-San Bernadino

190
Jacob Ortiz-Golden West
Rami Kiriakos San Bernardino
Donny Rider-Fresno
Mike Duran-Mt. San Antonio
Josh Smith-Santa Rosa
Dustin Silva-Sacramento
Jason King-Moorpark
Sean Malliet-Palomar

275
Gabe Zagata-Skyline
Jeff Ware-Cerritos
Francisco Duran-S Bernandin
Ruben Reynaga-Sacramento
David Wheeler-Cypress
Brendon Helston-Bakersfield
Chad Totina-Palomar
Larry Newton-Santa Rosa

Most Outstanding Wrestler
Brian Bowles-Santa Rosa
Coach of the Year
Jeff Smith-Cerritos
Assistant Coach of the Year
Greg Gascon-Cerritos

Team Scores
1	Cerritos	118.5
2	Palomar	79.5
3	Mt. SAC	77
4	Fresno	68
5	Rio Hondo	65.5
6	San Bernadino	60
7	Skyline	56.5
8	Golden West	56
9	R Santiago	53
10	East LA	46
11	Sacramento	42
12	West Valley	41.5
13	Santa Rosa	40
14	Bakersfield	34.5
15	Cuesta	34

Bill Musick Fresno City,
22 Years, 4 State Titles,
12 Northern California Titles,
17 Conference Titles,
2012 9-0 Duals and 9-0 in
Tournaments, 247-50-5

1995 134lb
6-David Lupinsky-Diabo Valley, 4-David Gayer-Cerritos, 2-Geovanny Aguilar-Rio Hondo, 1-Champion-Omar Diaz-Mt. SAC, 3-Patrick Hammond-Fresno, 5-Chris Wright-Palomar, 7-Jason Merrell-Bakersfield, 8-Nate Harrison-Santa Rosa(Not in Photo)

1995 Heavyweight
6-Brendon Helston-Bakersfield, 4-Ruben Reynaga-Sacramento, 2-Jeff Ware-Cerritos, 1-Champion-Gabe Zagata-Skyline, 3-Francisco Duran-San Bernardino, 5-David Wheeler-Cypress, 7-Chad Totina-Palomar, 8-Larry Newton-Santa Rosa(Not in Photo)

California Community College Champions - First Row: 190-Jacob Ortiz, Golden West; Second Row: (left to right) 167-Greg Jackson, Cerritos; 134-Omar Diaz, Mt. San Antonio; 150-Anthony Valencia, East LA; 118-David Rivas, East LA; 177-Brian Bowles, Santa Rosa; 275-Gabe Zagata, Skyline; Third Row: 158-Phil Holmgren, Mt. San Antonio; 126-Joe Estrada, San Bernardino; 142-Alfred Frausto, Rancho Santiago. Photo by A.G. Aldrich

1996 CCCAA Champions Left Front: 177-Raphael Davis-Golden West; 190-Outstanding Wrestler-Tito Ortiz-Golden West (undefeated in college wrestling); 158-Branden Rush-Sacramento City; 275-Dave Wheeler-Cypress. **Center Left:** 134-Stan Greene-Fresno City; 126-Paris Ruiz-Fresno City. **Left Back:** 142-Alfred Frausto-Rancho Santiago; 118-Mario Soloria-West Valley; 150-Mario Castillo-West Valley; 167-Albert Romero-Polomar College

1996 CCCAA State Wrestling Championships
December 19-20, 1996 Victor Valley College

118
Mario Solorio-West Vall 16-7
Julio Garcia-Skyline
Dave Leonard-Sierra Fall 3:59
Santos Garcia-Fresno
Justin Eisner-Cuesta Forfeit
Toon Alichanh-Modesto
Paco Arriaga-Mt. SAC 5-3
Aldo Broussaro-Palomar

126
Paris Ruiz-Fresno 7-4
Mark Kavanagh-Chabot
Kory Singh-Mt. SAC 14-9
Tom Vierra-Sacramento
Randy Bowers Cerrit Fall 3:20
Miguel Valencia-R Santiago
Levi Harbin-Palomar 15-3
Chad Andersen-Cuesta

134
Stan Green-Fresno 7-4
Justin Dersch-Sacramento
Joe Estrada-San Bernadin 4-2
Ty Jacob-Palomar
Matt Werner-Moorpark 4-3
Ed Morton-Cuesta
Javier Vasquez-Mt. SAC 8-6
Jason Lowe-Golden West

142
Alfred Frausto-R Santiago 9-2
Luis Rivas-Golden West
Juan Alvarez-Cerritos 9-4
Todd Adams-Cuesta
Jose Ramirez-Rio Hondo 11-2
William Brown-Fresno
Rafael Munoz-Chabot 4-3
Fred Molano-Moorpark

150
Mario Castillo-West Vall 10-7
Gabe Roman-Moorpark
Juan Lopez-Cerritos 6-4
Phil Wozniak-R Santiago
Ray Fonseca-Cerritos F 2:26
Rick Williamson-Palomar
M Ratanasurak-R Ho 5-2
Justin D'Amico-Santa Rosa

158
Branden Rush-Sacrament 7-6
Stefan Foley-Skyline
Ati Conner-Moorpark 19-4
Trever Strand-Modesto
Drew Hedlund-Cuesta 11-5
Daniel Prescott-Mt. SAC
Eric Taft-Palomar 7-4
Gabriel Ochoa-Cerritos

167
Alberto Romero-Paloma 13-9
Lawrence Johnson Bakfld
Peter Matheson-Chabot 11-7
Victor Perry-Sacramento
Cory Stropshire-Moorpa 13-6
Ryan Fasano-Santa Rosa
John Nogan-Diablo Valle 10-6
Chris Edwards-Golden West

177
Raphael Davis-Gold West 8-3
Joey Olivas-Modesto
Rodney Cooksey-Palo F 3:40
David Serrano-San Bernadino
Doug Burr-Cuesta 4-2
Steve Nielson-Mt. SAC
Carlos Miranda R Santiago 3-2
Darin Humphrey-Bakersfield

190
Tito Ortiz Golden West F 1:07
Jack Blosser-Sacramento
Scott Rojo-Cerritos 7-1
Danny Ramirez-Moorpark
James Gomez-R Santia F 1:35
Jim Hughes-West Valley
Eric Pack-Bakersfield 6-2
Donovan McHenry-Cuesta

275
Dave Wheeler-Cypress 5-3
Randy Leydecker Sacramento
Jim Ambriz-R Santiao Default
Scott Bonardi-Chabot 5-2OT
Ron Williams Mt. SAC Default
Gabe Zagata-Skyline
Jared Strauss-Cuesta 2-1
Richard Martin-S Bernadino

Most Outstanding Wrestler
Tito Ortiz-Golden West
Coach of the Year
Dave Pacheco-Sacramento
Assistant Coach of the Year
Brett Kranig-Sacramento

Team Scores
1	Sacramento	95.5
2	Palomar	79
3	R Santiago	75
4	Golden West	74
5	Cerritos	70
8	Moorpark	69.5
7	Fresno	68
8	Cuesta	67
9	West Valley	50
10	Mt. SAC	49.5
11	Chabot	48
12	Skyline	46
13	Modesto	38
14	Bakersfield	25.5
15	Cypress	25
16	San Berardino	24.5
17	Rio Hondo	21.5
18	Sierra	12
18	Santa Rosa	12
20	Diablo Valley	6

Career Record
Branden Rush 60-?

1997 CCCAA State Wrestling Championships
West Valley College

118
Dave Leonard-Sierra 3-0
Brian Gilliland-Cerritos
Fernando Serrato's-G Vall 4-3
Jason Bedsole-Palomar
Cleo Johnson-Bakersfield 5-3
Bert Clayton-Skyline
Jose Maroquin-Cypress 7-6
Ernie Nunez-Moorpark

126
Levi Harbin-Palomar 7-4
Wes Mayfield-Sierra
Juan Roman-Moorpark 11-6
Amir Noble-Mohamad Sacra
Steve Martin-Skyline Default
Camilo Gonzales-Mt. SAC
Pete Kuntz-Cypress 8-3
Omar Orozco-Santa Ana

134
Parris Ruiz-Fresno 6-5
George Moreno-Bakersfield
Irvin Michael-Palomar 7-3
David Jaramillo-Mt. SAC
Miguel Soto-Cerritos 13-0
Gabe Ochoa-Skyline
Eddie Sanchez- Santa Ana 9-6
Jeff Silveira-West Valley

142
Jonte Davis-Fresno Fall
Jesse Campos-Moorpark
Seth Garvin-Cerritos 6-4
Janie Alvarez Rio Hondo
Rafael Munoz-Chabot 8-2
Leo Perez-Palomar
Mario Gonzales-Bakfld 13-2
Luis Renteria-Santa Anna

150
William Brown-Fresno 9-5
Scott Erickson-Moorpark
Juan Gallardo-Bakersfield 9-5
Matt Gordon-Golden West
Chris Casares-Cerritos 11-8
Jeff Dickey-Modesto
Sherwood-Thomson Sac 13-7
Mike Zuckerman-Palomar

158
Bruno Bicocca-Cuesta Fall
Trevor Strand-Moorpark 10-2
Gabe Roman-Moorpark 10-2
Jose Landin-Bakersfield
Bill Miles-Sierra 5-1
Corey Hall -Cerritos
Abdullah Mohammed MS 13-6
Jeremy Bragg-Skyline

167
Ati Conner-Moorpark 17-5
Stefan Foley-Skyline
Heath Jones-Cuesta 11-7
Kevin Sanger-Palomar
Joel Perry-Modesto Default
Kyle Osborne-Mt. SAC
Matt Dusch-Santa Ana 11-3
James Williams-Sacramento

177
Chuck Sandlin-Moorp 2-0 OT
Davey Bowles-Santa Rosa
Brandon Bettencourt-Sier 9-3
Jake Shields-Cuesta
Steve Cooper-Golden We 9-2
Bradley Roberts-Sana Ana
Aaron Stanton-Skyline 2-1
Jared Westberg-Bakersfield

190
Tom Gohde-Fresno 10-2
Jay Wanier-Sierra
Adam Gilbert Cypress 6-4
Steve Ruiz-Santa Ana
Abner Morgan-Chabot 4-0
Ryan Shaw-Sacramento
Reginold Frayson-Skyline 3-1
Hassan Ayoub-San Bernadino

275
Randy Leydecker-Sacram 6-1
Ruben Reynaga-Sierra
Rigo Jimenez-Rio Hondo 8-6
John Devine-Skyline
Scott Bonardi-Chabot Default
Lloyd Marchbanks-Palomar
Dennis Garcia Santa Ana 10-5
Jason King-Moorpark

Most Outstanding Wrestler
Ati Conner-Moorpark
Coach of the Year
Paul Keysaw-Moorpark
Assistant Coach of the Year
Steve Payan-Moorpark

Team Scores
1	Moorpark	118.5
2	Sierra	98
3	Fresno	92
4	Palomar	75.5
5	Skyline	66.6
7	Cerritos	59
7	Bakersfield	56.6
8	Sacramento	53
9	Cuesta	49.5
10	Santa Ana	41
11	Modesto	38.5
12	Mt. SAC	31.5
13	Golden West	30.5
14	Chabot	30
15	Rio Hondo	26.5
16	Cypress	26
17	Santa Rosa	19
18	East LA	6
19	S Bernadino	4
19	West Valley	4
21	Diablo Valley	2.5
22	S J Delta	1.5

Career records
Parris Ruiz 67-4
Jonte Davis 32-2
Randy Leydecker 61-?
Season Records
Ati Conner 33-0
Juan Roman 29-2

1998 CCCAA State Wrestling Championships
December 4-5, 1998 Moorpark College

125
Camilo Gonzalez Mt. SAC*6-4
Jason Bedsole-Palomar
Eric Ferreira-Santa Rosa 9-2
Tony Madrigal-Bakersfield
Bert Clayton-Skyline 13-9
Froilan Gonzales-Goldn West
Joey Beaudoim-Modesto 4-1
Justin McLelland-Fresno

133
5abian Sandoval-Cuesta 6-4
Irvin Michael-Palomar
Alex Ortiz-Fresno 7-5
Robert Espejo-Cerritos
Ben Ashley-Bakersfield 10-6
Manuel Garcia-Sacramento
Pablo Sanchez-Skyline F 1:18
Brook Buonaccorsi-Sant Rosa

141
Ryan Meloche-Bakfld 9-7
Vince Elliot-Modesto
George Moreno-Fresno 3-1
Leo Perez-Palomar
Richard Dixson-San Rosa 6-1
David Gomez-Rio Hondo
Ken Coburn-Chabot 11-2
Jeremy Parker-Diablo Valley

149
Joey Martinez-Skyline 5-4
R J Arballo-Fresno
Juan Lopez-Cuesta 14-2
C J Johnson-Palomar
Cirillo Reyes-Bakersfield 4-2
Jason Lowe-Golden West
Mike Zuckerman-Sierra 10-4
Nate Coffin-Sacramento

157
Ken Murray-Chabot 8-1
Jeff Sereni-Skyline
Beau Taylor-Cuesta 6-1
Kenny Dixson-Santa Rosa
Adam Winters-Sierra 11-4
Jesse Fouch-Modesto
Beau Daniel-Fresno 13-9
Brian Pogue-Palomar

165
Heath Sims-Cerritos 9-1
Ciemente Moreno-Fresno
Shawn Henebry-W Valley 8-5
Jesse Standlea-Golden West
Monico Enriquez-East LA 5-3
Cornello Arreola-Mt. SAC
Jason Gigliotti-Palomar 8-3
Chris Schmidt-Santa Rosa

174
Brian Webster-S Ana 1-1 OT
Larry Silva-Fresno
Jose Ruano-East LA 11-9
Tim Heinrich-West Valley
Eric Ortegren-S Rosa 7-1
Jeff Dahi-Sierra
Bobby Chipman-Skyline 7-5
Bryan Ysais-Diablo Valley

184
Jason Rossotti-Fresno 5-4
Chuck Sandlin-Moorpark
Summer Brown-W Valley 5-1
Scott Smith-Sacramento
Todd Lesieur-Mt. SAC Default
Bill Tedd-Santa Ana
Allen Clegg-Palomar 12-7
Chris Fort-Santa Rosa

197
David Bonilla-Mt. SAC 3-1
Hector Ramirez-East LA
Jack Shields-Cuesta 9-0
Jay Wariner-Sierra
James Mason-Chabot 8-5
Gerold James-Skyline
Melon Melkonian M-park 5-4
Ryan Phips-Fresno

Heavyweight
Masoud Rahmani-Cerrit 14-5
Dan Maynard-Santa Ana
Mercedes Kinner-Fresno 6-0
Emmitt Brown-Chabot
Tony Gomez-San Berdo 7-1
Chris Arnold-Sierra
Darren Hill-Mt. SAC 13-7
Dave Knopfer-West Valley

Most Outstanding Wrestler
Camilo Gonzalez-Mt. SAC
Coach of the Year
Robert Arballo-Fresno
Assistant Coach of the Year
Yero Washington-Fresno

Team Scores
1	Fresno	128
2	Palomar	77
3	Skyline	71.5
4	Cerritos	67.5
5	Mt. SAC	66.5
6	Cuesta	65
7	Santa Rosa	62
8	Chabot	52.5
9	Santa Rosa	51
10	Bakersfield	48.5
11	Sierra	46.5
12	West Valley	42.5
13	East LA	38
14	Golden West	43.5
15	Modesto	32.5
16	Sacramento	26.5
17	Moorpark	23
18	S Bernadino	13
19	Rio Hondo	8.5
20	Diablo Valley	7.5
21	Cypress	3.5
22	Victor Valley	3
23	S J Delta	2.5

Records
Joey Martinez-Skyline
Undefeated
Masoud Rahmani Cerritos
Undefeated
Career Record
George Moreno-Fresno 63-5
Jake Shields-Cuesta 56-14

1998 CCCAA STATE CHAMPIONS: L-R 174-Brian Webster-Santa Ana; 149-Joey Martinez-Skyline; 141-Ryan Meloche-Bakersfield; 197-David Bonilla-Mt. SAC; 125-Outstanding Wrestler-Camilo Gonzales-Mt. SAC; 133-Fabian Sandoval-Cuesta; 184-Juson Rossotti-Fresno City; Heavyweight-Masoud Rahmani-Cerritos; 165-heath Sims-Cerritos; 157-Ken Murray-Chabot(not pictured)

1999 STATE CHAMPIONS L-R 133-James Guizar-Palomar; Heavyweight-Joe Vitomile-Palomar; 165-Arsen Aleksan-Mt. SAC; 184-David Bonilla-Mt. SAC; 174-Larry Johnson-Bakersfield; 141-Ryan Meloche-Bakersfield; 149-Casey Olson-Fresno; 125-Fernando Serratos-Golden West; 197-Hossin Oshani-Cerritos; 157-Brian Holt-Sierra

1999 CCCAA State Wrestling Championships
December 3-4, 1999 Skyline College

125
Fernando Serratos-G Vall 3-1
Nick Nakamura-Rio Hondo
J J Roberts-Palomar 1-0
Guy Horcasitas-Mt. SAC
Cleo Johnson-Bakersfield 3-2
James Blea-S J Delta
Chris Hammer-Sierra 14-2
Donnie Green-Santa Rosa

133
James Guizar-Palomar 14-5
Robert Sepulveda-Fresno
Marc Kavanagh-Chabot 7-2
Yonas Woldu-Moorpark
Bryce Escobar-Sierra 3-1
Frankie Alvarez-West Valley
Jose Palomares-San Ana 12-6
Frank Lara-Cerritos

141
Ryan Meloche-Bakfld 5-4
Juan Roman-Moorpark
Ben Baca-Fresno 7-2
Jesse Bastias-Sierra
Nick Hopping-Mod Default
Sal Garcia-Cerritos
Alex Garcia-Gol West Default
Ferando Flanagan-W Valley

149
Casey Olson-Fresno 12-4
Brett Gordon-Sacramento
Saul Lucatero-Moorp Default
Justin Fraser-Diablo Valley
C J Johnson-Palomar 17-4
Luis Renteria-Santa Rosa
Aaron Heinberger-Siea F 4:18
Cullen Rogers-Cuesta

157
Brian Holt-Sierra 12-2
Freddy Rivera-Mt. SAC
Eddie Lucatero-Moorpark 5-2
Shamar Pigg-Bakersfield
Shawn Betts-Cuesta 5-3
Ben Ward-Diablo Valley
Jesse Fouch-Modesto 8-3
Josh Delfin-Palomar

165
Arsen Aleksanyan-MP 2-1OT
Heath Sims-Cerritos
Art Martinez-Sac F 4:17
Alman Kerste-Bakersfield
Terrence Carter-Skyline 10-6
Bryan Pogue-Palomar
Monico Enriquez-East LA
Russell Smithson-Fresno

174
Larry Johnson-Bakfield 11-6
Brian Webster-Santa Ana
Sion King-Sacramento 5-3
Kevin Sanger-Palomar
Marc Banks-West Valley 4-0
Stuart Young-Moorpark
Aaron Spiller-Cuesta Default
Ricky Singh-Modesto

184
David Bonilla-Mt SAC 8-6
Chris Gonzalez-Moorpark
Dan Martinez-Cuesta 5-0
Phillip Miller-Victor Valley
Edgar Hernandez-WV Default
Nathan Loughran-Santa Rosa
Cortney Page-Sacrament 3-0
Asa Randolph-Cerritos

197
Hossin Oshani-Cerritos
Hector Ramirez-East LA
Bobby Chipman-Skyline 12-0
Piki Astudillo-Golden West
Ryan Philp-Fresno 8-7
Mike Mullin-Sierra
Ben Vendt-Pearce-S Rosa 9-7
Adam Benshea-Moorpark

285
Joe Vitromile Palomar Defaul
Masoud Rahmani-Cerritos
Freddie Aquitania Skyli F 1:47
J T Morales-Rio Hondo
Mercedes Kinner-Fresno 5-3
Rafael Lucero-Santa Ana
Tim Golia-Sierra 4-3
Richard Martin-S Bernadino

Most Outstanding Wrestler
Arsen Aleksanyan-Moorpark
Coach of the Year
Paul-Keysaw-Moorpark
Assistant Coach of the Year
Rich Bailey-Moorpark

Team Scores
1	Moorpark	107.5
2	Palomar	98
3	Fresno	78
4	Bakersfield	70
5	Cerritos	67.5
6	Sierra	66.5
7	Sacramento	60
8	Mt. SAC	48.5
9	Skyline	46.5
10	Golden West	44.5
11	Santa Ana	36.5
12	Cuesta	31
13	Rio Hondo	27
14	West Valley	26
15	East LA	22
16	Diablo Valley	21
17	Modesto	20
18	Santa Rosa	18
19	Chabot	14.5
20	Victor Valley	13.5
21	S J Delta	13
22	S Bernadino	3
23	Cypress	0

Career Record
Dan Martinez-Cuesta 42-8
Season Record
Saul Lucatero-Moorpark 31-2

2000 CCCAA State Wrestling Championships
December 1-2, 2000 Golden West College

125
Jack Anaya-Cerritos 1-0
Guy Horcasitas-Mt. SAC
Jesse Miramontes G W 6-5OT
Tommy Peralta-Santa Ana43
Chad McKenny-Fresno 11-2
Joey Beaudon-Modesto
Israel Navarro-Palomar 6-1
Jimmy Stevenson-Skyline

133
Robert Sepulveda-Fresno 5-2
Justin Bedwell-Chabot
Ricky Guzman-Rio Hondo 7-4
Adrian Velasquez-W Valley
Bumper Fleischman M 14
Juan Revuelta-Cerritos
Brandon Gushiken-WF 4:54
Travis Newton-Santa Rosa

141
Janes Guizar-Palomar 12-5*
Pablo Sanchez-Skyline
Scott Beck-Fresno 9-7
David Gomez-Rio Hondo
Fernando Flangan W Val 11-4
Jaret Newton-Santa Rosa
Camron Harris-G Val Default
Dylan Depue-Cuesta

149
Saul Lucatero-Moorpark 3-1
Casey Olsen-Fresno
Jesse Bastian-Sierra 5-3
Brett Gordon-Sacramento
Andrew Donaldson-S Ros 9-4
Josh Johnson Cerritos
Kevin Knall-S J Delta 9-2
George Smith-Skyline

157
Joey Martinez-Skyline F 4:37
Steve Hernandez-Moorpark
Jason Kochamp-Sierra 14-7
Ben Ward-Sacramento
Royce Thomas-Sa Rosa 12-4
Danny Hawkins-Fresno
Doc Ly-S J Delta Fall 6:43
Al Ledger-Palomar

165
Brian Holt-Sierra 4-0
Nick Tatum-Sacramento
Nick Cardenez-Palomar F1:01
Gerardo Rodriguez-Cypress
Alman Karste-Bakersfield 7-3
Ray Torres-Moorpark
Josh Jarrett-Golden West
Josue Tirado-Fresno

174
Wes Tielens-Palomar 8-7
Sion King-Sacramento
Shamar Pigg-Bakfld 2-2OT Ct
Shannon Sams-Moorpark
Terrence Carter-Sky F 4:50
Brian Burnett-Cerritos
Jesse Juarez-G Valley Default
Mike Beckman-Fresno

184
Chris Gonzalez-Moorprk 11-6
Phillip Miller-Victor Valley
Shane Clark Sacramento 4-2
Marc Banks-West Valley
Brandan Bear-Modest F 5:18
Joe Evano-Mt. SAC
Tim Neves-Santa Rosa F 1:53
Lucas Crabtree-Cuesta

197
Dan Martinez-Cuesta 11-8
Jeff Dahl-Sierra
Ben Fa Anunu-Chabot 5-4
Jay Foster-S J Delta
Sean Reid-Sacramento 3-1
Steve Grode-Golden West
Joe Stevenson-Victor Vay 3-1
Chris Sherley-Palomar

Heavyweight
Hossin Oshani-Cerritos 5-3
Ben Flores-Moorpark
Ken Kragie-Cuesta 8-3
Jason Paul-Palomar
Ricky Gamero-Sierra 6-1
Ron Davis-S J Delta
David Walker-Sky :29
Carlos Ceja-East LA

Most Outstanding Wrestler
James Guizar-Palomar
Coach of the year
Paul Keysaw-Moorpark
Assistant Coach of the Year
Tom Olejnik-Moorpark

Team Scores
1 Moorpark   110
2 Fresno   94.5
3 Palomar   89.5
4 Sacramento   87.5
5 Sierra   79
6 Skyline   73.5
7 Golden West   62.5
8 Cerritos   58
9 Cuesta   50
10 West Valley   43
11 Santa Rosa   42
12 S J Delta   41
13 Cypress   36.5
14 Rio Hondo   32.5
15 Chabot   32
16 Victor Valley 28.5
17 Santa Ana   28
18 Mt. SAC   27
19 Bakersfield   26.5
20 Modesto   19.5
21 East LA   6.5

Gary Meissner Cuesta
Coached 30 years, 124 wins, 7 Conference Championship Teams. Coached 4 State Champions, over 60 State Placers, 49 All-Americans, 1980 Small College Champions.

Season Records
James Guizar-Palomar 25.2
Saul Lucatero-Moorpark 34-0
Career Record
Sion King-Sacramento 60-?
Dan Martinez-Cuesta 42-8

2001 CCCAA State Wrestling Championships
November 30, December 1, 2001, Santa Rosa College

118
Jason Moreno-Bakfld 5-4
Chris Hammer-Sierra
Anthony Rodriquez-Ce F 4:13
Sergio Breceda-Fresno
Luis Fragoso-Rio Hondo 6-4
Ricky Aguirre-Moorpark
Israel Navarro-Pal T-Fall 19-3
Josh Hernandez-Chabot

133
Jose Palomares-S Ana 11-5
Rick Guzman-Rio Hondo
Damacio Page-Cerritos 4-3
Jorge Evangelista-Fresno
Justin Bedwell-Chabot Forfeit
Robert Pacheco-West Valley
Eric Higaonna-Pal MD 12-4
Jon Maitia-Sierra

141
Russell Miura-Fresno Default
Jaret Newton-Santa Rosa
Josh Johnson-Cerritos 6-5
Israel Sanchez-Santa Ana
Devon Zemp-Mp MD 8-0
Jason Rawlins-Golden West
Alex Jones Rio Hond MD 12-3
Jose Perez-Sierra

149
Nick Tatum-Sacramento 10-5
Scott Beck-Fresno
Steve Garcia-Cerrs T-Fall 16-0
Cody Wilkerson-West Valley
Anthony Reta-Chabot 8-6
Dante Curtola-Sierra
Todd Guevara-Bakfld F 2:00
Gonzalo Meza-Cypress

157
Eddie Lucatero-Mp 1-1 2 OT
Nick Davis-S J Delta
Buck Meridith-Palomar 9-3
Gabe Barragan-Cerritos
Ruby Lopez-Fresno 3-1
Maurice Washington-Rio Hon
Brendan Furnari-Cuesta
Fred Gonzalez-Bakersfield

165
Sam Sotelo-Chab Disqualified
Telly Sanders-Fresno
Karras Kalivas-Bakersfield 4-1
Ramior Carasa-Santa Ana
Greg Catton-West Vall Forfeit
Keith Ille-Modesto
Josh Williamson-Mt. SAC
Brad Martin-Sacramento

177
Andy Tufnell-Cerritos 2-1
Shann Sams-Moorpark
Jesse Vazquez-Modesto
Shawn Mahugh-West Valley
Jose Tirado-Fresno Forfeit
Aaron Spiller-Cuesta
Anthony Tedesco-S Rosa 7-2
Adam Neesby-Golden West

184
Jesse Juarez-Golen West Fall
Branden Bear-Modesto
Chris Rueckert-Moorpark
James Schumack-Santa Rosa
Justin Bixbe-Shasta 9-5
Kris Shirley-Palomar
Anthony Moreno-Fres F 2:41
Markus Powell-Sierra

197
Ralph Garcia-Moorpark 10-4
Nate Loughran-Santa Rosa
Chris Chambers-Palomar 9-3
Brian Scheesely-Fresno
Jeff Webster-Sant Ana Forfeit
Ryan Green-Sacramento
Ken Pamanian-Modes 1-1 TB
Kris Schwartz-Skyline

Heavyweight
Chase Gormley-Gol West 6-5
Brett Clark-Bakersfield
Erik Arevalo-Mt. San Antonio
Ben Flores-Moorpark
Taylor Schmidt-Pal Fall 1:46
Ricky Garnero-Shasta
Jason Smoyer-Fresno 9-7
Deniz Akmese-Skyline

Most Outstanding Wrestler
Jason Moreno-Bakersfield
Coach of the year
Anthony Camacho-Fresno
Assistant Coach of the Year
Jared Smith-Fresno

Team Scores
1	Fresno	146.5
2	Moorpark	118.5
3	Cerritos	113
4	Palomar	69.5
5	Santa Ana	66
6	Bakersfield	64.5
7	Golden West	64
8	Santa Rosa	61.5
9	Chabot	58
10	West Valley	56
11	Modesto	48.5
12	Rio Hondo	47.5
13	Sacramento	44
13	Sierra	44
15	Mt. SAC	29.5
16	Shasta	28.5
17	S J Delta	17.5
17	Cuesta	17.5
19	Skyline	12
20	Cypress	8
21	East LA	1
22	S Bernadino	.5
23	Victor Valley	0

Jeff Smith Cerritos Coached
12 South Coast Conference
Team Championships, 22
State induvial Champions, 75
All-Americans, 212-32-2

2002 CCCAA State Wrestling Championships
December 13-14, 2002 Cypress College

115
Jason Moreno-Bakfld Default
Jacob Palomino-Fresno
Jesse Miramontes-G We 11-3
Diwan Williams-Skyline
Nick Hein-Palomar 5-0
Steve Karlotski-Chabot
John Synhorst-Sacramen 5-4
Robbie Dashnow-Sierra

133
Damacio Page-Cerritos 11-9
Steve Avelar-Cypress
Darrell Goodpaster Fre F 6:25
Paul Lopez-Shasta
Alfonzo Paez-Modesto F 2:29
Joel Perez-Moorpark
Jeremy Waldram Cuesta 13-4
Tim Riscen-Palomar

142
Shannon Slack-Cerritos 12-5
Gabe Ruhkala-Sierra
Chris Chames-W Valley 18-5
Devon Zemp-Moorpark
Art Aguilar-Santa Ana 5-3
Joe Elliott-Santa Rosa
Marcos Austin-Bakfld 8-3
Joe Selinger-Palomar

149
Marco Lara-Cerritos 8-2
Kyle Bickford-Palomar
Cody Wilkinson-W Vly F4:33
Juan Serna-Santa Ana
Todd Guevara-Bakfld 8-4
Preston Irvin-Shasta
Steven Davis-East LA 10-7
Gonzalo Meza-Cypress

157
Matt Lambert-Palomar 6-2
Karras Kalivas-Bakersfield
Jonathan Keene-San Ana 6-2
R J Clifford-Golden West
Scoot Spratt-Sana Rosa 8-5
Dustin Hirashima-Chabot
Scott Oda Cerritos-Default
Matt Lantz-Sierra

165
Tony Morland-Bakfld 13-7
Carlos Montes-Mt. SAC
Chuong Le West-Valley 9-4
Buck Meredith-Palomar
Anthony Gaze-Sana Ana 6-4
Eli Reni-Shasta
Art Martinez-Sacram F 2:26
Emiliano Lopez-Cerritos

174
Jesse Vazquez-Modesto 5-4
Gerry Barragan-Cerritos
James Clay-Mt. SAC 8-2
Angelo Lago-Palomar
Cory Bonincontri-Sierra 8-7
Eddie Locke-Shasta
Tim Glass-Fresno 16-3
Justin Rivera-Moorpark

184
Chris Lopez-Cerritos 15-2
Jesse Taylor-Palomar
Sean Reid-Shasta 7-5
Jimmy Becerra-Santa Ana
Josh Jarrett-G West F 2:40
Josh Williamson-Mt. SAC
Jason Bovie-Santa Rosa 6-2
Pat Varela-Cuesta

197
Ralph Garcia-Moorpark 5-3
Chris Chambers-Palomar
Mariano Sanchez-Fall 1:35
Todd Barden-Sacramento
Matt Coonfield Shasta 8 6
Michael Hughes-East LA
Cheyne Cook-Mt. SAC 8-6
John Krieger-Chabot

282
Brett Clark-Bakersfield 3-2
Chas Gormley-Golden West
Brando Cash-Fresno Fall :21
Anthony Boone-Mt. SAC
Dan Kunkes-Moorpark 8-4
Nick Weaver-Sierra
Matt Tesoro-Cuesta Fall 6:20
Ben Brueske-Palomar

Most Outstanding Wrestler
Shannon Slack-Cerritos
Coach of the Year
Greg Gascon-Cerritos
Assistant Coach of the Year
Brian Ransom-Cerritos

Team Scores
1 Cerritos 128.5
2 Palomar 126
3 Bakersfield 100.5
4 Fresno 80.5
5 Shasta 69.5
6 Santa Ana 64
7 Moorpark 60
8 Golden West 58
9 Mt. SAC 56
10 West Valley 45
11 Sierra 44.5
12 Santa Rosa 34.5
13 Modesto 33.5
14 Sacramento 31.5
15 Chabot 29
16 Cuesta 27
17 Cypress 22.5
18 East LA 21.5
19 Skyline 13.5
20 S J Delta 3.5
21 Victor Valley .5
22 Rio Hondo 0

Season Records
Damacio Page 24-5
Matt Lambert 33-0
Gerry Barragan 20-3

John Keever Moorpark
Coached for 27 years, 244-111-4, 2 State Championship Teams, 53 All-Americans, 11 Individual State Champions, 17 Western State Conference Titles, 2-time State Coach of the Year

2003 CCCAA State Wrestling Championships
December 12-13, 2003 West Valley College

125
Logan Ingram-Cuesta 10-4
Diwan Williams-Skyline
Paul Magana-Modesto F 2:27
Eugene Yasutomi-Cerritos
Steve Karlotski-Chabot 5-0
Gerrard Contreras-Moorpark

133
Raul Lopez-Sierra 8-6
JJ Holt-Moorpark
Sergio Lopez-Modesto F 4:30
Abel Sadik-Rio Hondo
Nick Martinez-Bakersfield
John Synhorst-Sacramento

141
Drew Fredenburg-W Vall 9-2
Steven Davis-East LA
Chad Carmack-Cuesta 14-3
Virgil Lockett-Skyline
Ryan Garcia-Cerritos 7-2
Randy Aguire-Mt. SAC

149
Miguel Gutierrez-Bakfld 9-3
Kyle Bickford-Palomar
Mark Pfeifer-Sacramento 4-1
Brandon Lichtinger-Sierra
Jeff Covarrublas-Cuesta 6-2
Manuel Vasquez-Modesto

157
Micah Zachary-Shasta Defaul
Jeff Baker-Bakersfield
Anthony Gonzalez-Cuest 11-2
Bobby Stack-Skyline
Kevin Guinn Santa Rosa Forfe
Steve Garcia-Cerritos

165
Angelo Lago-Palomar 7-2
Russell Caldwell-Bakersfield
Matt Coonfield-Shasta 10-1
Casey Sullivan-Santa Rosa
Cory Bonincontri-Sierra F :18
Jose Sarabia-Fresno

174
Yasser Pezzat-Fresno 3-2OT
Chris Rueckert-Moorpark
Brandon Thomson-Sier 12-10
Jason Holt-Sacramento
Jerry Carollo-G West F 5:30
Ben Barrett-Mt. SAC

184
Jesse Taylor-Palomar 12-5
Jesse Ruiz-Santa Rosa
Pat Varela-Cuesta 8-3
Richard Escobar-West Valley
Jordan Polley-Sierra Default
Andrew Guzman-Bakersfield

197
Mariano Sanchez-Fresno 4-3
Jimmy Becerra-Santa Ana
Marcus Sousa-Bakfd F 1:08
Tyrell Blanche-Moorpark
Jeremiah Hunt-Sierra F 4:40
Oswaldo Avalos-Golden West

285
Jacob Hallmark-Fresno F 6:21
Aaron Hayes-East LA
Alex Becerra-San Ana 6-4OT
Dan Kunkes-Moorpark
Tanner Lovett-Shasta Forfeit
George Palmer-Cerritos

Most Outstanding Wrestler
Miguel Gutierrez-Bakersfield

Coach of the Year
Bill Kalivas-Bakersfield

Assistant Coach of the Year
Dan Lashley-Cuesta

Team Scores
1 Bakersfield   74.5
2 Cuesta   68
3 Sierra   57.5
4 Fresno   51.5
5 Moorpark   50.5
6 Palomar   44.5
7 Santa Ana   39
7 Shasta   39
9 Modesto   31
10 Skyline   30.5
11 Sacramento   28.5
12 Cerritos   27
13 East LA   26
14 West Valley 24.5
15 Santa Rosa   20.5
16 Golden West 18
17 Mt. SAC   9
18 Rio Hondo   8.5
19 Chabot   7

Career Record
Chad Carmack-Cuesta
33-9

Season Record
Logan Ingram Cuesta 32-1

2004 CCCAA State Wrestling Championships
December 10-11, 2004 Palomar College

125
Eugene Yasutomi Cerritos 8-2
Jean Leazard-Skyline
Gilbert Carrillo-Bakfld 5-3
Said Singh-Fresno
David Jagoda-Chabot 9-6
Sean Prentice-Rio Hondo
Jose Hernandez-San Ana12-2
Jason Le-West Valley

133
J J Holt-Moorpark 9-5
Darrell Goodpaster-Fresno
Tyus Torrean-Sierra Fall 5:21
Joey Monjure-Modesto
Carlos Alaniz-Cerritos 10-9
Tyler Gibson-Cuesta
Alvin Cacdac-W Valley 11-1
Cecil Sebastian-Mt. SAC

141
Matt Maldonado-Bakfld 12-8
Art Aguilar-Santa Ana
Benny Garcia-S J Delta 7-2
Jacob Salas-Fresno
Andy Bean-East LA 9-6
Chris Simms-Chabot
Anthony Cunha-Sierra F 3:55
Tony Arena-Sacramento

149
Miguel Gutierrez Bakld F 2:53
Mark Pfiefer-Sacramento
J J Lewis-Cerritos 11-4
Jeff Cox-Modesto
Ernie Aguilar-Santa Ana Def
Robert Dominguez-Mt. SAC
Ryan Waters-Shasta Default
John Lee-Victor-Valley

157
Jonathan Keene-San Ana7-3
Ryan Corn-Bakersfield
Ronnie Hopkins-Cerritos12-8
Eric Heldarov-Sierra
Matt Bryan-Modesto 11-4
Hector Sandoval-Santa Rosa
Stuart Cole-Palomar 18-6
James Coates-Chabot

165
Hurshid Haldarov-Sierra 7-2
Will Simmons-Sacramento
Jeff Baker-Bakersfield 12-5
Ernie Varela-Cuesta
Austin Torrez-Skyline Default
Ty Souza-Mt. SAC
Nathan Sare-Cerritos 7-6
Ty Minto-Shasta

174
Jason Points-Bakersfield 7-5
Brian Judd-Santa Ana
Eddie Locke-Shasta 15-6
Bryan Baker-Victor Valley
Konrad Schwartz SAC Default
Matt Lantz-Sierra
Jeff Cole-Fresno 13-3
Rickey Newsom-Palomar

184
Yasser Pazzat-Fresno 8-3
Jesse Ruiz-Santa Ana
Andrew Guzman-Bakfld 3-1
Michael Ullerich-G West
Jarred Dixon-Sacramento 6-3
Matt Lantz-Sierra
David Alexis-Palomar 4-2
Alexis Lara-Skyline

197
Danny Melendez-S Ana F4:23
Jordan Polly-Sierra
Eduardo Mercado-Fresno 6-4
Ben Faanunu-Chabot
Jay Thomas Mt. SAC 6-4
Dan Almanza Palomar
Jesse Velasquez Bakfld Def
Emanuel Newton Cerritos

285
Joe Espejo-Bakfld Default
Tyrell Blanche-Moorpark
Marcus Moore-Sierra Default
Tyler McKay-Palomar
Pedro Garcia-Cerritos F 1:00
Ryan Balletto-Santa Rosa
Donald Cosper-Chabot 6-4
Bryan Whetstone-Fresno

Most Outstanding Wrestler
Miguel Gutierrez-Bakersfield
Coach of the Year
Bill Kalivas-Bakersfield
Assistant Coach of the Year
Jesse Ortega-Bakersfield

Team Scores
1	Bakersfield	163
2	Santa Ana	114
3	Fresno	95
4	Sierra	89.5
5	Cerritos	75.5
6	Sacramento	64.5
7	Chabot	58.5
8	Palomar	47
8	Skyline	47
10	Modesto	37
11	Mt. SAC	34.5
12	Shasta	30
13	Cuesta	21.5
14	Victor Valley	20
15	Santa Rosa	18
16	S J Delta	15
16	West Valley	15
18	Golden West	14.5
19	Rio Hondo	13
20	East LA	11
21	Moorpark	5

Season Records
Eugene Yasutomi 28-1
Ronnie Hopkins 25-6

Career Record
Miguel Gutierrez 66-0 in 2 years, won 16 tournaments

Coaches
Bakersfield-Bill Kalivas
Santa Ana-Vince Silva
Fresno-Jared Smith
Sierra-Ken Wharry
Cerritos-Steve Glassey
Sacramento- Dave Pacheco
Chabot-Steve Siroy
Palomar-Byron Campbell
Skyline-James Haddon

2004 141lb
8-Tony Arena-Sacramento, 6-Chris Simms-Chabot, 4-Jacob Salas-Fresno, 2-Art Aguilar-Santa Ana, 1-Champion-Matt Maldonado-Bakersfield, 3-Benny Garcia-SJ Delta, 5-Andy Bean-East LA, 7-Anthony Cunda-Sierra

2004 149lb
8-John Lee-Victor Valley, 6-Robert Dominguez-Mt. SAC, 4-Jeff Cox-Modesto, 2-Mark Pfiefer-Sacramento, 1-Champion and Most Outstanding Wrestler-Miguel Gutierrez-Bakersfield, 3-J J Lewis-Cerritos, 5-Ernie Aguilar-Santa Ana, 7-Ryan Waters-Shasta

2004 157lb
8-James Coates-Chabot, 6-Hector Sandoval-Santa Rosa, 4-Eric Heldraov-Sierra, 2-Ryan Corn-Bakersfield, 1-Champion Jonathan Keen-Santa Ana, 3-Ronnie Hopkins-Cerritos, 5-Matt Bryan-Modesto, 7-Stuart Cole-Palomar

2004 165lb
6-Ty Souza-Mt. SAC, 4-Ernie Varela-Cuesta, 2-Will Simmons-Sacramento, 1-Champion-Hurshid Haldaron-Sierra, 3-Jeff Baker-Bakersfield, 5-Austin Torrez-Skyline, 7-Nathan Sare-Cerritos, 8-Ty Minto-Shasta(Not in Photo)

2004 184lb
8-Alexis Lara-Skyline, 6-Matt Lantz-Sierra, 4-Michael Ullarich-Golden West, 2-Jesse Ruiz-Santa Ana, 1-Champion-Yasser Pazzat-Fresno, 3-Andrew Guzman-Bakersfield, 5-Jarred Dixon-Sacramento, 7-David Alexis-Palomar

2004 197lb
6-Dan Almanza-Palomar, 4-Ben Faanunu-Chabot, 2-Jordan Polly-Sierra, 1-Champion, Danny Melendez-Santa Ana, 3-Eduardo Mercado-Fresno, 5-Jay Thomas-Mt. SAC, 7-Jesse Velasquez-Bakersfield, 9-Emanuel Newton-Cerritos(Not in Photo)

2004 STATE WRESTLING CHAMPIONS
Bakersfield College - 163 pts.

COACH OF THE YEAR: BILL KALIVAS
ASSISTANT COACH OF THE YEAR: JESSE ORTEGA
OUTSTANDING WRESTLER: MIGUEL GUTIERREZZ - 157
STATE CHAMPIONS: MATT MALDONADO - 141   JASON POINTS - 174
   JOE ESPEJO-HEAVYWEIGHT

2005 CCCAA State Wrestling Championships
December 10-11, 2005 Fresno City College

125
Sabi Sing-Fresno 9-3
Jimmy Valdivia-Cerritos
Jose Hernandez-S A Fall 6:00
Ismael Armendariz-East LA
Oscar Romero-Sierra F 1:05
David Navarrete-Palomar
Jonathan Macalolooy Cha 3-1
Keith Gibson-Bakersfield

133
Cory Hamabata-Mt. SAC 7-3
Cody Gibson-Bakersfield
Torrean Tyus-Sierra 9-7
Mike Waterson-Fresno
Shaun Jones Moorpark F 4:39
Paul Perez-East LA
Andrew Holmes-Cer Fall 1:11
Brandon Patterson-S Rosa

141
Danny Garcia-S J Delta 4-3
Bobby Gonzalez-Sierra
Andy Bean-East LA Fall 1:30
Tommy Machado-W Valley
Steve Schantin-S Ana F 1:57
T J Owens-Modesto
Dan Castro-Palomar 6-1
Andrew Cottrell-Moorpark

149
Mike O'Hara-Santa An 5-3
Alex Herrera-Bakersfield
Matt Giffin-Sierra Fall 2:40
Sinai Pezzat-Fresno
Josh Emmett-Sacramento 2-1
Octavio Lucatero-Moorpark
Louie Desantis-Palomar Def
Kelley Cromwell-Victor Valley

157
Zac Taylor-West Valley 12-4
Sabas Cruz-Santa Ana
J D Thrall-Sacramento 2-1
Orlando Landons-Bakersfield
Jason Hull-Golden Valley 6-3
Ben Barrett-Mt. SAC
Kyle Hames-Cuesta 6-3
Andres Lowen-Palomar

165
Jeff Davis-Cerritos Fall :22
Ty Sousa-Mt. SAC
Jesse Fernandez-Sac 5-3
Josh DeSherlia-West Valley
Royce Thomas-San Rosa 16-0
Mike Williams-Cuesta
Dan Barazza-Sierra 8-6
Jimmy Gallegos-Fresno

174
Konrad Schwartz-Sacro 16-7
Ronnie Hopkins-Cerritos
Jason Points-Bakfld 14-10
Tom Eaton-Santa Ana
Daniel Garay-Mt. SAC Default
Ryan Nejal-Palomar
Jeff Leama-Skyline 11-10
Justin Smith-Moorpark

184
Tom Hawkins-Mt. SAC 21-10
Brian Judd-Santa Ana
Brett Mooney-Bakfld 18-3
Shawn Riggs-Moorpark
Jordan Lefler-Modesto F 4:11
Luis Audelo-Cerritos
Sheldon Page-Sierra 6-2
Marquez Gales-Santa Rosa

197
Jacob Starr-Cuesta Fall 6:48
Alexis Lara-Skyline
Ryan Silviera-Mt. SAC 7-2
Jayson Collard-Santa Rosa
George Jimenez-Moor F 1:25
Cory Compton-Sacramento
Kenny Keller-S J Delta F 2:02
Tyler McKay-Palomar

Heavyweight
Marcus Moore-Sierra 14-7
Josh Marquez-Bakersfield
Ken Martin-Chabot 7-2
Bryan Whetstone-Fresno
Brandon Doran-Cerritos F :37
James Clark-Modesto
Juan Rodriguez-S Rosa F 2:31
Jose Arroyo-Rio Hondo

Most Outstanding Wrestler
Tom Hawkins-Mt. SAC
Coach of the Year
Vince Silva-Santa Ana
Assistant Coach of the Year
Veto Becerra-Santa Rosa

Team Scores
1 Santa Ana 106.5
2 Bakersfield 102.5
3 Sierra 99
4 Mt. SAC 93
5 Cerritos 82.5
6 Sacramento 68
7 Fresno 67.5
8 Moorpark 63.5
9 Palomar 50.5
10 West Valley 50
11 Cuesta 41.5
12 East LA 38.5
13 Santa Rosa 37
14 Modesto 32
15 S J Delta 29.5
16 Skyline 24.5
17 Chabot 19
18 Golden West 9
19 Rio Hondo 7.5
20 Victor Valley 0
20 Shasta 0

Season Records
Mike O'Hair-Samta Ana 33-0
Jeff Davis-Cerritos 28-1
Ronnie Hopkins-Cerritos 16-3

2006 CCCAA State Wrestling Championships
December 8-9, 2006 Fresno City College

125
Ivan Sanchez Santa Ana 14-4
Jason Carrillo Cerritos
Taylor McCorriston S R 19-18
Chauncey Phillips Sierra
Rick Bernal Rio Hondo 12-1
Kyle Crouch Fresno
Carl Riding Victor Valley 8-4
Sammy Saunders East LA

133
Carlos Alaniz Cerritos 14-7
Gabriel Aguilar Santa Ana
Ethan Hall Palomar 13-5
Cody Gibson Bakersfield
Mike Rigi Fresno Default
Armando Martinez S J Delta
Claudio Seanez Mt. SAC 8-4
Daymond Bland Sacramento

141
Leland Gridley Sierra 4-2OT
Joseph Serrato Santa Ana
Jordan Keckler Modesto 11-1
Andrew Holmes Cerritos
Tyson Knierim Palomar Def
Jonathan Ronny Chabot
Edgar Mercado Fresno 6-2
Bruce Wasserman Bakfld

149
Alfonso Sanchez Fresno 3-1
Henry Kofa Lassen
Ian Millan Rio Hondo 10-8
Travis Wood Sierra
Joe Barajas Palomar 7-6
Orlando Barragan Santa Ana
Tony Ruiz Cerritos Fall
Eric Timson Bakersfield

157
Devin Velasquez San Ana 2-1
Sinai Pezzat Fresno
Matt Giffi Sierra Fall
Stuart Cole Palomar
Zach Johnson Bakfld Default
Steve Saenz Rio Hondo
Jake Bridges Shasta 3-1
Shawn Schantin Chabot

165
Glenn Shawn Palomar 9-7
Nick Bardsley Fresno
Michael Williams Cuesta 9-5
Dan Barraza Sierra
Daniel Garay Mt. SAC
Eddie Sanchez Santa Ana
Jack Porter Cerritos 13-3
Tony Moser Lassen

174
Kyle Griffin Santa Rosa F 4:36
Tom Eaton Santa Ana
Shaun Ceremello Fresno 4-0
Celeb Smith Palomar
Ryan Sughrue Modest F 1:17
Eric Sanchez Rio Hondo
Matt Livley Lassen 7-6
Eric Gonzales Moorpark

184
Tim Hawkins Mt, SAC 8-6
Jason Carrasco Bakersfield
Mike Leslie Sierra Fall 1:09
Cory Compton Sacramento
Steven Urquizo Fresno 4-0
Louie Audelo Cerritos
Marques Gales S Rosa F 2:43
Shane Miller Lassen

197
Jerred Dixson Sac F 2:39
Jayson Collard Santa Rosa
Norman Nail W Hills F 1:07
Tyler Blair Fresno
Ryan Silvera Mt. SAC Default
Todd Moleworth Moorpark
Joseph Ramirez Modesto 8-3
Al Kinslow Cerritos

285
Erik Nye Sierra Fall 4:34
Brandon Doran Cerritos
Josh Marquez Bakfld F 1:50
Victor Leyva Fresno
Tyler Porras Santa Ana F 2:10
Steve Franklin Santa Rosa
Matt Klimek Palomar 6-2
Alex Arellano Rio Hondo

Most Outstanding Wrestler
Kyle Griffin Santa Rosa
Coach of the Year
Paul Keysaw Fresno
Assistant Coach of the Year
Sal Garcia Fresno

Team Scores
1 Fresno   135
2 Sierra   127
3 Santa Ana   126
4 Cerritos   101.5
5 Palomar   87
6 Santa Rosa   68.5
7 Bakersfield   68
8 Rio Hondo   51
8 Mt. SAC   51
10 Sacramento   41
11 Modesto   38.5
12 Lassen   31.5
13 West Hills   21
14 Chabot   14.5
15 Moorpark   13.5
16 Cuesta   12.5
17 S J Delta   9
18 Victor Valley 8.5
19 East LA   6.5
20 Shasta   0
20 West Valley 0

Records
Carlos Alaniz   27-3
Alfonso Sanchez 39-0
Tim Hawkins   36-0
Kyle Griffin   30-0
Brandon Doran   32-7

Coaches
Fresno Jared Smith
Sierra Ken Wharry
Santa Ana Vince Silva
Cerritos Steve Glassey
Palomar Byron Campbell
Santa Rosa Jake Fitpatrick

2007 CCCAA State Wrestling Championships
December 7-8, 2007 Fresno City College

125
Angel Olea-Fresno 11-1
Corey Houser-Lassen
Chauncey Philipps-Sierra Def
Jason Moorhouse-Skyline
Charles Chatman-S Rosa Def
Mark Ibarra-Palomar
Jason Carrillo-Cerritos 20-2
Fernando Munoz West Valley

133
Norman Richmond-Sierra 9-4
Paul Lyon-Cerritos
Eddy Ngo-West Valley F 5:29
Brett Land-West Hills
Cesar Renteria-Santa Ana 5-4
Rolando Velasco-Modesto
Paul Ruiz-Fresno 9-5
Benj Gomez-Moorpark

141
Juan Archuleta-Sacra 3-1OT
Brandon McKnight Vic Valley
Jonathan Ronny-Chabot 9-3
Mike Koehnlein-Cerritos
Brandon Drucker-Cuea F 2:27
Eathan Hall-Palomar
Edgar Mercado-Fresno 14-4
Nick Cardoza-Mt. SAC

149
Jose Serrato Santa-Ana 4-0
Octavio Lucatero-Moorpark
Chris Santana-Sierra 8-4
Diego Martinez-Rio Hondo
Aris Harutyunyan West V 4-0
Jonathan Anderson-Skyline
Jamie Rodriguez-Bakfld 6-4
Kyle Lew-Santa Rosa

157
Trinity Perkins-Lassen 4-0
Louie Desantis-Palomar
David Razo-Cerritos 10-6
Adrian Gonzales-East LA
Jake Bridges-Shasta Dfault
Travis Wood-Sierra
Mark Bartron-West Va F 2:15
Sean Barbor-Santa Ana

165
Luis Gonzales-Palomar 15-7
Jay Bogan-East LA
Nick Bardsley-Fresno 8-5
Zeth St, Clair-Sierra
Gene Choi-Cerritos 9-4
Robert Carothers-Sacramen
Bobby Vitatos-Santa Rosa 4-1
Sam Gaxioia-Mt. SAC

174
Victor Carazo-Modesto 4-2
James Clay-East LA
Shaun Ceremello-Fresno DQ
Mike Fucci-Sierra
Brad Muthart-Lassen F 2:59
Adam Hase-Cerritos
Eric Gonzales-Moorpa F 7:53
Mike Cavanaugh-Bakersfield

184
Ryan Sughrue-Modest F 2:05
Alex Howard-Sierra
Kellan Desmond-Palomar 5-0
Matt Garcia-West Hills
Lucas Duckwall-West Vall 9-6
Dan Righi-Fresno
Alex Alcala-Bakersfield 18-13
Jones Schenzel-Lassen

197
Shane Miller-Lassen 9-7
Jordan Lefier-Modesto
Mingo Grant-Sierra 10-5
Greg Villalobos-Palomar
Al Kinslow Cerritos-Fall 2:41
Andrew Capucetty-East LA
Todd Molesworth-Moo F1:22
Jimmy Gallegos-Fresno

285
Erik Nye-Sierra Fall 4:12
Timothy Guerrero-S J Delta
Juan Enriquez-Cerritos 6-1
Robert Elias-Santa Ana
Chris Kiel-Lassen Fall 1:56
Luis Leyva-Fresno
Josh Newman-W Hills F 7:43
Jeremy Pagaran-Cuesta

Most Outstanding Wrestler
Norman Richman-Sierra
Coach of the Year
Ken Wharry-Sierra
Assistant Coach of the Year
Don Martinez Sierra

Team Scores
1	Sierra	146
2	Cerritos	103
3	Lassen	97
4	Fresno	90.5
5	Palomar	81.5
6	Modesto	77
7	East LA	58.5
8	West Valley	50.5
9	Santa Ana	49
10	Moorpark	37.5
11	Sacramento	37
12	West Hills	35.5
13	Skyline	23.5
14	Bakersfield	21.5
15	Santa Rosa	21
16	Cuesta	20.5
17	S J Delta	17
18	Rio Hondo	16.5
19	Chabot	15.5
20	Victor Valley	15
21	Shasta	11
22	Mt. SAC	10

Seasons Records
Angel Olea (39-1))
Norman Richmond (35-1)
Paul Lyon (27-4)
Juan Archuleta (37-2)
Jose Serrato (28-3)
Trinity Perkins (28-5)
David Razo 26-5
Luis Gonzales (37-3)
Victor Carazo (27-1)
Ryan Sughrue (36-6)
Shane Miller (23-5)
Erik Nye (31-0)

2008 CCCAA State Wrestling Championships
December 12-13, 2008 Victor Valley College

125
Angel Olea-Fresno 10-1
Jaime Martinez-Santa Ana
Joe Cabanas-Cerritos 8-2
Brandon Benvenuti-Sierra
Charles Chatman-S Rosa 15-9
Alex Carrico-Rio Hondo
Tym Quigg-Victor Valley DQ
John Mort-Lassen

133
Todd Wilcox-Sierra 3-2
Gabe Aguilar-Santa Ana
Ryan Giovenco-Cerritos 12-9
Derek Ellis-Shasta
Marty Rubalcava-Fres F 4:10
Christian Hernandez-Bakfld
Julian Gonzalez-Rio Hon 13-8
Justen Locking-Sacramento

141
Mike Koehnlein-Cerritos 9-2
Bobby Scofield-Santa Ana
Mike Vassar-Sierra 12-2
Stephen Delacruz-Chabot
Jose Mondragon Palomar Def
Boy Medina-Mt.SAC
Kevin Thongseng-Fres F 1:31
Roy Bowen Victor-Valley

149
Brad Kummerer-Lassen 11-4
Ian Millan-Rio Hondo
Shad Maniigault West Hill 5-2
Jose Navarro-Santa Ana
Jaime Rodriguez-Bakfl F 4:40
Adam Obad-Modesto
Alfredo Solis Palomar Defaul

157
Alfonso Sanchez-Fresno 14-6
Robert Carothers-Sacrament
Matt Thomas-Shasta 14-4
Eric Sauvageau-Cerritos
David Stupplebeen-Mt. F4:45
Rafael Munoz-Lassen
Danny Kennedy-Santa A Def
Matt Klingler-Sierra

165
Zeth St. Clair-Sierra 9-3
Dustin Reid-Shasta
Adrian Gonzales-East LA 7-4
Sean Barbour-Santa Ana
Matt Cox-Fresno Fall 1:46
Blake Willard-Cuesta
Clayton Macfarlane-Palo 6-5
Anthony Clay-Lassen

174
Cody Vasconcellos-Sacra 2-0
Mike Fucci-Sierra
Mike Cavanaugh-Bakfld 6-3
James Hammontree-Lassen
Eric Smith- Fresno 9-5
Travis Tielens-Palomar
Cesar Ponce-East LA 8-0
Carlos Soto-S J Delta

184
Steven Urquizo-Fresno 5-3
Caleb Gerl-Cerritos
Edward Melitosyan-W V10-4
Derek Rottenberg-Shasta
Shawn Michalek Sacrom 10-4
Matt Garcia-West Hills
Tony Ferris-Lassen 8-6
Josh Villagomez-Mt. SAC

197
Tyler Garcia-Santa Ana F 1:52
Julian Silva-Mt. SAC
Sal Felicia-Rio Hondo F 1:53
Jacob Merrell-West Hills
B J Mosley-Sacramento Def
J T Minto-Shasta
Angel Romero-Palomar 2-1
Tyler Blare-Fresno

285
Matt Gibson-Sierra 9-3
Juan Enriquez-Cerritos
Kyle Roh-Santa Ana 9-7
Austin Garza-Fresno
Jeff Jones Victor Valley F 5:16
Tommy James-Mt. SAC
Carson Carman-Lassen F :54
Juan Durazo-Moorpark

Most Outstanding Wrestler
Angel Olea-Fresno
Coach of the Year
Paul Keysaw-Fresno
Assistant Coach of the Year
Sal Gonzalez-Fresno

Team Scores
1	Fresno	133
2	Santa Ana	118
3	Sierra	115
4	Cerritos	91.5
5	Sacramento	75
6	Lassen	68
7	Shasta	66
8	Mt. SAC	54.5
9	Rio Hondo	50
10	Palomar	44.5
11	West Hills	38.5
11	Bakersfield	38.5
13	Victor Valley	35
14	East LA	19.5
15	West Valley	15.5
16	Chabot	14
17	Modesto	12
18	Cuesta	9
18	Santa Rosa	9
20	S J Delta	4.5
20	Moorpark	4.5
22	Skyline	1

Season Records
Angel Olea (31-1)
Todd Wilcox (31-5)
Mike Koehnlein (39-4)
Alfonso Sanchez (31-1)
Zeth St. Clair (29-4)
Cody Vasconcellos (34-0)
Steven Urquizo (31-4)
Tyler Garcia (34-4)
Matt Gibson (34-1)

2008 CCCAA INDIVIDUAL CHAMPIONS

Front Row: Angle Olea-Fresno City, Todd Wilcox-Sierra, Mike Koenlein-Cerritos, Brad Kummerer-Lassen, Alfonso Sanchez-Fresno City. **Back Row:** Zeth St. Clair-Sierra, Cody Vasconcellos-Sacramento City, Steven Urquizo-Fresno City, Tyler Garcia-Santa Ana, Matt Gibson-Sierra.   Photo by John Sachs/Tech-Fall.com

2009 CCCAA INDIVIDUAL CHAMPIONS

Front Row: Jimmy Martinez-Santa Ana, Norm Richmond-Sierra, Bobby Scofield-Santa Ana, Jose Navarro-Santa Ana, Chris Urquizo-Fresno City, **Back Row:** Fernando Lucatero-Fresno City, Dustin Reid-Shasta, Caleb Gerl-Ceritos, JT Minto-Shasta, Jose Lopez-Cerritos.   Photo by John Sachs/Tech-Fall.com

2009 CCCAA State Wrestling Championships
December 11-12, 2009 Chabot College

125
Jimmy Martinez-S Ana 6-2OT
Brandon Benvenuli-Sierra
Galen Williams-Fresno F 6:57
Steve Salinas-Mt. SAC
Andy Yu-Cerritos 14-6
A J Jaramillo-West Hills
David Sok-S J Delta 12-10
Sophan Mey-Santa Ana

133
Norman Richmond-Sie F1:16
Pierce Lowry-Mt. SAC
Dan Osmer-Fresno 10-7
Jason Arreola-Santa Ana
Charlie Seang-S J Delta 9-8
Jeff Jancky-Cerritos
Jeremy Moreno-Shasta 11-7
Reggie Rubio-Victor Valley

141
Bobby Scofield-Santa Ana 4-3
Mike Vassar-Sierra
Stephen Delacruz-Cha F 2:14
John Marchena-East La
Tyler Diamond-Sacrame F :18
Danny Avila-Mt. SAC
T J Owens-Modesto 9-5
Anthony Agapaoa-West Vly

149
Jose Navarro-Santa Ana 7-2
Vlad Dombrovsky-Sierra
Tim Nevarez-Sac F 1:47
Mike Lopez-East LA
Jesse Ponce-Cerritos
Tim Randal-Palomar Default
Jesse Cruz-Rio Hondo 9-4
Amol Aroliga-Lassen

157
Chris Urquizo-Fresno 6-4
Tim Navarrette-Shasta
Ted Bristol-Santa Ana F 4:18
Bronson Gerl-Cuesta
Javier Avila-Cuesta 3-2
Adam Obad-Modesto
Shawn Brendle-Sac 6-3
Aaron Pickard-Sierra

165
Ferando Lucatero-Fresno 5-4
Joe Garner-Sacramento
Clayton MacFarane-Palo 4-3
R J Pilkington-Santa Ana
Travis Schaffer-Modesto 3-2
Alvaro Zemeno-Bakersfield
Mike Brady-Cuesta 6-4
Joey Forseth-Shasta

174
Dustin Reid-Shasta 14-5
Carlos Soto-S J Delta
Danny Kennedy-Santa An 7-3
Kale Degrandmont-Sac
Joe Cisneros-Fresno Fall 6:37
Nick Gill-Sierra
Nick Inclan-Rio Hondo Forfeit
A J Smith-Bakersfield

184
Caleb Gerl-Cerritos 3-2
Jesus Chavez-Sierra
Shawn Michalek-Sac 11-4
Luis Onofre-Santa Ana
Justin Walker-Fresno F 2:43
Todd Rucker-Shasta
Jeff Moran-Modesto Fall 7:00
Chris Herrera-Palomar

197
J T Minto-Shasta 6-3
Ryan Scarr-Sierra
Jimmy Brotheras-San Ana 3-1
Julian Silva-Mt. SAC
Kevin Keisler-Sac Forfeit
Adam O'Brien-Santa Rosa
Lucas Keene-Fresno 12-1
Jacob Eaton-Cerritos

283
Jose Lopez-Cerritos 5-2
Austin Garza-Fresno
Frank Ayala-Mt. SAC Fall 3:40
Jasmeet Basra-S J Delta
Brian Klieves-Sana Ana F 2:47
Anthony Gonzalez-Rio Hondo
Dan Colbert-Cuesta 12-1
Tyler Magart-Davis Shasta

Most Outstanding Wrestler
Norman Richmond-Sierra
Coach of the Year
Vince Silva-Santa Ana
Assistant Coach of the Year
Vito Becerra-Santa Ana

Team Scores
1	Santa Ana	158.5
2	Sierra	122
3	Fresno	115
4	Sacramento	101.5
5	Cerritos	92.5
6	Shasta	88.5
7	Mt. SAC	64.5
8	S J Delta	49.5
9	Modesto	37
10	East LA	27
10	Palomar	27
12	Cuesta	25
13	Rio Hondo	23
14	Chabot	20.5
15	Bakersfield	12.5
16	West Hills	11.5
17	Santa Rosa	10
18	Lassen	6.5
19	Victor Valley	5.5
19	West Valley	5.5
21	Skyline	0

Season Records
Jimmy Martinez 24-3
Brandon Benvenuli 30-7
Norman Richmond 23-2
Bobby Scofield 30-1
Mario Vassar 22-3
Jose Navarro 29-0
Chris Urquizo 24-5
Fernando Lucatero 30-3
Joe Garner 33-11
Dustin Reid 21-2
Carlos Sato 33-11
Caleb Geri 33-2
Jose Chavez 31-7
Jose Lopez 32-4
Austin Garza 35-3

2010 CCCAA State Wrestling Championships
December 10-11, 2010 Victor Valley College

125
Estevan Cabanas-Cerrito 10-6
A J Jaramillo-West Hills
Chris Padilla-Fresno 5-4
Aaron LaFarge-Palomar
Chris Diaz-Cuesta 5-2
Janik Santana-Chabot
Ruben Gonzalez-Default
Edgar Perez-Modesto

133
Charlie Seang-S J Delta 5-2
Bryan Magno-Bakersfield
Marty Rubalcaba-Fres F 4:27
Jon Gay-Cuesta
Alex Perez-West Hills 13-4
Alex Williams-Chabot
Hector Lopez 7-3
Ian Kelley-Palomar

141
Kevin Rojas-Fresno 3-2
Kyle Chene-Santa Ana
Tyler Diamond-Sac F 1:48
Terry Matthews-Shasta
Abel Avila-Rio Hondo 9-7
R J Pikington-Sierra
Nester Ruelas-Cuesta 8-1
Shane Kenihan-Santa Rosa

149
Conrad Rangel-Fresno T-F
Anthony Harris-Sacramento
Jesse Ponce-Cerritos 16-5
Spencer Anderson Cuesta
Westly Young Santa Ros 12-9
Chris Abeyla-Mt. SAC
Ernie Aguilar-Santa Ana 3-0
Jimmy Arazia-Santa Rosa

157
Eric Lopez-Victor Valley 10-2
Coby Bollinger-Cerritos
Craig Sherman-Chabot F 1:44
Taylor Sare-Mt. SAC
Aaron Lopez-San Ana Default
Tyler Johnson-Sierra
Jake Schilling Fresno 7-2
Russell Williams-Sacramento

165
Tigran Adzhemyan-Fresn 4-2
Vlad Dombrovsky-Sierra
Eric Sauvageau-Cerritos 3-1
Dustin Rocha-West Hills
Joe Madison-Lassen 7-2
Marco Orozco-Sacramento
Nick Hernandez 5-2
Thomas Marquez-Modesto

174
Martin Fabbian-Fresno 12-4
Sam Temko-Skyline
Nick Gill-Sierra 4-1
Alfredo Torres-Mt. SAC
A J Smith-Bakersfield 6-1
Thomas Estrada-Cerritos
Luis Vargas-Santa Ana 9-2
Chris White-Lassen

184
Jesse Hellinger-Sacra 3-1OT
Fito Juarez-Fresno
Sean Dougherty-Cuesta 13-9
Logan Paul-Eickhoff Shasta
Ryan Collins-Cerritos F 1:17
Matt Lewellen-Palomar
Milo Anderson-Chabot 7-4
Oscar Navarrete-Mt. SAC

197
Jordon Williams-Sie 12-3
Trever Gwin-Palomar
Brad Carls-Bakersfield 7-2
Colin Hart-Santa Rosa
Lucas Keene-Fresno 6-3
Kevin Keisler-Sacramento
Derek Sanchez-West Hills 6-5
Mario Delgado-Cerritos

285
Jose Lopez-Cerritos 4-0
Luis Contreras-Fresno
Quinn Moore-Bakfld F 1:55
Cheyne Cook-Victor Valley
Juan Lucero-East LA F 2:41
Tivo Cruz-Modesto
Jesse Green-Sacramento 5-3
Cameron McNeer-Palomar

Most Outstanding Wrestler
Eric Lopez-Victor Valley
Coach of the Year
Paul Keysaw-Fresno
Assistant Coach of the Year
Sal Garcia-Fresno

Team Scores
1	Fresno	185.5
2	Cerritos	125
3	Sacramento	92.5
4	Sierra	78
5	Cuesta	63
6	Bakersfield	61
7	Palomar	53.5
8	Mt. SAC	50
9	West Hills	49
10	Victor Valley	48
11	Chabot	47
12	Santa Ana	44
13	Shasta	39.5
14	Santa Rosa	31
15	S J Delta	26
16	Modesto	19
17	Skyline	17
18	Lassen	14.5
19	East LA	13
20	Rio Hondo	11
21	Moorpark	0
21	West Valley	0

Season Records
Estevan Estrada 27-6
Conrad Rangel 31-1
Martin Fabbian 29-2
Fito Juarez 29-6
Eric Lopez 33-1
Luis Contreras 29-8

Career Record
Tyler Diamond 62-?

2011 CCCAA State Wrestling Championships
December 9-10, 2011 Santa Rosa College

125
Pierce Lowery-Mt. SAC 4-2
Austin Wulfert-Sierra
Junior Davila-Fresno F1:54
Ray Delgado-Victor Valley
Marc Collier-Bakersfield 10-1
Nathan Monck-Sacramento
Mark Robbins-Santa Ros 10-5
Matt Correa-Cuesta

133
Eric Orozco-West Hills 1-0
Chris Padilla-Fresno
Isaiah Hurtado-Sac F 1:57
Jaydy Gonzales-Palomar
Jeff Lobos-Lassen 12-5
Phillip Hendrix-Mt. SAC
Aaron Pen-Kruger S Ros 10-4
Greg Barera-Cerritos

141
Frank Martinez-Rio
Kevin Rojas Fresno Hondo 7-4
Alberto Arreola-W Hills 10-0
Steve Melara-Mt. SAC
Anthony Vega-Sac 14-2
Rafik Havhannisyan-East LA
Richard Morris-Santa Ana 7-5
Jonathon Gomez-Bakersfield

149
Conrad Rangell-Fresno 9-0
Noel Blanco-Mt. SAC
Frank Ruiz-Rio Hondo F 1:41
Marcial Rodriguez-Lassen
Joe Martinez-East LA 10-2
Tim Nevarez-Sacramento
Will Deyoung-Palomar F 3:38
Voris Meeks-Cerritos

157
Brady Bersano-Fresno 7-5
Tim Randall-Palomar
Jesse Baldazo-Sierra 15-2
Shawn Porter-Sacramento
Alex Cruz-Mt. SAC 20-10
Owen Craugh Lassen
Ramon Estrada-Cerritos 8-3
Melvin Cabus-Santa Ana

165
Tigan Adzhemtan-Fresn 14-6
Gavin Ludwig-Sacramento
Aaron Lopez-Santa Ana 2-0
Alfonso Estrada-Cerritos
Jacob Pendleton Bakfld 8-6
Josh Lujan-West Hills
Michael Joseph-Palomar 13-8
Vinny Fausone-Santa Rosa

174
Martin Fabbian-Fresno F 4:30
Dylin Rodriguez-Sierra
Ryan McWatters-V Val Deflt
Mike McAlister-Cuesta
Lance Castaneda-Bakfld 5-3
Eric Gomez-Modesto
Dwight Flores-Chabot 8-6
Dalton Berncich-Santa Rosa

184
Fito Juarez-Fresno Fall 6:12
Daniel Allen-Rio Hondo
Matt Lewellen-Palom F 4:14
Ruben Pivaral-East LA
Gerson Nkunku-Sacra Forfeit
Jairo Chavez-Sierra
Carlos Arana-Santa Ana 13-0
Mike Anderson-West Hills

197
Logan Paul-Eickhoff Sh 4-3OT
Jesus Chavez-Sierra
Colin Hart-Santa Rosa 15-14
Justin Whitten-Fresno
Tommy Howard-Skyline 2-0
Aaron Dubois-Santa Ana
Jeff Monteirro-West Hills Def
Carl Stokes-Mt. SAC

285
Luis Contreras-Fresno 6-3
Brian Klevies-Santa Ana
Daniel Gusev-Sierra F 2:54
Martin Gonzalez-Mt. SAC
Richard Segovia-Chabot 5-2
Mike Perez-West Hills
Paul Buchanan-Sac Def
Spencer Smith-Cerritos

Most Outstanding Wrestler
Eric Orozco-West Hills
Coach of the Year
Paul Keysaw-Fresno
Assistant Coach of the Year
Doni Teran-Rio Hondo

Team Scores
1	Fresno	191
2	Sacramento	94
3	Mt. SAC	91
4	Sierra	85
5	West Hills	79
6	Palomar	62.5
7	Rio Hondo	53
8	Santa Ana	52
9	Santa Ana	45.5
10	Bakersfield	41
11	Cerritos	37
11	East LA	37
13	Lassen	35
14	Victor Valley	29
15	Cuesta	23
16	Shasta	22
17	Chabot	17.5
18	Skyline	14
19	Modesto	10
20	S J Delta	0

2012 CCCAA State Wrestling Championships
West Hills College

125
Andres Torres Santa Ros 10-9
Edward Estevez-Palomar
Gabe Ballesteros-Cerritos 6-0
Christian Betancort-Mt. SAC
Chris Martinez-Fresno 5-3
Silverio Esparza-S J Delta
Matthew Correa-Cuesta
Dieuminse Dore-Lassen

133
Juan Jaime-Santa Ana SV4-2
A J Valles-Fresno
Emilio Rivera-Palomar 8-1
Sean Melton-Sacramento
Rudy Delgado-Cerritos Def
Aaron Ceballos-S J Delta
Darrin Salazar-W Hills F 3:19
Travis Roberts-Sierra

141
Abel Avila- Rio Hondo86-3
Racelis Cardenas-Fresno
Michaël Ruiz-West Hills 4-2
Enriquez Barajas-Sacramento
Anthony Rubio-Chabot 13-4
Steven Melara-Mt. SAC
Max Ramirez-Bakersfield 8-3
Michael Behnke-Cerritos

149
Spencer Hill-Fresno 8-5
Bryant Wood-Sacramento
Nathan Meteo-San Ana 4-2
Jacob Dunning-Palomar
Dolin Mininni-Cuesta TF 19-2
Jose Rugama-Mt. SAC
Ryan Steibar-Bakersfield 15-4
Blake Burges-Santa Rosa

157
Brady Bersano-Fresno 14-0
Tyson Kuahine-Sacramento
Alexander Cruz-Mt. SAC 3-2
Jacob Blackwell-Santa Ana
Bryan Barocio-R Hondo Def
Francisco Rueda-West Hills
Robert Monta-Palomar 14-5
Zach Grove-Skyline

165
Matt Heckman-Fresno 9-3
Carlos Arana-Santa Ana
Michael Joseph-Palomar 8-7
Owen Crough-Lassen
Nathan Zarate-W Hills F 1:23
Jonathon Urango-Cuesta
Shawn Porter-Sacrament 6-2
Sergio Guerrero-Mt. SAC

174
Ryan McWatters V Vall 12-10
Kevin Corbett-Fresno
Tyler Brown-Sacramento 5-4
Joshua Newman-East LA
Broderick Goens-Mt. SAC 5-4
Quinten Becker-Sierra
Tyree Cox Cerrito-Fall 3:49
Awaad Yasin-Santa Ana

184
Kenneth Breux-Mt. SAC 4-3
Erik Gomez-Modesto
Will Gockel Figg-Fresno 12-0
Michael Middlebrooks-E LA
Angelo Travino-Sierra Fall :50
Tommy Howard-Skyline
Michael Anderson W Hills 4-2
Juan Hernandez-Santa Ana

197
Khymba-Johnson-Sierra 4-2
Paul Lujano-Fresno
Matt Reed-Palomar 6-2
Ryan Mackey-Modesto
Tyler Smith-Cerritos 4-2
Jared Matanane-Mt. SAC
Henry Campos-West Hills 2-0
Derek Jaunigue-Cuesta

285
Daniel Gusev-Sierra Fall 1:35
Derrick Lee-West Hills
Mike Branson-Shasta
An Ekeian-Santa Ana 1:02
Travis Smith-Modesto Def
Julian Zuniga-East LA
Weston Hawkins-Cerritos 2-0
Paul Buchanan-Sacramento

Most Outstanding Wrestler
Brady Bersano-Fresno
Coach of the Year

Assistant Coach of the Year

Team Scores
1	Fresno	149.5
2	Mt. SAC	100.5
3	West Hills	94
4	Sacramento	87.5
5	Santa Ana	85
6	Palomar	79
7	Sierra	67.5
8	Cerritos	59
9	Modesto	40
10	East LA	37.5
11	Cuesta	35
12	Rio Hondo	33
13	Santa Rosa	23
14	Lassen	20
15	Victor Valley	19
16	Skyline	18
17	Shasta	16.5
18	Bakersfield	14.5
19	S J Delta	12
20	Chabot	10

2013 CCCAA State Wrestling Championships
December 13-14, 2013 San Joaquin Delta College

125
Christian Betancort-SAC 6-4
Amifa Olea-Fresno
Dustin Kirk-Cerritos 10-1
Albert Landeros-Sacramento
Hugo Perez-East LA 8-4
Dieuminse Dore-Lassen
Christian Hauser-San Ana 9-5
George Sakkas-Cuesta

133
Nathan Pike-Mt. Sac 8-6
Alex Perez-West Hills
Michael Clemmensen-Cu 15-0
Aaron Pen-Kruger-Santa Rosa
Elias Mercado-Rio Hond Forf
Greg Barrera-Cerritos
Vincent Hernandez-Fresn 6-2
Brian Ha-Skyline

141
Ali Naser-Fresno 2-1
Andrew Schulte-Santa Ana
Anthony Duran-Mt. SAC 7-6
Julian Purdy-Cuesta
Adrian Gomez-Fresno 5-2
Laith Alnassiri-Sacramento
Ricky Lule-Palomar 9-7
Eric Ambriz-Cerritos

149
Martin Sandoval-Fresno 7-6
Junior Lule-Palomar
Joseph Ontiveras-Fresn 16-0
Richie Miranda-Santa Ana
Keanu Tom Cerritos-MD 18-5
Will Upson-Sacramento
Max Ramirez-Bakersfield 7-3
Monet Goldman-Skyline

157
Taylor Hodel-Sac F 8:19
Shervin Iraviha-Palomar
Marshall Palmer-Palomar 4-2
Nathan Mateo-Santa Ana
Josh Cortez-Cuesta TF 18-3
Daniel Larman-Santa Rosa
Austin Braddock-Fresn F 2:06
Zack Grove-Skyline

165
Desi Rios-Sacramento F 3:23
Tyson Kauhine-Sacramento
Robin Calles-Sierra Fall 3:37
Jacob Blackwell-Santa Ana
Cyrus Sanai-Mt. SAC 6-0
Peter Donchev-Palomar
Sebastian Suikowsky Fre 14-6
Dane Burgess-Chabot

174
A Campos-Chambers Sac 2:42
Kevin Corbell-Fresno
Brody Goens-Mt. SAC 8-0
Jovan Villalobos-Cuesta
Dillon Harroun-Bakfld 10-5
Jesse McDaniel-Modesto
Aaron Dubois-San Ana F 1:33
Isai Guzman-Santa Rosa

184
Kenny Steers-Sacrament 2-1
Ryan Mackey-Modesto
Alfredo Nava-Santa Ana 10-6
Drasko Bogdanovich-Palomar
Nathan Rodriguez-Mt. S 10-8
Thomas Cross-Shasta
Jeramiah Gerl-Cerritos F 4:05
Allen Emmons-Sacramento

197
Jaird Chavez-Sierra 7-3
Hudson Buck-Sacramento
Luke Brewer-Modesto F 1:30
Juan Hernandez-Santa Ana
Roman Ermolov-Skylin F 3:32
Geoff Merker-Cuesta
Ismael Alvarez-Fresno 5-2
Omar Ross-Mt. SAC

285
Nader Abdullatif-Mt. SAC 6-4
Dereck Lee-West Hills
Travis Smith-Modesto F 6:53
Robert Chism-Cerritos
Mike Branson-Shasta 2-1
Josh Davis-Bakersfield
Logan Paxton-Sacramen 12-3
Charlie Rassel-Palomar

Most Outstanding Wrestler
Alex Campos-Chambers Sac
Coach of the Year
Dave Pacheco-Sacramento
Assistant Coach of the Year
Walter Ulrich-Sacramento
Most Falls in Shortest Time
Luke Brewer-Modesto

Team Scores

1	Sacramento	171
2	Fresno	133.5
3	Mt. SAC	113.5
4	Santa Ana	98
5	Palomar	85
6	Cuesta	56.5
7	Modesto	60.5
8	Cerritos	56.5
9	Santa Rosa	36
9	West Hills	36
11	Sierra	35.5
12	Bakersfield	27.5
13	Skyline	27
14	Shasta	20
15	East LA	14
16	Rio Hondo	10.5
17	Lassen	9.5
18	Chabot	4.5
19	S J Delta	0

Career Record
Alex Campos Chambers-Santa Rosa 64-?
Season Record
Mike Clemmensen-Cuesta 30-3

2014 CCCAA State Wrestling Championships
December 12-13, 2014 Cuesta College

125
Aruffo Olea-Fresno Default
Adrian Camposano-Fresno
Gio Castillo-Mt. SAC Fall 1:54
Silverio Esparza-West Hills
Richie Taira-Mt. SAC 5-1
Gary Howe-Cerritos
Darren Nguyen-Chabot Deflt
Marcus Velasquez-Bakfld

133
Dustin Kirk-Cerritos 9-5
Alberto Garcia-Palomar
Albert Landeros-Sacram Def
Travis Roberts-Sierra
Vicente Hernandez-Fresn 6-0
Ronald Collister Santa Ana
Arik Onsurez-Bakfld F 2:17
Anwar Halteh-Skyline

141
Terrill Sidner-Mt. SAC F 4:40
Conner Pollock-Cuesta
Isiah Alva-Fresno Forfeit
Jonas Gaytan-Fresno
Daniel Romero-R Hondo 16-9
Trent Nicholson-Sierra
Lake Gee-Sacramento F 1:54
Dominic Cesena-Chabot

149
A J McKee-Cerritos 6-5
Anthony-Rubio Chabot
Brian Sergi-Sacramento 10-4
Joaquin Collister-Santa Ana
Ivan Govea-Fresno Fall 2:48
Johnny Callas-Cuesta
Rogelio Bravo-S J Delta 6-5
Justin Hill-Lassen

157
Keanu Tom-Cerritos 6-4OT
Adrian Gomez-Fresno
J. Magdalleno-Hudson LA3-2
Richard Miranda-Santa Ana
Sean Raftery-Lassen 15-0
George Medina-Mt. SAC
Vincent Gomez-Bakfld F 5:10
John Sinclair-Cuesta

165
Victor Pereira-Chabot 11-6
Daniel Allen-Rio Hondo
Eric Roberts-Santa Ana 10-6
Adrian Herrera-East LA
Peter Donchev-Palomr F 6:27
Joseph Else-Cuesta
Adam Busch-Sacrament 12-9
Eric Colin-Palomar

174
Mo Naser Fresno-Fall 2:38
Zach Wally-Chabot
Dylan Clarke-Cerritos 6-2
Kolton Martin-Mt. SAC
Cesar Luna-Bakersfield F 5:10
Micah Macias-Santa Ana
Tytin Johnson-Lassen F 5:42
Amir Bakhshi-Cuesta

184
Will Gockel-Figge-Fres 3-1OT
Max Kumashiro-Cerritos
Alex Groves-Palomar SV 6-1
Logan Paxton-Sacramento
Nathan Rodriguez-Mt. SA 9-3
Thomas Cross-Shasta
Paul Hernandez-San Ana 7-3
Jack Robinett-Cuesta

197
Jack Murphy-Bakersfield 3-2
Oscar Martinez-Cerritos
Jeremiah Geri-Cerritos 3-2
KeAndre Johnson-Mt. SAC
Francisco Vargas-Skyli F 1:39
Dom Freesha-Fresno
Talyn Latour-S J Delta Default
Fred Duerr-Santa Rosa

285
Robert Chism-Cerritos F 6:42
Jesse Gomez-Cerritos
Javier Gonzales-Rio Ho F5:24
Andrew Cruz-Mt. SAC
Timothy McMihelk-Delta 8-5
Andrew Singer-Fresno
Jimmy Dawson-Sierra F 4:52
Jacob Richards-Sacramento

Most Outstanding Wrestler
Mo Naser-Fresno
Coach of the Year
Donnie Garriot-Cerritos
Assistant Coach of the Year
Eric Gould-Cerritos
Most Falls Shortest Time
Francisco Vargas-Skyline
3 Falls in 9:09

Team Scores
1	Cerritos	167
2	Fresno	159
3	Mt. SAC	111.5
4	Chabot	72
5	Santa Ana	69
6	Sacramento	66.5
7	Cuesta	56.5
8	Bakersfield	55
9	Palomar	48
10	Rio Hondo	43
11	Sierra	32
12	East LA	29
13	Lassen	26
14	S J Delta	25
15	Skyline	18.5
16	West Hills	14
17	Shasta	13.5
18	Santa Rosa	5.5
19	Modesto	0

Records
Jack Murphy-Bakersfield 24-0
Victor Pereira-Chabot
Undefeated
Robert Chism-Cerritos
Undefeated
Dustin Kirk-Cerritos 36-1
Antonio (A J) McKee-Cerritos 28-1
Keanu Tom-Cerritos 34-3
Robert Chism-Cerritos 26-0
Jesse Gomez-Cerritos 26-7

2015 CCCAA State Wrestling Championships
December 11-12, 2015 Fresno City College

125
Gio Castillo-Mt. Sac 8-6
Julian Gaytan-Fresno
Adrian Camposano-Fre 18-12
Estevan Cabanas-Cerritos
Norman Abas-Bakfld 16-0
Christian Vasquez-Modesto
Tyler Poalillo-San Rosa F 6:22
Michael LeFuel-Shasta

133
Jonas Gaytan-Fresno 8-1
Anthony Vargas-Cerritos
Jake Schaefer-Palomar 10-2
Darren Nguyen-Chabot
Isaac Pilgrim-Sacramento 5-4
Chris Kimball-Palamar
Brady Huang-Skyline Fall 1:49
Seth Hood-Fresno

141
Josh Bennett-Sierra TB1 5-4
Daniel Romero-Rio Hondo
Isaiah Alva-Fresno 6-3
Andrew Gomez-Santa Ana
Mario Lopez-Mt. SAC SV 7-5
Antonio Jimenez-Sacramento
Ezra Clark-Skyline SV 1 6-4
Elias Mercado-Rio Hondo

149
Terrill Sidner-Mt, SAC 15-6
Martine Sandoval-Fresno
Kory Davis Cerritos-MD 15-5
Brock Dias-West Hills
Mark Taijeron-Modesto 8-0
Rees Chew-Sierra
Chris Vaughan Sacrament 9-6
Tristan Steinman-Santa Ana

157
Aaron Negrette-Cerritos 12-2
Jose Regama-Mt. SAC
Kaleio Romero-Sacrame10-6
Landon Myers-Santa Ana
Noor Kathem-Mod 17-2
Dylan Moreno-Cerritos
Josh Annis-Fresno Forfeit
Luis Quintero-Cuesta

165
Dylan Forzani-Sac 22-4
Derek Lee Loy-Sacramento
Eric Roberts-Santa Ana 9-5
Arman Fayazzi-Santa Ana
Roger Arce-Rio Hondo 4-1
Louie Delatorre-Palomar
Jamal Halvorson-Shas F 4:15
Eric Collin-Palomar

174
Mo Naser Fresno-MD 16-6
Trever Wright-Sacramento
Alex Callo-Palomar 6-5
Stephen Martin-Skyline
Isaiah Smith-Sacramento 7-6
Lukas Basham-West Hills
Juan Soto-East LA Fall 1:57
Javier Contreras-Lassen

184
Alex Graves-Palomar TF 20-5
Jhaylyn Hall-Santa Rosa
Nick Rohrer-Sacramen F 4:15
Kolton Martin-Mt. SAC
Will Thorton-Cuesta 3-1
Ty Freeman-Santa Ana
Zach Mitchell-Bakersfield 5-1
Patrick Penick-Shasta

197
Oscar Martinez-Cerrit F 6:49
Luke Brewer-Modesto
Jose Robledo-Bakersfield 4-3
Jason Zecchini-Sacramento
Fred Duerr-Santa Rosa F :46
Ned Estrada-East LA
Raul Briseno-Palomar F 3:43
Josh Escobedo-Rio Hondo

285
Sevile Hayes-Palomar 3-2
Jesse Gomez-Cerritos
Casey Jones-Fresno Forfeit
D'Juan Ewing Smalls-Sacrame
Kyle Lincoln-West Hills 10-1
Murrel Anderson-Chabot
Andrew Cruz-Mt. SAC 4-3
Josh Davis-Bakersfield

Most Outstanding Wrestler
Terrill Sidner-Mt. SAC
Coach of the Year
Dave Pacheco-Sacramento
Assistant Coach of the Year
Walter Ulrich-Sacramento
Most Falls in the least time
Fred Duerr-Santa Rosa 3 in 10:44

Team Scores
1	Sacramento	158
2	Fresno	137
3	Cerritos	116
4	Palomar	116.5
5	Mt. SAC	85.5
6	Santa Ana	61.5
7	Modesto	50.5
8	Santa Rosa	43.5
9	Bakersfield	41.5
10	West Hills	36.5
11	Rio Hondo	36
12	Sierra	27
13	Cuesta	25
14	Skyline	24
15	Shasta	22.5
16	Shasta	19.5
17	East LA	17
18	Lassen	8
19	SJ Delta	0
19	Victor Valley	0

Records
Aaron Negrette-Cerritos Undefeated,
Anthony Vargas-Cerritos 24-6
Oscar Martinez-Cerritos 20-3
Jesse Gomez-Cerritos 28-1

2016 CCCAA State Wrestling Championships
December 9-10, 2016 Victor Valley College

125
Julian Gaytan-Fresno 8-1
Landon McBride-Sierra
Norberto Buenrostro Cer12-7
Morgan Sauseda-Sacramento
Pedro Sarabia-Bakersfield 9-3
Elijah Diaz-Mt. SAC
A J Rosas-Fresno MD 17-4
Gilbert Martinez-Sierra

133
Alberto Garcia-Palomar 3-2
Jake Schaeffer-Palomar
Aaron Mora-Fresno Fall 3:16
Pedro Corona-Bakersfield
Adrian Marrufo-W Hills 20-5
Devon Lyle-Chabot
Leif Dominguez-Cuesta 14-3
Julian Melecio-Mt. SAC

141
Kevin Kelley-Mt. SAC 3-2
Casper Sherow-Mt. SAC
Hunter Minton-Sac 4-2
Richard Pocock-Cerritos
Andrew Gomez-San Ana 21-2
Clinton McAlester-Fresno
Eric Reyes-Palomar 13-8
Esteban Corona-Bakersfield

149
Dylan Martinez-Fresno 11-2
Dean Esquibel-Fresno
Joseph Dominguez-M S F5:58
Chris Kimball-Palomar
Wyatt Gerl Cerritos-Forfeit
Alex Aniciente-Lassen
Tristan Steinmon-S Ana F 4:08
Joshua Caro-Rio Hondo

157
Kevin James-Cerritos 6-4
Joshua Annis-Fresno
Noor Kathem-Modesto 26-12
Daniel Larman-Sacramento
Dylan Moreno Cerritos F 1:50
Nathan Pimentel-West Hills
Brandon Tierney-S An 12-10
Jessy Diez-Palomar

165
Derek Lee Loy-Sacrament 7-4
Ryan Soto-Victor Valley
Arman Fayyazi-Santa Ana 6-5
Blake Vasquez-Cerritos
Kevin Hope-Mt. SAC Forfeit
Andrew Brodland-Sierra
Kennith Kirk-Cerritos F 1:59
Ricardo Bribiescas-Skyline

174
Alex Garcia-Cuesta 9-6
Reed South-Mt. SAC
Niko Chapman Sac 9-3
Zach Wally-Chabot
Jerrin Dean-Fresno 2-0
Isaiah Leyva-Cerritos
Dupra Goodman-Skyline 6-0
Stephen Dixon-S J Delta

184
Kalan Hastey-Sac 13-4
Trevor Wright-Sacramento
Bruce Valdez-Palomar F 3:41
Barnabus Yi-Mt. SAC
Dom Freesha-Fresno TB 1 5-4
Bryant Vasquez-Cerritos
Isaac Delacruz-Cuesta 6-2
Ivan Sevilla-West Hills

197
David Van Weems Cerrito 4-3
Kelvin Stucky-Fresno
Wes Ruffer-Lassen MD 15-5
Andrew Ramos-Rio Hondo
Ben Sira-Chabot 4-2
Zack Mitchell-Bakersfield
Alex Gomez Palomar-F 2:29
Zavion Roberson-Bakersfield

285
Chance Eskam-Palomar 3-2
Bradon Sotomayor-East LA
Tristan Smith-Modesto 1-0
David Zavala-Cerritos
Ramiro Macias-Bakfld TB 4-3
Angel Mariscal-Fresno
Jarrad Kirk-Sacramento 5-0
Marco Valdivia-Rio Hondo

Most Outstanding Wrestler
Derek Lee Loy-Sacramento

Coach of the Year
Paul Keysaw-Fresno

Assistant Coach of the Year
George Moreno-Fresno

Most falls in the Least Time
Jerrin Dean-Fresno
3 in 7:53

Team Scores
1	Fresno	158.5
2	Cerritos	153.5
3	Sacramento	119.5
4	Palomar	114
5	Mt. SAC	113.5
6	Bakersfield	60
7	Santa Ana	42
8	Cuesta	40.5
9	Chabot	35.5
10	Sierra	31.5
11	Modesto	29
12	West Hills	27.5
13	Rio Hondo	24.5
14	Lassen	23
15	East LA	15
15	Victor Valley	15
17	Skyline	12
18	S J Delta	4
19	Santa Rosa	1
20	Shasta	0

Season Record
Alex Garcia Cuesta   32-2

2017 CCCAA State Wrestling Championships
December 8-9, 2017 San Joaquin Delta College

125
Brandon Bettancourt-Fre 7-1
Morgan Sauceda-Sacramento
Greg Viloria-S J Delta 3-1
Elijah Diaz-Mt. SAC
Danny Borrego-Skyline 3-2
Brandan Mendoza-Modesto
John Whisner-Mt. SAC
Isaac Guerrero-Palomar 3:22

133
Isaiah Perez-Fresno 8-1
Pedro Corona-Bakersfield
Adam Valdez-Mt. SAC SV11-5
Josh Brown-Cerritos
Josh Fuentes-Sana Ana F 2:41
Tyler Poalillo-Santa Rosa
Jeremy Newman-Sierra F :58
Zachary Moisner-Palomar

141
Aaron Mora-Fresno 8-5
Joseph Dominguez-Mt. SAC
Abraham Del Toro-Fresn20-8
Adrian Marufo-West Hills
Nick Camacho-Cerritos 13-2
Jeremy Huang-Sana Ana
Jacob Jimenez-Palomar Inj
Brandon Rullan-S J Delta

149
Dylan Martinez-Fresno F 3:44
Blake Boswell-Santa Rosa
Wolfgang Bernal-Santa A 9-2
Manuel Salcedo-Mt. SAC
Nathan Navida-Palomar inj
Emmett Kuntz-Bakersfield
Khalil Howard-Rio Hon F 2:18
Carlos Vasquez-S J Delta

157
James Schmidt-Rio Hon 12-4
Conrad Lopez-Fresno
Wyatt Gerl-Cerritos Fall 4:14
Muhammad Lateef-S J Delta
Josh McMillon-Fresno 5-4
Joseph Valdez-Mt. SAC
William Schwertscharf-M4-2
Jose Paiz-West Hills

165
Apollo Santos- Mt. SAC 3-2
Victor Vargas-Fresno
Matthew Mejia-Mt. SAC 13-5
Brandon Tierry-Santa Ana
Isaac Bartalotto-Sacrameo inj
Blake Vasquez-Cerritos
Josh Koning-Moorpark F :23
Brian Horn-Sacramento

174
Anthony Cress-Chabot F 2:52
Able Garcia-Sacramento
Hector Vargas-Mt. SAC 7-5
Braulio Banuelos-Palomar
Miguel Ruiz-Fresno 8-5
Cameron Casey-Santa Rosa
Zack Gonzalez-Cerritos F 6:18
Robert Flores-Moorpark

184
Adrian Godinez-Bakfld 10-4
Luis Melecio-Mt. SAC
Tevin Bailey-Lassen 14-2
Jeremy Mass-Bakersfield
Isaac Sillas-Sacramento F :41
Dylan Kranich-S J Delta
Angel Verduzco-Cerritos 14-7
Leo Perez-Santa Ana

197
David Van Weens-Cerrito 9-4
Rob Nickerson-Sacramento
Marcus Macias-Fresno F 2:13
Lazaro Carrasco-Chabot
David Warden-Sacram F 2:13
Zavion Roberson-Bakersfield
David Chavaria Mt.SAC OT4-4
Tristan Bergovic-Shasta

285
Chance Eskam-Palomar 3-2
Brandon Sotomayor-East LA
Cola Mair-Lassen 5-3
Chumkaur Dhaliwal-Chabot
Jesse Flores-Modesto 1-0
Casey Jones-Fresno
Ramon Guzman-Skyline 3-2
Ramiro Macias-Bakersfield

Most Outstanding Wrestler
Dylan Martinez-Fresno
Coach of the Year
Paul Keysaw-Fresno
Assistant Coach of the Year
George Moreno-Fresno
Most Fall in the Shortest Time
Josh Fuentes-Santa Ana
3 Falls in 3:44
Fresno 15TH CCCAA State Team Championship

Team Scores
1	Fresno	184
2	Mt. SAC	152
3	Sacramento	98
4	Cerritos	86
5	Bakersfield	71.5
6	Palomar	67.5
7	Santa Ana	66
8	San Joaquin Delta	56.5
9	Chabot	55
10	Santa Rosa	37.5
11	Rio Hondo	33.5
12	Lassen	30
13	Modesto	27.5
14	West Hills	22.5
15	Skyline	21.5
16	Moorpark	20
17	East LA	15
18	Sierra	7.5
19	Shasta	4
20	Cuesta	0
20	Victor Valley	0

2018 CCCAA State Wrestling Championships
December 8-9, 2018 Cerritos College

125
Greg Villoria-S J Delta 9-5
Mario Moreno-Fresno
Trevor Bagan-San Rosa 14-12
Isaac Guerrero-Palomar
Jacob Hiller-Shasta Forfeit
Marcus Hutcherson-Bakfld
Keithen Estrada-Bakfld 6-5
Zachary Cunningham-Mt.SAC

133
Isaiah Perez-Fresno 9-5
Raul Ortiz-Palomar
Oliver Rivera-Santa Ana 13-3
Eric Marquez-Palomar
Murtaza Nabaada-Sie F4:49
Jose Espinoza-Cerritos
Ivan Gomez-Modesto Forfeit
Kyle Jimenez-Fresno

141
Josh Brown-Cerritos 10-2
Luis Ramos-Fresno
Ezra Clark-Skyline MD 17-8
Michael Mello-Sacramento
Eric Reyes-Palomar 8-6
Josh Fuentes-Norikiyo-S Ana
Aaron Diaz-Mt. SAC Def
Logan Cota-Modesto 7-5

149
Daniel Ruiz-Fresno 6-5
Adam Valdez-Mt. SAC
Daniel Cota-Modesto 7-5
Larry Rodriguez-Cerritos
Josh Aveves-Skyline 4-3
Dylan Crawford-Sacramento
Humphry Quirie-Cuesta 10-4
Emmett Kuntz-Bakersfield

157
Luis Vargas-Santa Ana 8-2
Ruben Garcia-Fresno
Miguel Gallardo-Mt SAC 7-1
Conrad Garcia-Fresno
Joe Romero-West Hills 3-1
Conrad Trevino-Sacramento
Manny Curry-Sacramento 6-2
Jessy Diaz-Palomar

165
Augestine Garcia-Fresn 12-3
Marc Anderson-Palomar
Kenneth Kirk-Cerritos F 5:47
Abel Garcia-Sacramento
Devin Top-Moorpark 12-1
Kevin Garcia-Chabot
Jackson Blankenship-Sh 17-0
Kevin Mello-Bakersfield

174
Abner Romero-Fresno 8-1
Zac Gonzalez-Cerritos
Cameron Cox-Palomar 7-6
Hunter Gonzalez-Sierra
Isaiah Bertalotto-Sac 9-3
Robert Flores-Moorpark
Gabriel Rodriguez-E LA F 5:59
Juan Rosales-Modesto

184
Bronson Harmon-Sacram 3-2
Jhaylyn Hall-Santa Rosa
Steven Abbott-Sacram F 2:09
Trvin Bailey-Lassen
Nick Kimball-Palomar F 1:13
Victor Bryson-Cuesta
Jerrin Dean-Fresno 4-0
Victor Cruz-Modesto

197
Anthony Cress-Chabot 6-3
Brian Horn-Sacramento
Adrian Godinez-Bakfld 15-0
Karim Shakur-Santa Rosa
Tony Rogers-Lassen Forfeit
Matthew Martinez-Fresno
Andy Voong-Rio Hondo 4-0
Efren Velez-East LA

285
Cristian Ayala-Mt. SAC TB 3-2
Cole Mair-Lassen
Ramon Guzman-Skylin 3-1OT
Jacob Hall-Bakersfield
Randy Gonzalez-Cerritos 2-1
Diego Sanchez-Rio Hondo
Angel Mariscal-Fresno 4-2
Christopher-Alvizures Mt SAC

Most Outstanding Wrestler
Greg Viloria-S J Delta
Coach of the Year
Paul Keysaw-Fresno
Assistant Coach of the Year
George Moreno-Fresno
Most Falls in the Least time
Steve Abbott-Sacramento

Team Scores
1	Fresno	187
2	Sacramento	119.5
3	Palomar	109
4	Cerritos	103.5
5	Mt. SAC	79
6	Bakersfield	53.5
7	Santa Ana	52.5
8	Lassen	52
8	Santa Ana	52
10	Skyline	39.5
11	Modesto	32
12	Chabot	31
13	Sierra	25
14	Shasta	22.5
15	Moorpark	21.5
16	S J Delta	20.5
17	West Hills	18
18	Cuesta	17
19	Rio Hondo	16.5
20	East LA	12

Records
Josh Brown-Cerritos 22-0
Zac Gonzalez-Cerritos 21-7
Abner Romero-Fresno 28-0

David Pacheco-Sacramento
1983-2018, Championships Conference 17, Regional 3, State 4, All-Americans 99, Individual State 21, Regional 50, State Placers 186, Conference 129, Academic All-Americans 60, 301-114-4

2019 CCCAA State Wrestling Championships
December 13-14, 2019 Fresno City College

125
Jonathan Prata-Cerritos 3-2
Mario Moreno-Fresno
Brandon-Mendoza Mo 15-10
Nick Foster-Lassen
Ramiro Castillo-Fresno 6-1
Conner Diamond-Mt. SAC
Keithen Estrada-Bakfld 4-2
Gavin Sweeny-Sierra

133
Kahill Tucker-Rio Hondo 7-6
Houston Scibek-Modesto
Stefano McKinney Cerrit 14-5
Owen Jones-Santa Rosa
Louie Bravo-Fresno
Cole Kachmar-Sacramento
Andres Gonzalez-Cerritos 9-2
Jude Miranda-West Hills

141
Isaiah Mora-Cerritos 10-7
Christian Espinoza-Rio Hondo
Anthony Chavez-Fresno 15-8
Bradley Chirino-Mt. SAC
Ivan Gomez-Modesto 3-2
David Ortega-Victor Valley
Raul Ortiz-Sacramento 8-3
Al Kavehi-Santa Ana

149
Danny Ruiz-Fresno 1-0
Chris Gaxiola-Fresno
Greg Ewert-Santa Rosa 10-9
Logan Garcia-Lassen
Adrian Gonzalez-Bak F 4:25
Joe Kachmar-Sacramento
Vante Moore-Cerritos 6-1
Josue Aguilar-East LA

157
Josh McMillian-Fresno 8-3
William Schwetscharf-Modes
Larry Rodriguez-Cerrito 16-1
Ryan Ojeda-Sierra
Emmanuel Zepeda E LA Def
Hunter LaRue-Sacramento
Doroteo Lopez-East LA F 4:34
Gabriel Deharo-Lassen

165
Jacob Hansen-Moorpark 7-2
Augustine Garcia-Fresno
Wetzel Hill-Mt. SAC 25-12
Jeronimo Cardosa-West Hills
Darin Chick-S J Delta 10-9
Manny Curry-Sacramento
Drake Delacruz-Cerritos 19-4
Alex Thornburg-Sacramento

174
Jonathan Hunter-Bak F 4:25
Chase Miller-Sacramento
Arturo Rivas-Fresno F 4:17
Kevin Hope-Mt. SAC
Devyn Kreb-Sierra 19-8
Kevin Ayala-Mt. SAC
Bryan Samayoa-Cerrit F 3:25
Jamal Starks-S J Delta

184
Stephen Martin-Skyline 9-0
Jordan Annis-Bakersfield
Russell Rucklos-Lassen 8-0
Joey Conroy-Palomar
Breck Jeffus-Cuesta Fall 2:16
Angel Verduzco-Cerritos
Melad Ayyoub-Mt. SAC 14-5
Bobby Mello-Santa Rosa

197
Jack Kilner-Fresno 1-0
Hamza Al Saudi-Cerritos
Hunter Gonzalez-Sie F 2:45
Ricardo Gonzalez-Bakersfield
Andy Voong-Rio Hondo 11-1
Patrick Slatic-West Hills
Lazaro Carrasco-Chabot F :58
Steven Karas-Sacramento

285
Armando Barcenas-Fresn 5-2
Enrique Galica-Palomar
Juan Camacho-Cuesta 4-1
Victor Yakshin-Sierra
David Arriaga-East LA 5-3
Randy Arriaga-Cerritos
Alex Mosquada-Sierra Defaul
Ben Hodhodiabkena-Moorpk

Most Outstanding Wrestler
Jacob Hansen-Moorpark
Coach of the Year
Paul Keysaw-Fresno
Assistant Coach of the Year
George Moreno-Fresno

Team Scores
1 Fresno	186
2 Cerritos	137
3 Bakersfield	77
4 Sacramento	72
5 Sierra	70.5
6 Mt. SAC	70.5
7 Modesto	59
8 Lassen	53
9 Rio Hondo	48
10 East LA	41
11 Santa Rosa	34
12 West Hills	33.5
13 Palomar	30.5
14 Moorpark	29.5
15 Cuesta	23.5
16 Skyline	19
17 S J Delta	17
18 Chabot	11.5
19 Victor Valley	10
20 Santa Ana	8.5
21 Shasta	0

Records
Jonathon Prata-Cerritos 22-1
Isaiah Mora-Cerritos 21-7
Hamza Al Saudi-Cerritos 24-9

2021 CCCAA State Wrestling Championships
December 10-11, 2021 Cerritos College

125
Jonathan Prata-Cerritos 9-1
Alexis Tellez-Rio Hondo
Connor Diamond Mt. SAC 5-3
Christopher Betancort-M SAC
Austin Pimintel-Fresno 10-7
Victor Atherton-Rio Hondo
Salahdin Farukh-Sierra F :32
Alex Cardoza-Victor Valley

133
Jason Valencia-Mt. SAC 14-8
David Saenz-Mt. SAC
Dylan Duncan-Sac 7-4
Roland Dominguez-Cerritos
Trevor Bagan-Santa Ana 7-4
Adrian Chavez-Fresno
Owen Wilson-Palomar F 5:00
Joshua Mendoza-Cerritos

141
Wayne Joint-West Hills !0-8
Kendal Frank-Sacramento
Thomas Chapman-M SAC 7-2
Jose Cisneros-Victor Valley
Wyatt Carter-Modesto 10-8
Zayn Petel-Santa Ana
Stephen Lundquist-Bre Si 7-6
Hector Ramirez-East LA

149
Lupe Ayon-West Hills 6-1
Juan Lopez-Mt. SAC
Caoilte Drury-Cerritos 8-1
Jose Aguilar-East LA
Felix Osorio-Cerritos 6-2
Alfredo Mendoza-Sacrament
Donovan Sanin-R Hono F i:35
Everardo Rueda-Bakersfield

157
Noah Cortez-Fresno F 2:59
Daniel Bracamontes-Cerritos
Jerry Rubio-Mt. SAC 7-2
Conrad Trevino-Oceuo Sac
Gavin Kaminski-Palomar 8-3
Adrian Rios-Rio Hondo
Temistocle-Politi Shasta 3-1
Sami Barakat-Cuesta

165
Hassan Khan-Sacramento 2-1
Willy LaMacchia-Skyline
Armando Murillo-Cuesta Def
Saeed Perez-Santa Ana
Gracen Hayes-Bakersfield 9-6
Humphry Quirie-Cuesta
Gabe Carrillo-Cuesta 6-1
Bryan Thorne-Skyline

174
Wetzel Hill-Mt. SAC 2-1
Joseph Fernandez-Moorpark
Raymundo Raiz-Fresno 7-1
Stone Robledo-Sierra 7-4
Gabe Guzman-Sierra 7-4
Nick Lopez-East LA
Uriel Vasquez-Bakersfield 9-3
Jacob Turner-Modesto

184
Jonathan Hunter-Bak F 2:21
Eric Kasras-Sacramento
Luck Hansen-Moorpark 7-3
Justin Tripp-West Hills
Troy Garza-East LA 7-3
Melvin Naranjo-Fresno
Ahmed Khattab-Mt. SAC 12-8
Logan Cobert-Modesto

197
Angel Solis-West Hills F 2:21
Nate Kendrick-Mt. SAC
Steven Karas-Sacramento
Anthony Banuelos-Bakfld
Nicholas Echeveste-Fresn 6-3
Chente Trujillo-Bakersfield
Luc LaVasser-Moorpark 4-2
Devon Peries-East La

285
Jonovan Smith-Cerritos 8-3
Rudy Garcia-Fresno
Joseph Alaniz-Fall :42
Jacob Larsen-Santa Rosa
Corbin Hayes-Bakersfield Def
Taven Avila-Santa Rosa
Jesse Garcia-Mt. SAC F 5:41
Nathan Ramos-East LA

Most Outstanding Wrestler
Jonathan Hunter-Bakersfield
Coach of the Year
David Rivera-Mt. SAC
Assistant Coach of the Year
Robert Dominguez-Mt. SAC
Most Falls in the Least Time
Joseph Alaniz-Fresno
4 Falls in 3:52

Team Scores
1	Mt. SAC	167
2	Cerritos	138.5
3	Fresno	117
4	Sacramento	107.5
5	Bakersfield	85
6	West Hills	84.6
7	East LA	56
8	Rio Hondo	53
9	Moorpark	35
10	Cuesta	29.5
10	Santa Rosa	29.5
12	Santa Ana	27.5
13	Sierra	27
14	Modesto	23.5
15	Victor Valley	23
16	Palomar	22
17	Skyline	21
18	Shasta	5.5
19	Chabot	0
19	Lassen	0
19	S J Delta	0

Records
Jonathan Prata-Cerritos 21-1
Caoilte Drury-Cerritos 21-4
Armando Murillo-Cuesta 21-4
Jonovan Smith-Cerritos 31-1

2022 State Wrestling Championships
December 9-10, 2022 West Hills College

125
Chris Betancourt-M SAC 17-6
Chris Calderon-Mt. SAC
Alex Tellez-Rio Hondo 11-1
Blade Owens-Victor Valley
Eczequiel Jaurrieta-Fre 16-10
Darius Levan-Sacramento
Dylan Atherton-R Hono F1:57
Gabe Rivera-Cuesta

133
Devin Murphy-Fresno 8-6
David Saenz-Mt. SAC
Anthony Pererya-Cerrits 10-5
Devin Martinez-Rio Hondo
Derrek Alcantar-Bakfld 18-2
Joaquin Mosqueda-Sierra
Owen Wilson-Palomar F 1:55
Liam Nelson- Sierra

141
Wayne Joint-West Hills 3-0
Mario De La Torre-Cerritos
Abraham Cerda-Fresno 4-2
Wyatt Carter-Modesto
Salahdin Farukh-Sierra F 5:21
Riley Fitzsimmons-Mt. SAC
Jason Valencia-Mt. SAC 10-6
Zack Zernik-Moorpark

149
Felix Osorio-Cerritos !4-5
James Juarez-Bakersfield
Billy Looney-Mt. SAC 10-6
Matthew Arias-Fresno
Adam Hansen-Moorpk F 3:19
Chase Mirelez-Modesto
Joshua Padilla-East LA 6-4 SV
Jacob Benson-Shasta

157
Jackson Morgan-Fresno 8-1
Ethan Boyd-Sacramento
Noah Cortez-Fresno 8-4
Marcus Lobato-Mt. SAC
Kendall Frank-Sacrament 4-1
JJ Gutierrez-Palomar
Willy Lamacchia-Skyline 13-4
Trevor Thompson-Cerritos

165
Armando Murillo Cerritos 3-1
Jesus Gutierrez-Victor Valley
Jon Hernandez-Sac 2-0
Roman Mendez-Fresno
Gracen Hayes-Bakfld 11-2
Caidence Turner-Mt. SAC
Isaiah Castro-Sierra 16-6
Armando Renteria-Moorpark

174
Jake Prudek-Fresno 5-2
Reymundo Raiz-Fresno
Benicio Martinez-Sacr10-8 SV
Luke Combs-Bakersfield
Stone Robledo-Cerritos 2-0
Sergio Gutierrez-Santa Ana
Daniel Hernandez Palom13-5
Jacob Turner-Modesto

184
Luke Meyer-Fresno 9-3SV
Justin Tripp-West Hills
Justin Serra-Sacramento 7-0
Celso Silva-Palomar
Rafeal Guerra-Cerritos F 3:52
Leon Tippett-Cuesta
Jakob Hand-Mt. SAC 8-3
Tony Garza-East LA

197
Rudy Garcia-Fresno Fall 4:24
Malachi Lyles-Cerritos
Nate Kendricks-Mt. SAC 6-4
Denzel Mabry-Sacramento
Kevin Fernandez-Mod F 5:18
Joel Lopez-Shasta
Javante Gregoire-Sa Rosa 8-3
Devin Peries-East LA

285
Carson Hatch-Modesto 302
Corbin Hayes-Bakersfield
Kobe Pablo-Cerritos 3-1SV
Emitt Mercado-Rio Hondo
Javier Martinez-Fresno 11-1
Brandon Redd-Skyline
Jesse Garcia-Mt. SAC Fall :23
Garret Hicks-Modesto

Most Outstanding Wrestler
Wayne Joint-West Hills
Coach of the Year
Paul Keysaw-Fresno
Assistant Coach of the Year
George Moreno-Fresno
Most Falls in the Least Time
Salahdin Farukh-Sierra
4 Falls in 13:06

Team Scores
1	Fresno	214
2	Mt. SAC	154.5
3	Cerritos	153.5
4	Sacramento	103
5	Modesto	74.5
6	Bakersfield	71
7	Rio Hondo	60
8	Sierra	55
9	Palomar	45.5
10	West Hills	44.5
11	Victor Valley	42
12	East LA	29
13	Moorpark	28
14	Cuesta	21
15	Skyline	19
16	Shasta	16
17	Santa Ana	14
18	Santa Rosa	9
19	Chabot	3
20	S J Delta	.5
21	Lassen	0

Season Records
Bakersfield
Gracen Hayes   20-7
Luke Combs   21-4
Corbin Hayes   26-3

2022 CCCAA CHAMPIONS
FRESNO CITY COLLEGE

2023 CCCAA State Wrestling Championships
December 8-9, 2023 Cuesta College

125
Christoper-Calderon SAC 4-2
Adrian Limon-Mt. SAC
Scotty Moore-Skyline 16-8
Dylan Atherton-Rio Hondo
Dakota Sanders-Redwd 25-6
Abram Granados-Fresno
Tallon Chambers Fresn F 2:51
Cameron Fernando-Moorpar

133
Davin Martinez-Rio Ho 15-10
Adrian Chavez-Fresno
Derrek Alcantar-Bakfld F 2:01
Emilio Medina-Mt. SAC
Gio Urbieta-West Hills 16-5
Ben Quilpa-Sacramento
Dustin Merlos-Lassen Forfeit
Pedro Lacerdo-Mt. SAC

141
Zachary Parker-Mt. SAC F2:08
Evan Roy-Victor Valley
Matthew Terrence Fresn 12-4
Ahmaad Lewis-Sacramento
Kymani Capri-Redwd F 2:08
Finnegan Long-Rio Hondo
Jake Topartzer-Cerritos F 1:26
Zane Kowalkowski-Shasta

149
Brandon Bollinger-V Vall 10-3
Mario De La Torre-Cerritos
Anthony Nunes-Modesto 4-2
Matthew Arias-Fresno
Ammar Khan-Sac F 2:36
Dorian Parker-Palomar
Jasper Centeno Cerrito F 2:36
Brian Gleger-Mt. SAC

157
Alex Ramirez-Mt. SAC F 5:30
Caolite Drury-Cerritos
Alfredo T Mendoza-Sacr 11-2
Anthony Perez-Palomar
Gabe Carrillo-Moorpark
Chase Mirelez-Modesto
Nicholas Dehart-Fresno 9-1
Joshua Padilla-East LA

165
Etan Boyd-Sacramento F 5:21
Joshua Thomas-Sierra
Edward Ramirez-Sa Ana 12-2
Isaac R Martinez-Modesto
Adrian Juarez-Bakfld 12-1
Caidence Turner-Mt. SAC
Thomas Venezia-Skyline
Cael Garrett-Cerritos

174
Nathan Cruz-Mt. SAC 4-1
Jazziel Perez-Moorpark
D J Weimer-Palomar TF 17-2
Marcos Gamez-Fresno
Andrew Hamant-Sacram Forf
Joshua Shepard-Bakersfield
Anthony Hidalgo-Rio H F 4:20
Michael Negrete-Sierra

184
Adrian Morales-Sacra F 1:05
Bryan Thorne-Skyline
Rafael R-Amador-Bakfld 19-8
Adrian Garcia-Fresno
Andres Carrillo-Santa An 14-2
Isaac Villalobos-Bakersfield
Anthony Incantalupo-RH F3:56
Andrew Zarate-Lassen

197
Ethan Birch-Chabot 9-5
Rayhan Jaleel-Santa Rosa
Callan Ivy-Chabot TF 18-3
Christian Davidson-Cuesta
Frankie Pomilia-Sant Rosa 8-1
Uriel Vasquez-Bakersfield
Armando Sandoval-Cerri 14-6
Isaac Lopez-Mt. SAC

285
Isaish Perez-Chabot F 3:25
Joseph Nava-Santa Ana
Dib Sawaya-Mt. SAC TB 2-2-2
Koby Pablo-Cerritos
Evan Glines-Sacrament F 5:25
Gerard Marshall-Redwoods
Taven Avila-West Hills F :17
Mustafa Farha-Palomar

Most Outstanding Wrestler
Devin Martines-Rio Hondo
Manuel Gorriaran Award
Most Falls/Least Time
Adrian Chaves-Morales-Sacramento
National Coach of the Year
David Rivera-Mt. San Antonio College
National Assistant Coach of the Year Chris Mecate-Mt. San Antonio College

Team Scores
1	Mt. SAC	181.5
2	Sacramento	163.5
3	Fresno	122
4	Cerritos	94
5	Bakersfield	89
6	Rio Hondo	73
7	Palomar	56.5
8	Santa Ana	51.5
9	Skyline	48.5
10	Chabot	45.5
10	Victor Valley	45.5
12	Redwoods	42
13	Modesto	41.5
14	Moorpark	37
15	Sierra	30
16	West Hills	27
17	Santa Rosa	26.5
18	Lassen	20
19	Cuesta	16
20	Shasta	14.5
21	East LA	10
22	S J Delta	4.5

2024 CCCAA State Wrestling Championships
December 13-14, 2024 Lemoore College

125
Caden Hanover-Pal 9-3
Dakota Sanders-Cor
Jimmy Reyes-Lem 3-1
Rylan Madrid-Msac
Zane Cerda-Fre F 6:03
Eczequiel Jaurrieta-Fre
Dekek Ruffin-Src F 2:21
Jesse Hernandez-Cerr

133
Jason Saenz-Msac 5-0
Mason Carrillo-Moor
Gio Urbieta-Lem MD 21-8
Ricardo Solorio-Sa
Ben Quilpa-Scc Forfeit
Andrew Diaz-Vv
Dustin Merlos-Las TF 17-1
Erickson Edpao-Src

141
Diego Peraza-Pal 12-7
Yoshia Funakoshi-Cerr
Chris Guerrero-Vv 7-3
Aldo Quintero-Msac
Talon Niimi-Scc Injury S
hawn Torres-Rio
Brendon Ko-BC F :58
Azim Azimy-Chab

149
Alieza Kaveh-Sa 8-3 *
James Wright-Fre
Demarcus Turner-Mod 7-6
Brian Geiger-Msac
Michael Williams-Msac 7-1
Phu Le-Scc
Matthias Valdez-VV F 5:16
Vicente Rodarte-Src

157
Maxximus Martinez-Msac 4-1
Joe Anthony Perez
Isam Abodullaeu-Sie 8-6
Noah Reynolds-Fresno
Grant Eklund-Cues 7-5
Nicolas Pham-Cerr
Ceden Diamond-SCC 7-5
James Juarez-BC

165
Jack Estevez-Msac 7-3
Preston Scharf-Cues
Isaac Arroyo Lem 11-7
Philip Arroyo Lem
Marshall Beecham-Cues Forf
Max McWilliams Fre
D J Weimer-Pal 5-3
Khalid Ghani-Mod

174
Jake Prudek-Fre 4-2
Tyler Hanna-Cerr
Jakob Hand-Msac F 1:50
Adrian Juarez-BC
Maksim Sherstnev-Sie Inj
Fazal Mohammad-Chab
Javier Montes-Msac 4-0
Kelly Little-Scc

184
Frankie Stevenson-Vv 6-5
Roman Loya-Msac
Ivan Natceli-Pal MD 9-1
Andrew Zarate-Las
Farzad Hashimi-Cerr 6-2
Robert Felipe-Lem
Adrian P Pulido-Mod F :50
Ben Setum-Cerr

197
Mo Talebi-Msac F 3:48
Chance Evans-Cues
Rayhan Jaleel-Sa Injury
Daylan Henry-Pal
Vaea Salt-Scc Injury
Angel Cervantez-BC
Jaremiah Juarez-Rio Injury
Almazbekov Abdmanap-Chab

285
Javier Martinez-Fre 4-1
Joseph Alaniz-Fre
Kendrick Salcido-MD 14-4
Julian Bilezikjan-Rio
Jonathan Garcia-BC 5-0
Cody Ruiz-Mod
Mustafa Farha-Pal F 1:37
Bryce Meggers-Sierra

Most Outstanding Wrestler
Alireza Kaveh-Santa Ana
Coach of the Year
Tim Box-Palomar
Assistant Coach of the Year
Mike Box-Palomar
Gorriaran Award – Most Falls
Jakob Hand-Mt. San Antonio
4 Falls in 11:23

Team Scores
1	Mt. SAC-Msac	204
2	Fresno-Fre	138
3	Palomar-Pal	110
4	Sacramento-Scc	90.5
5	Cerritos-Cerr	79.5
6	Cuesta-Cues	70
7	Lemoore-Lem	61
8	Victor Valley-Vv	60.5
9	Modesto-Mod	58
10	Bakersfield-BC	47.5
11	Santa Ans-Sa	40.5
12	Rio Hondo-Rio	38.5
13	Santa Rosa-Src	38
14	Sierra-Sie	37.5
15	Lassen-Las	25.5
16	Chabot-Chab	25
17	Redwoods-Cor	18
18	Moorpark-Moor	17
19	Shasta-Sha	4
20	Delta-Del	3.5
21	Skyline-Sky	2.5
22	East LA-Elac	0

Records
James Wright-Fresno 37-2
Jake Prudek-Fresno 24-0
Javier Martinez-Fresno 24-4
Joseph Alaniz-Fresno 24-
Frankie Stevenson-Victor Valley 23-6

SECTION II

CCCAA REGIONAL WRESTLING CHAMPIONSHIPS

**1962 North Central Regional
March Fresno City College**

118
Larry Whitson-Bakfld Dec
Marchall Alcarez-Fresno

123
Roy Stucky-Fresno
Bob Parmelee-Bakersfield

130

Riojas-Fresno 3
Charles Bridgford-Bakersfield

137

Perez-Reedley 3
Norman Heiberger-Bakfld

147

Drew Washington-Bakfld 3
Luening-Reedley

157
Bill Lung-Fresno
Jim Bridger-Bakersfield

167
Don Nelson-Fresno
John Bigby-Bakersfield

177

Larry Carpender-Bakfld 3
Carlson-Reedley

191
Willard Roberson-Bakersfield
Doug Stiles-Modesto

Heavyweight

McGrew-Sequoia 3
Joe McDonald-Bakersfield

Team Scores
1 Fresno
2 Bakersfield   67

Others
Sequoia
Reedley
Modesto

Larry Whitson
Willard Roberson
Both undefeated

1963 North Central Regional
March 2, 1963 Modesto College

115
Bob Blanco-Modesto
Dan Ruiz-Bakersfield
Nick Saldiver-Hartnell
Akihiro Egerer-Fresno

123
Mario Marquez-Hartnell
Marshall Alcarez-Fresno
Lee Van Pelt-Modesto
Ernie Vasquez-Sequoias
Bob Parmalee-Bakersfield

130
Mike Stricker-Bakersfield OT
Jim Cox-Fresno
Manuel Souza-Modesto
Dan Morales-Hartnell

137
Chuck Fenton-Bakersfield
Andy Lukehart-Antelope Vly
John Ogas-Sequoias

147
John Oller-Fresno
Leroy Evans-Modesto
Allen Dillion-Antelope Valley
Bob Hammond-Sequoias
Mike Roberson-Bakersfield

157
Pete Delis-Bakersfield
John Harvey-Modesto
Art Valasquez-Hartnell
Joe Garcia-Fresno

167
Mike Stieler-Modesto
John Bigby-Bakersfield
Keith Boyer-
Gil Spinner-Antelope Valley

177
Ken Carman-Modesto
Ed Kerby-Fresno
Alvin Gatewood-Sequoias
Jerry Brownwood-Antelope V

191
Woody Knott-Fresno
Don Koontz-Bakersfield
Richard Kuhn-Antelope Valley
Mel Potter-Modesto

Heavyweight
Larry Martin-Bakersfield
Roland Fox-Antelope Valley
Jack Wernick-Fresno
Larry Palma-Hartnell

Most Outstanding Wrestler
Ken Carman-Modesto

Team Scores
1 Bakersfield   74
2
3

Coaches
Antelope Valley-Jack B. Frost
Bakersfield-Harry Kane
Sequoias-Al Baldock
Fresno-Paul Cookingham
Hartnell-Ed Adams
Modesto-Dean Sensenbaugh

Officials
Stan Pavko
Dan Gonsalves
Ed Jalli

1963 NORTH CENTRAL REGIONAL CHAMPIONS

L-R Bottom Row: 115-Bob Blanco-Modesto, 123-Mario Marquez-Harnell, 130-Mike Stricker - Bakersfield, 137-Chuck Fenton-Bakersfield, 147-John Oller-Fresno,
Top Row: 157-Pete Delis-Bakersfield, 167-Mike Stieler-Modesto, 177-Outstanding Wrestler-Ken Carman-Modesto, 191-Woody Knott-Fresno, Heavyweight-Larry Martin-Bakersfield

1963 South Regional
March 2, 1963

115

Dick Girard-Cerritos 2

123
Gary Harrison-Cerritos

130
Sam Garcia-El Camino X
Tom Warner-San Diego X

137

147
Don Holt-El Camino X

157
John Sowden-El Camino X

Clark McPherson-Cerritos 4

167
Bob Anderson-El Camino X

177
Sheldon Bromberg-Cerritos
Fred Aiken San Diego X

191
Bill Klump-Cerritos
Dennis Albright-El Camino X
Ned Murphy-Citrus X

Heavyweight

Team Results
1
2
3
4 Cerritos

Other Schools
El Camino-Dave Hengsteler
Imperial Valley
LA City
Oceanside
Palomar
Pierce
San Diego
LA Valley
Victor Valley

Results found on Cerritos Wrestling Web Page

X Results from the State not in any order

1964 North Central Regional
March 7, 1964 Fresno City College

115
Ron Marquez-Fresno
Frank Boado-Bakersfield
Fred Guerrero-Sequoias
Al Satake-S J Delta

123
Nick Nino-Sequoias
Gene Hess-Bakersfield
Nick Saldivar-Hartnell
Jim Armas-Fresno

130
Dave Rocha-Fresno
Larry Errea-Bakersfield
Ed Van Dyke-Modesto

137
Jim Norsworthy-Bakersfield
Jim Ashjian-Fresno
Jim Texiera-Merced
Phil Ogas-Sequoias

147
Armando Jacobo-Fresno
Frank Cole-Modesto
Mike Roberson-Bakersfield
Ray Naverro-S J Delta

157
Pete Delis-Bakersfield
Lee Ehrler-Modesto
Bart Casalis-S J Delta
Dennis Deliddo-Fresno

167
Frank Kirby-Fresno
Dan Lucas-Hartnell
Alvin Gatewood-Sequoias
Leroy Evans-Modesto

177
Jim Coerley-Modesto
Bob Cummings-SJ Delta
Ron Warwick-Hartnell
Bob Martini-Bakersfield

191
Woody Knott-Fresno
Jim Arnold-S J Delta
Mel Porter-Modesto
Bob Stone-Sequoias

Unlimited
Howard Dumble-Bakersfield
Frank Turner-Modesto
Joe Golis-Sequoias
John Obersham-S J Delta

Team Scores
1 Fresno		72
2 Bakersfield	66
3 Modesto		55
4 Sequoias	28
5 S J Delta	23
6 Hartnell	17
7 Merced		4

Coaches
Bakersfield-Vic Lindskog
Sequoias-Al Baldock
Fresno Hans-Weidenhofer
Hartnell-Ed Adams
Modesto-Dean Sensenbaugh
S J Delta-Larry Jones
Merced

1964 North Regional
March 7, 1964 Cabrillo College

115
Mike Remer-Chabot
Dick Vaughn-San Jose
Dan Smoothuers-San Mateo
Dave Chaves-Oakland

123
Dave Bruce-Diablo Valley
Teruo Yorita-Cabrillo
Wayne Lenhares-Chabot
Jim Elliott-Foothill

130
Harry Statts-Foothill
Al Hernandez-San Jose
Dean West-Sierra
Charlie Kretchman-Chabot

137
Ron Matheson-Diablo Valley
Mike McMahon-Chabot
Ed Hart-Cabrillo
Jack Wells-Foothill

147
Al Hughes-San Mateo
Chas Ballard-Cabrillo
Rich Hughes-Chabot
Jan Schultz-Foothill

157
Irv Rosenberg-San Jose
Larry Wilburn-Chabot
Laverne Carradine-Oakland
Bob Gibbons-Foothill

167
Cliff Gossett-Chabot
Mike Owens-Oakland
Sam Jones-San Mateo
Joe Guilian-San Jose

177
Alf Haerem-San Mateo
Benny Bendell-Foothill
Paul Buerg-Oakland
Bernard Mordret-Oakland

191
Roger Boeger-Diablo Valley
Phil Derr-San Mateo
Irvin Bailey-Oakland
Jack Erwin-Chabot

Unlimited
Jim Porter-Oakland
Walt Wenger-San Mateo
Ralph Wenzel-Foothill
Buck Deadrich-Chabot

Team Results
1
2
3

Coaches
Cabrillo-Paul Hodgins
Chabot-Bob Thomson
San Mateo-Hern Hudson
Ernie Cecaci
Foothill-Bill Walker
Oakland-Paul Chappell
San Francisco-Dutch Elston
San Jose-Jim Wheelihan
Sierra-Bud Ostrom

1964 South Central Regional
March 7, 1964 Chaffey College

115
George Lopez San Bernardino
Steve Calhoun-Southwestern
Pat Gosselin-Grossmont
Gary Ives-Orange Coast

123
Chet Bain-Fullerton
Andy Richard-San Bernardino
Andy Rosenberger Grossmon
David McCullough-Chaffey

130
George Shaeffer-Grossmont
Rich Paramo-San Bernardino
Curt Nichols-Fullerton

137
Roger Pickens-Grossmont
Al Rankin-San Bernardino
Ron Van Kaenel-Riverside
Fred Schubbert-Fullerton

147
George Taylor-San Bernardin
Jack Catton-Riverside
Chet Phillips- Grossmont
Ron Beitelspacher-Santa Ana

157
John Watmore-Grossmont
Tom Ester-Fullerton
Robin Duri-Chaffey
Elliott Fowler-San Bernadino

167
Gary White-Chaffey
Richard Whittington San Bern
Andy Smith-Orange Coast
John Black-Fullerton

177
Jim Wilson-Fullerton
Roy Williams-San Bernardino
Jim Ryan-Santa Ana
Don Johnston-Riverside

191
Tony Castello-Southwestern
Rob Braham-Fullerton
Joe Hollins-San Bernardino
Quito Sanchez-Orange Coast

Unlimited
Glenn Cook-Grossmont
Dick Birbeck-Riverside
George Corneal-Chaffey
Greg Wojcik-Orange Coast

Team Results
1
2
3

Coaches
Chaffey-Jack White
Fullerton-Oran Breeland
Grossmont-Mickey Shelley
Orange Coast-Fred Owens
Riverside-Don Birren
San Bernardino-Bob Smith
Santa Ana-Dan Shaughnessy
Southwestern-Richard Robinson

1964 South Regional
March 7, 1964 El Camino College

115
Rich Tamble-El Camino
Jack Sawatski-San Diego
Jim Martin-Imperial Valley
Bob Benavides-Cerritos

123
Tom McCann-El Camino
Bill Rose-Cerritos
Steve Kaplan-San Diego
Al Martinez-Imperial Valley

130
San Garcia-El Camino
Henry Bullinorouski-S Diego
Joe Moore-Cerritos
Luis Gonzales-Imperial Valley

137
Bob Munger-Imperial Valley
Paul Steinel-El Camino
Steve Hodges-Cerritos

147
Dennis Downing-Cerritos
Walter Coyle-San Diego
Ken Blight-El Camino
Paul Conner-Imperial Valley

157
Bob Pegram-San Diego
Dennis Albright-El Camino
Bob Burns-LA City
Nick Caputo-Cerritos

167
Bob Anderson-El Camino
George Shan-Imperial Valley
Dennis Snell -Cerritos
Ewald Briesk-San Diego

177
Larry Wolfe-El Camino
Fred Aiken-San Diego
Dave Bellamy-Imperial Valley
Craig Morze-LA City

191
Myron Miller-LA Valley
Virgil Carroll-Imperial Valley
Rod Mitchell-LA City
Paul Hopper-El Camino

Unlimited
Bob Hammas-San Diego
Ran Hampton-El Camino
Allen Miluso-LA City
Cris Cross-Cerritos

Team Results
1
2
3

Coaches
Cerritos-Hal Simonek
El Camino-Dave Hengsteler
Imperial Valley-Don Turner
LA City-Milton Hand
L A Valley-Nick Giovinazzo
San Diego-Mark Whittieton
Victor Valley-William Lacy

1965 North Central Regional
February 27, 1965 College of Sequoias

115
Ron Marquez-Fresno
Freddy Guerrero-Sequoias
Jerry Herring-Bakersfield
Al Satake-S J Delta

123
Robert Hernandez-Sequoias
Manuel Villerreal-Bakersfield
Fred Contreras-Fresno
Robert Hilley-Modesto

130
George Peveril-Fresno
Charl Henne-American River
Al Navarro-S J Delta
Steve Klein-Modesto

137
Jim Norsworthy-Bakersfield
Dennis Deliddo-Fresno
Jim Goodard-American River
Charles Blakeney-Sequoias

147
David Adams-Sequoias
Rick Morrison-Sacramento
Terry Moreland-Bakersfield
Jim Ashjian-Fresno

157
Armando Jacobo Fresno
Lee Ehrler-Modesto
Steve Ridolfi-S J Delta
Bill Kinnett-Bakersfield

167
Jim Widmer-S J Delta
Keith Boyer-Fresno
Jim Moshier-Bakersfield
Monty Miller- American River

177
Ray Mecedo-Modesto
Roger McClaughry-Fresno
Clydell Massey-Sequoias
Byrl Taylor-Bakersfield

191
Tim Cotton-Bakersfield
Robert Conley-Merced Ken
Carmen-Modesto Bob
Baird-American River

Heavyweight
Ben Brase-Fresno
Frank Stiger-Sequoias Mike
Pedigo-Sierra
Vic Guzman-American River

Team Scores
1
2 Bakersfield   60
3

Coaches
American River-John Lucerna
Bakersfield-Bruce Pfutzenruter
Sequoias-Al Baldock
Fresno-Hans Wiedenhoefer
Merced-Red Prichard
Modesto-Dean Sensenbaugh
Sacramento-Bob Towers
S J Delta-Larry Jones
Sierra-Homer D. Ostrom

1965 North Regional
February 27, 1965 Foothill College

115
John Yasuda-Diablo Valley
Dick Vaughn-San Jose
Gary Shouse-San Mateo
Joe Perales-Chabot
123
Wayne Lenhores-Chabot
Dave Bruce-Diablo Valley
Dave Chavez-Merritt
Dennis Uyehara-San Jose
130
Art Silva-San Jose
Ron Matheson-Diablo Valley
Ted Cano-San Mateo
Jim Edwards-Foothill
137
Tom Hook-Diablo Valley
Manual Austin-San Jose
Gary Loeeng-Foothill
Arnold Domingues-Foothill
147
Robert Hicks-West Valley
Eugene Teasley-Merritt
Scott Norris-Chabot
Dave Torres-Foothill
157
Sylvester Hodges-Merritt
Mike Weathers-Foothill
Manuel Navarro-Chabot
Bob Haskins-Cabrillo
167
Cy Lucas-Foothill
Ed Ferrell-Cabrillo
Cliff Gossett-Chabot
Greg Hobson-Merritt

177
Bob Buehler-Foothill
Frank Blichfeit-Chabot
Tony Epperson-San Mateo
Mike Pedroza-Hartnell
191
Buck Deadeick-Chabot
Mike Lobue-San Jose
Ron Buehler-Foothill
Gil Newcomb-San Francisco
Heavyweight
Mike McCarthy-Chabot
Bob Seymour-Foothill
John Shuford-West Valley
Gene Montori-Diablo Valley

Team Results
1
2
3

Coaches
Cabrillo-Will Pokriots
Chabot-Bob Thomson
Diablo Valley-Ernie Cecaci
Foothill-Bill Walker
Hartnell-Ed Adams
Merritt-John Marks
San Francisco-A.W. Elston
San Jose Jim-Wheelehan
San Mateo-Lee Allen
West Valley

1965 South Central Regional
February 27, 1965 Fullerton College

115
Andy Richards-San Bernardin
Dave Moore-Victor Valley
John Rice-Mt. SAC
Raul Duarte-Orange Coast

123
Tom Phillips-Orange Coast
Steve Lawson-Fullerton
Floyd Davis-San Bernardino
Guy Waller-Mt. SAC

130
John Geyer-Orange Coast
Frank Trujillo-Mt. SAC
Dave McCullough-Chaffey
Dave Villa-San Bernardino

137
Culver Ezel-Antelope Valley
Rich Paramo-San Bernardino
Dick Stevenson Fullerton
Rich Reeves Chaffey

147
Ken Cook Grossmont
Bill McMillian Orange Coast
Allen Rich Antelope Valley
Dave Ferro-San Bernardino

157
Bob Powell-Fullerton
Chuck Reynolds-Mt. SAC
Jim Hodge-Orange Coast
Lon Halcomb-San Bernardino

167
Jerry Butler-San Bernardino
Gary White-Chaffey
Stan Smith-Mt. SAC
Ed Maxwell-Orange Coast

177
Ralph Orr-Chaffey
Rich Wittington-San Bernardi
Terry Lorentzen Orange Coast
Andy Alvarez-Mt. SAC

191
Rich Hargrave-Chaffey
Bob Braham-Fullerton
Don Johnston-Riverside
Quito Sanchez-Orange Coast

Heavyweight
Dale Cranford-San Bernardin
Greg Wojcik-Orange Coast
Mike Bomar-Riverside
Norm Klemz-San Bernardino

Team Results
1
2
3

Coaches
Antelope Valley-Gary Taylor
Chaffey-Jack White
Fullerton-Oren Breeland
Grossmont-Mickey Shelly
Mt. SAC-Fred Burri
Orange Coast-Fred Owens
Riverside-Don Berrin
San Bernardino-Bob Smith
Victor Valley-Armondo Moreno

1965 South Regional
March 5, 1965 Southwestern College

115
Rich Tamble-El Camino
Dean Houchin-LA Valley
Lynn Cordova-San Diego
Dennis Runyon-Glendale
Lloyd Hill-Compton

123
Tom McCann-El Camino
Joe Moore-Cerritos
Ron Battey-Southwestern
Paul Shoenbeck-S D Mesa
Richard Parkhurst-San Diego

130
Norm Dean-El Camino
Jim McClenaghan-Glendale
Henry Buijnoruski-S D Mesa
Pete Phipott-Cerritos
Monroe Gray-LA City

137
Steve Johnson-Cerritos
Mike Martin-Southwestern
Gary deBeaubian-El Camino
Melvin Bonner-Compton
Jim Anderson-Pierce

147
Kent Wyatt-El Camino
Dennis Downing-Cerritos
Mike Danielson-Southwester
Gene Simpson-Compton
Lyn Naylor-San Diego

157
Don Apodaca-El Camino
John Bean Cerritos
Jack Ross-Southwestern
Richard Thompson-Compton
Bill Reese-Oceanside

167
Paul Hooper-El Camino
Ken Bos-Cerritos
John Laputz-S D Mesa
Tim Young-Southwestern
Hayward Nishioke-LA City

177
Wayne Partee-Cerritos
Dwight Fritz-El Camino
Lonnie Harris-Compton
Rex Honey-Southwestern
Tom Wilson-San Diego

191
Jim Palmer-Southwestern
Barry Schneider-Cerritos
Pat Harrison-LA Trade Tech
Jimmy Giesel-Oceanside
John Sowden-El Camino

Heavyweight
Nick Carollo-El Camino
Booker Williams-San Diego
Gary Densham-Cerritos
Al Niluso-LA Valley

Team Results
1
2 Cerritos
3

Coaches
Cerritos-Hal Simonek
Compton-Gene Farrell
El Camino-Dave Hengsteler
Glendale-Jim Hanafin
LA Valley-Nick Giovinazzo
LA Trade Tech-Bill Tom
Oceanside-Harry Phillips,
Ed Wiley
San Diego-Len Simorin
SD Mesa-E. Charles Popa
Southwestern-Dick Robinson

1966 North Central Regional
March 5, 1966 Modesto Junior College

115

Emmitte Herrera-Bakfld 2

123

Art Chavez-Bakersfield 2

130

John Kileen-Bakersfield 4

137

Mike Brown-Bakersfield 3

145

Frank Sousa-Bakersfield 2

152

Terry Moreland-Bakersfield 2

167

Ben Welch-Bakersfield 2

177

Joe Barton-Bakersfield 2

191

Byrl Taylor-Bakersfield 4
Heavyweight
Rocky Rasley-Bakersfield 1

Team Scores
1 Bakersfield 92
2 Fresno 78
3 Sequoia 62
4

Results from the Bakersfield College Wrestling Guide

MIKE BROWN - 137

BEN WELCH - 167

ART CHAVEZ - 123

1966 South Regional
March 5, 1966 El Camino College

115
Rolan Garza-Cerritos
Dan Gucvara-El Camino
Joe Stein-LA Valley
George Kyle-Mira Costa

123
Shep Bloom-Cerritos
Jim Abrams-Southwestern
Sam Hand-Pierce
Jess Sandoval-S D Mesa

130
Ed Acosta-El Camino
Jim McClenaghan-Mira Costa
Kent Lee-Southwestern
Pete Phillpott-Cerritos

137
Kurt Adler-El Camino
John Chuckta-S D Mesa
Brian Richards-Mira Costa
Brian Shoup-Cerritos

147
Kent Wyatt-El Camino
Steve Johnson-Cerritos
Lynn Nayler-San Diego
Harold Dugger-Grossmont

152
Ken Cook-Grossmont
Fern Arsenault-Cerritos
Tom Hawkes-Mira Costa
Rich Byrne-El Camino

160
Charles Hauartes-El Camino
Ken Bos-Cerritos
Terry Westlin-Grossmont
Richard Reed-S D Mesa

167
Don Apodaca-El Camino
Charles Bishop-Cerritos
Tim Pittman-Grossmont
Ken Morris-Pierce

177
Wayne Partee-Cerritos
Dwight Fritz-El Camino
Bill Hoffman-S D Mesa
Leri Fackrell-San Diego

191
Barry Schneioer-Cerritos
Jim Palmer-Southwestern
Glen Engle-El Camino
John Ferlin-Grossmont

Heavyweight
Nick Carollo-El Camino
Jeff Smith-Cerritos
Bud Lane-Southwestern
Mark Nelson-Grossmont

Team Results
1 Cerritos
2
3

Official representing the Southern Section
Reed Nelson

1967 North Central Regional
March 4, 1967

115
Jack Serros-Bakersfield
Alex Dochary-Sacramento
Ed Moraga-Fresno
David Zevely-S J Delta

123
Jim Sunderland-Cuesta
Dan Tarver-Fresno
Chris Olivera-Porterville

130
Jay Yaudegis-Sacramento
Carlos Hernandez-Sequoias
Joe Marquez-Fresno
John Baker-American River

137
Russ Simpson-Fresno 11-3
Frank Sousa-Bakersfield
Sam Turner-Sequoias
Ron Baldwin-Sacramento

145
Mike Collier-Bakersfield
Pedro Rios-Fresno
Wayne Hubbard-Sierra
Roger Ulmer-Yuba

152
Tom Moule-Sierra
Tony Eutra-S J Delta
Sam Gollmyer-Bakersfield
Ken Wilson-Yuba

160
Pat Mathews-S J Delta
Tom Opperman-Fresno
Bill Kinnett-Bakersfield
Bob Bailey-Merced
Jim Gavel-Sierra

167
Larry Brewer-Bakersfield
Ted Fitzpatrick-Modesto
Dave Ruhkala-Sierra

177
Ed Ortiz-Fresno 11-3
Don Lundgrun-Bakersfield
John Bulgheroni-Modesto
Chip Storts-Sierra

191
Joe Barton-Bakersfield
John Medarin-Fresno
Mike Avila-Porterville
Willie McDaniel-Reedley

Heavyweight
Rocky Rasley-Bakersfield
Dennis Petracek-Amer River
John Perez-Merced
Ben Brase-Fresno

Most Outstanding Wrestler
Tom Moule-Sierra

Team Scores
1 Bakersfield 99
2 Fresno 91
3 Sierra 53
4 S J Delta 33
5 Sacramento 28

15 Teams

Coaches
American River-John Lucerna
Bakersfield-Bruce Pfutzenreuter
Sequoias-Al Baldock
Cuesta-Warren Hansen
Fresno-Bill Musick
Merced-Red Prichard
Modesto-Dean Sensenbaugh
Porterville-Don Kavadas
Reedley-Maury Fitzpatrick
Sacramento-Bob Towers
S J Delta-Larry Jones
Sierra-John Murillo
Yuba-Lou Menghini

Rocky Rasley - Bakersfield

1967 North Regional
March 4, 1967

115
Ben Barrientos-San Mateo
Joe Perales-Chabot
Ray Chavez-San Jose
John Shinault-Diablo Valley

123
Don Ellison-Diablo Valley
Mike Rizzo-Chabot
Wendell Chun-San Mateo
Bill Chapman-Laney

130
Scott Lewis-Diablo Valley
Art Olmos-Foothill
Frank Mason-Gavilan
Earl Brown-San Mateo

137
Mike Taylor-Diablo Valley
Dennis Burns-Chabot
Wendell Jefferson-Laney
Jeff Raybould-San Jose

145
Doug Parsons-West Valley
Gary Westford-Chabot
Steve McKeown-Foothill
John Berg-Diablo Valley

152
Scott Rehm-Foothill
Pete Laughton-Chabot
Oliver Wesson-San Mateo
Gene Rochelle-Cabrillo

160
Bob Hicks-Foothill
Saul Nava-Chabot
Gene Arthur-Marin
Nathan Harrison-Merritt

167
Don Shelton-San Mateo
Ron Taylor-West Valley
Jeff Baker-Chabot
Bill Green-Diablo Valley

177
Phil Baylis-Chabot
Steve Brown-Foothill
Tom Phillips-San Mateo
Mike Cowan-West Valley

191
Stan Hackett-Foothill
Paul Weston-Chabot
Bennie Guerra-Hartnell
Bryan Loehr-Cabrillo

Heavyweight
Tom Powell-San Mateo
Ric Rosenquist-Foothill
Ken Roberts-Diablo Valley
Evan Weir-Merritt

Team Scores
1 Chabot   93
2 Foothill   74
3 San Mateo   70
4 Diablo Valley   62

Coaches
Cabrillo-Ken Flynn
Chabot-Bob Thomsen
Diablo Valley-Ernie Cecaci
Foothill-Bill Walker
Gavilan-Wayne Howard
Hartnell-Ed Adams
Laney-Bob Power
Marin-Jim McGowan
Merritt-Paul Chappelle
San Mateo-Lee Allen
San Jose-Jim Wheelehan
West Valley-Bob Sutter

Over 90 Junior Colleges had
Wrestling Teams in California

1967 South Central Regional
March 4, 1967

115
Terry Hall-San Bernardino
Ubane Standifird-Chaffey
Don Stephenson-Golde West
Jim Vallejo-Mt. SAC

123
Roger LaPointe-San Bernardi
Ricardo Ruiz-Golden West
Jim Galvan-Rio Hondo
Tom Kerr-Golden West
Jay McKeown-Chaffey

130
Katsuji Nerio-Golden West
Chuck Newman-San Bernardi
Dan Dean-Santa Ana
Rusty Stiffler-Chaffey

137
Al Rivera-Santa Ana
Rich Neal-San Bernardino
Mark Timeus-Mt. SAC
Henry Compos-Riverside

145
Gordon Leavy-Fullerton
Richard Dees-San Bernardino
Bob Burrett-Santa Ana
Jim Harding-Mt. SAC

152
Steve Moran-San Bernardino
Ralph McDaniels-Golde West
Rick Peterson-Orange Coast
Steve Abramoritz-Fullerton

160
Dan Churchill-San Bernardino
Dave Pollard-Riverside
John Miller-Citrus
Greg Kaiser-Santa Ana

167
Greg Tribble-San Bernardino
Glenn Brush-Mt. SAC
Charles Smith-Golden West
Steve Pearson-Fullerton

177
Rich Davis-Chaffey
Ray Nayler-Orange Coast
Randy Straphman-San Bernar
Don Guinn-Riverside

191
Gary Myers-Riverside
Don Long-Mt. SAC
Dave Failing-San Bernardino
Mark Hallet-Santa Monica

Heavyweight
Ken Oyer-San Bernardino
Mike Fristoe-Mt. SAC
Henry Lee-Citrus
Frank Davidson-Golden West

Team Results
1	San Bernadino	119
2	Golden West	43
2	Mt. SAC	43
4	Santa Ana	39

Coaches
Chaffey-Jack White
Citrus-Phil Brown
Fullerton-Oran Breeland
Golden West-Fred Owens
Mt. SAC-Fred Burri
Orange Coast-Jack Fair
Riverside-Don Berrin
San Bernardino-Bob Smith
Santa Ana-Frank Addleman
Santa Monica-Bob Blix

1967 South Regional
March 4, 1967

115
Jim Fester-S D Mesa
Art Stone-Southwestern
Frank Hernandez-Mira Costa
Randy Tucker-Imperial Valley

123
Shep Bloom-Cerritos
Jim Galvin-Rio Hondo
Jesse Sandoval-S D Mesa
George Kyle-Mira Costa

130
Bob Hall-Cerritos
Luis Provencio-Imperia Valley
Dan Acosta-El Camino
Brian Richards-Mira Costa

137
Steve Warren-El Camino
Bob Richards-Pierce
John Mitchell-Palomar
Bill Nelson-S D Mesa

145
Mark Racousky-Pierce
Gary deBeaubien-El Camino
Steve Sanson-Cerritos
Mike Hofreiter-S D Mesa
Denver Williams-Mira Costa

152
Curtis Elder-El Camino
Fern Arsenault-Rio Hondo
Doug Shoulders-Palomar
Bill Henderson-Cerritos

160
Dave Patterson-El Camino
Jim West-Cerritos
Kent Geyer-Grossmont
Armando Medina-Rio Hondo

167
John Hall-Cerritos
Tim Pittman-Grossmont
Pat Farner-Palomar
Walter Thatcher-Southwester

177
Glen Engle-El Camino
Bill Halsey-Cerritos
Dave Reed-Pierce
John Ferlin-Grossmont

191
Glen Bernard-Cerritos 1
Ken Morris-Pierce
Jerry Gray-San Diego

Heavyweight
Jeff Smith-Cerritos
Ed Villalobos-Rio Hondo
Carl Black-Grossmont
Robert Callahan-Southwester

Team Scores
1 Cerritos   93
2 El Camino   72
3 Pierce   37
4 Rio Hondo   34

Coaches
Cerritos-Harold Simonek
El Camino-Dave Hengsteler
Grossmont-Mickey Shelley
Imperial Valley-Don Rogers
S D Mesa-Al Walker
Mira Costa-Larry Nugent
Palomar-Mack Wiebe
Pierce-Edwin Goldbloom
Rio Hondo-Clint South
San Diego-Len Smorin
Southwestern-Wes Foreman

1967-68 South Central Regional

118
Ed Moraga Fresno

123
Ray Conteras Fresno
Jim Galvan-Rio Hondo
Terry Hall-San Bernadino X
Nash Martinez-Riverside X

134
Don Dean Santa Ana

142

150
Greg (Ray) Kaiser-Santa Ana

160
Dan Churchill-S Bernadino X

Richard Rhode-Rio Hondo 4

167
Steve Pearson-Fullerton X

177
Victor Holloway-S Bernadi X

190

Heavyweight
Ken Oyer-San Bernadino X

Team Results
1
2
3

Results found on the Rio Hondo Wrestling History

Joe Alvarado-Rio Hondo 4
Brian Mahaffey-Rio Hondo 6
Weights not given

X From State results not in any order
From Santa Ana Program

1968 North Central Regional
March 2, 1968 Allan Hancock College

115

Herb Cosme-Bakersfield 3

123

Karl Herrera-Bakersfield 2

130

137

David Jones-Bakersfield 3

147

Steve Varner-Bakersfield 3

152

Rich Bridges-Bakersfield 2

160

Al Dorris-Bakersfield 2

167
Joe Nigos-Bakersfield 1

177
Don Lundgren-Bakersfield 1

191

Tom Estrada-Bakersfield 2

Heavyweight
Jim Robesky-Bakersfield 1

Most Outstanding Wrestler
Joe Nigos-Bakersfield

Team Scores
1 Fresno   122
2 Bakersfield   117
3 American River 52

Results found on the Bakersfield College Wrestling Guide

1968 South Regional
March 2, 1968

115
Bob Mousaw-Cerritos 2

123
Dave Raptis-Cerritos 1

130
Tony Searing-Cerritos 2

137
Frank Kuhn-Cerritos 1

145
Ron Kenworthy-Cerritos 1

152
John Norfleet-Cerritos 1

160
John Hall-Cerritos 1

167
Bill Henderson-Cerritos 1

177
Gene Bernard-Cerritos 3

190
Gary Maiolfi-Cerritos 1

Heavyweight
Ben Struve-Cerritos 1

Team Result
1 Cerritos
2
3

Results found on the Cerritos Wrestling web page

1968-69 North Central Regional
March 1, 1969 Modesto Junior College

115
Ray Hernandes-Sequoia 7-3
Herb Cosme-Bakersfield
Ruben Valenzuela Fresno Dec
John Rilla-S J Delta

123
Vic Gonzales-Sequoia 3-0
Ray Conterras-Fresno
Karl Herrera-Bakersfield Dec
Dave Mendoza-S J Delta

130
Gene Warner-Cuesta 7-3*
Mike Carr-Fresno
Eugene Walker-Bakfld 4-1
Gene Bigelow-Sacramento

137
Dan Montgomery-Fresno 5-3
Bruce Burnett-Bakersfield
Dan Sear-Sequoia
Don Bunch-Hancock

145
Brad Draktenle-Hancock
Steve Varner-Bakersfield
Tony Fuentes-Modesto
Cliff Eastman-Fresno

152
Lee Torres-Fresno 4-1
Joe Smart-Bakersfield
Al Palmer-Modesto
Ray Hanson-Hancock

160
Wes Williams-Sequoia 13-4
Bill Morgan-S J Delta
Jim Byrd-Bakersfield
Corky Napier-Fresno

167
Joe Nigos-Bakersfield
Ruben Diaz-Sequoia
Ted Young-Fresno Dec
Clyde George-Sacramento

177
Charles O'Brian Modes F 3:18
Tom Giamprieto-Sequoia
Richard Brand-Bakfld F 2:20
Ray Harner-Cuesta

191
John Miller-Bakersfield 6-0
Boyd Jones-Cuesta
Mike Viser-S J Delta Dec
John Ming-Sacramento

Heavyweight
Jim Robesky-Bakfld F 5:57
Henry Allison-Sequoia
Aquino Fresno-Fall
Scott Lawson-Sacramento

Most Outstanding Wrestler
Gene Warner-Cuesta

Team Scores
1 Bakersfield   131
2 Fresno   103
3 Sequoia   97
4 S J Delta   47
5 Cuesta   43
6 Modesto   38
7 Sacramento   30
8 Hancock   28
9 American River 11
10 Reedley   8
11 Merced   6
12 Coalinga   0
12 Porterville   0

Joe Smart - Bakersfield College

1969 North Regional
March 1, 1969

115
Bernie Olmas-Foothill
Arman Brett-San Mateo
Kuno Boydston-La Canda
Sal Muniz-De Anza

123
David Tomori-Diablo Valley
Dick Furuya-Foothill
Ron Rhodes-Chabot
Bob Paiz-San Mateo

130
Ken Wright-San Mateo
Gary Wolt-Butte
Jerry Biggan-West Valley
Ron Montgomery-De Anza

137
Ed King-Chabot
John Zenith-Lassen
Grant Connell-San Mateo
Howard Zink-Hartnell

145
Rick Slack-Foothill
Norm Hale-Diablo Valley
Warner Hasse-West Valley
Ray Jimenez-San Jose

152
Don Loflin-Lassen
Elliot Smith-Merritt
Steve Sanchez-Diablo Valley
Brian Adamson-West Valley

160
Tom Bell-Butte
Marc Grunseth-Contra Costa
Gordan George-West Valley
Cort Wiegand-Diablo Valley

Tom Williams Redwoods 6

167
Bill Bolar-Chabot
Chauncey Turnbow-Merritt
Stock Schleuter-Redwoods
Ralph Vandro-San Mateo

177
Ron Lucas-Hartnell
Marc Likens-San Mateo
Semas Owen-Merritt
Vic Mitchell-Shasta
Dwight Wallace Redwoods

191
Jim Schlueter-Redwoods
Noah Rollins-Laney
Gene Hansen-Diablo Valley
Bob Crutcher-Solano

Heavyweight
Ed Galigher-Chabot
John Johnston-Redwoods
Bill Tippett-Laney
Alan McQuire-De Anza

Team Results
1
2 Redwoods
3

Coaches
Chabot-Bob Thomsen
Redwoods-Jim Sylvia
San Mateo-Lee Allen
De Anza-Bill Walker
Diablo Valley-Bob Ericson
Foothill-Jim Noon
Hartnell-Ed Adams
Laney-Bob Pawek
Merritt-Paul Chappelle
San Jose-Jim Wheelehan
Shasta-Marion Serafin
West Valley-Bob Sutter

Top 3 qualify for state

1969 South Central Regional
March 1, 1969

115
Ed Oquendo-San Bernardino
Willie Garcia-Rio Hondo
Mark Christian-Orange Coast
Steve Andrilla-Mt. SAC

123
John Abad-San Bernardino
Bob Leinger-Cypress
Larry Watanabe-Mt. SAC
Bill Harris-Golden West
Bob Ybarra-Rio Hondo

130
Jim Rodrigues-Riverside
Kevin Schubert San Bernardin
John Terry-Cypress
Joe Alvarado-Rio Hondo
Ben Benjamin-Santa Ana

137
Katuji Nerio-Golden West
Phil Jackson- Cypress
Gabe Ruiz-Santa Ana
Ralph Apply-Fullerton
Jim McKay-Antelope Valley

145
Pat Burris-Santa Ana
Bill Ehler-San Bernardino
Joe Garcia-Chaffey
Bob De La Torre-Fullerton
David Brier-Riverside

152
Al Price-Santa Ana
Ron Scott-San Bernadino
Harold Lundell-Orange Coast
Rich Cunningham-Mt. SAC
Oscar Valenzuela-Fullerton

160
Steve Dildine-San Bernardino
W. D. Martin-Santa Ana
Mark Haygood-Mt. SAC
Richard Rhode-Rio Hondo
Larry Vaughn-Riverside

167
Lee Corley-Mt. SAC
Dick Gillett-Fullerton
Dennis Price-Santa Monicia
Ernell Smith-San Bernadino
Teddy William-Ventura

177
Jim Shields-Cypress
Dave Alexander-Santa Ana
Ed Carroll-Chaffey
Victor Holloway San Bernadin
Dennis Collins-Mt. SAC

191
Pete Lutz-San Bernardino
John Mooney-Cypress
Ken Linn-San Bernardino
Steve Peterson-Fullerton
Dan Gann-Riverside

Heavyweight
Dave Hacker-Santa Monica
Ernie Pilar-Mt. SAC
Alva Smith-Fullerton
Carl Beach-San Bernardino
Dan Hillard-Orange Coast

Team Results
1
2
3

Coaches
Chaffey-Jack White
Cypress-Ray Hass
Fullerton-Oren Breeland
Golden West-Fred Owens
Mt. Sac-Fred Burri
Orange Coast-Jack Fair
Rio Hondo-Clint South
Riverside-Don Birren
San Bernardino-Bob Smith
Santa Ana-Fred Addleman
Santa Monica-Robert Blix

1969 South Regional
March 1, 1969

115
Dave Raptis-Cerritos
Terry Tambel-El Camino
Steve Ray-Grossmont
Rick Johnson-S D Mesa
Henry Takeguchu Southwest

123
Ken Turner-Cerritos
Al Gonzales-El Camino
Ramiro Sandoval-S D Mesa
Charles Howell-Grossmont
Bob Martony-Palomar

130
John Norris-El Camino
Anthony Searing-Cerritos
Robert Ito-S D Mesa
Tim Reed-Grossmont
Dan Shepard-Pierce

137
Ron McCormick-Cerritos
Steve Jackson-Grossmont
Randy Lawrence-Pierce
Gary Naud-El Camino
Ron Calkins-Southwestern

145
Ron Kenworthy-Cerritos
Marty Harris-El Camino
Duane Conte-Grossmont
Roger Thomas-LA City
Phil Guskin-Pierce

152
John Norfleet-Cerritos
Richard Acosta-Pierce
Michael McIntyre-El Camino
Mike Bradley-Grossmont
Albert Macias-Southwestern

160
Joe Hall-Pierce
Bob Sasser-Cerritos
Chuck Eaton-S D Mesa
Rick Ricker-Grossmont
Erik Ray-Palomar

167
Pat Miller-S D Mesa
George Maddox-Cerritos
Tim Tuner-Palomar
Tom Wenbourne-Grossmont
Alan Cohen-El Camino

177
Greg Uttecht-Cerritos
Frank Barnardt-Palomar
Greg Whillock-Grossmont
Randy Schneider-LA City
Joe Kmet-Southwestern

191
Gary Maiolfi-Cerritos
Frank Lucio-El Camino
John Weatherup-Pierce
Rick Klaman-S D Mesa
Tom Peterson-Grossmont

Heavyweight
Dan Felix-El Camino
Bill Struve-Cerritos 2
Tuffy Avil-Southwestern
Joe Ashe-LA City
Vance White-S D Mesa

Team Results
1
2
3

Coaches
Cerritos-Hal Simonek First
El Camino-Dave Hengsteier
Grossmont-Bob Haywood
LA City-Milton Hand
Pierce-Erwin Goldbloom
Palomar-Tony Lynds
S D Mesa-Al Walker
Southwestern-Dick Mason

1970 North Central Regional
March 7, 1970 Sacramento City College

118
Ray Hernandez-Sequoias
Tom Tatarakis-West Hills
Rosey Fonfeca-Modesto
George Marquez-Fresno
126
Larry Little-Bakersfield 4-3
Pete Holeman-Fresno
Tony Guerrero-Sequoias
Lincoln Lee-Sacramento
Mike Chism-American River
134
Jose Rivera-Hancock
Pete Gomez-Sequoias
Eugene Walker-Bakersfield
Ed McIntyre-Fresno
Rod McDowell-Reedley
142
Bruce Burnett-Bakersfield
Jay Ervine-Cuesta
Pat Colip-American River
Martin Ugalde-Modesto
Jim Clark-Sacramento
150
Joe Smart-Bakersfield
Bob Greco-Fresno
Dennis Bunch-Hancock
Bill Curtis-Cuesta
Stu Walthall-Sacramento
158
George Howe-Fresno
Bill Drennan-Bakersfield
Everett Robbon-Porterville
Sig Mayers-American River
167
Jerry Greer-Bakersfield
Doug Porter-Modesto
Mike Mendez-Fresno
Jesse Scoggins-Merced
Bob Whitley-American River

177
Tim Del Toro-Fresno
Mike O'Brian-Modesto
Wayne Cagle-Bakersfield
Richard Bacciarini-Hancock
Steve Curtis-Sequoias
190
Doyle Nelms-Porterville
Mike Duncan-Fresno
Roy McDaniels-Cuesta
Lynn Dearmand-S J Delta
Unlimited
Al Aquino-Fresno
Dan Graham-Modesto
Larry Ramos-Cuesta
Chris Hanson-Reedley
Les Kaiser-Sacramento

Team Scores
1 Fresno 103
2 Bakersfield 97
3 Sacramento 53
4 Modesto 50
5 Cuesta
6 Sequoias

Coaches
American River-Bob Towers
Bakersfield-Bruce Pfutzenreuter
Cuesta-Sid Bennett
Fresno-Bill Musick
Hancock-Barny Eames
Merced-Richard Rohrke
Modesto-Dean Sensenbough
Porterville-Darryl Williams
Reedley-Frank Kirby
Sacramento-Bill Hickey
S J Delta-Larry Jones

1970 North Regional
March 7, 1970

118
Dan Cabrel-San Jose
Tom Morrison-De Anza
Pat Wheeler-West Valley
Terry Prunty-Lassen
John Gallegos-Hartnell

126
Dave Brummer-Diablo Valley
Leroy Kerby-Lassen
Mike Jauregui-Canada
Scott Carnes-Redwoods
George Whaley-Cabrillo

134
Manuel DeLuna-Diablo Valley
Gary Garcia-Chabot
Tom Eckes-Solano
Dennis Luster-Redwoods

142
Don Wright-Skyline
Bruce Blanchard-Foothill
Gary Ferdinand-Chabot
Deey Converse-San Jose
Bob McNeil-Diablo Valley

150
Ed King-Chabot
Wally Knakabayaski-De Anza
Werner Haase-West Valley
Mike Ornelas-Skyline
Tom Micome-San Jose

158
Norman Hale-Diablo Valley
Ken Berribge-De Anza
Greg Mason-Redwoods
Tex Corson-Laney
Terry Melnin-Cabrillo
Dave Frost Redwoods

167
Lancer Smith-Diablo Valley
Bill Bohler-Chabot
Chris Hurchanik-Canada
Jerod Whitley-West Valley
Monty Hobbs-Ohlone

177
Ken King-Diablo Valley
Ron Lucas-Foothill
Jim Smith-Skyline
Bill Fell-San Jose
Dave Frost-Redwoods

190
Jim Schlueter-Redwoods
John Shea-Diablo Valley
Dann Highins-Chabot
Terry Pholmon-Contra Costa
Jim Schwitzer-San Mateo

Unlimited
Tim Kopitar-Diablo Valley
John Johnson-Redwoods
Bill Tippitt-Laney
Bob Bonner-Contra Costa
Frank Randon-Foothill

Team Results
1 Diablo Valley 115
2 Redwoods 69
3 Chabot 65
4 DeAnza 45
5 Skyline 43

Coaches
Cabrillo-Don Montgomery
Chabot-Zach Papachrisos
Redwoods-Jim Sylvia
Contra Costa-Paul Farris
De Anza-Bill Walker
Diablo Valley-Bob Ericson
Foothill-Jim Noon
Hartnell-Wes Williams
Laney-Nock Garedakis
Lassen-Dave Foster
San Jose-Sam Huerta
Skyline-Lee Allen
Solano-Jack Harvath
West Valley-Bob Sutter
Canada
San Mateo
Ohlone

1970 South Central Regional
March 7, 1970

118
Ed Oqueno-San Bernardino
Maurice Howard-Riverside
Ray Villrgas-Barstow
Dave Breen-Mt. SAC
Frank Jacobson-Ventura

126
Jim Rodriquez-Riverside
Larry Watanabe-Mt. SAC
Luis Blanco-San Bernardino
Robert Ybarra-Rio Hondo
Bob Lyle-Orange Coast

134
John Abad-San Bernardino
Parry Molony-Cypress
Bruce Bogart-Fullerton
Larry Wilson-Ventura
Bob Wood-Antelope Valley

142
Ed Oquendo-San Bernardino
Wayne Branstetter-Ventura
Bob Manley-Mt. SAC
Chris Louisell-Santa Monica
Mayo Oshi-Fullerton

150
Pat Burris-Santa Ana
Bill Swanson-Cypress
Terry Trout-Mt. SAC
Darryl Murphy-Ventura
Steve Perry-Chaffey

158
W. D. Martin-Santa Ana
Ron Scott-San Bernardino
Bob Curry-Orange Coast
John Wilkins-Golden West
Tom Cromwell-Mt. SAC

167
Don Swanson-Cypress
Jeff Schwarz-Rio Hondo
Bob Post-Riverside
Mark Taul-Fullerton
Jim Williams-Santa Ana

177
Dave Alexander-Santa Ana
John Bell-Cypress
Jim Wassink-San Bernardino
Bill Evens-Barstow
Mike O'Shann-Rio Hondo

190
Ed Carroll-Chaffey
Jim Bishop-Fullerton
Bob Prible-Mt. SAC
Steve Speck-Cypress
Mike Oshann-Rio Hondo

Unlimited
John Stahl-Riverside
Bob Raymond-Golden West
Dan McLain-Moorpark
Oshi Tuitama-Ventura

Team Results
1
2
3

Coaches
Antelope Valley-
Bill Van Osdel
Barstow-George Koualick
Chaffey-Jack White
Cypress-Ray Haas
Fullerton-Oran Breeland
Golden West-Fred Owens
Long Beach-Wayne Skill
Moorpark-John Keever
Mt. SAC-Fred Burri
Orange Coast-Jack Fair
Rio Hondo-Clint South
San Bernardino-Bob Smith
Santa Ana-Frank Addleman
Santa Monica-Bob Blix
Ventura-Jerry Dunlap

John Keever - Moorpark College
Two-Time CCCAA Coach of the Year

1970 South Regional
March 7, 1970

118
Dan Kida-Grossmont
Jim Lingle-S D Mesa
Stacy Cody-Cerritos
Rocky Chavez-El Camino
Frank Tuitama-Ventura

126
Hal Jordan-Cerritos
Rick Johnson-S D Mesa
Mike Raikes-Pierce
Harold Russell-Grossmont

134
Alex Verduzco-El Camino
Ken Turner-Cerritos
Mike Ito-S D Mesa
Larry Wilson-Ventura
Joe Rodriguez-East LA

142
Jerrett Williams-Cerritos
Wayne Branstetter-Ventura
Joe Tice-S D Mesa
Mitch Anderson-Southwestn
Dave Johnson-Pierce
Tom Johnson-Imperial Valley

150
Henry Macernie-El Comino
Mack Byrge-Cerritos
Darryl Murphy-Ventura
Larry Davidson-Grossmont

158
Mike McIntyre-El Camino
Darry Coe-Pierce
Chuck Molnar-S D Mesa
Keith Richards-Cerritos
Dick Turner-Southwestern

167
Dave Starr-El Camino
George Maddox-Cerritos
Tom Wenbourne-Grossmont
Larry Miller-S D Mesa
Pierre Lievre-Pierce

177
Chester Bosek-Cerritos
Ken Wright-El Camino
Dayle Mazzarella-Southwest
Tili Tuitama-Ventura
Al Davis-S D Mesa
John Connally-Grossmont

190
Ben Ohai-Cerritos
Frank Barnhart-Palomar
Phil Arkin-Pierce
Steve Downer-El Camino
Paul Beauchamp-Southwestn

Unlimited
Dave Campbell-Cerritos
Brian Lukas-Pierce
Gary Pool-Grossmont
Ron Boling-Mira Costa
Oshi Tuitama-Ventura

Team Results
1
2
3

Coaches
Cerritos-Hal Simonek First
East LA-Benny Bohlander
El Camino-Dave Hengsteler
Grossmont-Bob Hayward
Mira Costa-John Oakley
Palomar-Tony Lyrids
Pierce-Edwin Goldbloom
S D Mesa-Al Walker
Southwestern-Dick Mason

1971 North Central Regional
March 6, 1971 Fresno City College

118
Dave Exline-Cuesta
Gene Hughes-Fresno
Dick Masuda-American River
Dave Hernandez-Reedley
Paul Gonzales-Bakersfield

126
Robert Arballo-Fresno
John Zehnder-Sacramento
Bill Seaborn-Bakersfield
George Palmer-Cuesta

134
Pete Holeman-Fresno
Carl Lindholm-Sequoias
Dave Giggy-Bakersfield
Tom Zehnder-Sacramento
Martin Ugalde-Modesto

142
Charles Freeman-Fresno
Eldon Ross-Bakersfield
Cliff Acosta-Modesto
Steve Bennette-Sierra
Lincoln Lee-Sacramento

150
Lonnie Paterson-Fresno
Keith Wecker-American River
Richard O'Brien-Modesto
Clyde Adams-Sequoias
Harvey Wilson-Sacramento

158
George Howe-Fresno
Doug Stone-Bakersfield
Horace Wallace-Porterville
Dick Kersh-Shasta
Lionel Selda-Sequoias

167
Bob Herndon-Bakersfield
Nat Harris-Sacramento
Ron Myers-Butte
Bryant Wissenbach-Sierra

177
Jerry Greer-Bakersfield
Mike Mendez-Fresno
John White-Merced
Reed Shaffer-Sequoias
Lynn DeArmand-S J Delta

190
Tim Del Toro-Fresno
Doyle Nelms-Porterville
Mark Padilla-Bakersfield
Chuck Sufeldt-Modesto

Unlimited
Dan Hart-American River
Chris Hansen-Reedley
Bud Ruschhaupt-Fresno
Leo Kaiser-Sacramento
Jose Reyes-Merced

Team Scores
1
2 Bakersfield 84
3

Coaches
American River-Bob Towers
Bakersfield-Bruce Pfutzenreuter
Butte-Remo Ferretti
Sequoias-Al Branco
Cuesta-Lennis Cowell
Fresno-Bill Musick
Merced-Ricard Rohrke
Modesto-Dean Sensenbaugh
Porterville-Darryl Williams
Reedley-John Perkins
Sacramento-Bill Hickey
S J Delta-Larry Jones
Shasta-John Bunton
Sierra-John Horrillo

1971 North Regional
March 6, 1971

118
Glen Maxon-Redwoods
Mike Graham-Santa Ana
Dee Rosario-Chabot
Dan Salinas-San Jose
Dave Randall-San Mateo
126
Dave Brunner-Diablo Valley
Ed Bournaccrsi-Santa Ana
Manny Sanchez-Foothill
Vince Perez-Gavilan
Scott Carnes-Redwoods
134
Mitch Pinney-De Anza
Derry Converse-San Jose
Roger Eckes-Solano
Bob Loflin-Lassen
Mark O'Neal-Diablo Valley
142
Don Wright-Skyline
Bob McNeil-Diablo Valley
Bruce Blanchard-Foothill
Jerry Ruggiero-San Jose
Mark Smith-West Valley
150
Roger Warner-Diablo Valley
Bruce Bicocca-West Valley
Bob Marsella-De Anza
Gary Garcia-Chabot
Bob Morris-Skyline
158
Monty Hobbs-Ohlone
Cliff Hatch-Diablo Valley
Gary Ballard-Chabot
Barney Strickland-Laney
Greg Mason-Redwoods
167
Chris Hurchanik-Canada
Rick Lewis-De Anza
Bert Dalton-Chabot
Jerome Cortese-San Jose
Dave Montgomery-Lassen

177
Dave Osterkamp-Solano
Jim Smith-Skyline
John Needham-Chabot
Bob Kistner-San Jose
190
Harold Morris-Canada
Dann Higgins-Chabot
Doug Holt-De Anza
Tony Buccellato-Diablo Valley
Mike Gould-Contra Costa
Unlimited
Terry Gorman-Chabot
Ron Tate-Hartnell
Alvin Davis-Diablo Valley
Steve Boschetti-San Mateo
Mike Kornes-Solano

Team Results
1
2
3
4
5
6
7
8
9-Redwoods
Coaches
Canada-Sam-Nicolopulos
Chabot-Zack-Papachristos
Redwoods-Jim Sylvia
Contra Costa-Paul Ferris
De Anza-Tuck Halsey
Diablo Valley-Bob Ericson
Foothill-Jim Noon
Gavilan-Bob Garcia
Hartnell-Wes McWilliams
Laney-Ashley Sherman
Lassen-Dave Foster
Ohlone-Pat English
San Jose-Sam Huerta
San Mateo-Jim Jacques
Santa Rosa-Marv Mays
Skyline-Lee Allen
Solano-Jack Harvath
West Valley-Bob Sutter

1971 South Central Regional
March 6, 1971

118
Eddie Lee-Mt. SAC
Robert Vargas-San Bernardin
Maurice Howard-Riverside
Ray Villegas-Barstow

126
Bob Leininger-Cypress
David Womask-Golden West
Victor Oquendo-San Bernardi
Marshall Thompson-Mt. SAC

134
Bob Manley-Mt. SAC
Louis Blanco-San Bernardino
Glen Suel-Riverside
Tom Foss-Golden West
Kiki Sanchez-Moorpark

142
Burni Molony-Cypress
Bruce Brown-Riverside
Bruce Bogart Fullerton
Tom Kurth Chaffey
Greg Lau Mt. SAC

150
Phillip Brown Riverside
Harris Osni-Fullerton
Steve Kurtz-Golden West
Richey Donathan-Cypress
John Sandlin-Chaffey

158
Bill Long-Mt. SAC
Greg Hertzler-Fullerton
David Yates-San Bernardino
Harold Dotson-Riverside
Bert Shirley-Rio Hondo

167
Malcolm Poemoceah-Fullerto
Bill Swanson-Cypress
Ike Seny-Antelope Valley
Joe Beaty-Mt. SAC
John Noble-Golden West

177
Jim Bishop-Fullerton
Steve Shine-Antelope Valley
Doug Hilliard-Golden West
Charles Asmus-Moorpark
Ed Beaune-Mt. SAC

190
Glen Cosman-Fullerton
Sammy Davis Jr.-San Bernardi
Bill Postmes-Cypress
George Vaughn-Riverside
Tom Whitten-Mt. SAC

Unlimited
John Stahl-Riverside
Steve Thuralde-Cypress
Jerry Small-Mt. SAC
Jack Simmons-Moorpark
Zack Tatum-Fullerton

Team Results
1
2
3

Coaches
Antelope Valley-Richard Curtis
Barstow-George Koualick
Chaffey-Paul Iaeger
Cypress-Ray Haas
Fullerton-Oran Breeland
Golden West-Dale Deffner
Moorpark-John Keever
Mt. SAC-Fred Burri
Rio Hondo-Clint South
Riverside-Don Birren
San Bernardino-Glen Baggrtt

1971 South Regional
March 6, 1971 Grossmont College

118
Alan Gonzales-El Camino
Stacy Cody-Cerritos
Lim Lingle-S D Mesa
David Legaspi-Long Beach

126
Mark Surber-El Camino
Paul Strait-Cerritos
Richard Lackey-Grossmont
Rick Riofrio-Long Beach

134
Harold Jordan-Cerritos
Ivan Meadows-Santa Ana
Conrad Kauble-El Camino
Scott Murdock-Pierce

142
Guy Morrison-Orange Coast
Dan MacErnie-El Camino
Bill Amadon-Cerritos
Chris Lousell-Pierce

150
Mark Racowsky-Pierce
Richard Riker-Grossmont
Robert Carreon-Long Beach
Roger Thomas

158
John Hardy-Southwestern *
Tracey Mitchell-Pierce
Bob Curry-Orange Coast
John Wilkins-Long Beach
Ernie Zouras-Cerritos

167
Dave Starr-El Camino
Chris Ehrentraut-Grossmont
James Zumuda-Cerritos
Alvin Davis-S D Mesa
Marty Stewart-Long Beach

177
James Kauble-El Camino
Bob Fate-Orange Coast
Andy Halsey-Cerritos
Grey Whillock-Grossmont
Roger Lee-San Diego

190
Ben Ohi-Cerritos
Keith Smith-Imperial Valley
Darrell Smith-Compton
Al Otteman-Santa Ana
Elard Tom-San Diego

Unlimited
Tom Hazell-El Camino
David Campbell-Cerritos
Gerald Peeke-Pierce
Lawrence Rhodes-S D Mesa

Most Outstanding Wrestler
John Hardy-Southwestern

Team Scores
1 El Camino   96
2 Cerritos   83
3 Pierce   41
4 Orange Coast   32
5 Grossmont   28
6 S D Mesa   19
7 Long Beach   18
8 Santa Ana   16
9 Southwestern   14
10 Imperial Valley 11
11 Compton   9
12 East LA   7
13 San Diego   4
14 Mira Costa   1
15 Palomar   0

Coaches
Cerritos-Hal Simonek
Compton-Chalk Ramsey
East LA Benny-Bohlander
El Camino-Dave Hengsteler
Grossmont-Bob Haywood
Imperial Valley-Leon Kelsoe
Long Beach-Wayne Skill
Orange Coast-Jack Fair
Pierce-Edwin Goldbloom
San Diego-Mark Whittleton
S D Mesa-Al Walker
Santa Ana-Frank Addleman
Southwestern-Dick Mason

1972 North Central Regional
February 25, 1972 Sierra College

118
Gene Hughes-Fresno 3-1
Dick Molina-Bakersfield
Mario Arce-Modesto
Dave Hernandez-Reedley
Steve Garcia-Yuba

126
George Palmer-Cuesta
Steve Combs Fresno
Dennis Burnett-Bakersfield
Jay Nightingale-Yuba
Roger Ozbira-Modesto

134
Eldon Ross-Bakersfield
John Apodaca-Cuesta
Steve Barrero-Lassen
Jerry Rebbel-Modesto
Rube Foseca-Sequoias

142
Charles Freeman-Fresno
Bob Loflin-Lassen
Rich Santana-American River
Bruce Johnson-Cuesta
Cliff Acosta-Modesto

150
Steve Tirapelle American Rive
Greg Anderson-S J Delta
Tom Ramos-Bakersfield
Larry Shubat-Yuba
Don Borges-Sierra

158
Doug Porter-Modesto
Dan Hutching-Sequoias
Miguel Avitia-Bakersfield
Camilio Alarcio-Cuesta
Bob Domingues-Fresno

167
Brady Hall-Modesto
Bob Henderson-Sierra
Abe Oliveras-Bakersfield
Gary Macagni-Cuesta
Nick Quintana-Reedley

177
Brent Wissenback-Sierra *
John White-Merced
Paul Vallagomez-Fresno
Reed Shaffater-Sequoias
Dave Kadel-Bakersfield

190
Chuck Seefeldt-Modesto
Gary Ramos-American River
Gary Nunnelly-Shasta
John Campbell-Bakersfield

Unlimited
Bill Van Worth-Bakersfield
Dan Hart-American River
Dan Watson-Fresno
Frank Peifer-Cuesta
Rich Newton-S J Delta

Most Outstanding Wrestler
Brent Wissenbeck Sierra

Tean Scores
1 Bakersfield   103.5
2 Modesto   79
3 Fresno   77

Coaches
American River-Bob Towers
Bakersfield-Bruce Pfutzenreuter
Sequoias-Al Branco
Cuesta-Lennis Cowell
Fresno-Bill Musick
Lassen-Dave Foster
Merced-Richard Rohrke
Modesto-Dean Sensenbaugh
Reedley-John Perkins
S J Delta-Larry Jones
Shasta-John Bunton
Sierra-John Horrillo
Yuba-Lou Menghini

1972 North Regional
February 25, 1972

118
Steve Siroy-Chabot
Ken Crumley-Redwoods
Louie Luna-Cabrillo
Sam Nishamota-Diablo Valley
David Ybarra-Hartnell

126
Glenn Maxson-Redwoods
Alex Gonzales-Solano
Roy Rios Diablo-Valley
David Gonzales-San Jose
Ed Ortiz-De Anza

134
Simon Flores-Chabot
Ed Bournaccrsi-Santa Rosa
Juan Pitchardo-Diablo Valley
Dave Mendez-West Valley
Cal Norman-Solano

142
Brent Jacinto-Chabot
Pete Araujo-De Anza
Ruben Ramos-Diablo Valley
Mitch Vierra-West Valley
Tom Cherhoniak-Skyline

150
Roger Warner-Diablo Valley *
Bill Cline-Ohlone
Dennis Bardsley-Santa Rosa
Dan Cunningham-West Valley

158
Cliff Hatch-Diablo Valley
Bob Marsella-De Anza
Gary Ballard-Chabot
Leif Grunseth-Contra Costa
Logan Cox-Redwoods

167
Andy Soares-West Valley
Mike Schantz-Chabot
Jay Lawson-De Anza
Dave Eller-Cabrillo
Scott Davis-Diablo Valley

177
Brett Noon-Foothill
Ray Needham-Chabot
Richard Calderon-San Jose
Rick Lewis-De Anza
Roger McLaughlin-Hartnell

190
Bill Fritz-Foothill
Doug Holt-De Anza
Hal Morris-Canada
Mall Alexander-San Jose
Tom Roberts-Diablo Valley

Unlimited
Ron Tate-Hartnell
Terry Gorman-Chabot
Tom Douglas-San Mateo
Steve Hogan-Redwoods
Dan Touplin-Diablo Valley

Mos Outstanding Wrestler
Roger Warner-Diablo Valley

Team Results
1
2
3
4 Redwoods

Coaches
Cabrillo-Don Montgomery
Canada-Sam Nicolopulos
Chabot-Zack Papachristos
Redwoods-Jim Sylvia
Contra Costa-Paul Farris
De Anza-Tuck Halsey
Diablo Valley-Bob Ericson
Foothill-Jim Noon
Hartnell-Wes McWilliams
Ohlone-Pat English
San Jose-Sam Huerta
San Mateo-Jim Jacques
Santa Rosa-Marvin Mays
Skyline-Lee Allen
Solano-Jack Harvath
West Valley-Robert Sutter

1972 South Central Regional

118
Ed Lee-Mt. SAC *
Jerry Munoz-San Bernardino
John Cox-Cypress
Steve Joannes-Orange Coast
Jim Myers-Fullerton
126
Tom Foss-Orange Coast
Lyle Dalby-Moorpark
Ted Wilton-Cypress
Victor Oquendo-San Bernardi
Tom Bravo-Chaffey
Joe Malave-Rio Hondo
134
Victor Vorobiefft-SAC
Mike Flook-Cypress
Pat Buono-Golden West
David Branstetter-Ventura
Stan Phillips-Antelope Valley
142
Tom Kurth-Chaffey
Paul LaBlanc-Orange Coast
Bill Miller-Mt. SAC
Sian Mansfield-Moorpark
Duane Patton-Cypress
Mike Snow-Rio Hondo
150
John Sandlin-Chaffey
Ben Goodwin-Moorpark
Guy Morrison-Orange Coast
Greg Lau-Mt. SAC
Gene Leininger-Cypress
158
Bill Long-Mt. SAC
Terry Newsome-Chaffey
Mickey Abers Antelope Valley
Bob Davis-Cypress
Scott Burns-Moorpark
167
Dan Lewis-Orange Coast
Tim Kalcevick-Cypress
Greg Cook-Victor Valley
Rod Harvey-Ventura
Brynn Downey-Chaffey

177
Tim Bandel-Orange Coast
Steve Shine-Antelope Valley
Steve Hoyt-Moorpark
Bill Postmus-Cypress
Willis Pringle-Victor Valley
190
Mike Mueller-Cypress
Steve Fisher-Riverside
Mike Hayden-Rio Hondo
Jim Lupinetti-Chaffey
Bob Fate-Orange Coast
Unlimited
Jim Kish-Antelope Valley
Steve Goodyear-Ventura
Terry Fisher-Moorpark
Mike Henry-Cypress
John Suter-Golden Valley

Most Outstanding Wrestler
Ed Lee-Mt. SAC

Team Results
1
2
3
4
5
6
7
8
9
10
11 Rio Hondo

Coaches
Antelope-Valley Jim Curtis
Chaffey-Paul Iaeger
Cypress-Ray Haas
Golden West-Dale Deffner
Moorpark-John Keever
Mt. SAC-Fred Burri
Orange Coast-Jack Fair
Rio Hondo-Ken Bos
Riverside-Don Birren
San Bernardino-Clyde Williams
Ventura-Jerry Dunlap
Victor Valley-Ken Garver

1972 South Regional
February 25, 1972 Cerritos College

118
James Hamada-Palomar 6-0
Mitch Steinauer-Grossmont
Terese Villegas-S Western FF
Rosalio Fonseca-East LA
Mark Suger-El Camino

126
Gary Tackett Imperial Va 10-4
Conrad Kauble-El Camino
Carl Slocum-Santa Ana 4-2
Jim Samson-Pierce
John Shea-Cerritos

134
Paul Strait-Cerritos Fall 1:47
Wilson Guzman-El Camino
Fred Taylor-Grossmont 2-0
Bill Spencer-S D Mesa

142
Dan Macernie-El Camin 18-7
Bill Amadon-Cerritos
Jeff Howell-Grossmont 10-2
Scott Murdock-Pierce
Ed Wilson-S D Mesa

150
Larry Willeman El Camino 7-3
Spencer Call-Cerritos
Chris Fagan Grossmont OT7-3
Mike Woodcraft-S D Mesa

158
Bob Snowden-S D Mesa 11-7
Julian Fernandez-Cerritos
Russ Turner-Pierce 9-2
Clay Clifford-Palomar
Ken Meffan-El Camino

167
Bill Kalivas-Pierce 4-3
Jim Zmuda-Cerritos 3
John McAndrews-I Valley 8-2
Ed Spann-Santa Ana
John Bree-El Camino

177
Larry Perales-Cerritos 11-5
Frank Gonzales-Santa Ana
Wayne Mickerson Palomar FF
Jack Bell-Pierce
Greg McCulley-Long Beach

191
Rich Brown-L Beach F 1:19
Paul Beauchamp-Southwestn
Andy Halsey-Cerritos Default
George Smith-Imperial Valley
Don Buck-Grossmont

Unlimited
Tom Hazell-El Camin F 7:48 *
Rudy Huerta-Imperial Valley
Bruce Rockwell-S Ana F 1:35
Pat Barron-Long Beach
Mike Badsky-Palomar

Most Outstanding Wrestler
Tom Hazell-El Camino

Team Scores
1 Cerritos   63.5
2 El Camino   55
3 Imperial Valley 29
4 Pierce   26.5
5 Grossmont   25.5
6 Palomar   19
7 Long Beach   18.5

East LA   3

Coaches
Cerritos-Hal Simonek
East LA-Benny Bohlander
El Camino-Dave Hegsteler
Grossmont-Robert Haywood
Imperial Valley-Leon Kelsoe
Long Beach-Wayne Skill
Palomar-Tony Lynds
Pierce-Edwin Goldbloom
S D Mesa-Alfred Walker
Santa Ana-Frank Addleman
Southwestern-Dick Mason

1973 North Central Regional
February 23, 1973 Bakersfield

118
Jack Serros-Bakersfield 10-4

126
Robert Arballo-Fresno

Manuel Ibarra-Bakfl F 1:43   5
134
Jess Ortiz-Hancock *F 6:50
Dennis Burnett-Bakersfield

142
David East-Bakfld 3-2 OT
Grant Arnold-Modesto

150
Jim Anderson-S J Delta 3-1
Fred Porter-Bakersfield

158

Miguel Avitia-Bakfld 12-6   5

167
Tony Alvarez-Bakfld 19-14

177

Russell Dickson-Bakersfield 3

190

Heavyweight
Bill Van Worth-Bakfld F 1:36

Most Outstanding Wrestler
Jess Ortiz-Alan Hancock

Team Scores
1 Bakersfield   112.5
2 Modesto   102.5
3 Fresno   73.5
4 S J Delta   71
5 Hancock   36.5
6 Sierra   32.5

Bill Van Worth pinned all four opponents

1973 North Regional
February 23, 1973 Chabot College

118
Steve Siroy-Chabot
Roger Flook-Gavilan
Ken Crumley-Redwoods
Ben Gonzales-San Jose

126
Rich Torres-Chabot
Ed Ortiz-De Anza
David Gonzales-Solano

134
Juan Pichardo-Diablo Valley
Steve Dick-Chabot
Greg Hill-De Anza
Cal Norman-Solano

142
Kenny Lewis-Diablo Valley
Brent Jacinto-Chabot
Mike Walker-West Valley
Tom Cherhoniak-Skyline

150
Tom Rosenthal-Chabot
Bob Zucker-Foothill
Dennis Bardsley-Santa Rosa
Logan Cox-Redwoods

158
Leif Grunseth-Contra Costa
Russ Barcelona-Foothill
Gary Goodrich-Skyline
Jerry Strangis-San Jose

167
Mike Hatch-Diablo Valley
Chris Anaya-Chabot
Hilario Lopez-San Jose
Ross Dove-Skyline

177
Richie Hale-Diablo Valley
Jay Lawson-De Anza
Jim Thompson-Hartnell
Bob Loyst-San Jose

190
Bob Green-Diablo Valley
Paul Schantz-Chabot
Rich Calderon-San Jose
Bob Figas-Redwoods

Heavyweight
Don Barbitts-San Mateo
Paul Brown-Diablo Valley
Randy Hudson-Chabot
Bob Figas-Redwoods?

Not in any order of place in weights – in the North Regional – state results

Team Results
1
2
3

1973 South Central Regional
February 23, 1973

118
Bob Martinez-Antelope Valle
John Cox-Cypress
Steve Pivac-Mt. SAC
David Cruse-Rio Hondo *

126
Steve Siliceo-Cypress
John Hinojose-Fullerton
Lyle Dalby-Moorpark
Duane Dennis-Riverside

134
Ron Vaughan-Golden West
Brent Dyer-Canyons
Ted Wilton-Cypress
Todd Stocks-Citrus

142
Gene Leninger-Cypress
Rocky Escalante-Ventura
Paul LaBlanc-Orange Coast
Pat Buono-Golden West

150
Gerry Kurth-Chaffey
Ben Goodwin-Moorpark
Jeff Noon Orange-Coast
Randy Larson-Rio Hondo *

158
Tom Brooks-Chaffey
Lewis Pringle-Barstow
Bob Long-Mt. SAC
Ron Jones-Riverside

167
Ken Kalcevich-Cypress
Ed Sauls-Fullerton
Dan Lewis-Orange Coast
Rich Masters-Golden West

177
Stan Combs-Chaffey
Willie Pringle-Victor Valley
Dan Rollins-Golden West
Gary Casey-Orange Coast

190
Dave Duck-Fullerton
Steve Fisher-Riverside
Tim Bandel-Orange Coast
Rob Jackson-Moorpark

Heavyweight
Mike Henry-Cypress
Julius Askew-Canyon
Roy Kreitner-Fullerton
John Sutter-Golden West
Frank Nancini-Santa Ana

Team Results
1
2
3

Not in any order of place in weights – From the State results
* Both from the Rio Hondo Wrestling History

1973 South Regional
February 23, 1973

118
George Hunsaker-Cerritos
Mitch Steinhauer-Grossmont
Jesse Villegas-Southwestern
Roy Shimomura-Santa Ana

126
John Shea-Cerritos
George Moreno-Imperial Vall
Carl Slocum-Santa Ana
Marlo Lacasse-East LA

134
Rich Boyle-El Camino
Gary Tackett-Imperial Valley
Mike Bertetto-Long Beach
Rob Lundren-Santa Ana

142
Wilson Guzman-El Camino
Richie Legarra-Imperial Valley
Marcus McAnally-Palomar

150
Ernie Zouras-Cerritos
Larry Willeman-El Camino
Mike Woodcraft-S D Mesa
Ernie Zarp-Cerritos
Ivan Meadows-Santa Ana

158
Bob Snowden-S D Mesa
Eusebo Sams-El Camino
Wayne Mason-Cerritos
Jon Leifer-Long Beach

167
Gil Johnson-Southwestern
Mark Schuff-Grossmont
Ken Mettan-El Camino
Jim Norris-Santa Ana

177
Don Wakefield-Cerritos
Jack Bell-Peirce
George Allen-Palomar
Ed Spann-Santa Ana

190
Joe Botello-Cerritos
Chuck Couvretto-Grossmont
Steve Stone-Southwestern
Jeff Jackson-Pierce

Heavyweight
Rudy Huerta-Imperial Valley
John Sawyer-Cerritos
Bill Palmer-Southwestern
Frank Mancini-Santa Ana

Not in any order of place in weights - in the South Regional – state results

Team Results
1 Cerritos
2
3

1973-74 South Central Regional

118

177

Team Results
1
2
3

126

190

Results found on the Rio Hondo Wrestling History
Results found on the Santa Ana Program

134
Frank Gonzales-Santa Ana

Heavyweight

Chris Wernicke-Rio Hondo 4

142
Jim Wood-Santa Ana

150

158
Jeff Jaquot-Santa Ana

167
Don Shuler-Santa Ana

1974 North Central Regional
February 23, 1974 Lassen College

118

Glen Dilley-Butte Forfeit
Doug Klinchuch-Bakfld 3

126
Ed Alves-Modesto 10-7
Manuel Ibarra-Bakersfield

177
Tony Alvarez-Bakersfield 12-6
Don Burtschie-Modesto

190
Mike Bull-Bakersfield 7-5
Jim Brazil-Sierra

Team Scores
1 Bakersfield   136
2 Modesto   110.5
3 Fresno   103.5
4 S J Delta   58
5 Butte   50

134

Mike Peevyhouse-Bakfld 5

142

David East-Bakersfield 9-2 3
Mike Zimmerman-Sacrameno

150

Heavyweight

Duane Williams-Bakfld OT3
Ref Dec Todd Starr-Modesto

158
Mike-Anderson Bakfld 3-2
Rich Gallentine-S J Delta

167
Florencio Rocha-Bakfld 11-3
Scott Ricardo-Modesto

1974 South Regional
February 23, 1974

118
Mark Baker-Cerritos 17-4
Terry Drew-Palomar
Steven Guilland S D Mesa 7-2
Larry Moore-Mira Costa
126
Mike Salcido-Cerritos 9-2
Craig Mitufuka-El Camino
Marino Lacasse-East LA 5-4
John Phillips-Pierce
134
Frank Gonzales Santa Ana 7-4
Joe Zeller-El Camino
Jorge Moreno Imperial Va 5-2
Jerry Tingle-Southwestern
142
Jim Wood-Sa Ana 8-8 OT Dec
Gordon Cox-El Camino
Paul Gibbs-Cerritos 7-4
Lee Brannen-Southwestern
150
Kevin Clark-Grossmont 4-2
Kirk McConchia-Santa Ana
Tom Tice-S D Mesa 3-0
Perfirio Huerta-Imperial Valle
158
Jon Leifer-Long Beach 5-4
Jeff Jacouet-Santa Ana
Mark Schuff-Grossmont
Jim Ullray-Santa Moncia
167
Don Shuler-Santa Ana 8-2 *
Warren Nikilis-Palomar
Justin Rowinsk-Palomar 16-9
Woody Van Oocsbree Grossm

177
Don Wakefield-Cerritos 7-5
Dave Hill-El Camino
Rich Weather-Grossmo F 1:32
Dennis Zebinsky-Palomar
190
Ed Acosta-Mira Costa 6-1
Jeff Sharp-Grossmont
Robert Jones-Cerritos 5-3
Chris Poma-Palomar
Heavyweight
Russ Snyder-Pierce 15-0
Mark Oahs-Grossmont
Joe Cascioppo-Palomar
Ken Bogner-Cerritos

Most Outstanding Wrestler
Don Shuler-Santa Ana

Team Scores
1 Santa Ana   97.5
2 Cerritos   90.5
3 Grossmont   69
4 Palomar   67.5
5 El Camino   65
6 Pierce   34
7 S D Mesa   28.5
8 Mira Costa   28
9 East LA   26
10 Imperial Valley 24
10 Southwestern   24

1975 North Central Regional
February 28, Fresno City College

118
Ernie Flores-Fresno
Doug Klinchuch-Bakersfield
Robert Smith-Sacramento
Carlos Garrido-Modesto
Brock Chamberlain-Butte

126
Guy Reilly-Lassen
David Gantzer-Merced
Gene Guerraro-Sequoias
Joe Montes-Sierra
Art Serros-Modesto

134
Tom Gongora-Fresno
Franc Affentranger-Bakfld
Reynolds Capps-Sierra
Marlin Moreno-Modesto
Joel Preheim-Reedley

142
Rod Balch-Fresno
Melvin Harris-Merced
Mike Peevghouse-Bakfld
Bill Zimmerman-Sacramento
Don Roy-Sierra

150
Bob Weaver-Merced
Randy Baxter-Fresno
Warren Hutchings-Sequoias
Manuel Perez-Modesto
Don Ellison-S J Delta

158
Dusty Clark-Butte
Albert Valadez-Lassen
Randy Lopez-Fresno
Paul Zepp-Cuesta
John Russell-Sequoias

167
Florencio Rocha-Bakersfield
Joe Bracamonte-Fresno
Ben Emana-Lassen
Russ Wardrip-Hancock
Steve Satterwhite-Cuesta

177
Tony Manning-Fresno
John Shallenberger-Merced
Vince Cotton-Sacramento
Cardell Geary-Yuba
Andy Huyck-Hancock
Craig Tobin-Bakersfield

190
Kevin Hunstad-Cuesta
Jim Sams-Yuba
Manual Gomez-Fresno
Stan Carter-Merced
Rod Gaines-S J Delta
Mike Anderson-Bakersfield

Heavyweight
Charles Harman-Fresno
Terry Watson-Yuba
Gene Gonzales-Merced
Bob Gregerson-Cuesta
John Del Carlo-Sierra

Team Scores
1 Fresno 155.5
2 Merced 98.5
3 Bakersfield 72.5
4 Cuesta 45
5 Sierra 43.5

Coaches
Hancock-Wayne King
Bakersfield-Bruce Pfutzenreuter
Butte-Remo Ferretti
Sequoias-Rudy Duarte
Cuesta-Gary Meissner
S J Delta-Larry Jones
Fresno-Bill Musick
Lassen-Dave Foster
Merced-Rich Rohrke
Modesto-Dean Sensenbaugh
Reedley-Vance Stanley
Sacramento-Bill Hickey
Sierra John Horrillo
Yuba-Ron Peterson

Florencio Rocha 30-0 as of 2-28-75

1975 North Regional
February 28, 1975 Skyline College

118
Curt Kawabata-Chabot
Andrew Gonzales-San Jose
George Naranjo-Gavilan
Robert Hill-Monterey
Jim Lewers-Santa Rosa

126
Joe Stallworth-Chabot
Baltazr Mamon-San Jose
Dale Brumette-De Anza
Dave Lane-Diablo Valley
Greg Chapell-Hartnell

134
Carlos Rodriguez-San Jose
Anthony Richardson-Sa Rosa
Greg DeJongh-Chabot
Mike Ross-Diablo Valley
Kurt Seeter-Cabrillo

142
Jerry Nobles-San Jose
Tim McTighe-West Valley
Mark Wilwand-Chabot
Terry Bautista-Gavilan

150
Kevin Hejnal-West Valley
Emanuel Miller-San Jose
Mike Gerton-Chabot
Pat Dunn-Monterey
Brooke Wentner-Diablo Valle

158
Jerry Hoffman-Chabot
Steve Cook-Skyline
Craig Thiessen-Diablo Valley
Dave Rodriguez-West Valley

167
Bob Parker-Cabrillo
Rich Blanton-Chabot
Mike Mercure-Diablo Valley
Bill Merriot-San Jose
Phil Lankford-Canada

177
Jeff Ramona-San Jose
Ron Jones-Chabot
Steve Carnes-Cabrillo
Brian Jordan-Marin
Ken Mercure-Diablo Valley

190
Eric Woolsey-Redwoods
Jim Ainley-Cabrillo
John Fritz-Skyline
Bob Andrade-Chabot
Robin Hutchins-San Jose

Heavyweight
Jeff Ricketts-San Jose
Ralph Kuehn-Foothill
Clinton Miller-Contra Costa
Chuck Martinez-De Anza

Team Scores
1 San Jose   145
2 Chabot   127.5
3 West Valley   62
4 Diablo Valley   60.5
5 Cabrillo   57.5

Coaches
Cabrillo-Don Montgomery
Canada-Sam Nicblopolous
Chabot Zack-Papachristos
Redwoods-Jim Syliva
Contra Costa-Paul Ferris
Diablo Valley-Bob Ericson
Foothill-Dave Reed
Gavilan-Ed Johnson
Hartnell-Mark Sindel
Marin-Jim McGowin
Monterey-Chuck Smith
San Jose-Sam Huerta
Santa Rosa-Marv Mays
Skyline-Lee Allen
West Valley-Jim Root

1975 South Central Regional
February 28, 1975 Antelope Valley College

118
Mike Flemming-Fullerton
Rick Alley-Rio Hondo
Brad Wendt-Cypress
Mike Brock-Moorpark
Frank Clemeni-Santa Barbra

126
Butch Escalante-Ventura
Ray Yocum-Antelope Valley
Terry Kemp-Mt. SAC
Vick Yslas-Cypress
Pete Breslin-Moorpark

134
Mark Okoorian-Cypress
Andy Guzman-Mt. SAC
Greg Pollard-Victor Valley
Tim Wallstrom-Fullerton
Jim Luster-Canyon

142
Steve Thompson-Cypress
Pete Paldsovic-Fullerton
Tony Gonnella-Mt. SAC
Jeff Vogel-Ventura
Greg Dishman-Victor Valley

150
Bob Rhinehart-Moorpark
Dave Edgeworth-Antelope Va
Jess Wilson-Cypress
Glen Arenas-Mt. SAC
Neils Buys-Ventura

158
Dan Rutschke-Cypress
Frank Sulick-Chaffey
Toshi Tochikubo-Orange Coas
Lewis Gonzales-Mt. SAC
Gary Cavender-Riverside

167
Mark Smith-Golden West
Eddie Lopez-Moorpark
Bob Vidana-Cypress
Henry Heidebreeder-San Ber
Abdon Pena-Santa Barbara

177
Charles Cacciata-Cypress
Richard Rose-Moorpark
Karl Stupke-Mt. SAC
David Budgen-Golden West
Bob Geottsche-Fullerton

190
Les Austin-Golden West
Craig Foster-Cypress
Reed Goettsche-Fullerton
Ben Velasquez-Moorpark
George Kovalick-San Bernardi

Heavyweight
Greg Metcalf-Santa Barbara
Chris Wernicke-Rio Hondo
Andy Guthrie-Cypress
Tom Malloy-Moorpark
Derwin Morris-Ventura

Team Scores
1 Cypress   142
2 Moorpark   90.5
3 Fullerton   70.5
4 Mt. SAC   70
5 Golden West   53
4
5
6
7
8
9 Rio Hondo

Coaches
Antelope Valley-Richard Curtis
Chaffey-Paul Laeger
Canyon-Lee Corbin
Cypress-Ray Haas
Fullerton-Oran Breeland
Golden West-Dale Deffner
Moorpark-John Keever
Mt. SAC-Fred Burri
Orange Coast-Vern Wagner
Rio Hondo-Ken Bos
Riverside-Don Birren
San Bernardino-Don Seintuer
Santa Barbara-George Gordon
Ventura-Jerry Dunlap
Victor Valley-Gary Charles

1975 South Regional
February 28, 1975 Grossmont College

118
Mark Baker-Cerritos 11-3
Terry Drew-Palomar
Jeff Morton-El Camino 4-1
Larry Moore-Mira Costa
Sonny Bernal-Southwestern

126
Mike Salcido-Cerritos 12-5
John Phillips-Pierce
Frank Sabala-Grossmont 14-5
Kim Cline-Palomar
Steve Thompson-East LA

134
Frank Gonzales-Sa Ana F 3:35
Dan Field-Palomar
Jim Zeller-El Camino 5-2
John Bottger-Southwestern
Rudy Garcia-Pierce

142
Spencer Call-Cerritos
Bob Northridge-Palomar
Joe Zellers-El Camino 11-1
Bart Bertetto-Long Beach
Ron Pullen-Santa Ana

150
Gordon Cox-El Camino F 7:53
James Brown-Palomar
Kevin Clark-Grossmont 5-4
Jim Woud-Santa Ana
James Tingle-Southwestern

158
Paul Grisafi-Grossmont 5-3
Don Barrios-Palomar
Ted Kelley-El Camino 4-2
Bob Sanders-Santa Ana
Porfirio Huerta-Imperial Valle

167
Don Shuler-Santa Ana 11-4
Eusedio Sams-El Camino
Mike Karges-Palomar 9-2
Gary White-Cerritos
Charles Walker-Pierce

177
Dave Hill-El Camino Fall 3:49
Dave Rottenberg-S D Mesa
Larry Chrisman-Palomar 12-9
Bob Zantos-Santa Ana
Steve Hart-Cerritos

190
Stewart Felker-El Camino
Paul Hart-Grossmont
Warren Nikles-Palomar
Pat Devine-Cerritos
John Cannels-Santa Ana

Heavyweight
Ernest Binggelli-Mira Costa
Wayne Nickerson-Palomar
Foster Harrison Cerrito F 3:05
Larrick Crawford-El Camino
Mike Geer-Pierce

Team Scores
1	El Camino	138
2	Palomar	130.5
3	Cerritos	96.5
4	Santa Ana	73
5	Grossmont	58.5
6	S D Mesa	37.5
7	Pierce	21
8	Southwestern	11
9	Long Beach	10.5
10	Mira Costa	10
11	Imperial Valley	7
12	LA Trade Tech	.5
12	East LA	.5
14	LA Valley	0

Coaches
Hal Simonek-Cerritos
Ben Bolander-East LA
El Camino Dave-Hengsteller
Don Rohrke-Grossmont
Mark Meka-Imperial Valley
Jim Murphy-Long Beach
Al Waibel-Mira Costa
John Woods-Palomar
Erwin Goldbloom-Pierce
Al Walker-SD Mesa
Frank Addleman-Santa Ana
Southwestern-Art Stone

1976 North Central Regional
February 28, 1976 Sierra College

118
Ed Franco-S J Delta
Duane Fidel-Sacramento
Ruben Rios-Merced
Randy Alford-Modesto
Fred Daniels-Fresno

126
Gene Guerrero-Sequoias
Robert Johnson-Sacramento
Ray Garza-Bakersfield
Hal Dillashaw-S J Delta

134
Franc Affentranger-Bakfld
Reynold Capps-Sierra
Bob Burkett-Modesto
Jess McCushom-Shasta
Mike McGann-American Rive

142
Tom Gongora-Fresno OT
Joe Lopez-Bakersfield
Jim Gagliardi-Modesto
Mario Betti-Sacramento
Julian Gurrero-Butte

150
Eugene Royal-Fresno
Jeff Williams-Butte
Paul Bristow-Sacramento
John Parreira-Modesto
Warren Hutchings-Sequoias

158
Dean Reichenberg-Ame River
Victor Adkins-Sacramento
Randy Baxter-Fresno
Joe O'Brian-Modesto
Pat Riley-S J Delta

167
Joe Bracamonte-Fresno
Rudy Burtschi-Modesto
Craig Tobin-Bakersfield
Tom Tirapelle-American River
Bruce Grosebeck-Sequoias

177
John Parrish-American River
Mike Diaz-Modesto
Amos Scott-Fresno
Paul Trout-Yuba
Andy Huyck-Hancock

190
Kevin Hunstad-Cuesta
Al Retziperis-Modesto
Brent Causey-American River
Manuel Gomez-Fresno
Gary Pierson-Bakersfield

Heavyweight
Gene Gonzales-Merced
Jess Ponce-Bakersfield
Gary Krigbaum-Modesto
Ken Karbuck-American River
Gary Weldon-Sierra

Team Scores
1 Modesto   119.75
2 Fresno   101
3 American River 83.75
4 Bakersfield   81
5 Sacramento   78.25
6 Cuesta   45.75
7 S J Delta   44
8 Sequoias   42.5
9 Merced   27
10 Sierra   25.5

Coaches
Hancock-Wayne King
American River-Bob Towers
Bakersfield-Bruce Pfutzenreuter
Butte-Remo Ferretti
Cuesta-Gary Meisser
Fresno-Al Kiddy
Merced-Rich Rohrke
Modesto-Dean Sensenbaugh
Sacramento-Bill Hickey
S J Delta-Larry Jones
Sequoias-Dave Adams
Shasta-Leon Donahue
Sierra-John Horrillo
Yuba-Ron Peterson

Coach of the Year Nominees
Dean Sensenbaugh-Modesto
Bob Towers-American River

1976 North Regional
February 28, 1976 Chabot College

118
Jesus Flores-Chabot
Andy Gonzales-San Jose
Greg Ford-Diablo Valley
Baron Wong-Santa Rosa
Ed Stringer-Skyline

126
Dwight Miller-Foothill
Mark Needham-Chabot
David Cotti-San Jose
Eddie Lewis-Diablo Valley
Larry Bates-Contra Costa

134
Jim Nelson-Solano
John Sabenorio-Chabot
Frank Olms-Foothill
Steve Knabe-Skyline
Greg Chappel-Hartnell

142
Frank Peterson-Chabot
Mark Lindin-Foothill
Rich Bredengard-Skyline
Pat Larson-Santa Rosa
Tim McTighe-West Valley

150
Wes Burris-Chabot
Ken Cushman-Redwoods
Dan Overkamp-Diablo Valley
Pete Klee-Foothill

158
Kevin Hejnel-West Valley
John Noble-Chabot
Tony Brewer-Foothill
Ed Solario-San Jose
Gary Anderson-Solano

167
Kirk Poppay-West Valley
David Hines-Chabot
Bill Merriott-San Jose
Mike DeArman-Ohlone
Scott Overholt-Contra Costa

177
Rich Blanton-Chabot
Ted Woerner-Diablo Valley
Frank Lockett-Contra Costa
Jesus Aboytes-Cabrillo
Mark Martinez-Redwoods

190
Eric Woolsey-Redwoods
Curt Bledsoe-Chabot
Terrell Duran-Ohlone
Jim Robinson-Santa Rosa
Nelson Ahistrom-Diablo Valle

Heavyweight
Dave Shaw-Cabot
Joe DaRosa-Cabrillo
Mike Fox-Redwoods
Nick Provecchio-San Jose
John Glass-Gavilan

Top three qualify for the state championships

Team Scores
1 Chabot   176
2 San Jose   77.25
3 Foothill   70.25
4 West Valley   59.5
5 Redwoods   55
6 Diablo Valley 53.75
7 Solano   41.5
8 Santa Rosa   40.5
9 Contra Costa   34.75
10 Skyline   31.5

Coaches
Cabrillo-Don Montgomery
Chabot-Zack Papachristos
Contra Costa-Gary Murr
Foothill-George Avakian
Gavilan-Ed Johnson
Hartnell-Mark Sindel
Ohlone-Mike Cowan
Redwoods-Jim Sylvia
San Jose-San Huerta
Santa Rosa-Marv Mays
Skyline-Lee Allen
Solano-Jack Harvath
West Valley-Jim Root

Coach of the Year Nominees
Zack Papachristos-Chabot
Jim Root-West Valley

1976 South Central Regional
February 28, 1976

118
Terry Kamp-Mt. SAC
Pete Breslin-Moorpark
Jim Platts-Antelope Valley
Kevin Smith-Golden West
Paul Tuscher-Chaffey

126
Butch Escalante-Ventura
Vic Yslas-Cypress
Jim Fernandez-Moorpark
Paul Sowa-Orange Coast
Terry Palnely-San Bernadino

134
Mark Okoorian-Cypress
Pierre Smith-Moorpark
Ruben Lopez-Rio Hondo
Dan Lehor-Chaffey
Dan Carlson-Canyons

142
Greg Okoorian-Cypress
Tony Gonelle-Mt. SAC
Jim Blazej-Moorpark
Jeff Vogel-Ventura
Greg Pollard-Victor Valley

150
Jeff Wilton-Cypress
Frank Hernandez-Golde West
Pierre Arsenault-Rio Hondo
Gary Murphy-Moorpark
Dana Ellison-Canyons

158
Ron Shillyiday-Orange Coast
Bob Vidans-Cypress
Neils Buus-Ventura
Steve Sparks-San Bernadino

167
Eddie Lopez-Moorpark
Greg Johnson-Cypress
Vince Mele-Rio Hondo
Joe Barragan-Mt. SAC
Eric Peterson-Chaffey

177
Craig Foster-Chaffey
Lance Marcus-Moorpark
Jim Mayo-Canyons
Mario Polanco-Rio Hondo
Kevin Thorderson-Mt. SAC

190
Roy Austin-Cypress
Andy Lasak-Orange Coast
John Rudolph-Mt. SAC
Benny Mendoza-Chaffey
Steve Padilla-Ventura

Heavyweight
Ron Hegge-Canyons
Gil Martinez-Rio Hondo
Mike King-Cypress
Bob Miller-Chaffey
Eugene Ortega-San Bernadin

Team Scores
1 Cypress   156.25
2 Moorpark   95
3 Mt. SAC   63.25
4 Rio Hondo   52.5
5 Orange Coast   49.25
6 Ventura   43.5
7 Chaffey   41.25
8 Canyons   37.23
9 Golden West   25.5
10 San Bernadino   21

Coaches
Antelope Valley-Dick Curtis
Canyons-Lee Corbin
Chaffey-Paul Iaeger
Cypress-Ray Haas
Dale Deffner-Golden West
Moorpark-John Keever
Mt. SAC-Bob Combs
Orange Coast-Vern Wagner
Rio Hondo-Ken Bos
San Bernadino-Don Seinturer
Ventura-Jerry Dunlap
Victor Valley-Gary Charles

Coach of the Year Nominees
John Keever-Moorpark and
Ken Bos-Rio Hondo

1976 South Regional
February 28, 1976

118
Joe Gonzales-East LA
Brad Morton-El Camino
Dan Hallinan-Grossmont
Jim Hamada-Palomar
Joaquin-Moldanado Cerritos

126
Ben Martinez-El Camino
Jerry Manckia-Grossmont
Aaron Thomas-Santa Ana
Mario Gardes-Cerritos
Tak Overmire-Palomar

134
Allen Willeman-El Camino
Jack Scruggs-Santa Ana
Paul Thompson-Cerritos
Dan Jacobson-Grossmont
Brian Canuda-Palomar

142
Marty Maciel-Cerritos
Jim Zeller-El Camino
Leonard Jacobson-Grossmont
Bob Northridge-Palomar
Tony Huscuja-East LA

150
Bill Cripps-El Camino
Jim Mattie-Grossmont
Don Barrios-Palomar
Robert Clair-S D Mesa
Jim Scott-Santa Ana

158
Ted Kelley-El Camino
Bob Zantos-Santa Ana
Mike Berger-Palomar
Ken Clark-Grossmont
Ralph Valli-East LA

167
Tony Fuertsch-Cerritos
Steve Draper-Santa Ana
Pete Grisafi-Grossmont
Don Zeller-El Camino
Don Hill-East LA

177
Robert Jones-Cerritos
Robert Maskell Southwestern
Glenn Thoreson-Palomar
Fred Gebart-S D Mesa
Keven Harvey-Santa Ana

190
Dennis Zabinsky-Palomar
Steve Hart-Cerritos
Tom Dorsey-Long Beach
Carlos Durazo-East LA

Heavyweight
Don Alamon-Santa Ana
Scott Moore-Grossmont
John Dineen-Palomar
Bart Nikoletish-Long Beach

Team Scores
1 El Camino 84.75
2 Cerritos 67.75
3 Grossmont 64.25
4 Palomar 62
5 Santa Ana 54.5
6 East LA 25
7 Southwestern 18.5
8 S D Mesa 18
8 Long Beach 18
10 LA Valley 4
11 LA City 3.5
12 Imperial Valley 2
13 Mira Costa 1.5
13 LA Trade Tech 1.5

Coaches
Cerritos-Hal Simonek
East LA-Bob Lander
El Camino-Dave Hengsteler
Grossmont-Don Rohrke
Long Beach-Jim Murphy
Palomar-John Woods
S D Mesa-Al Walker
Santa Ana-Frank Addleman
Southwestern-Art Stone

Coach of the Year Nominees
Dave Hengsteller-El Camino
and John Woods-Palomar

1976-77 North Central Regional
February 25, 1977 Bakersfield College

118
Robert Wurm-Yuba 2-1 *
Duane Fidel-Sacramento
Pete Gonzales-Bakersfield
Paul Bolanos-Fresno
Eddie Prance-S J Delta

126
Guy Reiley-Lassen 13-2
Brent Rocha-Modesto
William Gonzales-Bakersfield
Chris Ehrke-Sacramento
Carl Cox-Cuesta

134
Bill Jones-Sequoias 7-4
Robert Burkett-Modesto
Hal Delashaw-S J Delta
Primo Torres-Bakersfield
Brad Arvance-Fresno

142
Joe Lopez-Bakersfield 15-5
Craig Vejvoda-Sequoia
Jim Gagliardi-Modesto
Tim O'Kelly-American River
Neil Freeman-Fresno
Jim Martin-Sacramento

150
John Parreira-Modesta 12-8
Mario Betti-Sacramento
Rick Scicluna-Sierra
Andy Wilson-American River
Grover Lee-Shasta
Ted Hunter-Bakersfield

158
Bob Roberts-Cuesta 12-2
Don Johnston-Fresno
Doug Kepner-Sacramento
Kevin Erewin-American River
Dennis Brown-S J Delta
Ed Scantling-Sierra

167
Mark Hall-Allen Hancock 9-1
Dan Tyson-Modesto
Bob Grimes-Fresno
Dave Pacheco-Sacramento
Dixon Allen-American River
Al Castellanos-Sierra

177
Eugene Wais-Cuesta 4-3
Curt Wiendenhoefer-Fresno
Rich England-American River
Rudi Buurtschi-Modesto
Paul Trout-Yuba
Glenn Mosley-Bakersfield

190
Amas Scott-Fresno 10-5
George Smith-Allen Hancock
Norman Williams-Bakersfield
John Parrish-American River
Neal McClellan-Lassen
George Crawford-S J Delta

Heavyweight
Ken Harbuck-Ameri Riv F 1:52
Dave McKeehan-Bakersfield
Gary Weldon-Sierra
Mitch Bridenstine-Lassen
John Diaz-Fresno
Tom Martin-Merced

Most Outstanding Wrestler
Robert Wurm-Yuba

Team Scores
1 Modesto 87.25
2 Fresno 86.25
3 Bakersfield 86
4 American River 84.75
5 Cuesta 69.75
6 Sacramento 61
7 Lassen 45.75
8 Hancock 36.75
9 Sierra 33.75
10 Sequoia 33
11 S J Delta 29.5
12 Yuba 24.5
13 Shasta 9.5
14 Merced 3.5
Reedley, Porterville, Butte All 0

20 Teams in the tournament
Joe Lopez Bakersfield as of 2-25-77 34-4

1976-77 North Regional
February 25, 1977

118
Jesus Flores-Chabot
David Cotti-San Jose

126
Joel Chavez-Santa Jose
Garu Bocci San Mateo

134
Tyrone Rose-Dialo Valley
Mark Needham-Chabot
Bert Van Duzer-Redwoods

142
John Sylvia-Redwoods *
Brad Vadnais Chabot

150
Bill Wiley-Chabot
Mario Lomas-Ohlone

158
Kevin Dugan-Chabot
Bill Baker-Ohlone

Dave Phillips-Redwoods 4

167
Tony Brewer-Foothill
Tom Pender-Santa Jose

177
John Wilhite-Chabot
Jesus Aboytes-Cabrillo

190
Curtis Bledsoe-Chabot
Robert Ashue-Skyline

Heavyweight
Dave Shaw-Chabot
Craig Schoene-Skyline

Team Scores
1 Chabot
2 Diablo Valley
3 San Jose
4 Cabrillo
5 Ohlone

Result from the Amateur Wrestling News

John Sylvia was a Small College Champion

1976-77 South Central Regional

118
Dan LeMelle-Mt. SAC
Joe Young-Orange Coast

126
Mike Engle-Cypress
Dean Busk-Rio Hondo

134
Gerald Singh-Mt. SAC
Nick Restivo-Rio Hondo 2

142
Greg Okoorian-Cypress
John Blasez-Moorpark

Bob Saul-Rio Hondo 5
150
Rick Brazney-Cypress
Gary Murphy-Moorpark

158
Greg Johnson-Cypress
Ron Cota-Mt. SAC

Mike Schumm-Rio Hondo 5
167
Joe Barragan-MT. SAC
Jeff Camire-Orange Coast

177
Roy Austin-Cypress
Mark Vick-Golden West

190
Bob Allen-MT. SAC
Bob Prince-Cypress

Charles Ogle-Rio Hondo 4
Heavyweight
Lydell Harris-Cypress
Dave White-Chaffey

Nick Coats-Rio Hondo 5

Team Results
1 Cypress   161.25
2 Mt. SAC   120.75
3 Moorpark   100.25
4 Rio Hondo   70
5 Orange Coast 50.5

Results Found on the Rio Hondo Wrestling History and Amateur Wrestling News

1976-77 South Regional

118
Dan Hallinan-Grossmont
Edwin Dilbeck-Palomar
Dave Suarez-Cerritos 3

126
Joaquin Maldonado-Cerritos
Ben Martinez-El Camino

134
Alan Willeman-El Camino
Aaron Thomas-Santa Ana
Al Morita-Cerritos 3

142
Marty Maciel-Cerritos
Nathan Holland-Palomar

150
Bill Cripps-El Camino
Mike Burgher-Palomar

158
Rick Worel-Palomar
Pinto Parra-El Camino
Don Maciel-Cerritos 3

167
Glen Thoreson-Palomar
Mike Couch-Cerritos

177
Steve Draper-Santa Ana
Javier Romero-Southwestern

190
Don Hill-Santa Ana
Cam Herrick-Grossmont

Jon Lhli-Cerritos 4
Heavyweight
Allan Tanner-Palomar
Pat Devine-Cerritos

Team Results
1 Palomar   96
2 El Camino 75
3 Cerritos   64.5
4 Santa Ana 52.5
5 Grossmont 30.75

Results from the Cerritos Wrestling web page and Amateur Wrestling News

1977-78 North Central Regional
February 4, 1978 Allan Hancock

118
Pete Gonzalez-Bakersfield 4-2
Bob Delgado-Cuesta

126
William Gonzales-Bakfld 11-7
Charlie Chaney-Alan Hancock

134
Bob Tuner-Modesto 11-4
Jeff Hull-Bakersfield

142
Marlin Royal-Fresno*
Don Mills-Modesto*

150
Craig Vejvoda-Sequoias*

158

167

177
Bob Grimes-Fresno*

190
John Diaz-Fresno*

Heavyweight
Doug Severe-Modesto*
Casey Delliford-Shasta*
Larry Lee-Sequoias 9-3
Tom Van Arkel-Bakersfield

* Name from state results not in order – Bakersfield result is from the Bakersfield Wrestling History

Top four to state

Team Scores
1 Fresno 102.5
2 Modesto 96.5
3 Bakersfield 63.5
4 Sacramento 59.25
5 Shasta 58
6 A Hancock 49.25
7 Lassen 45.25
8 Cuesta 40.25
9 Sierra 29.5
10 Sequioa 26
11 A River 18.5
12 Yuba 17.5
13 Porterville 13.5
14 Merced 10.5
15 S J Delta 4
16 Butte 0

1977-78 North Regional
February 4, 1978

118

177

Co-Coach of the Year
Jim Sylvia-Redwoods
Mike Coawn-Ohlone

125

190

Team Results
1
2
3

134

Heavyweight

4
5
6
7
8

142

9
10
11
12 Redwoods

150

158

167

Rocky Harrison-Redwoods 2

1977-78 South Central Regional
February 4, 1978

118
Paul Sevillano-Rio Hondo

177

Most Outstanding Wrestler
Dean Busk-Rio Hondo

126
Dean Busk-Rio Hondo *

Walt McNichol-Rio Hondo 5
190

Team Results
1 Rio Hondo
2
3

134
Nick Restivo-Rio Hondo

Bill Sollars-Rio Hondo 5
Heavyweight

Result from the Rio Hondo Wrestling Guide

142

Bob Soul-Rio Hondo 5
150

158

167

Mike Schumm-Rio Hondo 5

1977-78 South Regional
February 4, 1978

118
Dave Suarez-Cerritos 1

126
Al Morita-Cerritos 1

134
Ed Delgado-Cerritos 2

142

Bob Legaspi-Cerritos 4
150

158

Rick Maciel-Cerritos 3

167
Bill Choate-Chabot 6-3

Mike Couch-Cerritos 3

177

Mike Miller-Cerritos 4
190
Jim Lhli-Cerritos 1

Heavyweight

Greg Tait-Cerritos 4

Team Scores
1
2
3

Results found on the Cerritos Wrestling web page

1978-79 North Regional
February 2, 1979

118
Steve Lutz-Ohlone

177
Rich Sykers-Diablo Valley
Roy Coudright-Chabot

Team Scores
1 Chabot   158.5
2 Diablo Valley 118.5
3 San Jose   110.75
4 West Valley   43.5
5 Ohlone   39
6 Santa Rosa   38
10 Foothill   36.5
11 Cabrillo   34.75
12 San Mateo   26
13 Canada   18
14 Skyline   17.5

126
Terry Burton-Chabot

190
Bruce Kopitar-Diablo Valley
Ron Freeman-Chabot

134
Cody Tanner-Chabot

Heavyweight
Tom Tomsen-Chabot
Mike Malkovich-Diablo Valley

No real order the results is from the state results

142
George Crower-San Jose

150
Lee Noble-West Valley

158
Eddie Carver-Chabot
Joey Guillroy-San Jose

167
Mike Roberson-Chabot
Ron Garcia-Diablo Valley

1978-79 North Regional
February 2, 1979

118
Steve Lutz-Ohlone

126
Terry Burton-Chabot

134
Cody Tanner-Chabot

142
George Crower-San Jose

150
Lee Noble-West Valley

158
Eddie Carver-Chabot
Joey Guillroy-San Jose

167
Mike Roberson-Chabot
Ron Garcia-Diablo Valley

177
Rich Sykers-Diablo Valley
Roy Coudright-Chabot

190
Bruce Kopitar-Diablo Valley
Ron Freeman-Chabot

Heavyweight
Tom Tomsen-Chabot
Mike Malkovich-Diablo Valley

Team Scores
1 Chabot   158.5
2 Diablo Valley   118.5
3 San Jose   110.75
4 West Valley   43.5
5 Ohlone   39
6 Santa Rosa   38
10 Foothill   36.5
11 Cabrillo   34.75
12 San Mateo   26
13 Canada   18
14 Skyline   17.5

No real order the results is from the state results

1978-79 North Regional
February 2, 1979

118
Steve Lutz-Ohlone

126
Terry Burton-Chabot

134
Cody Tanner-Chabot

142
George Crower-San Jose

150
Lee Noble-West Valley

158
Eddie Carver-Chabot
Joey Guillroy-San Jose

167
Mike Roberson-Chabot
Ron Garcia-Diablo Valley

177
Rich Sykers-Diablo Valley
Roy Coudright-Chabot

190
Bruce Kopitar-Diablo Valley
Ron Freeman-Chabot

Heavyweight
Tom Tomsen-Chabot
Mike Malkovich-Diablo Valley

Team Scores
1	Chabot	158.5
2	Diablo Valley	118.5
3	San Jose	110.75
4	West Valley	43.5
5	Ohlone	39
6	Santa Rosa	38
10	Foothill	36.5
11	Cabrillo	34.75
12	San Mateo	26
13	Canada	18
14	Skyline	17.5

No real order the results is from the state results

1978-79 South Central Regional
February 2, 1979

118

Karl Glover-Rio Hondo

126

Paul Tucker-Rio Hondo 2

134

142

150

Tim Kelley-Rio Hondo 3

158

Dan Mather-Rio Hondo

167

177

190

Jim Batson-Rio Hondo 2

Heavyweight

Calvin Kelly-Rio Hondo 2

Team Results
1
2 Rio Hondo
3

Results found on the Rio Hondo Wrestling History

1979 North Central Regional
February 2, 1979 Modesto College

118
Paul Bolanos Fresno 12-3
Fred Gonzalez Bakersfield

177
Mark Hall A Hancock 12-3
Marty Jones Bakersfield

Team Scores
1 Fresno   103.75
2 Bakersfield   99
3 Modesto   83.25
4 Sequoias   61.25

126

Mike Powell Sequoias Default
Glenn McCullough Bakfld 4

190

134

John McSwain Modesto 3-2
Jeff Hull Bakersfield 4

Heavyweight

Daniel Barrios Cuesta 5-2
Juan Lujan Bakersfield 4

142
Steve Nichell Bakersfield
Matt Clark Sacramento

150

158

167

Casey Cridelich Bakfd
Gary Wilds Sacramento 4

1979-80 South Central Regional
February 1, 1980

118
Ron Anaya-Cerritos 2
Fernando Venegas-Cypress
Bill Brookkens-Golden West
Mike Paulsen-Rio Hondo 4

126
Tony Ovalle-Rio Hondo
Mike Saucedo-Cypress
Bill Ball
Dave Serber-Santa Ana 4
Darryl Kimes-Golden West

134
Bob Wallender-Cerritos
John Ogata-Orange Coast

142

Tim Kelley-Rio Hondo 3

150
Bill Weiskopf-Cypress

158
Dan Mather-Rio Hondo*
Frank Bitetto-Cypress
Ed Thorp-Golden West

167
John White-Santa Ana Cris
Fuertsch-Cerritos
Jeff Hickok-Cypress
Todd Boyer-Golden West
Ted Martinez-Orange Coast

177
Dave Deal-Cerritos
Terry Todd-Golden West
Dennis Reed-Orange Coast

190
Jim Batson-Rio Hondo
Jack Fanning-Cypress
Cedric Reed-Orange Coast
Craig Theines-Cerritos

Heavyweight
Mitch Clark-Cypress
Darryl Davis-Golden West

Most Outstanding Wrestler
Dave Matter-Rio Hondo

Team Results
1 Rio Hondo
2
3 Cypress

Results found on the Rio Hondo Wrestling History

No real order from the Orange County Register

1980 North Central Regional
February 2, 1980 College of the Sequoias

118
Al Gutierrez-Sequoias 8-6
Fred Gonzales-Bakersfield
Robert Simpson-Sacram 12-8
Vic Tarkley-Lassen
Jeff McKay-Modesto
Tom Harautnlan-Fresno

123
Mike Powell-Sequoias 7-6
Darrell Harris
Percy Richards-Bakersfield
Kenny Tisdale-Delta Forfeit
Ty Angle-Modesto 6-1
Bruce Byerly-Sacramento

134
Glenn McCullough-Bakfld 6-4
Rod Lewis-Lassen
Tony Elinski-Sequoias 13-6
Rod Wright-Modesto
Bill Stansbury-Butte 6-2 OT
Rich Gross-Cuesta

142
Steve Nickell-Bakersfield 8-7
Charlie Chaney-Alan Hancock
Jim Valentine-Sequoias Def
Theo Beutler-Lassen
Loring Turrell-Sierra Forfeit
Rich Phillips-American River

150
Alvaro Cano-Sequoias 4-2
Tim Santos-Modesto
Mike Mills-Cuesta 5-3
John Evans-Lassen
Russ Lichti-Fresno Fall :46
Lawrence Bettencourt

158
Scott Teuscher Sacrament 7-1
Kelly Boyd-Cuesta
Allan Thacker-Sierra 15-11
Frankie Scott-Fresno
John Taylor-American Riv 5-3
Joe Knoblauch-Sequoias

167
Dave Allen-Butte 6-0 OT
Gary Wilson-Alan Hancock
Fred Ribeiro-Modesto 6-5
Darren Lee-Shasta
John Buford-Fresno 5-2
Tim Morres-Sierra

177
Marty Jones-Bakersfield 6-0
Dave Ernaga-Lassen
Robin Green-Fresno Forfeit
Richard Lawellin-S J Delta
Dennis Townsend-Sequoi 8-0
Fran O'Brian-Modesto

190
Mark Loomis-Sacrament 14-4
Bill Kropog-Sequoia
Lewis McNabb-Bakfld 17-0
Fred Hernandez-Modesto
Don Brantley-Fresno Fall 5:57
Ken Chastain-Butte

Heavyweight

Team Scores
1 Sequoias   128.25
2 Bakersfield 92.25
3 Lassen   88.75
4 Modesto   60.5
5 Sacramento   59.75

Records as of 2-2-1980
Robert Simpson 33-1
Mike Powell 32-2-1
Joshua Washington 36-2

Steve Nickell - Bakersfield College
1980 CCCAA 142lb-State Champion

1980-81 North Central Regional
January 30, 1981 Sierra College

118
Al Gutierrez-Sequoias 16-11
Robert Simpson-Sacrament
Victor Tanksley-Lassen 19-5
Vince Vanni-Porterville
126
Thom Harautuneian-Fres 4-3
Benjie Gutierrez-Sequoias
David Araini-S J Delta 13-8
   John Rucker
134
Brian Miller-Modesto F 7:06*
Rod Lemos-Fresno
Joseph Guerro-S J Delta 9-6
Dale Dow-Bakersfield
Tony Elinsky-Fresno
142
Ty McGuire-Sequoias 17-7
Brian Smith-Sierra
Lawrence Thompson-B F 4:50
Joe Pacello-Sacramento
150
Tim Santos-Modesto Fall 6:03
Airron Duckworth-Porterville
Allen Thacker-Sierra 9-8
Robert Frusetta-S J Delta
David Fry-Fresno
156
Gene Allison-Sequoias F 5:53
   Workman-Lassen
Lawrence Bettencourt-Si 11-4
Neal Focha-Lassen
167
Scott Teuscher Sacram 3-2 OT
   Welch-Sequoias
Randy Thacker-Sierra 13-8
Bill Laveille-Lassen

177
John Taylor-America Riv F:55
Dennis Townsend-Sequoias
Jim O'Brian-Modesto 11-6
Greg Reilly-Sacramento
190
Olivio Salazar-Modesto 11-3
Lewis McNabb-Bakersfield
Mike Allen-Butte 11-9
   Scott-Cuesta
Dan Castaneda-Fresno
Heavyweight
Joshua Washington-Seq 14-5
Dennis Martin-Bakersfield
Daniel Sodan-S J Delta 8-6
Mike Bond-Butte

Most Outstanding Wrestler
Brian Miller-Modesto
Coaches of the Year
Dave Adams-Sequoias
Dean Sesnsenbaugh-Modesto

Team Scores
1 Sequoias   137.5
2 Modesto   101.25
3 Sacramento   66.25
4 Bakersfield   60.25
5 S J Delta   56.75
6
7
8
9 Porterville
10 Fresno

Total 14 teams

1980-81 North Regional
January 30, 1981 Chabot College

118
Bruce Bennett-Chabot

177
Carl Newman-Skyline

Most Outstanding Wrestler
Lance Anzivine-Diablo Valley
Coaches of the Year
Zack Papachristos-Chabot and Bob Ericson-Diablo Valley

126
Cliff Gosse-Chabot

190
Ali Nazari-Skyline

Team Scores
1 Chabot   140.75
2 Diablo Valley 104.25
3 San Jose   85.5

134
Armondo Gonzalez-San Jose

Heavyweight
Roger Herrera-Chabot

Rocky Costa-Redwoods
142
Steve Markey-Chabot

Mike Rick-Redwoods 4
150
Woody Smith-Chabot

158
Lance Anzivine-Diablo Valley

Greg Small-Redwoods
167
Mike Hairston-Ohlone

1980-81 South Central Regional
January 30, 1981 Mt. San Antonio College

118
William Taylor-Golden West

Brian Heinselman-Moorpar 3

126
Mike Saucedo-Cypress

Brian Mills-Rio Hondo 4
134
Victor Lizama-Mt. SAC

Dave Barona-Moorpark 3

142
Tony Martin-Rio Hondo

150
Chris Cordovia-Moorpark *
Ray Hammond-Rio Hondo

158
Chris Schulz-Golden West
Rex Davis-Moorpark

Mike Bell-Rio Hondo 4
167
Steve Short-Ventura

177
Rob Mella-Orange Coast
Scott Crow-Rio Hondo

190
Jeff Stewart-Ventura

Brian Necke-Rio Hondo 4
Heavyweight
Joe Kaminski-Ventura
Craig Broderick-Rio Hondo

Terry Fredette Moorpark 4

Most Outstanding Wrestler
Chris Cordova-Moorpark
Coaches of the Year
John Keever-Moorpark and
Ken Bos-Rio Hondo

Team Scores
1 Moorpark   111.5
2 Rio Hondo   105
3 Mt. SAC   101.75

Moorpark results found on the Moorpark Wrestling Pressbook and the Rio Hondo Wrestling History

Others weight not given
Cerritos Wrestlers
Jeff Bowers 3
Tim Savoy 5
Randy Randall 4
Mark Ball 3

1980-81 South Regional
January 30, 1981 Palomar College

118
Scott Schneider-Cerritos

126
James Cortez-Pierce

134
Mike Grosberg-Palomar

142
Ken Jenkins-Palomar

150
David Knox-El Camino

158
John Holbrook-Palomar

167
Kerry Hiatt-Palomar

177
Louie Garcia-Chaffey

190
Mike Porcelli-San Diego

Heavyweight
Mike Van Hoven-El Camino

Most Outstanding Wrestler
Kerry Hiatt-Palomar
Coaches of the Year
John Woods-Palomar
Jeff Smith-Cerritos

Team Scores
1 Palomar   126
2 Cerritos   116
3 El Camino   106.25

1981–1982 South Central Regional
January 29, 1982 Moorpark College

118
Jose Martinez-Mt. SAC

Adrian Jacobo-Rio Hondo 4

126
Dan Ducan-Cypress

Henry Yturralde-Rio Hondo 3
Brian Heinselman-Moorpark
    Dinfing-Porterville

134

Dondi Teran-Rio Hondo 2
Ram Bryant-Cypress

142
Lee Patrick-Bakersfield 1
George Ishak-Rio Hondo 2

Frank Torres-Mt. SAC

150
Ray Hammond-Rio Hondo *
Larry Tevis-Ventura

158
Fred Little Bakersfield 1
Chris Cordova-Moorpark 2
Dave Nahay-Cypress
Mitch Pagano–Rio Hondo

167
Todd Stragler-Mt. SAC
Ray Cox-Bakersfield
Bob Campuzano-Cypress

177
Tim Olson-Mt. SAC
Randy Randell-Moorpark

190
James Blevins-Bakersfield 1
Wendell Valliere-Rio Hondo 2
Tom Kelley-Porterville

Heavyweight
Craig Broderick-Rio Hondo
Bill Pierce-Bakersfield 2

Most Outstanding Wrestler
Ray Hammond-Rio Hondo

Team Results
1 Rio Hondo   124.5
2 Cypress   98
3 Bakersfield 93
4 Moorpark   87
5 Porterville 78.25
6 Mt. SAC   77
7 Ventura   43.5
8 Cuesta   30

Moorpark results came from the Moorpark Wrestling Pressbook and the Rio Hondo Wrestling History, Bakersfield Wrestling History – others from state results

Others with no weight given
Moorpark Wrestlers
John McCarthy 4
Robert Connelly 5
Larry Cook 3
Greg Wendling 5
Jeff Collins 4

1982 North Central Regional
December 11, 1982

118
Wes Gaston-Sacramento

177
Bill Elbin-Sequoias

Team Scores
1 Modesto 76.75
2 Sequoias 61.50
3 Bakersfield 61.25
4 Sacramento 44.25
5 Sierra 42.25
6 S J Delta 41.25

126
Marty Gonzales-Sequoias

190
James Bivins Bakersfield
Troy Elmer-S J Delta

134
Tim Mattos-Butte

Heavyweight
Craig Edling-Modesto

142
Lee Patrick Bakersfield
Dan Casey-Modesto

150
Barry LaBass-Modesto

158
Fred Little Bakersfield
Barry Cole-Modesto

167
Steve Haxby-Butte

1982 North Regional
December 10, 1982 Skyline College

118
Brett McNamer-Diablo Valley

177
Vic Ceja-Chabot
Dale Delaney-Redwood 3-2
Herb Wheeler-Chabot 3

Team Scores
1 Chabot   120.5
2 Diablo Valley 55.5
3 West Valley   34.50
4 Skyline   31
5 Santa Rosa   12.75

126
John Leandro-Chabot

190
Tim Boyd-Chabot

Bryan Hyder-Redwoo F 5:20
4
Rob Prjnak-Cabrillo 5

134
Joe Triggs-Chabot

Heavyweight
Alonzo West-Chabot

Records as of 1-29-82
Greg Small-Redwood 31-8
Jack Horton-Redwood 21-3
Dale Delaney-Redwood 16-1

Rob Landergen-Redwood 6
142
Dave-Wood-Chabot

150
Chuck Justice-Chabot

Dan Sanchez-Redwood 5

158
Doug Carnation-Chabot

Greg-Small-Redwood 7-1 3
Jim Anderson-Diablo Valley 4

167
Tim Martire-Skyline
Sylvester Carver-Chabot 11-1
Jack Horton-Redwood 3

142- Dave Wood - Chabot 1982 *OW (Spring) and CA HOF Coach Zach Papachristos

1982 South Central Regional #1
December 10, 1982 Moorpark College

118
Jim Estrella-Rio Hondo * 1
Steve Martinez-Cypress

126

Brian Mills-Rio Hondo 2
Ram Bryant-Cypress
    Dinfing-Porterville

134

Dondi Teran 2
Ernie Geronimo-Bakersfield
Danny Nunes-Cuesta

142
Lee Patrick Bakersfield
George Ishak-Rio Hondo 2
Glen Evens Cypress
Todd Giurlani-Bakersfield
150
Mitch Pagano-Rio Hondo
Richie Sinnott-Bakersfield
Dave Nahay-Cypress
Larry Tevis-Ventura
158
Fred Little-Bakersfield
Jack Ward-Cypress
Barry Cole-Cypress
Frank Torres-Mt. SAC
Robert Connelly-Moorpark
Cres Cordova-Moorpark
167
Kent Davis-Mt. SAC
Bob Camposano-Cypress

177
Todd Stralger-Mt. SAC
Craig Bogard-Cypress
Dan Castaneda-Bakersfield
Tim Olson-t SAC
    Randall-Moorpark
190
James Bevins-Bakersfield
Scott Crow-Rio Hondo
Dana Ott-Rio Hondo

Heavyweight
John Smith-Cerritos
Jim Traffenstedt-Bakersfield

Most Outstanding Wrestler
Jim Estrella-Rio Hondo

Team Results
1 Rio Hondo   124.5
2 Cypress   98
3 Bakersfield   93
4 Moorpark   87
5 Porterville   78.25
6 Mt. SAC   77
7 Ventura   43.5
8 Cuesta   30

Result from state results in no order and found on the Rio Hondo, Cerritos and Bakersfield Wrestling History

1982 South Regional
January 29, 1982 Cerritos College

118
Scott Schneider-Cerritos
Alex Duarte-Golden West
Chris Laudise-Palomar

126
Dan Hopkins-Santa Ana *
Joe Ismay-Palomar
Ron Anaya-Cerritos 3

134
Jon Vega-Cerritos 1
Roger Blackshear-El Camino
David Avina Palomar
James Cortez-Pierce

142
Doug Ruiz-Cerritos
Ken Jenkins-Palomar
Dan Hartano-El Camino
Doug Ruiz-Cerritos

150
Jeff Boyko-Pierce
    Sims-Palomar
    Glynn-San Diego
Clark Cavanaugh-Cerritos 4

158
Ky Segfugash-El Camino
    Hall Golden-West
Larry Mowatt-Cerritos 3
Kie Fortier-Pierce

167
Ken Battle-Cerritos 1
Steve Glore-Golden West

177
Phil Dunford-Cerritos 1
John Head-Palomar

190
Jeff Young-Palomar
Steve McGee-San Diego
    Pat Burns

Heavyweight
Tim Reilly-Golden West
Steve Cataifamo-Cerritos
Marcus Johnson-Santa Ana

Most Outstanding Wrestler
Dan Hopkins-Santa Ana

Team Scores
1	Cerritos	87.75
2	Palomar	69.25
3	Golden West	46
4	El Camino	43.25
5	San Diego	32.75
6	Pierce	23.25
7	Santa Ana	20.75
8	Imperial Valley	2

No real order results from the state – Cerritos results from the Cerritos webpage

1982 South Regional
December 10, 1982 San Marcos College

118
Steve Martinez-Cypress *1
Tony Trabucco-El Camino
Alex Duart-Golden West
Paul Okimoto-Cerritos 4
Scott Schneider- Cerritos

126
Brian Mills-Rio Hondo 2
Jack Mejazi-El Camino 3
Ram Bryant-Cypress
Dan Duncan-Cypress
Jon Love-Santa Ana
Ron Sigler-Palomar
Dan Hopkins-Santa Ana
Ray Anaya-Cerritos

134
Joe Ismay-Palomar
John Verga-Cerritos
Josi Soni-Cerritos 3
Roger Blackshear-El Camino
David Avina-Palomar

142
Glen Evans-Cypress
Tom Valentine-Palomar
Doug Ruiz-Cerritos

150
Gary Williams-Cerritos
Dave Nahay-Cypress
Les Lewis-El Camino
Clark Cavanaugh-Cerritos
    Sims-Palomar
    Glynn-San Diego

158
Jack Ward-Cypress
Barry Cole-Cypress
Anthony Porcelli-San Diego
Ky Segfugash El Camino
    Hall-Golden West
Larry Mowatt-Cerritos

167
Chris Duran-Cerritos 1
Steve Glore-Golden West
Steve Camposano-Cypress

177
Craig Bogard-Cerritos
Dave Virik-Palomar
Phil Dunford-Cerritos
John Head-Palomar

190
Jeff Young-Palomar
Chris Roll-Santa Ana

Heavyweight
John Smith-Cerritos
Ernie Ortega-Palomar

Most Outstanding Wrestler
Steve Martinez-Cypress

Team Scores
1 Palomar   91.5
2 Cypress   88.25
3 Cerritos   37.5
4 San Diego City 23.5

Others
El Camino
Golden West
Imperial Valley
Santa Ana

Not in any order names from state results – some information from Rio Hondo, Cerritos Wrestling History

1983 South Central Regional

118

Moses Martin-Rio Hondo 2
Erine Neri-Moorpark 3

126

Tony Ramires Bakersfield
Aaron Jackson-Moorpark 2
Zalen Liley-Rio Hondo 3

134

Ernie Geromino Bakersfield

142

Scott Palmer-Rio Hondo

Tom Brekke-Moorpark 3

150

Mike Ponce-Rio Hondo 2

158

Dan Van Brabant-Rio Hond 3

167

Frank Barajas-Moorpark 2
Dan Rodriguez-Rio Hondo 3

177

190

Heavyweight

Team Results
1
2
3
4 Rio Hondo
5 Bakersfield   47.5

Moorpark results from the Moorpark Wrestling Pressbook and the Rio Hondo Wrestling History, Bakersfield College Wrestling History

Others with no weight given
Moorpark Wrestlers
Joe Hernandez   2
Ivan Marpel   4
Dan Martin   2
Vicente Agular 4
Ken Resnick   4
Allan Paicius   3

1984 South Central Regional

118

Tim Atkinson-Moorpark 2
Wynn Ray-Bakersfield 3

126

Pete Clemment-Moorpark 3

Tony Ramirez-Bakersfield 5
134

James Hembree-Bakersfield 3

142

Brooke Ashjian-Bakersfield 4
150

Paul Arbon-Moorpark 2

Mike Lathrop-Bakersfield 4
158

Dean Pfutzenreuter-Bakfld 3

167

Keith Hodges-Bakersfield 3

177

Blake Garnand-Bakersfield 4
190

Emmitt Flores-Bakersfield 3

Heavyweight

Team Results
1
2
3
4
5 Bakersfield   49

Moorpark results found on the Moorpark Wrestling Pressbook and Bakersfield results on Bakersfield Wrestling History

Other with no weight from Moorpark
Ivan Marpel   2
Joe Lansden   4

1984 South Regional

118

177

Team Results
1
2
3

126

190

4 Rio Hondo

John Brown-Rio Hondo 2

Results Found on the Rio Hondo Wrestling History

Richard Martinez-Rio Hondo

134

Heavyweight

142

Scott Palmer-Rio Hondo 3

150

158

Homero Sanin-Rio Hondo 4

167

1985 South Central Regional

118
John Esquivel-Rio Hondo*
Ray Esparza-Moorpark 2

126

Arine Bautista-Moorpark 3

134

John Hidaka-Rio Hondo 4
142

Ruben Chavez-Rio Hondo 4
150
Al Martinez-Rio Hondo

Eric Cortez-Moorpark 3

158

167
Brain Bennett-Moorpark
Robert Rico-Rio Hondo

177

190

Heavyweight

Most Outstanding Wrestler
John Esquivel-Rio Hondo

Team Results
1
2
3
4
5 Rio Hondo

Moorpark results found on the Moorpark Wrestling Pressbook and the Rio Hondo Wrestling History and the Rio Hondo Wrestling History

Others weight not given
Moorpark Wrestlers
Kurt Mathey   4
Jeff Butler   3
Joe DePrio   3

1986 South Central Regional

118

Keith Hernandez-Moorpark 2

126

Ray Esparza-Moorpark 1

134

147

Steve Fuess-Moorpark 2

150

158

167

177

190

Ross Boomhower-Moorpk 3

Heavyweight

Team Results
1
2
3

Moorpark found on the Moorpark Wrestling Pressbook

Others no weight given
Moorpark Wrestlers
Kurt Mathy   2
Brian Bennett   2
Ali Rahnavardi   3
Paul Delgado   4

1986 South Regional

118

Gus Gutierrez-Rio Hondo

126

134
Arnold Alpert Santa Ana

142

Eddie Solis-Reo Hondo

150

158

Jay Martinez-Rio Hondo

167

Eric Espinal-Rio Hondo

177

John Geanakos-Rio Hondo

190

Heavyweight

James Varnum-Rio Hondo

Team Results
1
2 Rio Hondo
2

Results found on the Rio Hondo Wrestling History Results from the Santa Ana Program

1987 South Central Regional

118
Luis Nebel-Rio Hondo

177

Jay Martinez-Rio Hondo 3

Most Outstanding Wrestler
Scott Schumm-Rio Hondo

126

190
Mark Reimers-Rio Hondo

Team Results
1
2 Rio Hondo
3
4
5 Bakersfield   41

134

Richard Caballero-Rio Hondo

Heavyweight

Michael Tellez-Rio Hondo 3

Results found on the Rio Hondo Wrestling History

142

150
Marty Kouyoumtjian- Hondo

158
Scott Schumm-Rio Hondo *

167

John Geanakos-Rio Hondo 4

1987 South Regional

118

126
Bo Leyva Rancho Santiago

134

142

150

158
Denny Furnish R Santiago

167
Matt Fletcher R Santiago

177

184

190

Heavyweight

Team Results
1
2
3
4

Rancho Santiago result found on the Rancho Santiago Program

1988 South Central Regional
December 3, 1988 Rio Hondo College

118
Robert Kawamura-Rio Honda
Eric Millsap-Moorpark
Hugh Northington-Bakfld

126
Tom Goodman-Bakersfield
Bill Montgomery-Cypress
    Yosteum-Mt. SAC
Sheldon Kim-Rio Hondo

134
Doug Haring-Cypress
Lewis Nebel-Rio Hondo
Martin Cisneros-Mt. SAC

142
Serge Mezheritsky-Moorpark
Dante Terramani-Rio Hondo
Mokie McGee-Bakersfield

150
Ralph Rucker-Cypress
Scott Herndon-Bakersfield
Oscar Rodriguez-Rio Hondo

158
Art Orozco-Cypress
Manuel Gallegos-Moorpark
Lane Stapp-Bakersfield
Eddie Garcia Rio Hondo

167
Greg Monteith-Cypress
    Acuna-San Bernadino
Polo Ornelas-Rio Hondo

177
Veto Becerra-Cypress
Luis Castro-Bakersfield
Travis Roquet-Rio Hondo

190
Carsen Wollert-Moorpark
Leo Garnand-Cypress
    Freeman-San Bernadino
Fred Myers-Rio Hondo

Heavyweight
Vince Plymire-Moorpark
Randy Gonzales-Cypress
Derrick Cooper-Mt. SAC
Todd Beatse-Rio Hondo

Most Outstanding Wrestler
Robert Kawamura-Rio Hondo
Coach of the Year
Mike Flook-Cypress

Team Scores
1 Cypress   96
2 Moorpark   85.25
3 Rio Hondo   57.75
4 Bakersfield   46
5 Mt. SAC   13.5
6 San Bernadino   13

Others no weights given
Diego Pena 4 Moorpark
Sam Marquez 4 Moorpark

1988 South Regional
December 3, 1988 Cerritos College

118
Casey Hankin-Palomar
   Iwanagas-Rancho Sant
     Rabata-El Camino

126
Don Garrett-l Camino
Fred Mora-Rancho Santiago
   Besterlaia-Golden West

134
Armando Morales-Cerritos
Bret Fry Rancho-Santiago
   Woodbury-Golden West

142
Antonio McGee-Cerritos
   Dallas-Golden West
Mike Saletta-Palomar

150
Gordan Stacer-Cerritos
R J Fairless-Palomar
Trent Kenney-Golden West

158
Aaron Gaier-Palomar
  Torres Golden-West
    Everett-San-Diego

167
Chad Sessions-Rana Santiago
Carl Perce-El Camino
Brian Millun-Palomar

177
Matt Hoffman-Golden West
Chuck Leptich-Palomar
   Grease-Rancho Santiago

190
Tedd Williams-Cerritos
Raab Rydeen-Palomar
Ken Cominsky-Ranc Santiago

Heavyweight
Hossein Kalabi-Ranc Santiago
Nick Barrios-Palomar
    Salinas-Cerritos

Team Scores
1	Palomar	78
2	Rancho Santiago	68.5
3	Cerritos	62.5
4	Golden West	52
5	El Camino	31.5
6	San Diego	5

1989 North Central Regional

118
Brian Ramirez-Fresno
Jim Feckner-Sierra
Steve Munson-Modesto
Tony Araon-Sacramento

126
Brad East-Fresno
Hugo Culebro-Modesto
Shann Inman-Sierra
Tony Fulwider-Sacramento

134
John Petty-Fresno
Steve Hillier-Butte
Shawne Silvia-Sacramento
Brian Johnston-Sierra

142
Ray Rangel-Fresno
Sigurd Asp-Sacramento
Jose Juarez-Modesto
Jon Hamel-Sierra

150
Darren Stauts-Sierra
Scott Saltz-Sacramento
Kelvin Olivas-Fresno
Chad Allen-Butte

158
Ociel Zarate-Fresno
Chopper Melo-Modesto
Clint Burch-Sacramento
John Hittle-S J Delta

167
Pal Laneg-Modesto
John Brook-Fresno
Todd Carlson-Sacramento
Erin Mankins-Butte

177
Robert Zapata-Fresno
Vance Rea-Modesto
Mitchel Evans-S J Delta
Deron Knarr-Sierra

190
Glenn Nye-Butte
Jack Sperry-Modesto
Mike Morin-Fresno
No Entry

Heavyweight
Brian Ormson-Sacramento
Ken Fontes-Fresno
Mike Rodgers-Butte
Tony Golic-Sierra

Team Scores
1 Fresno   110
2 Modesto   60
3 Sacramento   51.25
4 Sierra   35
5 Butte   29
6 S J Delta   6

Coaches
Butte-Larry Turner
S J Delta-Larry Jones
Fresno-Bill Musick
Modesto-Lee Elrler
Sacramento-Dave Pacheco

1989 North Regional

118
Albert Lelonde-Lassen
Brando Keosky-Cuesta
Clint Hunter-Santa Rosa
Ralph Shoukry-West Valley

126
Maurice Hernandez-Lassen
Juan Padilla-West Valley
Paul Hunt-Cuesta
Kirk Wheeler-Diablo Valley

134
Shawn McGhee-Lassen
John Peavier-Skyline
Luis Salcido-West Valley
B. Fortenbaugh-Cuesta

142
Chris Lovato-West Valley
Russ Allyn-Lassen
Reuben Tomayo-Skyline
Sean Brooks-Cuesta

150
Robert Nieto-West Valley
Casey Rhyan-Diablo Valley
Billy Reid-Lassen
Rod Thompson-Chabot

158
Todd Burk-Lassen
Jim Grundler-Cuesta
Brian Swisher-Diablo Valley
Carlos Salazar-West Valley

167
Kevin Ivie-Cuesta
Matt Davis-Lassen
Dudley Perry-West Valley
Dan Coffin-Diablo Valley

177
Torry Clemers-Lassen
Robert Hogue-Cuesta
Keith Spataro-Skyline
Alfed Fontes-Chabot

190
Terry Kennedy-Lassen
Rodney Harr-Cuesta
K. Walukiewicz-West Valley
Adam Aikman-Santa Rosa

Heavyweight
Abram Salazar-Lassen
Tony Barajas-West Valley
Steve Carlson-Cuesta
Kevin Phillips-Chabot

Team Scores
1 Lassen   116
2 West Valley   67
3 Cuesta   66
4 Diablo Valley   24
5 Skyline   19
6 Santa Rosa   10
7 Chabot   9

Coaches
Chabot-Steve Siroy
Cuesta-Gary Meissner
Diablo Valley- Cliff Hatch
Lassen-Dave Foster
Santa Rosa-Jake Fitzpatrick
Skyline-Lee Allen
West Valley-Jim Root

1989 South Central Regional

118
Sam Lopez-Cypress
Delfino Ochoa-Moorpark
Pedro Fambona-Bakersfield
Jim Garcia-Rio Hondo

126
Bill Scannell-Moorpark
Pete Gomez-Rio Hondo
Brian Bertrand-Cypress
Steve Ward-Bakersfield

134
Robby Cook-Moorpark
Ben Mauriello-Bakersfield
Vincent Mayorga-S Bernard
Tony Hernandez-Rio Hondo

142
Serg Mezheritsky-Moorpark
Efrian Gonzalez-Mt. SAC
Doug Haring-Cypress
Ray Manchaca Bakersfield

150
Derek Patton Bakersfield
Neil Truax-Mt. Sac
Oscar Rodriguez-Rio Hondo
Chris Malavar-Cypress

158
Mokie McGhee-Bakersfield
Rey Molina-Mt. SAC
Pete Lutz-Moorpark
Eddie Garcia Rio Hondo

167
Greg Monteith Cypress
Ty Stricker-Bakersfield
Pete Atwater-Moorpark
Tony Chapa-Rio Hondo

177
Tony Flores-Moorpark
Jim Froehlich-Bakersfield
Mike Robles-Cypress
John Beresford-S Bernardino

190
Carson Wollert-Moorpark
Ken Stegall-Cypress
Steve Shearer-Bakersfield
Derk Hamilton-San Berdo

Heavyweight
George Anderson-Bakersfield
Trevor Hargrave-Cypress
Don Young-Moorpark
Eric Cooper-Mt. SAC

Team Scores
1 Moorpark   88.75
2 Bakersfield 81.25
3 Cypress   64.25
4 Mt. SAC   30.5
5 Rio Hondo   12.5
6 S Bernardino 4.5

Coaches
Moorpark-John Keever
Bakersfield-Bill Kalivas

1989 South Regional

118
Eric LeGarreta-Golden West
Kyle Onaga-El Camino
Ken Workman=Cerritos
Ravi Ramsamodj-Ra Santiago

126
Orlando Montero-Cerritos
Sam Bailey-Palomar
Pat Kinney Rancho-Santiago
Pat Santo-Golden West

134
Chris Winkler-Palomar
Jorge Montero-Cerritos
Jeff Combs-Rancho Santiago
Augie Hooker-San Diego

142
Antonio McKee-Cerritos
Rusty Espinoza-Ran Santiago
Frank Milsap-Palomar
Danny Merlino-Golden West

150
Ron Fairless-Palomar
Mario Preciado-Cerritos
Craig Garriott-El Camino
Jack Pacheco-Ranch Santiago

158
Aaron Gaier-Palomar
Tom Henderson-Cerritos
Ryan Owings-Ranch Santiago
Jerry Decker-El Camino

167
Carl Pierce-Cerritos
Chris Shaul-Golden West
Chuck Lepyich-Palomar
John Prefontaine-El Camino

177
Steve Clemmer-Palomar
Marc Aguirre-Ranch Santiago
Russell Corbin-Golden Valley
Gabriel Garcia-Cerritos

190
Ted Williams-Cerritos
Phil Myer-Golden West
Ben Rice-El Camino
Antonio DaSilva-Palomar

Heavyweight
Robert Avila-El Camino
Phil Jones-Palomar
Chris Yagerlener-Ra Santiago
Mike Harris-San Diego

Team Scores
1 Cerritos   83.5
2 Palomar   80.5
3 R Santiago   42
4 Golden West   38.75
5 El Camino   38.5
6 San Diego City 6

1990 North Central Regional
December 1, 1990

118
Brian Ramirez-Fresno
Erin Razo-Lassen
Terry Munson-Modesto
Robert Gonzales-Gavilan

126
Albert LaLonde-Lassen
Jeff Barry-Gavilan
David Gobeli-Fresno
Donnie Fontana-Modesto

134
Shawn McGhee-Lassen
Angelo Gama-Modesto
Mike Ortega-Fresno
Scott Winn-Sierra

142
Greg Valencia-Lassen *
Ralph Olivas-Fresno
Howie Bair-Sierra
Tim Luis-Modesto

150
Country Taylor-Lassen
Rex Rabine-Modesto
Ismael Quintana-Fresno
Craig Sweeney-Sierra

158
Marcus Boness-Lassen
Heath Heapt-Fresno
Jorge Mena-Gavilan
Chopper Mello-Modesto

167
Todd Burk-Lassen
John Wallace-Butte
Doug Smith-Fresno
Deron Knarr-Sierra

177
Scott Sperry-Modesto
Richard Estrada-Fresno
Keith Craig-Sacramento
Jason Zubieta-Lassen

190
Hercules Ward-Lassen
Matt Scanavino-Sacramento
Mike Morin-Fresno
Curt Maddon-Sierra

Heavyweight
Lamar Washington-Lassen
Jesse Frost-Modesto
Mike Rogers-Butte
Joe Islas-Gavilan

Most Outstanding Wrestler
Greg Valencia-Lassen

Team Scores
1 Lassen   113
2 Fresno   70.5
3 Modesto   57.75
4 Gavilan   25
5 Sierra   22.5
6 Sacramento   17
7 Butte   13.5

1990 North Regional
December 1, 1990

118
Leroy Rivers-Diablo Valley
Clint Hunter-Santa Rosa
David Dawal-Chabot
Ralph Shoukry-West Valley

126
Al Reyes West-Valley
Brandon Keosky-Cuesta
Dennis Hunter-Santa Rosa
James Wang-Chabot

134
Paul Hunt-Cuesta
Gustavo-Ceja Skyline
Carlos Padilla-West Valley
Pedro Loaiza-Chabot

142
John Peavier-Skyline
B Fortunbaugh-Cuesta
Pete Hedrick-West Valley
Kyle Behmiander-Diablo

150
Jorge Lopez-Santa Rosa
Tyler Burbank-Cuesta
Rodney Thompson-Chabot
Luis Salcido-West Valley

158
Clark Conover-Chabot
Brian Swisher-Diablo Valley
Gung Lee-West Valley
John Giufere-S J Delta

167
Kevin Ivie-Cuesta *
Craig Doerfert-Diablo Valley
Joe Ciprian-West Valley
Greg Mack-Chabot

177
Shawn Slaven-Cuesta
Dan Corah-West Valley
Dennis Weibe-S J Delta
Aaron Bach-Diablo Valley

190
Keith Spataro-Skyline
Steve Bach-Chabot
Danny Stonebarger Dia Valley
Rodney Harr-Cuesta

Heavyweight
Luis Recio-Cuesta
Tyron Smith-Santa Ros
Bill Davis-West Valley
Ron Spataro-Skyline

Most Outstanding Wrestler
Kevin Ivie-Cuesta

Team Scores
1 Cuesta   83
2 West Valley   63.5
3 Chabot   48.75
4 Diablo Valley 48.25
5 Skyline   41.5
6 Santa Rosa   40
7 S J Delta   12

1990 South Central Regional
December 1, 1990 Bakersfield College

118
Sam Lopez-Cypress 6-5
Billy Scannell-Moorpark
Tommy Gallegos-San Ber 9-3
Keith Richards-Golden West

126
Delfino Ochoa-Moorpark 8-5
Anthony Hamelett-San Berna
Hugh Northington-Bak 6-1
Bryon Schultz-Cypress

134
Ben Mauriello-Bakfld F 2:40
Derek Hele-Golden West
Richard Allen-Cypress 6-0
Hiep Hong-Rio Hondo

142
Rob Cook-Moorpark 10-4
Ray Salazar-Bakersfield
Brent Holmes-Cypress 2-0
Kevin Burgess-Golden West

150
Scott Herndon-Bakfld 6-2
John Luksa-San Bernardino
Ray Castellamos-Rio Ho 10-8
Wade Caddin-Moorpark

158
Neil Mason-Moorpark 11-3
Dan Kirger-Golden West
Ty Stricker-Bakersfield 18-4
Jose Lopez-Rio Hondo

167
Brandon Procter-Mt SAC 8-4
Mike Biss Golden-West
Pete Lutz-Moorpark 19-6
Brandon Rogers-Bakersfield

177
Phil Guerrero-Moorpark 3-2
Luis Castro-Bakersfield
Leo Perez-Rio Hondo 17-5
Saul Lopez-Cypress

190
Ken Seagall-Cypress Fall 4:40
Tommy Flores-Moorpark
Omar Delgado-Rio Hondo 2-0
Russell Corbin-Golden West

Heavyweight
Fred Ruiz-Mt. SAC Fall 3:30
John Woltz-Bakersfield
Tony Flores-Moorpark Def
    Hargrave-Cypress

Team Scores
1 Moorpark   82.5
2 Bakersfield 68.5
3
4

Others
Cypress
San Bernardino
Cypress
Rio Hondo
Golden West

1990 South Regional
December 1, 1990

118
Jason Booth-Rancho Santiago
Calixto Jimenez-East LA
Kevin Mabry-Palomar
Mike Molina-Cerritos

126
Orlando Montero-Cerritos*
D Uyematsu-El Camino
Pat Kenny-Palomar
Lupe Jimenez-East LA

134
Abraham-Sanchez Palomar
Bo Leyva-Ranch Santiago
Ken Prefontaine-El Camino
Bak Pheng-Cerritos

142
Dusty Harless-Palomar
Augie Hooker-San Diego
John Hueter-Ranch Santiago
Troy Monge-Cerritos

150
Dondi Terramani-East LA
Leman Wells-Cerritos
Daryle Brenner-Palomar
David Piquette-Ran Santiago

158
Richard Freeman-Palomar
Ryan Owings-Ran Santiago
Doug Hammond-Cerritos
Joe Black-El Camino

167
Eddie Luna-Palomar
Polo Ornelas-Cerritos
John Prefontaine-El Camino
John Serrato-Ranch Santiago

177
Monday-Eguabok East LA
Willis Bangham-Cerritos
Joe Falk-Palomar
Matt Luker-Ranch Santiago

190
Rick Herman-El Camino
Eric Johnson-Palomar
Tom Proprosky-Ranc Santiago
Scott Lawson-Cerritos

Heavyweight
Mike Purnell-Palomar
Art Sanchez-Cerritos
Jon Sprague-Rancho Santiago
    Hudson-San Diego

Most Outstanding Wrestler
Orlando Montero-Cerritos

Team Scores
1 Palomar   86
2 Cerritos   71.5
3 R Santiago   55.5
4 East LA   42.75
5 El Camino   33
6 San Diego   14.5

1991 North Central Regional
December 7, 1991

118
Mike Fore-Santa Rosa

126
Jeff Hobart-Sacramento
Eric La Garreta-Fresno

134
Ben Ervin-Fresno
Angelo Gama-Modesto
Jon Peterson-Santa Rosa

142
Dustin Riley-Fresno
Chad Lavezzo-Sacramento

150
Randy Moti-Fresno
Vance Wheatly-Sacramento

158
Heath Heapt-Fresno
Chris Anderson-Modesto

167
Luke Corona-Gavilan
Lance Thurman-Sacramento
Ben Van Staavern-Modesto

177
Ryan Miller-Sacramento

190
Todd Parham-Sacramento
Clint Madden-Sierra

Heavyweight
Ed Neal-Fresno
Bob O'Diorne-Santa Rosa
John Meade-Modesto

Team Results
1
2
3

Coaches
Sacramento-Dave Pacheco
Sierra-John Horrillo
Modesto-Lee Ehrler
Fresno-Bill Musick
Santa Rosa-Jake Fitzpatrick
Gavilan-Zeke Contreras

No real order in the results the names are taken from the state results

1991 North Regional
December 7, 1991

118
Fernando Garcia-Cuesta Paul Gilman-West Valley

126
Andy Norden-West Valley Dave Dawal-Chabot

134
Richard Gutierrez- West Valley
Gus Ceja-Skyline
Chris Pena-Cuesta

142
Marcial Cruz-West Valley
Geof Hayden-Diablo Valley

150
Kyle Behmlander-Diablo Valley

158
Cung Lee-West Valley
Wendell Jefferson-Chabot

167
Clark Conover-Chabot

177
Trent Williams-Cuesta
Dan Corah-West Valley

190
Dan Stonebarger-Diablo Valley
Richard Garcia-West Valley

Heavyweight

Team Results
1
2
3

Coaches
Diablo Valley-Bill Martell
West Valley-Jim Root
Chabot-Steve Siroy
Skyline-Lee Allen
Cuesta-Gary Meissner
S Joaquin Delta-Dean Heath

No real order of results the results were from the state results

1991 South Central Regional
December 7, 1991

118
Valo Barajas-Moorpark
Steve Ward-Bakersfield

126
Anthony Hamlett-Cerritos
Brad Miya-Moorpark

134
Albert Morales-Cerritos
Richard Delselva-Moorpark

142
Troy Monge-Cerritos
Chris Camarena-Moorpark

150

Homer Ruiz-Cerritos 3

158
Leman Wells-Cerritos
Kent Davis-Mt. SAC
Neal Mason-Moorpark

167
Josh Gale-Cypress

Steve Egg-Cerritos 3
Walter Muirhead-Moorpark

177

Manfred Blum-Cerritos 2
Richard Aguila-Rio Hondo
Todd Hoult-Moorpark
Mike Parcells-Cypress

190
Phil Guerrero-Moorpark

Heavyweight

Dan Bracamonte-Cerritos 2
Adan Flores-Moorpark
Tom Beavers-Bakersfield

Team Results
1
2 Cerritos
3

Cerritos results from Cerritos Wrestling web page – All other are not in any order taken from state results

Coaches
Bakersfield-Bill Kalivas
Cypress-Mike Flook
Cerritos-Jeff Smith
Moorpark-John Keever
Rio Hondo-John Rosales
Mt. SAC-Fred Burri

1991 South Regional
December 7, 1991

118
Jason Booth-R Santiago
Tom Gallegos-San Bernadino
Lkaika Molina-Palomar

126
Steve Morales-San Bernadino
Mike Wilkey-Palomar

134

142
Raul Hurta-Palomar
Lee Heigi-Golden West

150
Dustin Harless-Palomar
Kenny Richards-Golden West
Wayne Blasingame-El Camino

158
Damian Botero-El Camino

167
Erick Gaunt-El Camino
Dan Kriger-Golden West

177
Monday Equabar-East LA
Todd Falk-Palomar

190
Eric Johnson-Palomar
Leo Perez-East LA

Heavyweight
Josh Gormley-El Camino
Brain Tomazic-Ranc Santiago
Phil Martinez-Palomar

Most outstanding Wrestler
Monday Eguabar-East LA

Team Results
1
2
3

Coaches
Palomar-Joe Ismay
San Bernadino-Bobby Vargas
Golden West-Dale Deffner
El Camino-Tom Hazell
Rancho Santiago-Gary de Beaubien
East LA-Ben Bohlander

Results is in no real order
results comes from the state results
Santa Ana result from the Santa Ana Program
No weights given first place
David Vizzini-Rancho Santiago
Brian Burgess-Rancho Santiago

Monday Equabar
East Los Angeles - 1991

1992 South Regional

118
Jesse Espinosa-Cerritos 1

126
David Niedringhaus R Santai

Rudy Garcia-Cerritos 4
134
Brian Burgess

Mark Cody-Cerritos 5
142

Sal Raza-Cerritos 5
150
Kevin Burgess R Santiago

Homer Ruiz-Cerritos 4
158
Rod Ludington-Cerritos 1

167

Jesse Bueno-Cerritos 2

177

James Hill-Cerritos 5
190
Brian Tomazic R Santiago

Hicham Semaan-Cerritos 3

Heavyweight

Matt Deller-Cerritos 4

Most Outstanding Wrestler
Jesse Espinosa-Cerritos

Team Results
1 Cerritos
2
3

Cerritos Result found on
Cerritos Wrestling web page
Rancho Santiago results from
the Rancho Santiago Program

**1993 North Regional
Modesto Junior College**

118
Orlando DeCastroverde-Cues
Victor DeLaCruz-Fresno
Luis Alejo-Gavilan
Dave Benning-Modesto
Brian Kanakaris-Skyline
Jeremy Petterson-Sacrament
125
Yero Washington-Fresno
Gus Banuelos-West Valley
Danny Hernandez-Cuesta
Kevin Carter-Skyline
Josh Augusto-Modesto
Lance Wargo-Santa Rosa
Ruben Modesto-S J Delta
Scott Ozawa Sacramento *
134
Detren Gant-Fresno
Aaron Reeves-Sacramento
Saul Gomez-West Valley
Sergio Mar-Gavilan
Vince Elliott-Modesto
Chris Pena-Cuesta
Dugenny Viacheslaw Skyline
Kenny Shaffer-Santa Rosa
Lavonce Yeargin-Chabot *
142
Eddie Ramos-Fresno
Pat Coffin-Sacramento
Pete Hedrick-West Valley
Joe Lasaga-Skyline
Jeff Rodrigues-Chabot
Shane Roberts-Santa Rosa
Toby Reyes-Modesta
Davd Lupinsky-Diablo Valley
Frank Montoya-Gavilan *

150
Tony Cooper-Sacramento
Emilio Vadnais-Diablo Valley
Timmy Perez-S J Delta
Doug Gaines-Santa Rosa
Jeff Dickey-Modesto
Ryan Johnson-Fresno
Joshua Benkman-Chabot
Tim Partee-Cuesta
Paul Doushgounian-W Valle *
158
Alfonzo Tucker-Fresno
Todd Oliver-Sacramento
Mike Perez-West Valley
Clayton Schneider-Cuesta
Mark Shin-Skyline
Mike Roper-Diablo Valley
Aaron Archbold-Modesto
Andy Reindel-S J Delta
167
Trent Williams-Cuesta
Chris Delgado-Gavilan
Brian Haupt-Fresno
Rich Pederson-Santa Rosa
Jerry Broughton-S J Delta
Ben Collier-Modesto
Akira Nakan-Diabolo Valley
Warren Newsome-W Valley
Jack Villagomez-Chabot *
177
Dave Crumpier-West Valley
Johann Geriach-Santa Rosa
Noah Thompson-Modesta
Fred Douthat-Fresno
Travis Skarda-Sacramento
Tim Bruce-Diablo Valley
Jack Fanning-Cuesta
David Naverro-S J Delta
Eric Dabragnano-Skyline *

190
Brian Campbell-Modesto
Brandon Burks-Sacramento
Amilar Chacon-Skyline
Michael Barns-Gavilan
Kory Westbury-Fresno
Rick Carasco-Cuesta
Elliot Booker-West Valley
Kevin Phillips-Chabot
Kevin P ? *
275
Mike Caroian-Diablo Valley
Dan Jones-Sacramento
Chris Wellisch-West Valley
Jack Keener-Gavilan
Jaimi Garcia-Cuesta
Marcos Gams-Modesto
Leonard Schneyder-Chabot
Alfredo Rivas-Skyline
Luis Briseno-Fresno *

Team Scores
1 Fresno   130.75
2 Sacramento   115
3 West Valley   84.75
4 Modesto   81.25
5 Cuesta   79
6 Gavilan   68.25
7 Diablo Valley 53.75
8 Santa Rosa   44.5
8 Skyline   44.5
10 S J Delta   23.5
11 Chabot   12

*= Alternate

1993 South Regional
Golden West College

118
Charlie Valencia-East LA
Stanley Packer-Palomar
Bobby Campos-R Santiago
Phai Hoang-Rio Hondo
Gil Zavala-Moorpark
Tam Nehei-Mt. SAC
Matt Jackson-Bakfld
Kelly Martinez-Cerritos
David Kelley-Golden West

126
Shane Holloway-R Santiago
Randy Garcia-Cerritos
Armik Bagramjan-East LA
Ruben Loera-Rio Hondo
Phil Dampier-Mt. SAC
Ty Jacob-Palomar
Sam Reyna-Bakersfield
Jerry Goodspeed-Cypress
Robert Calariza-Moorpark
Alternate

134
David Nirdringhaus-R Santiag
Rico Morel-Palomar
Mark Cody-Cerritos
Ryan Kerr-Moorpark
Gabe Rios-Rio Hondo
Bulmaro Nunez-Mt. SAC
Steve Alfano-Golden West
Jereme James-Cypress
Andy Sheffield-Bakersfield
Alternate

142
Jason Gaer-Bakersfield
Jorge Ruiz-Moorpark
Craig Weik-Palomar
Billey Myer-Cerritos
Anthony Valazquez-R Hondo
Derek Fitsimmons-G West
Greg Niedringhaus-R Santiag
Terry Villegas-Mt. SAC
Mario Ruiz-East LA
Alternate

150
Dan Santana-Cerritos
Anthony Valencia-East LA
Kyle Plummer-Moorpark
Reza Khayat-Cypress
Chris Hafer-Palomar
Ryan Gates-Bakersfield
Scott Herman-Golden West
Mike Prefontaine-Mt. SAC
Jim Little-Rancho Santiago
Alternate

158
Jason Pratt-Moorpark
Rick Carreon-Cerritos
Joe Toth-Palomar
Doug Blake-Mt.SAC
Ron Davis-Bakersfield
Mike Nicholson-Palomar
Carlos Miranda-R Santiago
Scott Pantington-Cypress
No Entry

167
Matt Padgett-R Santiago
Jesse Bueno-Cerritos
Atti Toth-Palomar
Gabe Garcia-Bakersfield
Mario Varela-Moorpark
Oscar Balderama-Mt. SAC
Israel Gomez-Rio Hondo
Tolio Estrada-East LA
No Entry

177
Bisolt Delsiev-Cerritos
Nayif Abdullah-R Santiago
Dan Burdis-Moorpark
Israel Franco-Rio Hondo
Vagan Adzhenyan-East LA
Eric Gaunt-Golden West
Sean Garlock-Palomar
Adam Gilbert-Cypress
No Entry

190
Todd Hoult-Moorpark
James Hill-Cerritos
Joe Lipps-Rancho Santiago
Anthony Palacia-East LA
Robert Alva-Rio Hondo
Sal Bandin-Mt. SAC
Tony Anderson-Palomar
David Fagel-Mt. SAC
John Vargas-Cypress
Alternate

275
Mike Gambel-Palomar
Mike Bolster-Golden West
Jeff Ware-Cerritos
Zenen Pena-Cerritos
Joe Damirjian-East LA
Paul Jaramillo-Moorpark
Gabrial Godinez Moorpark
Tom Willis-Cypress
Rigo Garcia-Bakersfield
Alternate

Team Scores
1 Cerritos   141.75
2 Ranch Santiago   121.5
3 Moorpark   112.75
4 Palomar   100.5
5 East LA   77.25
6 Rio Hondo   71.5
7 Bakersfield   47.75
8 Mt. SAC   41
9 Golden West   35
10 Cypress   17
11 San Bernardino

1994 North Regional
November 19, 1994 Fresno City College

118
Isaac Pomarejo-Fresno

177
Elias Zamorno-Fresno*

Team Scores
1 Fresno   194
2 Sierra   102.5
3

126
Vic De LaCruz-Fresno

190

Results from the Fresno Bee
All Champions
*Didn't give place

134
Yero Washington-Fresno

Heavyweight
Chad Mast-Fresno

142
Eddie Ramos Fresno

150

Ray Benavides-Fresno *

158
Doug Miller-Fresno

167
Jeremiah Muhammed-
Fresno Fall 4:10
Brian Campbell

1994 South Regional

118

Brian Gilliland-Cerritos 7

126

Ahid Diab-Cerritos 3

134
Shane Holloway R Santiago

David Gayer-Cerritos 3

142
Juan Alverez-Cerritos 1

150
Rudolph James-Cerritos 1

158

Mario Moreno-Cerritos 5

167
Matt Padgett-R Santiago

Rick Carreon-Cerritos 7

177
Terry Tuzzolino-R Santiago
Jake Harman-Cerritos 2

190

Adimu Madyun-Cerritos 3

Heavyweight

Dan Bracamonte-Cerritos 2

Dan Bracamonte-Cerritos 2

Team Results
1 Cerritos
2
3

Results found on the Cerritos Wrestling web page Rancho Santiago results found in the Rancho Santiago Program Kevin Burgess Rancho Santiago Champion no weight given

1995 South Regional

118

Kelly Martinez-Cerritos 2

126

Randy Bowers-Cerritos 3

134

David Gayer-Cerritos 3

142
Fred Leavy-Cerritos 1

150

Mario Moreno-Cerritos 3

158
Rudolph James-Cerritos 1

167
Greg Jackson-Cerritos 1

177
Terry Tuzzsolino-R Santiago

Dave Moyer-Cerritos 4

190

Tony Rojo-Cerritos 5
Heavyweight

Jeff Ware-Cerritos 4

Team Results
1 Cerritos
2
3

Results found on the Cerritos Wrestling web page
Rancho Santiago results found on the Rancho Santiago Program
Alfredo Fausto Rancho Santiago weight not given

1996 South Regional

118

Julio Soto-Cerritos 8

126

Randy Bowers-Cerritos 2

134
Paul Fonseca-Cerritos 2

142
Juan Alvarez-Cerritos 2

150
Phil Wozniak R Santiago

Ray Fonseca-Cerritos 4
158

Gabriel Ochoa-Cerritos 7
167

Dan Moyer-Cerritos 3

177

Joshua Lewis-Cerritos 8
190

Scott Rojo-Cerritos 2

Heavyweight

Kelly Richardson-Cerritos 4

Team Results
1
2
3
4 Cerritos

Results found on the Cerritos Wrestling web page
Results found on the Rancho Santiago Program

Alfredo Fausto Rancho Santiago weight not given

1997 North Regional

118
Dave Leonard-Sierra
Bert Clayton-Skyline
Tee Sar-Cuesta
Simon Triggs-Chabot
Jason Grim-Sacramento
Sun Ngo-Diablo Valley
Belissa Minjarez-S J Delta
Brian Tacke-Modesto

126
Steve Martin-Skyline
Alex Ortiz-Fresno
Wes Mayfield-Sierra
Brock Brown-Santa Rosa
Amir Noble-Muhammad Sacr
Luis Mendez-West Valley
Rico Molina-S J Delta
Doug Silva-Cuesta

134
Paris Ruiz-Fresno
Gabe Ochoa-Skyline
Jeff Silveira-West Valley
Brad Takenaka-Cuesta
Anthony Chavira Chabot
Ray Leija-Modesto
Ray Castellon-S J Delta
Bablo Ortiz-Santa Ros

142
Jonte Davis-Fresno
Rafael Quintana-Skyline
Rafael Muniz-Chabot
Terry Blesso-Sierra
Tom Trevino-West Valley
Colin Mattison-Santa Rosa
Steve Valgas-Modesto
Armondo Gonzalez-Cuesta

150
Jeff Dickey-Modesto
William Brown-Fresno
Dan Urbancic-Skyline
Sherwood Thomson-Sac
Bashar Amso Diablo-Valley
Dustin Jones-Cuesta
David Hose-S J Delta
Tom Henry-Santa Rosa

158
Clemente Moreno-Fresno
Trevor Stran-Modesto
Bruno Biccoca-Cuesta
Jay Morrow-Diablo Valley
Jeremy Bragg-Skyline
Bill Miles-Sierra
David Littrell-Sacramento
Pete Sotiras-Santa Rosa

167
Stefan Foley-Santa Rosa
Heath Jones-Cuesta
Tim Heinrich-West Valley
James Williams-Sacramento
James Smith-Diablo Valley
Joel Perry-Modesto
Kevin Lewis-S J Delta
Oscar Espinoza-Santa Rosa

177
Davey Bowles-Santa Rosa
Jake Shields-Cuesta
Brandon Bettencourt-Sierra
Dean Vinson-West Valley
Jim Tauber-Sacramento
Josh Flora-Modesto
Aaron Stanton-Skyline
Stephen Stewart-Chabot

190
Tom Gohde-Fresno
Jay Warnier-Sierra
Abner Morgan-Chabot
Brian Stilwell-Cuesta
Ryan Shaw-Sacramento
Reginald Grayson-Skyline
Jorge Castillo-S J Delta
Frank Grengo-West Valley

275
John Devine-Skyline
Randy Leydecker-Sacramento
Ruben Reynaga-Sierra
Scott Bohardi-Chabot
Zeb Gromm-S J Delta
Ben Pearce-Santa Rosa
Adam Ruiz-West Valley
Scott Gohde-Fresno

Coach of the Year
Keith Spataro-Skyline

Team Scores
1	Skyline	181.5
2	Fresno	143
3	Sierra	123.5
4	Cuesta	118.5
5	Sacramento	85.5
6	Chabot	85
7	Modesto	77.5
8	West Valley	75
9	Santa Rosa	67
10	S J Delta	48
11	Diablo Valley	45

1997 South Regional

118
Jason Bedsole-Palomar 3-0
Cleo Johnson-Bakersfield
Ernie Nunez-Moorpark 7-6
Brian Gilliland-Cerritos
Fernando Serratos-G Wes 3-1
Jose Maroquin-Cypress
Alex Oropeza-East LA 13-4
Kris Winemiller-San Bernadio

126
Juan Roman-Moorpark 12-6
Levi Harbin-Palomar
Peter Kunz-Cypress 5-2
Camilo Gonzales-Mt. SAC
Omar Orozco-Sac 15-4
Robert Lopez-Rio Hondo
Jimmy Solis-East LA 11-3
Dave Deville-Cerritos

134
George Moreno-Bakfld 4-2
Miguel Soto-Cerritos
Irvin Michaels-Palomar 6-4
David Jaramillo-Mt. SAC
Eddie Sanchez-Sacrament 3-2
Mark Gillen-Rio Hondo
Frank Ramirez-Moorpar 13-4
Matt Perez-Golden West

142
Jessie Campos-Moorpark 8-7
Seth Garvin-Cerritos
Luis Renteria-Sacramento 7-5
Mario Gonzales-Bakersfield
Jamie Alvarez-Rio Hondo 7-5
Leo Perez-Palomar
Dru Morton-Mt. SAC 13-9
Roman Hernandez-G West

150
Juan Gallardo-Bakersfield 6-4
Scott Erickson-Moorpark
Chris Casares-Cerritos 3-2
Mike Zuckerman-Palomar
Matt Gordon-East LA Default
Brian Burnett-Golden West
Moises Camacho-Sacra 12-10
Jason Lowe-Mt. SAC

158
Gabe Roman-Moorpark 12-3
Jose Landin-Bakersfield
Corey Hall-Cerritos Fall 2:50
Gerardo Rodriguez-Cypress
Dan Righter-Palomar 8-3
Mohammed Abdullah-Mt. S
Cutter Chanley-San Ber 12-10
Tom Salcido-Sacramento

167
Ati Conner-Moorpark F 3:55
Kevin Sanger-Palomar
Landon Parker-Cerritos F 1:00
Matt Dusch-Sacramento
Kyle Osborne-Mt. SAC Defaut
Jose Ruano-East LA
Ben Sherley-Bakfld Default
Danny Torres-Cypress

177
Chuck Sandlin-Moorpark 8-6
Steven Cooper-Golden West
Todd Le Sieur-M. SAC Default
Bradley Roberts-Sacramento
Marlin Shaw-Palomar F 4:09
Jared Westberg-Bakersfield
Mike Plesnicher-S Berd F 3:29
Luis Robles Rio-Hondo

190
Adam Gilbert-Cypress 11-6
Steve Ruiz-Sacramento
Josh Lewis-Cerritos 8-1
Dan Ramirez-Moorpark
Hassan Ayoub-Palomar 7-2
Chad Totina-San Bernadino
Steve Grode-Gold West 12-3
Joe Rojas-Bakersfield

275
Lloyd Marshbanks-Palo 10-8
Rigo Jimenez-Rio Hondo
Dennis Garcia-Sacramet 11-2
Jason King-Moorpark
Kelly Richardson-Cerr Default
Mike Ketcham-Golden West
Rick Viramontes-East LA Defa
Ron Williams-Mt. SAC

Coach of the Year
Paul Keysaw-Moorpark

Alternates
Jeff Smith-Cerritos
Joe Ismay-Palomar

Most Outstanding Wrestler
Gabe Roman-Moorpark

Team Scores
1 Moorpark   165.5
2 Palomar   136.5
3 Cerritos   116.5
4 Bakersfield   103
5 Santa Ana   86
6 Mt. SAC   56.5
7 Cypress   52.5
8 Golden West   42.5
9 Rio Hondo   35
10 East LA   31.5
11 San Bernadino 17.5
12 Victor Valley 0

1998 North Regional
November 28, 1998 Fresno City

125
Eric Ferreira-Santa Rosa
Bert Clayton-Skyline
Joe Beaudoin-Modesto
Justin McLelland-Fresno
    Wightman-Cuesta
    Langille-Sacram
    Berard-Sierra
    Tran-S J Delta

133
Sabian Sandoval-Cuesta
Alex Ortiz-Fresno
Pablo Sanchez-Skyline
Manuel Garcia-Sacramento
Brook Buonaccorsi-Sana Rosa
    Walke-Modesto
DeMarco-Dialo Valley
    Sagnep-Chabot

141
George Moreno-Fresno
Richard Dixson-Santa Rosa
Vince Elliott-Modesto
    Blackner-Cuesta
Jaxson Kochamp-Sierra
    Castillo-Sacramento
Ken Coburn-Chabot
Jeremy Parker-Diablo Valley

149
Joey Martinez-Skyline
R J Arballo-Fresno
Juan Lopez-Cuesta
    Valgos-Modesto
Mike Zuckerman-Sierra
Nate Coffin-Sacramento
    Brown-Santa Rosa
    Rivera-Chabot

157
Ken Murray-Chabot
Adam Winters-Sierra
Beau Taylor-Cuesta
Jason Sereni-Skyline
Beau Danieli-Fresno
Jesse Fouch-Modesto
Kenney Dixon-Santa Rosa
    Goins-S J Delta

165
Clemente Moreno-Fresno
Shawn Henebry-West Valley
    Davis-Cuesta
Chris Schmidt-Santa Rosa
    Green-Diablo Valley
    Yothers-Chabot
    Cochran-S J Delta
    Hopping-Modesto

174
Larry Silva-Fresno
Tim Heinrich-West Valley
Eric Ortegren-Santa Rosa
Bryan Ysais-Diablo Valley
Bobby Chipman-Skyline
Jeff Dahl-Sierra
    Randolph-Chabot
    Williams-Sacramento

184
Jason Rossotti-Fresno
Scott Smith-Sacramento
Summer Brown-West Valley
Mike Mullen-Sierra
Chris Fort-Santa Rosa
    Allen-Skyline
    Paul-Diablo Valley
    Tong-Cuesta

197
Jay Wariner-Sierra
Jake Shields-Cuesta
Ryan Philp-Fresno
James Mason-Chabot
Gerold James-Skyline
    Foster-S J Delta
    Hernandez-West Vly
    Croskey-Diablo Valley

285
Mercedes Kinner-Fresno
Emmitt Brown-Chabot
Dave Knopfer-West Valley
    Davis-S J Delta
    Rellaford-Sacramento
Chris Arnold-Sierra
    Barajas-Skyline
    Peramaki-Cuesta

Team Scores
1	Fresno	177.5
2	Cuesta	100
3	Skyline	92
4	Santa Rosa	88
5	West Valley	65.5
6	Chabot	62.5
7	Modesto	58
8	Sacramento	53
9	Diablo Valley	29
10	S J Delta	24

1998 South Regional
November 28, 1998 East Los Angeles College

125
Jason Bledsole-Palomar
Camplo Gonzalez-Mt. SAC
Froilan Gonzalez-G West
Tony Madrigal-Bakersfield
    Ramirez-East LA
    Sandoval-San Berdo
    Olivas-Sacramento
    Kadi-Victor Valley

133
Ervin Michael-Palomar
Robert Espejo-Cerritos
    Torres-Moorpark
    Garcia-Santa Ana
Ben Ashley-Bakersfield
    Yearry-Cypress
    DeLeon-San Bernardino
    Cartagena-Victor Valley

141
Ryan Meloche-Bakersfield
Leo Perez-Palomar
Dave Gomez-Rio Hondo
    Jaramillo-Mt. SAC
    Sear-Cypress
    Weber-Santa Ana
    Baldwin-Moorpark
    Sal Garcia-Cerritos

149
Jason Lowe-Golden West
Cirillo Reyes-Bakersfield
    Kleekley-Mt. SAC
    Diaz Rio-Hondo
C J Johnston-Palomar
    Smith-San Bernard
    Rodrigues-Moorpark
    Garcia-East LA

157
Brian Pogue-Palomar
Joe Velasquez-Cerritos
    Humphry-Golden West
    Gillen-Rio Hondo
Jim Solis-East LA
    Avila-Cypress
    Casa-San Bernard
    Stephens-Mt. SAC

165
Heath Sims-Cerritos
Jesse Standlea-Golden West
Cornello Arriola-Mt. SAC
Monico Enriquez-East LA
Jason Gigliotti-Palomar
    Vargas-Cypress
    Bagby-Moorpark
    Penalber-San Berdo

174
Brian Webber-Santa Ana
Jose Ruano-East LA
    Robles-Rio Hondo
    Blanco-Golden West
    Mayer-Bakersfield
    Padilla-Palomar
    McGlaughlin-Cypress
    Drimi-Cerritos

184
Chuck Sandlin-Moorpark
Bill Tedd-Santa Anna
Todd Leseur-Mt. SAC
    Helwig-Golden West
Allen Clegg-Palomar
    Rios-Cerritos
    Eagon-Victor Valley
    Rocha-East LA

197
David Bonilla-Mt. SAC
Hector Ramerez-East LA
Melkonian-Moorpark
Asa Randolph Cerritos
    Godínez-Santa Ana
    Lobo-Bakersfield
Victor Bonilla-Rio Hondo
    Cross-Cypress

285
Masoud Rahmani-Cerritos
Dan Maynard-Santa Ana
Tony Gomez-San Bernadino
Van Winkle-Golden West
    Paul-East LA
    Ruano-Palomar
Darren Hill-Mt. SAC
    Forman-Victor Valley

Team Scores
1 Moorpark
2 Cerritos
3 Mt. SAC
4 Golden West
5 Santa Ana

Santa Ana Program list Brian Webster 150 and Don Maynard Heavyweight as Champions

1999 North Regional
November 20, 1999

125
Joey Taylor-Skyline 9-2
James Blea-S J Delta
Justin Mclelland-Fresno Deft
Donnie Green-Santa Rosa
Chris Hammer-Sierra 8-2
Ryan Krugh-Modesto
Josh Hernandez-Chabot Deft
Sean Matulac-Cuesta

133
Robert Supulveda-Fresno Def
Marc Kavanagh-Chabot
Frankie Alvarez-W Vly 13-5
Russ Walke-Modesto
Bryce Escobar-Sierra Deft
Nathan Fafard-Skyline F 3:18
Brian Brandon-Diablo Valley

141
Anthony Reta-Chabot 6-1*
Fernando Flanagan-W Valley
Ben Baca-Fresno 6-1
Nick Hopping-Modesto
Nick Saldivar-Sacramento Def
Jesse Bastian-Sierra
Kevin Knall-S J Delta 9-4
Jason Sevigny-Skyline

149
Casey Olsen-Fresno 8-3
Duc Lee-S J Delta
Aaron Heinberger-Sierra 8-7
Justin Fraser-Diablo Valley
Dan Urbancic-Skyline 11-4
Brett Gordon-Sacramento
Eric Roberson-Modesto 6-3
Joseph Furman-Santa Rosa

157
Dan Castillo-Sacramento 5-4
Brian Holt-Sierra
Jesse Fouch-Modesto 4-1
Gabe Felix-Fresno
Shawn Betts-Cuesta 9-7
Ben Ward-Diablo Valley
Pavel Gonzalez-Skyline 9-4
John Britz-Wast Valley

165
Art Martinez Sacrament 8-2*
Anthony Gonzalez-Modesto
Terrence Carter-Skyline 8-4
Zach Hopkins-Sierra
Russell Smithson-Fresno Deft
Bruno Bicocca-Cuesta
Shawn Mahugh W Valley Deft
Says Keoveunxay-S J Delta

174
Aaron Spiller-Cuesta 9-5
Sion King-Sacramento
Robert Thomas-Skyline F 2:00
Marc Banks-West Valley
Tim Neves-Santa Rosa Deft
Ricky Singh-Modesto
Michael Gonzalez-Fresno Def

184
Dan Martinez-Cuesta 9-5
Edgar Hernandez-West Valley
Cortney Page-Sacramento T F
Marcus Randolph-Chabot
Art Pezzat Fresno-Default
Nathan Loughran-Santa Rosa
Jody Smith Modesto-Default
Marcos Hernandez-Skyline

197
Ryan Philp-Fresno 7-5
Bobby Chipman-Skyline
Pancho Freer-Sacramento 3-2
Mike Mullen-Sierra
Chris Martin-Chabot Default
Ben Van-Pearce-Santa Rosa
Seth Myers Diablo Valley 3-2
Amos Tong-Cuesta

285
Freddie Aquitania-Skyline 5-2
Mercedes Kinne-Fresno
Tim Golia-Sierra
Glenn Campbell-Cuesta
John Abbott-Diablo Valley 4-3
Mike Womack-Modesto
Tolen Miller-Sacramento Deft
Ernesto Mello-S J Delta

Most Outstanding Wrestlers
Lower Weight
Anthony Reta-Chabot
Upper Weight
Art Martinez-Sacramento
Coach of the Year
Robert Arballo-Fresno
Assistant Coach of the Year
Gary Quintania-Fresno

Team Scores
1	Fresno	150
2	Skyline	107.5
3	Sacramento	105
4	Sierra	89
5	Modesto	79
6	Cuesta	63
7	Chabot	62
8	West Valley	61
9	S J Delta	41
10	Santa Rosa	37
11	Diablo Valley	30

1999 South Regional
November 20, 1999 Rio Hondo College

125
Nick Nakamura-Rio Hond 5-3
J J Roberts-Palomar
Fernando Serratos-G Wes 3-2
Cleo Johnson-Bakersfield
Guy Horcasitas-Mt. SAC 6-4
Andre Deville-Cerritos
Kent Victor-Valley Default
Tito Olivas-Sacramento

133
Yonas Waldu-Moorpark 8-6
Jose Palomares-Sacramento
James Guizar-Palomar TF 20-5
Jim Solis-East LA
Jose Carrillo-Golden West 8-2
Frank Lara-Cerritos
Joey Martinez Bakersfield 8-6
Ernie Santos-Mt. SAC

141
Ryan Meloche Bakersfield 6-1
Sal Garcia-Cerritos
Josh Roman-Moorpark 4-1
Chris Payne-Palomar
Andrew Donaldson-Sac Defal
Alex Garcia-Golden West
Morales Cypress-Default
Darren Jaramillo-Mt. SAC

149
Sal Lucatero-Moorpark 13-8
C J Johnson-Palomar
Jamie Alvarez-Rio Hond 14-9
Luis Renteria-Sacramento
Sam Lopez Cerritos 12-0
Ralph Lopez-Cerritos
David Baker-Bakersfield 7-5
Kazeka Muniz-Golden West

157
Eddie Lucatero-Moorpark 5-1
Freddy Rivera-Mt. SAC
Shamar Pigg-Bakfld Default
Steve Avalos-Golden West
Josh Delfin-Palomar 2-0
Mora-Sacramento
Jason Burch-Cypress Fall 1:35
Alex Lefort-East LA

165
Heath Sims-Cerritos
Arsen Aleksanyan-Moorpark
Alman Kerste-Bakersfield 8-5
Monico Enriquez-East LA
David Pierce-Golden Wes 6-4
Alex Errico Santa Ana
Classen-Victor Valley Def
Bryan Pogue-Palomar

174
Larry Johnson Bakfld Fall :28*
Bryan Webster-Sacramento
Kevin Sanger-Palomar 8-2
Ryan Painter-San Bernardino
Stewart Young-Moorpark 2-0
Robert Driml-Cerritos
Joe Evano-Mt. SAC 15-5
Haward Janec-Cypress

184
David Bonilla-Mt S 9-9 Ri Out
Chris Gonzalez-Moorpark
Hector Carreon-East LA 8-5
Phil Miller-Victor Valley
Asa Randolph-Cerritos F 4:36
Al Leglar-Palomar
Grant Entsminger-S A F 3:05
Fred Gutierrez-Bakersfield

197
Hector Ramirez-East LA 13-5
Hossin Oshani-Cerritos
Piki Astudillo-Go West F 3:22
Shawn Canfield-Rio Hondo
Adam Benshea-Moorpk 3:35
Gilbert Garcia-Sacramento
Donny Farmer-Palomar
No Eighth

285
J T Morales-Rio Hondo Deft
Joe Vetromile-Palomar
Masoud Rahmani Cerritos 7-3
Rafael Lucero-Santa Ana
Chris Jansen-Moorpark 3-2
Richard Martin-San Bernadin
Aaron Cross-Cypress Fall 4:00
Dewayne Hogan-Bakersfield

Most Outstanding Wrestler
Larry Johnson-Bakersfield
3 Falls

Coach of the Year
Paul Keysaw-Moorpark

Assistant Coach of the Year
Richard-Bailey

Team Scores
#	Team	Score
1	Moorpark	139
2	Palomar	120.5
3	Cerritos	98.5
4	Santa Ana	94.5
5	Bakersfield	90.5
6	Rio Hondo	67.5
7	East LA	67
8	Golden West	64
9	Mt. SAC	56
10	Victor Valley	23.5
11	Cypress	19
12	San Bernadino	15.5

Coaches
Bakersfield-Bill Kalivas
Cerritos-Greg Gascon
Cypress-Mike Flook
East LA-Ralph Valle
Golden West-Dale Deffner
Moorpark-Paul Keysaw
Mt. SAC-Larry Watanabe
Palomar-Joe Ismay
Rio Hondo-Paul La Blanc
San Bernadino-Bobby Vargas
Santa Ana-Alan Clinton
Victor Valley-Lance Smith

1999 Coach of the year
Paul Keysaw - Moorpark

2000 South Regional
November 25, 2000 Palomar College

125
Jack Anaya-Cypress 6-4
Guy Horcasitas-Mt. SAC
Tommy Peralta-Sana Ana 5-3
Israel Navarro-Palomar
Jess Miramontes G West 12-8
Ricky Aguirra-Moorpark
Branden-McDonald Vic Valley

133
Ricky Guzman-Rio Hond 10-3
Bumper Fleischman-Moorpar
Parris Whitley Bakersfield 9-7
Joel Sanchez-Santa Ana
Brandon Gushiken-G Wes 4-3
Nick Randall-Palomar
Juan Revuelta-Cerritos 5-0
Anthony Cartagena-Vic Valley
Quiche Roura-East LA

141
Javes Guizar-Palomar 3-1
David Gomez-Rio Hondo
Gabriel BarraganCerr TF 19-1
Camron Harris-Golden Valley
Brett Homesly Bakersfield 6-0
Matt Javid-Moorpark
Johnny Hoong-Mt. SAC F 6:40
Joseph Pallon-East LA

149
Saul Lucatero-Moorpark 11-3
Andrew Donaldson-Sant Ana
Josh Johson-Cerritos 10-9
Bryan Bone-Palomar
Marcos Austin-Bakfld 8-1
  Batres-Rio Hondo Default
Vince Parra-Rio Hondo Defau
Duey Tran-Cypress

157
Steve Hernandez-Moorpk 3-2
Sam Lopez-Cerritos
Hector Mora-Santa Ana 8-2
Jay Casas-Golden West
Al Leglar Palomar Fall 3:48
Yaroslav Kudryshen- LA Def
  Cox-Cypress

165
Nick Cardenez-Palomar Defa
Rey Torres-Moorpark
Alman Kerste- Bakfld 12-8
Gerardo Rodriguez-Cypress
Josh Jarrett-Golden West Def
David Magote-East LA
John Cary-Victor Valley Defau
  Badillo-Rio Hondo
Mike Lee-Cerritos

174
Shamar Pigg-Bakfld 17-8
Wesley Tielens-Palomar
Jesse Juarez Golden West Def
Brian Burnett-Cerritos
Shannon Sams-Moorp F 4:24
  Ryen-East LA

184
Chris Gonzalez-Moorpark 9-6
Phil Miller-Victor Valley
Joe Evano-Mt. SAC 9-2
Isaac McMann-Palomar
Daniel Melendez-Sn Ana Def
Dan Contreras-Rio Hondo
Robert Volga-Golden Wes 8-7
Andrew Zubia-Cerritos

197
Joe Stevenson-Vic Valley 10-4
Jeremiah Peterson-Moorpark
Steve Sanchez-Santa Ana 3-2
Steve Grode-Golden West
Tom Meza-Rio Hondo 3-2
Kris Sherley-Palomar
Brain Van Fossen Mt. SAC Def
Josh O'Neal-Bakersfield

Heavyweight
Ben Flores-Moorpark 10-2
  Jason Paul
Anthoy Boone-Mt. SAC Juan
Prado-Golden West Def Carlos
Ceja-East LA
Bobby Shin-Rio Hondo Defaul
Beetle Bettencourt-Vic Valley

Team Scores
1	Moorpark	148
2	Palomar	141
3	Golden West	96.5
4	Cerritos	83
5	Bakersfield	76
6	Santa Ana	73.5
7	Rio Hondo	73
8	Victor Valley	62
9	Mt. SAC	57.5
10	Cypress	40
10	East LA	40
12	San Bernardino	0

Teams
Bakersfield-Bill Kalivas
Cerritos-Greg Gascon
Cypress-Mike Flook
East LA-Ralph Valle
Golden West-Dale Deffner
Moorpark-Paul Keysaw
Mt. SAC-Larry Wantanabe
Palomar-Joe Ismay
Rio Hondo-Paul LeBlanc
San Bernadino-Bobby Vargas
Santa Ana-Vince Silva
Victor Valley-Lance Smith

2001 South Regional
November 24, 2001 San Bernardino Valley College

125
Jason Moreno-Bakfld 12-5
Anthony Rodriguez-Cerritos
Luis Fragoso-Rio Hondo Deft
Brandon Gushiken-Gold West
Ricky Aguirre-Moorpark
Hamilton Alvarenga-Mt. SAC
Israel Navarro PalomarTF18-2
Fabian Alizo-San Bernardino
Chris Goffredo-Victor Valley

133
Jose Palomares-Santa An 9-5
Rick Guzman-Rio Hondo
Damacio Page-Cerritos 9-7
Bumper Fleischmann-Moorp
Chad Flook-Cypress 2-0
Eric Higaonna-Palomar
Steve Lindo- San Bernardino
Jose Chavez-Victor Valley

141
Josh Johnson-Cerritos 7-3
Israel Sanchez-Santa Ana
Devon Zemp-Moorpk F 5:39
Tim Riscen-Palomar
Alex Johns-Rio Hondo F 2:51
Victor Wise-Cypress
Jason Rawlins-Gol Valley Deft
Steve Elisondo-Bakersfield
Quiche Roura-East LA

149
Steve Garcia-Cerritos 16-4
Richard King-Mt. SAC
Ralph Lopez-East LA Fall 4:55
Gonzalo Meza-Cypress
Marty Brown-Palomar F 4:55
Todd Guevara-Bakersfield
Jordon Goodrich-Vic Valley
Carlos Anaya-Moorpark 15-4
Devin Willette-Rio Hondo

157
Eddie Lucatero-Moorpark 6-4
Buck Meredith-Palomar
Maurice Washington-RH15-10
Gabe Barragan-Cerritos
Fred Gutierrez-Bakfld 7-2
Randall Clifford-Golden West
Aaron Miller-Vic Valley 10-4
Jamie Chavez-Santa Ana
Brian Ekeda-East LA

165
Rey Torres-Moorpark 3-2
Karras Kalivas-Bakersfield
Ramiro Carasa-Santa An 12-1
Aaron Hacker-Golden West
Andy Lopez-Cerritos Fall 1:07
Josh Williamson-Mt. SAC
Tam Nguyen-San Bern F 2:02
Leo Langarica-Victor Valley
Matt Cook-Palomar

174
Shannon Sams-Moorpark 3-1
Andy Tufnell-Cerritos
Richard Willemstein-MSAC 7-3
Adam Neesby-Golden West
Victor Contreras-Palomar Def
Brian Wike-Victor Valley
Saad Awad-San Bernardino

184
Jesse Juarez-Golden West 3-0
Chris Rueckert-Moorpark
Kris Shirley-Palomar 10 2
Kouji Nerio-Mt. SAC
Dustin Finley-R Hondo F 2:09
Tad Millane-Cerritos
Jason Figueroa-Cypress F2:16
Gustavo Alvarado-East LA

197
Ralph Garcia-Moorpark 3-2
Chris Chambers-Palomar
Jeff Webster-Santa Ana 5-2
Deron Ward-Cerritos
Alejandro Cruz-East LA Deft
Braian Carroll-Golden West
Richard Esparza-Mt. SAC

Heavyweight
Brett Clark-Bakersfield 5-4
Chase Gormley-Golden West
Ben Flores-Moorpark 8-1
Taylor Schmidt-Palomar
Matt Frembling-Cypress Deft
Eric Arevalo-Mt. SAC
Steve Covarrubias-San Be Def
John McCoy-Victor Valley
Antonio Cruz-East LA

Team Scores
1	Moorpark	151
2	Cerritos	148.5
3	Palomar	115
4	Golden West	105
5	Bakersfield	85.5
6	Mt. SAC	77.5
7	Santa Ana	71.5
8	Rio Hondo	68
9	Cypress	48.5
10	Victor Valley	31.5
11	San Bernadino	30.5
12	East LA	28.5

2002 North Regional
December 7, 2002 Sacramento City

125
Jacob Palamino-Fresno
Diwan Williams-Skyline
John Synhorst-Sacramento
Robbie Dashnow-Sierra
Steve Karlotski-Chabot
Jed Davis-Cuesta
Tommy Flores-S J Delta

133
Raul Lopez-Shasta
Alfonso Paez-Modesto
Darrell Goodpaster-Fresno
Alek Butler-S J Delta
Virgil Lockett-Skyline
Alvin Cacdac-West Valley
Jeremy Waldram-Cuesta
Jose Ortiz-Chabot
Eric Ticas-Sacramento

141
Gabe Ruhkala-Sierra
Chris Chames-West Valley
Josh Sha-Skyline
Adam Berry-Fresno
    Robbie Fogliasso
Mark McChesney-Chabot
Joe Elliott-Santa Rosa
Marcus Moore-Sacramento
Josh Bye-Cuesta

149
Fernando Razo-Fresno
Cody Williamson-West Valley
Zack Evans-Chabot
Preston Ivin-Shasta
Darrib Unenoyama-Skyline
Carl Arevalo-S J Delta
Ikaika Arakaki-Santa Rosa
Alex Aguilar-Sacramento
Nick Panziera-Cuesta

157
Matt Lantz-Sierra
Dustin Hirashima-Chabot
Scott Spratt-Santa Rosa
David Lee-Sacramento
John Villapando-Cuesta
Bobby Slack-Shasta
Eric Sorenson-Skyline
Rocco Lucero-West Valley
Jose Sarabia-Fresno

165
Choung Le-West Valley
Jared Shullz-Fresno
Art Martinez-Sacramento
Eli Reni-Shasta
Pavel Gonzalez-Skyline
Bradley Sausser-Modesto
Chris Adams-Sierra
Joshua Wooley-S J Delta
Andrew Miranda-Chabot

174
Cory Bonincontri-Sierra
Jesse Vasquez-Modesto
Jason Hanson-Chabot
Tim Glass-Fresno
Justin Stine-Santa Rosa
Eddie Locke-Shasta
Ray Gastelum-Skyline
Brian Hooker-Sacramento
Danny Guerrero-Cuesta

184
Richard Escobar-West Valley
Sean Reid-Shasta
Jason Bolvie-Santa Rosa
Jason Holt-Sacramento
Jack Weaver-Fresno
Pat Vareia-Cuesta
Ty Thompson-Skyline
Amanjot Tamana-Modesto
Gus Corona-S J Delta

197
Mariano Sanchez-Fresno
Todd Barden-Sacramento
Matt Coonfield-Shasta
Kenneth Pamanian-Modesto
John Krieger-Chabot
Charles Waiz-Cuesta
Miguel Medina-West Valley
Mark Smith-Santa Rosa
Kyle Torre-Skyline

Heavyweight
Nick Weaver-Sierra
Damian Mason-Santa Rosa
Russell Lexau-S J Delta
Brandon Cash-Fresno
Matt Tesors-Cuesta
Chris Serrano- Skyline
Andy Ramirez-hasta
Jansher Asher-West Valley
Greg Vandestreek-Sac

Most Outstanding Wrestler
Choung Le-West Valley
Outstanding Head Coach
Max Burch-Shasta
Outstanding Assistant Coach
Garrett Spooner-Fresno

Team Scores
1 Fresno   145
2 Shasta   113.5
3 West Valley   102.5
4 Sierra   100.5
5 Skyline   90.5
6 Santa Rosa   80
7 Chabot   78
8 Sacramento   76.5
9 Modesto   65.5
10 Cuesta   61.5
11 S J Delta   53

2002 South Reginal
December 7, 2002 Victor Valley College

125
Jason Moreno Bakersfield 5-3
Jesse Miramontes-Gold West
Robert Delira-Mt. SAC 5-1
Nick Hein-Palomar
Joel Sanchez Santa Ana 13-9
Ibrahim Atalla-Rio Hondo
No Seventh
No Eighth

133
Joel Perez-Moorpark Default
Damacio Page-Cerritos
Steve Avelar-Cypress Default
Tim Riscen-Palomar
Erick Hopkins-Bakersfield 8-1
Arman Delarocha-East LA
Frank Angulo-S Ana Default
Chris Goffredo-Victor Valley

141
Shanon Slack-Cerritos 10-4
Devon Zept-Moorpark
Marcos Austin-Bakfld 9-4
Joe Selinger-Palomar
Art Aguilar-Santa Ana Default
Adrian Enriquez-East LA
Chad Flook-Cypress 9-3
Garrett Pewsey-Mt. SAC

149
Juan Serna Santa-Ana 7-5
Kyle Bickford-Palomar
Marco Lara-Cerritos 12-8
Todd Guevara-Bakersfield
Steven Davis-East LA 21-12
Nam Phan-Golden West
Josh Gaskins-Moorpark 5-4
Gonzalo Meza-Cypress

157
Matt Lambert Palomar 8-5
Karras Kalivas-Bakersfield
R J Clifford-Golden Valley 4-2
Jonathon Keene-Santa Ana
Scott Oda-Cerritos 15-5
David Castelli-Victor Valley
Edgar Mejia-East LA TF 17-0
Jose Rosa-Mt SAC

167
Buck Meredith-Palm Fall 6:09
Tony Morland-Bakersfield
Carlos Montes-Mt. SAC 14-13
Emiliano Lopez-Cerritos
Joe Cobo-Gold Valley Default
Dustin Alleman-Moorpark
Anthony Gaze-Sa Ana Default
Erik Mejia-East LA

174
James Clay-Mt. SAC 6-3
Jerry Barragan-Cerritos
Angelo Lago-Palomar 6-4
Jose Sagrero-Santa Ana
Justin Rivera-Moorpark 15-4
Japheth Nunez-East LA
Dennis Balough-G West Deflt
Dan Pagnella-Victor Valley

184
Chris Lopez- Cerritos 4-3
Josh Jarrett-Golden West
Paul Gutierrez-Gol West 11-4
Jimmy Becerra-Santa Ana
Mike Hidalgo-Moorpark 5-3
Josh Williamson-Mt. SAC
Gus Alvarado-East LA Default
Jesse Taylor-Palomar

197
Ralph Garcia-Moorpark 3-2
Chris Chambers-Palomar
Michael Hughes-East LA 6-1
Anthony Tobin-Bakersfield
Cheyne Cook-Mt. SAC F :26
Juan Elias-Santa Ana
Tad Millane-Cerritos
No Eighth

Heavyweight
Brett Clark-Bakersfield 3-2
Chase Gormley-Golden West
Anthony Boone-Mt. SAC 2-1
Dan Kunkes-Moorpark
Ben Brueske-Palomar 9-6
Mark Martinez-East LA
Diego Garcia-Cerritos
No Eighth

Team Scores
1	Palomar	135
2	Bakersfield	128
3	Cerritos	122
4	Moorpark	115
5	Santa Ana	99
6	Golden West	84
7	Mt. SAC	81
8	East LA	71
9	Cypress	21
10	Victor Valley	16
11	Rio Hondo	7

Coaches
Bakersfield-Bill Kalivas
Cerritos-Greg Gascon
Cy press-Mike Flook
East LA-Ralph Valle
Golden West-Dale Deffner
Moorpark-Paul Keysaw
Mt. SAC-Larry Watanabe
Palomar-Joe Ismay
Rio Hondo-Paul LaBlanc
Santa Ana-Vince Silvia
Victor Valley-Lance Smith

Santa Ana Program list Jimmy Becerra 184 as Champion

2003 South Regional
December 6, 2003 Mt. San Antonio College

125
Gerrard Contreras-Moor 10-2
Eugene Yasutomi-Cerritos
Nuoy Bun Santa-Ana Fall 1:20
Manuel Vasquez-Bakersfield
Jacob Durant Palomar-Defaul
Brett Bond-Mt. SAC

133
JJ Holt-Moorpark-11-4
Abdel Sadik-Rio Hondo
Nick Martinez-Bakersfield 3-0
Corey Hamabata-Mt. SAC
James Leon-Palomar Default
Martin Bautista-East LA

141
Steven Davis-East LA 2-1
Dan Castro-Palomar
Randy Aguirre-Mt. SAC 4-3
Ryan Garcia-Cerritos
Mat Maldonado-Bak F 2:00
Cody Eigelbach-Golden West

149
Miguel Gutierrez-Bak F 2:43
Kyle Bickford-Palomar
Sabas Cruz-anta Ana 9-6
Jason Claproth-Mt. SAC
Gilbert Rodriguez-E LA F 2:00
Jimmy Carr-Golden West

157
Jeff Baker-Bakersfield 17-13
Steve Garcia-Cerritos
Josh Walters-Palomar 7-4
AJ Cessario-Moorpark
Erik Mejia-East LA Fall 3:59
Ed Murguia-Mt. SAC

165
Angelo Lago-Palomar 18-6
Edgar Mejia-East LA
Russell Caldwell-Bak Fall 2:00
Justin Rivera-Moorpark
Bryan Clavecilla-Rio Hon Defl
Jon Andry-Mt. SAC

174
Chris Rueckert-Moorpar 16-7
Rickey Newsome-Palomar
Jerry Carollo-G West F 5:50
Ben Barrett-Mt. SAC
Kris Subia-Bakersfield-Default
Michael Gomes-Cerritos

184
Jese Taylor-Palomar 17-12
Jesse Ruiz-Santa Ana
Andrew Guzman-Bakfld 10-3
Chris Eyre-Golden West
Mike Nava-Mt. SAC 13-4
Jon Sanchez-Moorpark

197
Jimmy Beccera-Santa Ana 9-6
Tyrell Blanche-Moorpark
Marcus Sursa-Bakersfield 9-5
Oswaldo Avalos-Golden West
David Corson-Palomar Defaut
Joe Alvarez-Mt. SAC

282
George Palmer-Cerritos 9-4
Dan Kunkes-Moorpark
Alex Beccera-Santa Ana 3-2
Aaron Hayes-East LA
Ozzie Preclado-Rio Hon 12-6
Joe Espejo-Bakersfield

Team Scores
1 Palomar   108
2 Bakersfield   104.5
3 Moorpark   91
4 Mt. SAC   65
5 East LA   53
6 Santa Ana   52
7 Cerritos   51
8 Golden West   40
9 Rio Hondo   30
10 Victor Valley .5

2003 and 2004 CCCAA 149 pound State Champion and named Most Outstanding Wrestler both years.
Miguel Gutierrez-Bakersfiled College

2004 North Regional
December 4, 2004

125
Jean Leazard-Skyline
Said Sing-Fresno
Jason Lee-West Valley
133
Darrell Goodpaster-Fresno
Tyus Torrrean-Sierra
Joey Monjure-Modesto
Tyler Gibson-Cuesta
Alvin Cacdac-West Valley
141
Benny Garcia-S J Delta
Jacab Salas-Fresno
Chris Simms-Chabot
Anthony Curha-Sierra
Tony Arena-Sacramento
149
Mark Pfiefer-Sacramento
Jeff Cox-Modesto
Ryan Walters-Shasta
157
Eric Heldarov-Sierra
Matt Ryan-Modesto
Hector Sandoval-Santa Rosa
James Coates-Chabot
167
Hurshid Haldarov-Sierra
Will Simmons-Sacramento
Austin Torrez-Skyline
Ty Souza-Mt. SAC
Ty Minto-Shasta
174
Eddie Locke-Shasta
Konrad Schwartz-Sacramento
Matt Lantz-Sierra
Jeff Cole-Fresno

184
Yasser Pazzat-Fresno
Jarred Dixson-Sacramento
Matt Lantz-Sierra
Alexis Lara-Skyline
197
Jordan O'Polly-Sierra
Eduardo Mercado-Fresno
Ben Faanunu-Chabot
285
Marcus Moore-Sierra
Ryan Balletto-Santa Rosa
Donald Cosper-Chabot
Bryan Whetstone-Fresno

Team Results
1
2
3

Results from state placers not in any order

Coaches
Chabot-Steve Siroy
Cuesta-Joe Dansby
Fresno-Jarred Smith
Modesto-Lee Ehrler
Sacramento-Dave Pacheco
S J Delta-Mike Sandler
Santa Rosa-Jake Fitzpatrick
Shasta-Max Burch
Sierra-Ken Wharry
Skyline-Braumon Creighton
West Valley-Jim Root

2004 South Regional
December 4, 2004 Mt. San Antonio College

125
Eugene Yasutomi-Cerritos 5-4
Jose Hernandez-Santa Ana
Sean Prentice-R Hon Default
Gilbert Carrillo-Bakersfield
Ray Saucedo-East LA Default
Ricardo Figueroa-Palomar
Edwin Rodriguez-G V Default
Marc Marroquin-Mt. SAC

133
J J Holt-Moorpark 10-4
Justo Rodolfo-Santa Ana
Colby Heppler-Bakfld Default
Carlos Alaniz-Cerritos
Mike Noriega-Rio Ho Default
Cecil Sebastian-Mt. SAC
No Seventh
No Eighth

141
Art Aguilar-Santa Ana 7-2
Mat Maldonado-Bakersfield
Daniel Brito-Go West 10-6
Andy Beam-East LA
Ryan Garcia-Cerritos Default
Chris Beal-Moorpark
Caleb Mullinax-V Vall Default
Randy Aguirre-Mt. SAC

149
Miguel Gutierrez-Bak Fall :45
J J Lewis-Cerritos
Robert Dominguez M SAC 7-4
Ernie Aguilar-Santa Ana
John Lee Victor- Valley 13-5
Jimmy Carr-Golden West
Andrew Lowen-Palomar 8-7
Saul Lopez-East LA

157
Ronnie Hopkins-Cerritos 8-4
Ryan Corn-Bakersfield
Jonathan Keene-Sta Ana 11-0
Eric Sanchez-Rio Hondo
Joe Foss-Golden West
Sam Choi-Mt. SAC
Stuart Cole-Palomar 12-0
Tyrone Mendez-Moorpark

165
Jeff Baker-Bakersfield Fall :09
Ty Souza-Mt. SAC
Garett Williams-MP Default
Nathan Sare-Cerritos
Ellis Trotter-East LA 15-7
Devin Williams-Rio Hondo
A J Hagan-Palomar 3-2
Bazan Gabrakristos-Sa Ana

174
Jason Points-Bakersfield 18-9
Brian Judd-Santa Ana
Bryan Baker-Vic Valley 13-0
Rickey Newsom-Palomar
Wil Ayon-G West-Fall 1:51
Nick Loiacano-Rio Hondo
No Seventh
No Eighth

184
Jesse Ruiz-Santa Ana 12-4
Michael Ullerich-G West
Andrew Guzman-Bakfld 8-3
David Carson-Palomar
Brandon Davis-Cerritos 10-0
Steve Boulay-Moorpark
No Seventh
No Eighth

197
Danny Melendez-S Ana 22-8
Dan Almanza-Palomar
Emanuel Newton Cerritos 8-2
Jay Thomas-Mt. SAC
Jesse Velasquez-Bakfld 6-4
Sam Liera-Golden West
Sam Sitchler-Victor Valley
No Eighth

285
Tyrell Blanche Moorpark 11-1
Pedro Garcia-Cerritos
Joe Espejo-Bakfld Default
Tyler McKay-Palomar
Eric Garcia-Mt. SAC 7-2
Dana Morgan-East LA
Robert Elias-Santa Ana 10-5
Gary Bradshaw-Victor Valley

Team Scores
1 Bakersfield 175
2 Santa Ans 149
3 Cerritos 146
4 Moorpark 80
5 Palomar 78.5
6 Mt. SAC 76
7 Golden West 70
8 Rio Hondo 53
9 East LA 48.5
10 Victor Valley 43

Coaches
Bakersfield-Bill Kalivas
Cerritos-Steve Glassey
East LA-Ralph Valle
Golden West-Dale Deffner
Moorpark-Paul Keysaw
Mt. SAC-Larry Watanabe
Palomar-Joe Ismay
Rio Hondo Paul LaBlanc
Santa Ana-Vince Silva
Victor Valley-Mike Labrosse

Santa Ana Program list
Jonathan Keene 157 as Champion

Miguel Gutierrez (Bakersfield) 2003 & '04

2005 North Regional
December 3, 2005

126
Sabi Sing-Fresno
Oscar Romero-Sierra
Jonathan Macalolooy-Chabot

133
Torrean Tyus-Sierra
Mike Waterston-Fresno
Brandon Patterson-Sant Rosa

141
Benny Garcia-S J Delta
Tommy Machado-West Valley
T J Owens-Modesto

150
Matt Griffin-Sierra
Sinai Pezzat-Fresno
Josh Emmett-Sacramento

157
Zac Taylor-West Valley
J D Thrall-Sacramento
Kyle Hames-Cuesta

165
Jesse Fernandez-Sacramento
Jeff Lema-Skyline

174
Konrad Schwartz-Sacramento
Justin Smith-Moorpark

184
Jordan Lefler-Modesto
Sheldon Page-Sierra
Marques Gales-Santa Rosa

197
Jacob Starr-Cuesta
Alexis Lara-Skyline
Jayson Collard-Santa Rosa
Cory Compton-Sacramento
Kenny Keller-S J Delta

285
Marcus Moore-Sierra
Ken Martin-Chabot
Bryan Whetstone-Fresno
James Clark-Modesto

Team Results
1
2
3

In no order names are from the state results

2005 South Regional
December 3, 2005

126
Jimmy Valdivia-Cerritos 6-2
Ismael Armendariz-East LA
Jose Hernandez-Sa Ana 19-6
David Navarrete-Palomar
Keith Gibson-Bakersfield Def
Travis Patterson-Rio Hondo
Eric Medina-Moorpark F :26
Jessica Chaplin-Mt. SAC

133
Corey Hamabata-Mt.SAC 7-3
Cody Gibson-Bakersfield
Rudy Justo-Santa Ana F 1:30
Paul Paez-East LA
Andrew Holmes-Cerrito 10-8
Shawn Jones-Moorpark
Luis Mercardo-Palomar
No Eighth

141
Steve Schantin-Sa Ana F 1:02
Adam Beam-East LA
Brian Secaida-Mt SAC Def
Dan Castro-Palomar
Derrick Hunter-BakFld F 3:25
Andrew Cottrell-Moorpark
Jon McCaleb Cerritos
No Eighth

149
Mike O'Hara-Santa Ana 4-2
Alex Herrera-Bakersfield
Octavio Lucatero-Moorp 10-2
Kelly Cromwell-Victor Valley
Louie Desantis-PalomarF5:40
Eric Fehrs-Mt. SAC
David Razo-Cerritos 6-3
Steven Saenz-Rio Hondo

157
Ben Barrett-Mt. SAC 12-8
Jason Hull-Golden West
Orlando Landois-Bakfld 8-3
Sabas Cruz-Santa Ana
Andrew Lowen-Palomar 5-2
Daniel Salcido-East LA
Evan Rodriguez-Moor TF 17-2
Jordan Cope Victor Valley

165
Jeff Davis-Cerritos 5-2
Ty Sousa-Mt. SAC
Randy Doherty-Bakfld 5-4
Bhnom Khaki-Moorpark
Charleton Thayn-Vi Valley 5-4
Duayne Guile-Palomar
Frank Vergara Santa Ana 12-5
Derek Perry-Golden West

174
Ryan Nejal-Palomar 8-6
Jason Points-Bakersfield
Ronnie Hopkins-Cerrit F 2:45
Tom Eaton-Santa Ana
Justin Smith-Moorpark 15-5
Daniel Garay-Mt. SAC
Scott Hert-Victor Valley
Matt Lightner-Golden West

184
Brett Mooney-Bakersfield 3-2
Brian Judd-Santa Ana
Tim Hawkins-Mt. SAC 4-2
Luie Audelo-Cerritos
Shawn Riggs-Moorpk F 2:08
Mike Cascioppo-Palomar
Navarre Perry-Golden West
No Eighth

197
Ryan Silvera-Mt. SAC 10-2
George Jimenez-Moorpark
Tyler McKay-Palomar F 2:32
Gerald Carollo Golden West
Miguel Ruano-East LA
Bye
Paul Martinez-Rio Hondo Def
Kyle McGraw-Santa Ana

185
Josh Marquez-Bakfld 17-6
Brandon Doran-Cerritos
Juan Rodrigoez-Sa Ana F 6:57
Jose Arroyo-Rio Hondo
John Terndrup-Moorpark 4-2
Matt Klimek-Palomar
Manuel Gomez-East LA
No Eighth

Team Scores
1	Santa Ana	145
2	Bakersfield	139.5
3	Mt. SAC	124.5
4	Palomar	108.5
5	Moorpark	107
6	Cerritos	105
7	East LA	66.5
8	Golden West	42
9	Victory Valley	33
10	Rio Hondo	32

184-Tim Hawkins-Mt. San Antonio College
*OW 2005

2006 North Regional
December 2, 2006 S J Delta College

125
Chauncey Philips-Sierra
Taylor McCorriston-Sant Rosa
Kyle Couch-Fresno
Albert Tapia-Sacramento
Patrick Dominguez-Lassen
Jesus Felix-Modesto

133
Eddy Ngo-West Valley
Daymond Bland-Sacramento
Mike Righi-Fresno
Aaron McCrea-Chabot
Mitch Schroder-Lassen
Armando Martinez-S J Delta

141
Leland Gridley-Sierra
Edgar Mercado-Fresno
Jordan Keckler-Modesto
Jonathan Ronny-Chabot
Richie Nole West-Valley
Caleb Mack-S J Delta

149
Alfonso Sanchez-Fresno
Henry Kofa-Lassen
Travis Wood-Sierra
John Daly-Sacramento
Will Matulich-Santa Rosa
Bayardo Sanchez-West Valley

157
Sinai Pezzai-Fresno
Jack Bridges-Shasta
Matt Griffin-Sierra
J D Thrall Sacramento
Shawn Schantin-Chabot
Matthew Coit-Santa Rosa

165
Nick Bardsley-Fresno
Tony Moser-Lassen
Dan Barraza-Sierra
Zac Wichi-West Valley
Josh Dixon-Sacramento
Martin Beeler-Modesto

174
Kyle Griffin-Santa Rosa *
Shawn Ceremello-Fresno
Marcus Garcia-West Hills
Ryan Sughrue-Modesto
Carlos Ordonez-SJ Delta
Matt Livley-Lassen

184
Steve Urquizo-Fresno
Marques Gates-Santa Rosa
Mike Leslie-Sierra
Cory Compton-Sacramento
Shane Miller-Lassen
Matt McGarry-Shasta

197
Jayson Collard-Santa Rosa
Jerred Dixon-Sacramento
Joseph Ramirez-Modesto
Tyler Blair-Fresno
Norman Nail-West Hills
Tim Wallace-Shasta

285
Eric Nye-Sierra
Steve Franklin-Santa Rosa
Victor Leyva-Fresno
Nick Thompson-Sacramento
Robbie Roman-Marin W Hills
Nolan Verga-West Hills

Most Outstanding Wrestler
Kyle Griffin-Santa Rosa

Team Scores
1 Fresno   158.5
2 Sierra   116
3 Santa Rosa 101
4 Sacramento 99
5 Lassen   65.5
6 Modesto   47.5
6 West Valley 47.5
8 West Hills 39
9 Chabot   38
10 S J Delta 31
11 Shasta   25
12 Skyline   18

Coaches
Chabot-Steve Siroy
Cuesta-Joe Danby
Fresno-Jared Smith
Modesto-Gary Fisher
Sacramento-Dave Pacheco
S J Delta-Mike Sandler
Santa Rosa-Jake Fitpatrick
Shasta-Justin Bxbye
Sierra-Ken Wharry
Skyline-James Haddon
West Valley-Jim Root

174-Kyle Griffin-Santa Rosa JC *OW 2006

2006 South Regional
December 2, 2006 Cerritos College

125
Ivan Sanchez-Santa Ana 12-6
Jason Carrillo-Cerritos
Carl Riding-Victor Valley 8-4
Sammy Saunders-East LA
Rick Bernal-Rio Hond TF 16-0
  Medina-Moorpark
Brandon Silvia-Bakersfield

133
Carlos Alaniz-Cerrit Fall 4:25
Gabriel Aguilar-Santa Ana
Ethan Hall-Palomar
Cody Gibson-Bakersfield
  Lopez-Rio Hondo Default
Claudio Seanez-Mt. SAC
  Prado Moorpark-15-10
  Jones-Cuesta

141
Joseph Serrato-S Ana Default
Bruce Wasserman Bakersfield
Andrew Holmes-Cerrit F 3:45
Tyson Knierim-Palomar
  Drucker-Cuesta Fall 3:40
  Fehrs-Mt. SAC
  Aguirre-East LA 11-3
  Aguilera-Victor Valley

149
Orlando Barragan-Sa Ana 5-4
Joe Barajas-Palomar
Tony Ruiz-Cerritos Fall 2:01
Eric Timson-Bakersfield
Ian Millan-Rio Hondo 9-5
  Kamaakala-Cuesta
  Cottrell-Moorpark Fall 1:10
  Marroquin-East LA

157
Devin Velasquez Santa An 2-0
Steve Saenz-Rio Hondo
Emilio Rojas-Chavez-Cerri 3-2
Stewart Cole-Palomar
Zach Johnson-Bakersfield 8-3
  Orewyler-Mt. SAC
  Pachon Moorpark-Default
  Peterson-East LA

165
Glen Shaw-Palomar 6-1
Jack Porter-Cerritos
Daniel Garay-Mt. SAC 13-7
Michael-Williams-Cuesta
  Reifstahl Moorpark- Default
Orlando Landon-Bakersfield
Eddie Sanchez-Santa An 15-1
  Loiacano-Rio Hondo

174
Tom Eaton-Santa Ana 2-1
Celib Smith-Palomar
Eric Gonzalez-Moorpark Deflt
Gene Choi-Cerritos
  Lemus East-LA Default
Eric Sanchez-Rio Hondo
Thayn Victor-Valley Fall 3:10
  Gibson-Cuesta

184
Tom Hawkins Mt. SAC Default
Jason Carrasco-Bakersfield
Luie Audelo-Cerritos16-8
  Hauss-Moorpark
  Guzman-Santa Ana 5-3
  Tielens-Palomar
  Melendez-Rio Hondo 12-1
  Bradley-Cuesta

197
Ryan Silvera-Mt. SAC F 3:25
Todd Moleworth-Moorpark
  Desmond-Palomar 15-8
Al Kinslow-Cerritos
  Hernandez-Santa Ana 9-6
  Ramon-Perez-Bakersfield
  Abeyta-Rio Hondo

285
Brandon Doran-Cerritos 10-9
Josh Marquez-Bakersfield
Tyler Porras-Santa Ana F 6:35
Matt Klimek-Palomar
  Chavez-Moorpark Fall 2:20
  Pagaran-Cuesta
Alex Arellano-Rio Hondo

Team Scores

1	Cerritos	168
2	Santa Ana	165
3	Palomar	130
4	Bakersfield	103
5	Moorpark	93.5
6	Mt. SAC	88.5
7	Rio Hondo	75
8	Cuesta	52
9	East LA	36
10	Victor Valley	23

Coaches
Bakersfield-Bill Kalivas
Cerritos-Steve Glassey
East LA-Ralph Valle
Golden West-Dale Deffner
Moorpark-John Kever
Mt. SAC-Larry Watanabe
Palomar- Byron Campbell
Rio Hondo-Paul LaBlane
Santa Ana-Vince Silva
Victor Valley

2007 North Regional
November 30, 2007

125
Angel Olea-Fresno
Corey Houser-Lassen
Chauncey Philipps-Sierra
Jason Moorhouse-Skyline
Charles Chatman-Santa Rosa
Fernando Munoz-West Hills
133
Norman Richmond-Sierra
Eddy Ngo-West Valley
Brett Land-West Hills
Rolando Velasco-Modesto
Paul Ruiz-Fresno
141
Juan Archuleta-Sacramento
Jonathan Ronny-Chabot
Edger Mercado-Fresno
149
Chris Santana-Sierra
Aris Harutunyan-West Valley
Jimmy Anderson-Skyline
Kyle Lew-Santa Rosa
157
Trinity Perkins-Lassen
Jake Bridges-Shasta
Travis Wood-Sierra
Mark Berton-West Valley
165
Nick Bardsley-Fresno
Zeth St. Clair-Sierra
Robert Carothers Sacramento
Bobby Vitatoe-Santa Rosa

174
Victor Carazo-Modesto
Shaun Ceremello-Fresno
Mike Fucci-Sierra
Brad Muthart-Lassen
184
Ryan Sughrue-Modesto
Alex Howard-Sierra
Matt Garcia-West Hills
Dan Righi-Fresno
Jonas Schenzel-Lassen
197
Shane Miller-Lassen
Jordan Lefler-Modesto
Mingo Grant-Sierra
Jimmy Gallegos-Fresno
Heavyweight
Erik Nye-Sierra
Timothy Guerrero-S J Delta
Chris Kiel-Lassen
Luis Leyva-Fresno
Josh Newman-West Hills

Team Results
1
2
3

No real order names taken from state place winners.

133-Norman Richmond - Sierra College *OW 2007

2007 South Regional
November 30, 2007

125
Jason Carrillo-Cerritos 1
Mark Ibarra-Palomar

133
Paul Lyon-Cerritos 1
Cesar Renteria-Santa Ana
Benji Gomez-Fresno

141
Mike Koehnlein-Cerritos 1
Brandon McKnight-Vict Valley
Ethan Hall-Palomar
Nick Cardoza-Mt. SAC
149
Jose Serrato-Santa Ana
Octavio Santana-Sierra
Diego Martinez-Rio Hono
Jaime Rodriguez-Bakersfield
157
Louie Desantis-Palomar
Sean Barbour-Santa Ana
David Razo-Cerritos 3

165
Lewis Gonzales-Palomar
Jay Bogan East-LA
Gene Choi-Cerritos 3
Sam Gaxiola-Mt. SAC
174
James Clay-East LA
Eric Gonzales-Moorpark

Adam Hase-Cerritos 5

184
Kellan Desmond-Palomar
Alex Alcala-Bakersfield

Mike Mehegan-Cerritos 5
197
Al Kinslow-Cerritos 1
Greg Villalobo-Palomar
Andrew Capucetti-East LA
Todd Molesworth-Moorpark
285
Robert Elias-Santa Ana
Juan Enriquez-Cerritos 2
Jeremy Pagaran-Cuesta

Team Results
1 Cerritos
2
3

Not in order the results from state results, the Cerritos wrestlers with a number is the place from the regional found of the Cerritos web page.

2008 North Regional
December 5, 2008

125
Angel Olea-Fresno
Brandon Benvenuti-Sierra
John Mort-Lassen

133
Todd Wilcox-Sierra
Derek Ellis-Shasta
Marty Rubalcava-Fresno
Justen Locking-Sacramento

141
Mike Vassar-Sierra
Stephen De La Cruz-Chabot
Keven Thongseng-Fresno

149
Brad Kummerer-Lassen
Adam Obad-Modesto

157
Alfonso Shanchez-Fresno
Robert Carothers Sacramento
Matt Thomas-Shasta
Rafael Munoz-Lassen
Matt Klingler Sierra

165
Zeth St. Clair-Sierra
Dustin Reid-Shasta
Matt Cox-Fresno
Anthony Clay-Lassen

174
Cody Vasconcellos Sacrament
Mike Fucci-Sierra
James Hammontree-
Eric Smith-Fresno
Carlos Soto-S J Delta

184
Steven Urquizo-Fresno
Edward Melitosyan-W Valley
Derek Rottenberg-Shasta
Shawn Michalek-Sacramento
Tony Ferris-Lassen

197
B J Mosley-Sacramento
J T Minto-Shasta
Tyler Blair-Fresno

285
Matt Gibson-Sierra
Austin Garza-Fresno
Carson Carman-Lassen

Team Results unofficial
1 Fresno
2 Sierra
3 Sacramento
4 Lassen
5 Shasta

Not in any order names taken from state results

125-Angel Olea- Fresno City College
*OW 2008

2008 South Regional
December 6, 2008

125
Jamie Martinez-Santa Ana
Joe Cabanas-Cerritos
Alex Carrico-Rio Hondo
Tym Quigg-Victor Valley

133
Gabe Aguilar-Santa Ana
Ryan Giovenco-Cerritos
Christian Hernandez-Bakfld
Julian Gonzalez-Rio Hondo

141
Mike Koenlein-Cerritos
Bobby Scofield-Santa Ana
Joes Mondragon-Palomar
Bobby Medina-Mt. SAC
Ray Bowen-Victor Valley

149
Ian Millan-Rio Hondo
Sad Manigault-West Hills
Jose Navarro-Santa Ana
Jamie Rodriguez-Bakersfield
Alfred Solis-Palomar

157
Eric Sauvageaum-Cerritos
David Supplebeen-Mt. SAC
Danny Kennedy-Santa Ana

165
Adrian Gonzales-East LA
Sean Barbour-Santa Ana
Blake Willard-Cuesta
Clayton MacFarland-Palomar

174
Mike Cavanaugh-Bakfld
Travis Tielens-Palomar
Cesar Ponce-East LA

184
Caleb Gerl-Cerritos
Matt Garcia-West Hills
Josh Villagomez-Mt. SAC

197
Tyler Garcia-Santa Ana
Julian Silva-Mt. SAC
Sal Felicia-Rio Hondo
Jacob Merrell-West Hills
Angel Romero-Palomar

285
Juan Enriquez-Cerritos
Kyle Roh-Santa-Ana
Jeff Jones-Victor Valley
Tommy James-Mt. SAC
Juan Durazo-Moorpark

Team Results
1
2
3

No real order results from the state results

2009 North Regional
December 5, 2009 Fresno City College

125
Brandon Benvenuti-Sie F 6:33
Galen Williams-Fresno
Sophan Mey-Sacramento 8-2
David Sok-SJ Delta
Josh Delgado-Modesto Deft
Joshua Aveno-West Valley
Lewis Mercado-Lassen F 4:22
Brian Vierra-Chabot

133
Dan Osmer-Fresno 9-6
Norman Richmond-Sierra
Justen Lockling-Sacramen 3-2
Charlie Seang-S J Delta
Jeremy Moreno-Shasta 8-4
Sam Orozco-Modesto
Jairo Rodriguez-Skyline F 4:11
Steve Parodi-Chabot

141
Mike Vassar-Sierra 7-5
Stephen De La Cruz-Chabot
T J Owens-Modesto Fall 4:15
Pete Escandon Fresno
Tyler Diamond-Sacrame Deft
Wesley Young-Santa Rosa
Derek Ellis-Shasta 10-9
Anthony Agapoa-West Valley

149
Vlad Dombrovskiy-Sierra 8-3
Tim Nevarez-Sacramento
Arnol Aroliga-Lassen Fall 3:58
Kyle Lew Santa-Rosa
Kyle Means-Chabot 10-7
Kevin Miller-Fresno
Will Horton-Modesto 13-7
Kris Swatsbaugh-Skyline

157
Tim Navarrette-Sierra 7-2
Chris Urquizo-Fresno
Aaron Pickard-Sierra 3-2
Shawn Brendle-Sacramento
Adam Obad-Modesto 11-7
Mitchell Arreguin-Santa Rosa
Spencer Phillips-Chabot 6-4 X
Jonah Estrella-Lassen

165
Joe Garner-Sacramento 2-1
Fernando Lucatero-Fresno
Travis Schaffer-Modesto 12-4
Dwight Flores-Chabot
Joey Forseth Shasta 7-3
Bruce Arndt-Sierra
Joe Madison-Lassen Fall :14
Hiram Torrecilas-West Valley

174
Dustin Reid-Shasta 9-4
Nick Gill-Sierra
Carlos Soto-S J Delta
Joe Cisneros-Fresno
Kale Degrandmont-Sacramen
Milo Anderson-Chabot
Blair Bergman-Modesto
Jesus Gonzalez-West Valley

184
Jesus Chavez-Sierra 6-4
Justin Walker-Fresno
Shawn Michalck-Sacramento
Todd Rucker-Shasta
Jeff Moran-Modesto
Kevin Reed-Skyline
Robert Hoggle-Chabot
Omar Ortiz-Santa Rosa

197
Ryan Scarr-Sierra 6-4
J T Minto-Shasta
Adam O'Brien-Santa Rosa
Kevin Keisler-Sacramento
Lucas Keene-Fresno
Cruz Zawedeah-Skyline
Frank Keach-Modesto
Carlos Castro-Chabot

285
Austin Garza-Fresno
Richard Segovia-West Valley
Jasmette Basra-S J Delta
George Palmer-Chabot
Tyler Magart-Davis Shasta
Dimitrius Berry-Sacramento
Kevon Tillotson-Sierra
James Gonzalez-Skyline

Most Outstanding Wrestler
Brandon Benvenuti-Sierra

Team Scores
1	Sierra	169
2	Fresno	154
3	Sacramento	138.5
4	Shasta	112.5
5	Chabot	82.5
6	Modesto	76.5
7	S J Delta	57
8	Santa Rosa	40.5
9	West Valley	38
10	Lassen	33.5
11	Skyline	22.5

X = True Sixth

133-Norman Richmond
Sierra College *OW 2009

2009 South Regional
December 5, 2009 Cypress College

125
Jimmy Martinez-Santa Ana
Steve Salinas-Mt. SAC
Andy Yu-Cerritos
A J Jaramillo-West Hills
Alex Gonzalez-Palomar
Anthony Cruz-East LA
Carlos Reyes-Cuesta

133
Jason Arreola-Santa Ana
Pierce Lowry-Mt. SAC
Jeff Janecky-Cerritos
Victor Rubio-Victor Valley
Jesus Pacheco-East LA
Angel Garcia-Palomar
M. Langford-West Hills

141
Bobby Scofield-Santa Ana
John Marchena-East LA
Frank Ruiz-Rio Hondo
F. Amador-West Hills
Sam Smith-Victor Valley
Danny Avila-Mt. SAC
Danny Varela-Palomar
Sean Martin-Bakersfield

149
Jose Navarro-Santa Ana
Jesse Cruz-Rio Hondo
Mike Lopez-East La
Jesse Ponce Cerritos
John Banke-Cuesta
Tim Randall-Palomar
Bryce Horton-Bakersfield
J. Araiza Victor-Valley

157
Ted Bristol-Santa Ana F 1:36
Bronson Gerl-Cerritos
Javier Avila-Cuesta 9-8
Chris Abeyta-Mt. SAC
Adolfo Rojo-Bakersfield 7-2
Rudy Conant-Rio Hondo
J. Whittington-West Hills
Addie Sann-East LA

165
Alvaro Zermeno-Bakfld Def
Clayton McFarlane-Palomar
Alfonso Estrada-Cerritos 7-6
R J Pilkington-Santa Ana
Alfred Torres-Mt. SAC 4-2
Mike Brady-Cuesta
Andy Riding-Victor Valley
   Bestgen-West Hills

174
Daniel Kennedy-S Ana Deft
A J Smith-Bakersfield
Nick Inclan-Rio Hondo Deft
Nico Phillips-Mt. SAC
Hunter Baird-Cuesta 8-6
Oren Dramen-Palomar
Daniel Walton-Cerritos F 2:12
C. Dean-West Hills

184
Caleb Gerl-Cerritos 3-2
George Munoz-Mt. SAC
Jack Robinett-Cuesta 6-3
Chris Herrera-Palomar
Luis Onofre-Santa Ana F 1:10
Dan Thomas-Rio Hondo
R. Garcia-West Hills

197
Julian Silva-Mt. SAC 7-2
Jimmy Botheras-Santa Ana
   Aguirre-Victor Valley 8-2
Jacob Eaton-Cerritos
Anthony Meza-Rio Ho F 2:05
C J Marvin-Cuesta
Q. Willingham-W Hills 13-2
Lucas Marty-Palomar

285
Jose Lopez-Cerritos 5-2
Frank Ayala-Mt. SAC
Anthony Gonzalez-Rio Ho 4-2
Dan Colbert-Cuesta
Kasey Cowan-Palomar 3-2
Brian Klieves-Santa Ana
T. Underwood-W Hills F 5:58
K. Walker-Victor Valley

Team Scores
1	Santa Ana	177.5
2	Mt. SAC	139
3	Cerritos	132
4	Rio Hondo	91
5	Cuesta	89.5
6	Palomar	85.5
7	West Hills	55.5
8	Bakersfield	54
9	East LA	48
9	Victor Valley	48

2010 North Regional
December 4, 2010 Modesto College

125
David Soc-S J Delta 6-4
Chris Padilla-Fresno
Janik Santana-Chabot 9-3
Ruben Gonzalez-Shasta
Issac Taz Pilgrim-Santa Rosa
Edgar Paez-Modesto
Jack Hagan-Skyline
Eric Down-Sierra

133
Marty Rubalcaba-Fresno 5-3
Charlie Seang-S J Delta
Alex Williams-Chabot 15-7
William Sepulvada-Lassen
Tyler Christiansen-Santa Rosa
Ralph Rioja-Skyline
Jason Gagnon-Modesto
Ben Gacayan-Sacramento

141
Kevin Rojas-Fresno 12-4
R J Pilkington-Sierra
Tyler Diamond-Sacrame Deft
Terry Matthews-Shasta
Paul Kellam-S J Delta
Shane Kenihan-Santa Rosa
Dio Cerda-Skyline
David Pimentel-Modesto

149
Conrad Rangel-Fresno Fall
Anthony Harris-Sacramento
Marcial Rodriguez-Lassen 3-2
Wesley Young-Santa Rosa
Victor Tubera-Modesto
Marquez Ford-Sierra
Joe Wettstein-Skyline
Alex LeCoco-S J Delta

157
Jake Schilling-Fresno Default
Tyler Johnson-Sierra
Craig Simmons-Shasta Deft
Craig Sherman-Chabot
Russell Williams-Sacramento
Von Borges-Santa Rosa
Eric Munoz-Modesto
Miguel Garcia-S J Delta

165
Tigan Adzhemyan-Fresno 3-1
Vlad Dombbrovsky-Sierra
Joe Madison-Lassen 5-3
Marco Orozco-Sacramento
Cody Bagley-Santa Rosa
Thomas Marquez-Modesto
Steven Yale-Shasta
Alex Trevizo-Skyline

174
Martin Fabbian-Fresno Deft
Sam Temko-Skyline
Nick Gill-Sierra Fall
Ira Goosby-Chabot
Tyler Edwards-Sacramento
Christian Moore-Modesto
Chris White-Lassen X
Adam Cruz-Santa Rosa

184
Jesse Hellinger-Sacrame 3-2
Fito Juarez-Fresno
Milo Anderson-Chabot 6-4
Adam Charles Skyline
LoganPaul Eickhoff Shasta
Eric McCary-Modesto
Alfonso Estrada-Lassen
Alex Cerda-Santa Rosa

197
Jordan Williams-Sierra 3-1
Marco Delgado-Modesto
Lucas Keen-Fresno 11-6
Colin Hart-Santa Rosa
Kevin Keisler-Sacramento
Alvaro Tellez-S J Delta
Jared Minoletti-Shasta

285
Luis Contreras-Fresno 9-2
Jesse Green-Sacramento
Anthony Chu-S J Delta Fall
Tivo Cruz Modesto
Wesley Swafford-Shasta
Eric Hesterberg-Santa Rosa
Rafael Iriarte-Sierra
Sam Garcia-Chabot

Team Scores
1 Fresno   202
2 Sacramento   119
3 Sierra   103
4 Santa Rosa   90.5
5 Modesto   87
6 Shasta   77.5
7 S J Delta   71.5
8 Chabot   67.5
9 Skyline   56
10 Lassen   53.5

X = True Sixth

2010 South Regional
December 4, 2010 Santa Ana College

125
Estevan Cabanas Cerritos 7-6
A J Jaramillo West Hills
Aaron LaFarge Palomar 4-2
Chris Diaz Cuesta
Marc Collier Bakersfield 8-3
Ivan Garibay East LA
Anthony Bonalas Rio Ho Deft
Nick Danna Santa Ana

133
Alex Perez West Hills 5-1
Jon Gay Cuesta
Brian Magno Bakersfield 5-0
Hector Lopez Mt. SAC
Ian Kelly Palomar 15-9
Danny Rosas East LA
Hector Martinez Rio Ho 4-3 X
Chad Thornock Cerritos

141
Kyle Chene Santa Ana Default
Tillman Tran Cerritos
Abel Avila Rio Hondo 13-2
Audric DeCastro Palomar
Eric Orozco West Hills F 1:18
Joseph Martinez East LA
Nestor Ruelas Cuesta 10-3 X
Renee Garcia Bakersfield

149
Spencer Anderson 5-2
Chris Abeyta Mt. SAC
Ernie Aguilar Default
Jimmy Arazia Victor Valley
Jesse Ponce Cerritos 7-4
Nick Okley Palomar
Ryan Steiber Bakfld 14-12 X
Jose Maldonado Rio Hondo

157
Eric Lopez Victor Valley Deft
Taylor Sare Mt. SAC
Josh Lujan West Hills Default
Cody Bollinger Cerritos
Aaron Lopez Santa Ana 13-0
Carson Garcia Cuesta
Jose Marroquin Est LA F 3:41
Mark Nevarez Bakersfield

165
Eric Sauvageau Cerritos 5-0
Dustin Rocha West Hills
Eric Gutterman Santa Ana 3-2
Nick Hernandez Cuesta
Christian Ruvaicaba Cuest 2-0
Thomas Negrette Rio Hondo
Orlando Lopez V Valley Def X
Giovanni Vasquez East LA

174
A J Smith Bakersfield 3-1
Alfredo Torres Mt. SAC
Thomas Estrada Cerritos 2-1
Charlie Galaviz Cuesta
Chase Mirassou Rio Hon 5-3
Luis Vargas Santa Ana
Oren Dramen Sa Ana TF 15-0
Edward Carbajal East LA

184
Sean Dougherty Cuest F 2:30
Matt Lewellen Palomar
Oscar Navarrete Mt. SAC 7-1
Dan Thomas Rio Hondo
Ryan Collins Cerritos 6-4
Santino Delfino Bakersfield
Adrian Macias East LA Fall :22
Alex Cholmakijan West Hills

197
Brad Carls Bakersfield 10-0
Mario Delgado Cerritos
Trever Gwin Palomar 14-2
Derek Sanchez West Hills
Rudy Calderon East LA F 2:03
Carl Stokes Mt. SAC
Chad Rodriguez Santa Ana

282
Jose Lopez Cerritos Fall 3:00
Cheyene Cook Victor Valley
Quinn Moore Bakersfield 5-3
Juan Lucero East LA
Cameron McNeer Paloma 4-1
George Pacheco Mt. SAC
Robert Contreras R Hon F:13
Barry Gee Santa Ana

Team Scores
1 Cerritos   143
2 Cuesta   112
3 Bakersfield   100.5
4 Palomar   97.5
4 West Hills   97.5
6 Mt. SAC   90
7 Santa Ana   81
8 East LA   70
9 Rio Hondo   67
10 Victor Valley 59

X = True Sixth

Record
A J Jaramillo West Hills 31-7

157- Eric Lopez
Victor Valley College *OW 2010

2011 North Regional
December 3, 2011 Skyline College

125
Merk Robbins-Sa Rosa 8-6 OT
Austin Auston Wufert-Sierra
Nathan-Sacramento Fall 1:38
Junior Davila-Fresno
Carson Homuth-Mode F 3:59
Daniel Nguyen-Chabot
Froyan Valencia-Delta F 1:46
Chase Mari-Shasta

133
Isaiah Hurtado-Sacra TF 21-4
Jeff Lobos-Lassen
Chris Padilla-Fresno Default
Aaron Pen Kruger-Santa Ana
Jeremy Newman-Siera 9-7 OT
Dan Mai-Chabot
Jason Cortez-Modest F 2:24 X
Atom Garcia-S J Delta

141
Kevin Rojas-Fresno 7-4
Anthony Vega-Sacramento
Richard Morris- Rosa F 6 :04
Mike Sepulveda-Lassen
John Claitor-Skyline 4-2
Nick Ghannam-Sierra
Joey Castery-Shasta Fall 1:05
Ernesto Villegas-Modesto

149
Conrad Rangell-Fresno 5-3
Tim Nevarex-Sacramento
Alex Rodriguez Lassen
Marcus Gebhardt-Skyline D Q
Victor Tubera-Modesto
Nolen Kajiware-Chabo14-4 X
Andrew Collins-Santa Rosa

157
Brady Bersano Fresno Default
Shawn Porter-Sacramento
Monet Goldman-Skyline Deft
Jesse Baldazo-Sierra
Josh Dye-Shasta 4-3
Owen Craugh-Lassen
Anthony Spinella-Modest 6-1
Nico Serrano-Santa Rosa

165
Tigran Adzhemyan Fresn 10-4
Gavin Ludwig-Sacramento
Vinny Fausone-Santa Ros 3-2
A J Estrada-Lassen
Richie Green-Shasta 12-3
Derrick Hoo-Skyline
Adam Lagos Modesto Default
Trey Edmunds-Sierra

174
Martin Fabbian-Fresno 4-3
Rick Gomez-Modesto
Dwight Flores-Chabot Default
Dalton Berncich-Santa Rosa
Dylin Rodriguez Sierra Fall :20
Garret Marinelli-Sacramento
Kyle Towler-Lassen Fall 3:44 X
Ellizon Dizon-Skyline

184
Fito Juarez-Fresno 6-0
Jairo Chavez-Sierra
Josh Cutts-Lassen Fall 1:57
Gerson Nkunku-Sacramento
Neweed Zemaryalal-Cha 19-8
Xavier Bahena-Santa Rosa
Coleman Myer-Skyline 17-5
Isaiah Amaya-Modesto

197
Jesus Chavez-Sierra Default
Colin Hart-Santa Rosa
Logan Paul-Eickhoff Shas 18-1
Justin Whitten-Fresno
Tommy Howard-Skyline 4-2
Milton Nkunku-Sacramento
Thomas Marshall-Las F 2:52 X

285
Paul Buchanan-Sacramen 3-1
Richard Sigovia-Chabot
Daniel Gjusey Sierra Default
Leonard Castellanos San Rosa
Luis Contreras-Fresno 4-1
Anthony Chu-S J Delta
Jose Avina-Shasta Default X
Michael Robles-Modesto

Team Scores
1	Fresno	198.5
2	Sacramento	198.5
3	Sierra	153.5
4	Santa Rosa	136.5
5	Lassen	96.5
6	Modesto	71.5
7	Chabot	69
8	Skyline	61
9	Shasta	59
10	S J Delta	20

X = True Seventh

2011 South Regional
December 3, 2011 Palomar College

125
Michael Ruiz-West Hills
Marc Collier-Bakersfield
Pierce Lowry-Mt. SAC
Matt Correa-Cuesta
Jake Harrison-Cuesta
Ray Delgado-Victor Valley
Emilio Rivera-Palomar

133
Eric Orozco-West Hills
Jaydy Gonzales-Palomar
Greg Barera-Cerritos
Phillip Hendrix-Mt. SAC
Brandon Brown-Santa Ana
Jonathan Gay-Cuesta
Josh Ho-East LA

141
Frank Martinez-Rio Hondo
Alberto Arreola-West Hills
Steve Melara-Mt. SAC
Rafik Havhannisyan-East LA
Jonathan Gomez-Bakersfield
Matt Deyoung-Palomar
Sean Pitoniak-Santa Aa

149
Noel Blanco-Mt. SAC
Frank Ruiz-Rio Hondo
Voris Meeks-Cerritos
Will Deyoung-Palomar
Joe Martinez-East La
Cory Flores Santa Ans
Jawayne Fambrough-Bakfld

157
Tim Randall-Palomar
Alex Cruz-Mt. SAC
Ramon Estrada-Cerritos
Marty Legaspe-Rio Hondo
Melvin Cabus-Santa Ana
Adrian Virgen-East LA
Frankie Mariscal-West Hills

165
Aaron Lopez-Santa Ana
Alfonso Estrada-Cerritos
Jacob Pendleton-Bakersfield
Josh Lujan-West Hills
Michael Joseph-Palomar
Josh Newman-East La
Daniel Guzman-Rio Hondo

174
Ryan McWalters-Victor Valley
Mike Macalister-Cuesta
Tyree Cox-Cerritos
Lance Castaneda-Bakersfield
Adrian Macias-East LA
Angel Ramirez-Palomar
Corey Ramos-Mt. SAC

184
Daniel Allan-Rio Hondo
Keith Nieves-Cerritos
Matt Lowellen-Palomar
Ruben Pivaral-East LA
Mike Anderson-West Hills
Brad Beaudette-Cuesta
Carlos Arana-Santa Ana X

197
Jeff Monteirro-West Hills
Carl Stokes-Mt. SAC
Matt Lopez-Rio Hondo
Aaron Dubois-Santa Ana
Dale Fuller-Cuesta
Tyson Pinon-Bakersfield
Edward Carajoi-East LA

285
Brian Klevies-Santa Ana
Martin Gonzales-Mt. SAC
Mike Perez-West Hills
Weston Hawkins-Cerritos
Travis Horn-Rio Hondo
Spencer Smith-Cerritos
Jose Cortez-Palomar
Marshall Thrasher-Cuesta

Team Scores
1
2
3
4 Cerritos

X = True Sixth

Teams
West Hills
Bakersfield
Mt. SAC
Cuesta
Victor Valley
Palomar
Santa Ana
East LA
Rio Hondo
Cerritos

133-Eric Orozco West Hills College
*OW 2011

2012 North Regional
San Joaquin Delta College

125
Chris Martinez-Fresno
Andres Torres-Santa Rosa
Dieuminse-Dore Lassen
Abor Adilov-Sierra
Jeshua Aveno-Chabot
Rickie Castillo-SJ Delta X
Kevin Reber-Skyline

133
A J Valles-Fresno
Travis Roberts-Sierra
Aaron Ceballos-S J Delta
Sean Melton-Sacramento
Dominic Cesena-Chabot
Yesier Alvarez-Lassen X
Jimmy Zhen-Skyline
Andrew Wolocatiuk-San Rosa

141
Racelis Cardenas-Fresno
Anthony Rubio-Chabot
Enriquez Barajas-Sacramento
Atom Garcia-S J Delta
Ishi Silva-Santa Rosa
Justin Belnap-Skyline
Ryan Byleven Shasta X

149
Spencer Hill-Fresno
Bryan Wood-Sacramento
Blake Borges-Santa Ana
Terry Matthews-Shasta
Marcus Gebhardt-Skyline
Adam Lagos-Modesto
Jake Thompson-Zanarini Sie X

157
Brady Bersano-Fresno
Yyson Kuahine-Sacramento
Zach Grove-Skyline
Aaron Demay-Sierra
Eric Figueroa-Santa Rosa
Jacob Bohland-Chabot

165
Matt Hickman-Fresno
Owen Craugh-Lassen
Marquis Ford-Sierra
Shawn Porter-Sacramento
Kaden Martin-Santa Rosa
Atoine Lopez-S J Delta
Dakota Johnson-Chabot
Derrick Hoo-Skyline

174
Tyler Brown-Sacramento
Quinten Becker-Sierra
Kevin Corbett-Fresno
Roman Ermolov-Skyline
Greg Robinson-Santa Ana
Eric Munoz-Modesto X
Robert Uhalde-Chabot
Anthony Williams-S J Delta

184
Fric Gomez-Modesto
Will Gockel-Figge Fresno
Matt Dakin-Sacramento
Tommy Howard-Skyline
Angelo Travino-Sierra
James Windom-Chabot
Jon Creech-Shasta X
Ashton Morales-San Rosa

197
Khymba Johnson-Sierra
Paul Lujano-Fresno
Ryan Mackey-Modesto
Alex Compos-Sacramento
Mick McElvogue-Chabot
Stephen Whiteman-S J Delta
Otilio Carrillo-Santa Rosa X

285
Daniel Gusey-Sierra
Mike Branson-Shasta
Bud Guinn-Santa Rosa
Paul Buchanan-Sacramento
Travis Smith-Modesto
Narcisco Juarez-Fresno X
Temo Cervantes-Skyline
Jose Cisneros-S J Delta

Team Scores
1 Fresno 180.5
2 Sacramento 141
3 Sierra 126
4 Santa Rosa 94.5
5 Chabot 78
6 Skyline 71
7 Modesto 61.5
8 S J Delta 59
9 Shasta 38.5
10 Lassen 37

X=True Sixth

157-Brady Bersano-Fresno City
*OW 2012

2012 South Regional

125
Silverio Esparza-W Hills F2:16
Edwardo Estevez-Paloma
Matthew Correa-Cuesta 5-1
Christian Betancort-Mt. SAC
Gabe Ballerteros-Cerrito 10-4
Hugo Perez-East LA
Brandon Brown-S Ana F 3:57
Cleo Johnson-Bakersfield

133
Juan Jaime-Santa Ana 6-1
Emilio Rivera-Palomar
Darrin Salazar-W Hills F 7:30
Rudy Delgado-Cerritos
Matt Fregoso-Rio Hondo
Ty Young-Bakersfield
Joseph Padilla-East LA 10-6
   Lopez-Mt. SAC

141
Abel Avila-Rio Hondo TF 17-0
Michael Ruiz-West Hills
Michael Behenke-Cerritos
Max Ramirez-Bakersfield
Steven Melara-Mt. SAC 5-2
Julian Purdy-Cuesta
Ascary Lule-Palomar F 2:52
   Catalan-Santa Ana

149
Jacob Dunning-Palomar 6-3
Jose Maldonado-Rio Hondo
Dolin Mininni-Cuesta 15-10
Jose Rugama-Mt. SAC
Nathan Mateo-ant Ana 10-7
Omar Ochoa-East LA
Ryan Steibar-Bakfld 10-1 X
   Medley West-Hills

157
Jacob Blackwell-Sant Ana 3-1
Alexander Cruz-Mt. SAC
Bryan Barocio Rio-Hondo 4-1
Francisco Rueda-West Hills
Joe Else-Cuesta
Robert Monta-Palomar 3-2
Eddie Rodgers-Cerritos X
   Reel-East LA

165
Carlos Arana-Santa Ana 12-7
Jonathon Urango-Cuesta
Nathan Zarate West-Hills 5-3
Michael Joseph-Palomar
Sergo Guerrero-Mt. SAC F :55
   Correa Victor-Valley
Cesar Luna-Bakfld F 4:20 X
Dylan Clark-Cerritos

174
Ryan McWatters-V Vly 12-7
Tyree Cox-Cerritos
Joshua Newman East LA F :38
Brody Gorns-Mt. SAC
Awaad Yasin-Santa Ans 8-3
Chris Bacon-Palomar
Lance Casteneda-Bakf F 1:06
   Cortez-West Hills

184
Kenneth Breaux-Mt. SAC 5-2
Middie Brooks-East LA
Mike Anderson-W Hills F 1:05
Adrian Garcia-Rio Hondo
Juan Hernandez San Ana Deft
Kyle Pivovaroff-Cerritos
Juan Valladores-Cuesta 4-2
   Desantis-Palomar

197
Matt Reed-Palomar
Tyler Smith-Cerritos
Henry Campos-West Hills
Derek Jaurigur-Cuesta
Victor Cisneros-East LA
Jared Matanana-Mt. SAC
Arko Petrosyan-Bakersfield
   Rodreguez-Santa Ana

285
Derrick Lee-West Hills
An Ekezian-Santa Ana
George Pacheco-Mt. SAC
Weston Hawkins-Cerritos
Julian Zuniga-East LA
   Auxier-Rio Hondo
Quinn Moore-Bakersfield
   Castle-Palomar

Team Scores
1	West Hills	141.5
2	Santa Ana	119
3	Mt. SAC	118
4	Palomar	117
5	Cerritos	94.5
6	Rio Hondo	81
7	East LA	80
8	Cuesta	79
9	Bakersfield	54.5
10	Victor Valley	27

X = True Sixth

2013 North Regional
December 7, 2013 Sierra College

125
Arnlfo Olea-Fresno 8-3
Dieuminse Dore-Lassen
Albert Landeros Sacram Forfe
Robert Smith-Santa Rosa
Daniel Nguyen-Chabot F 2:50
Joey Vigil-Sierra
Manny Borrego-Skyline 1-0
Justin Osuna-Skyline

133
Brian Ha-Skyline 4-3
Vincent-Hernandez-Fresno
Aaron PenKruger-Sa Rosa 7-6
Anthony Sakaoka-Sacrament
Logan Fore-Santa Rosa 20-4
Randy Howell-Lassen
Frankie Oceguera Chab 12-10
Anwar Halteh-Skyline

141
Ali Naser-Fresno 1-0
Adrian Gomez-Fresno
Laith Alnassiri-Sacrament 7-0
Carson Homuth-Modesto
Quinn Walker-Sierra Fall :55
Kenji Gutierrez Santa Rosa
Peter Berrington-Delta F 5:45
Ryan Blyleven-Shasta

149
Martine Sandoval-Fresno 1-0
Joseph Ontiveras-Fresno
Will Upson Sacramento Deft
Monet Goldman-Skyline
Jacob Pratt-Chabot Fall 4:18
Regelio Bravo-S J Delta
Bobby Rocha-Sierra 5-4
Giovanni Murillo-Modesto

157
Taylor Hodel-Sacrament 15-0
Austin Braddock-Fresno
Daniel Larman-San-Rosa 9-6
Latrell Benjamin-Modesto
Alex Grijalba-Modesto 14-0
Jeiko Da Silvera Lassen
Zack Grove-Skyline F :42 X
Wes Jensen Shasta

165
Desi Rios-Sacramento Default
Tyson Kuahine-Sacramento
Robin Callas-Sierra 14-1
Sabastian Suikowsky-Fresno
Dane Burgess-Chabot 11-3
Antoine Lopes-S J Delta
Kaden Martin-San Rosa 8-1 X
Leo Arredondo-Skyline

174
Kevin Corbett-Fresno F 4:59
Alex Campos-Chambers Sac
Jesse McDaniel-Modesto TF
Oscar Flores-Sierra
Isai Guzman-San Rosa F 2:00
Robert Uhalde-Chabot
Alan Gonzales-Lassen 14-2
Joel Keough-S J Delta

184
Thomas Cross-Shasta 17-7
Allen Emmons-Sacramento
Ryan Mackey-Modesto 4-3
Kenny Steers-Sacramento
Preston Hill-Fresno F :55
Keith Wanger-Sierra
Sarbjit Sepla-Chabot 9-1
Jose Anaya-Santa Rosa

197
Hudson Buck-Sacramento 3-1
Jairo Chavez-Sierra
Luke Brewer-Modesto Fall
Ismael Alvarez-Fresno
Jordan Davis-Sierra Default
Stephen Wilbert-Lassen
Roman Ermolov-Skyline 15-0
James Liggett-Santa Rosa

285
Mike Branson-Shasta F 2:51
Travis Smith-Modesto
Logan Paxton-Sacrament 2-1
Narsico Juarez-Fresno
Buddy Barraza-Chabot 8-4
Chris Vasquez-Sierra
Jacob Clausen-Chabot Deft
Emmanuel Leon-Chabot

Team Scores
1	Sacramento	187.5
2	Fresno	180.5
3	Modesto	98.5
4	Sierra	95
5	Santa Rosa	79.5
6	Chabot	56.5
7	Shasta	39
8	Lassen	37
9	Skyline	36.5
10	S J Delta	22.5

X= True Sixth

2013 South Regional
December 7, 2013

125
Christian Betancourt M SAC-4
Dustin Kirk-Cerritos
Hugo Perez-East LA
Christian Hauser-Santa Ana
George Sakkas-Cuesta 4-0
Jose Lenddro Bakersfield
Gabe Ballesteros-Cerritos
Jonas Tirado-West Hills

133
Michael Clemmensen Cu 1-0
Connor Pollock-Cuesta
Alex Perez West-Hills 3-1
Nathan Pike-Mt. SAC
Greg Barrera-Cerritos 3-2
Elias Mercado-Rio Hondo
Travys Carus-Palomar 7-6
Joshua Quezada-East LA

141
Andrew Schulte-Sant Ana 4-0
Julian Purdy-Cuesta
Anthony Duran-M SAC F 4:34
Ricky Lule-Palomar
Ryan Maldonado-R Hond 4-3
Eric Ambriz-Cerritos
Omar Ochoa-East LA Fall 1:34
Efrain Velasquez-Victor Valley

149
Max Ramirez-Bakersfield 6-4
Keanu Tom-Cerritos
Richie Miranda-San Ana 12-2
Jr Lule-Palomar
Jonathan-Gomez Bakfl F2:38
Landon Myers-Santa Ana
Jon Hernandez-Mt. SAC F :29
Jonny Callas-Cuesta

157
Shervin Iraniha-Palomar 1-0
Marshal Palmer-Palomar
Nathan Mateo Santa Ana 4-1
Adrian Herrera-East LA
J Magdaleno-Hudson ELA10-3
Josh Cortez Cuesta
Marcos Villarreal-Mt.SA F1:27
Jawayne Fambrough-Bakfld

165
Jacob Blackwell Santa Ana 4-1
Peter Domchev-Palomar
Cyrus Sanai-Mt. SAC 3-1
Jason Zecchini-West Hills
John Sinclair-Cuesta Default
Alex Gallo-Palomar
Max Kumashiro-Cerritos 1-0
Tim Garmica-Cerritos

174
Brody Goens-Mt. SAC 9-1
Jovan Vilalobos-Cuesta
Dillion Harroun-Bakfld 11-3
Lukas Basham-West Hills
Aaron Dubois-Santa Ana 1-0
Raul Hernandez-Santa Ana
Wes Burreisci-Palomar F 3:53
Armando Saldana-Bakersfield

184
Jared Matanane-Mt. SAC 7-3
Jeramiah Gerl-Cerritos
Nathan Rodriguez Mt.SAC Def
Drasko Bogdanovich-Palomar
Alfredo Nava-Santa Ana 13-3
Nate Mesa-Cuesta
Juan Rosales-West Hills Deft
Francisco Aceves-East LA

197
Juan Hernandez-San Ana 4-2
Geoff Merker-Cuesta
Omar Ross-Mt. SAC 8-3
Tyler Moulton-Palomar
Vernon Willis-Mt. SAC 16-7
Josef Ramirez-West Hills
Ian Poling Rio-Hondo F :28
Joseph Ovalle-East LA

285
Dereck Lee-West Hills 11-4
Nader Abdullatif-Mt. SAC
Josh Davis-Bakersfield F 4:39
Robert Chism-Cerritos
Charlie Rassel-Palomar Deft
William Smith-Victor Valley
William Amelong-East LA 7-3
Jared Dorado-Cuesta

Champ of Champs
Christian Bentancourt
Mt. SAC

MVP Upper Weight
Dereck Lee-West Hills

MVP Lower Weight
Andrew Shulte-Santa Ana

Coach of the Year
David Rivera

Team Scores
1	Mt. SAC	184
2	Cuesta	146
3	Palomar	142
4	Santa Ana	141.5
5	Cerritos	98.5
6	West Hills	83.5
7	Bakersfield	79.5
8	East LA	68.5
9	Rio Hondo	29
10	Victory Valley	15.5

2014 North Regional
December 6, 2014 Chabot College

125
Arnulfo Olea-Fresno 1-0
Adrian Camposano-Fresno
Juan Garza-Sacrament F 4:05
Darren Nguyen-Chabot
Riko Quintana-Sierra Forfeit
Jaime Cruz-Skyline

133
Vicente Hernandez-Fresn 4-2
Albert Landeros-Sacramento
Travis Roberts-Sierra Fall 6:24
Eric Royfman-Skyline
Anthony Locke-Sacram F 6:42
Anwar Haltah-Skyline

141
Isiah Alva-Fresno-Fall 4:36
Trent Nicholson-Sierra
Lake Gee-Sacramento 9-4
Dominic Cesena-Chabot
Jonas Gaytan-Fresno-Default
Richard Morris-Santa Rosa
Mark Canapi-Modesto
Jacob Orner-S J Delta

149
Anthony Rubio-Chabot Deft
Brian Segi-Sacrament
Branden Matu-Sierra 13-8
Regelio Bravo-S J Delta
Ivan Govea-Fresno Fall 1:00
Justin Hill-Lassen

157
Adrian Gomes-Fresno 3-2
Sean Raftery-Lassen
Terin O'Callaghan Chabo 14-4
Rocklin Loranger-Sierra
Isaiah Smith-Sacramento
Michael Hodge-Modest 17-7

165
Victor Pereira-Chabot Fall :14
Adam Busch-Sacramento
Jiovanni Paredes-Chabot Deft
Tony Magalhaes-Sierra
Colton Reed-Lassen 11-8
Isidro Arroyo-Fresno

174
Mo Nasser-Fresno 11-3
Zack Wally-Chabot
Tylin Johnson-Lassen 11-8
Kalan Hasley-Sacramento
Jeiko DeSilvera-Lassen F 4:46
Dupra Goodman-Skyline

184
Loagan Paxton Sacrament 4-2
Will Gockel-Figg Fresno
Thomas Cross-Shasta Fall :44
Chad Thodos-Skyline
Hakeem Sanusi-Sant Rosa 7-4
Christian Yanes-Sierra
Elijh Johnson-Chabot X

197
Mark Papish-Sacrament 10-3
Fred Duerr-Santa Rosa
Francisco Vargas-Skyline 7-0
Dom Freesha-Fresno
Ben Sira-Chabot 4-2
Talyn Latour-S J Delta
Andrew Teats-Sierra

285
Jimmy Dawson-Sierra 8-0
Andrew Singer-Fresno
Jacob Richards-Sacramen 5-1
Chumkaur Dhaliwal-Chabot
Cesar Garcia-Sacrament Deft
Timothy Mcmihelk-S J Delta
Wyatt Williams-Lassen Deft
Arthur Georrgiyev Skyline

Team Scores
1 Fresno 210
2 Sacramento 186.5
3 Chabot 156
4 Sierra 141
5 Lassen 76
5 Skyline 76
7 Santa Rosa 75.5
8 S J Delta 53
9 Shasta 16.5
10 Modesto 13

X = True Sixth
Top 6 wrestlers to state

174- Mo Nasser-Fresno City College *OW

2014 South Regional
December 6, 2014

125
Gio Castillo-Mt. SAC 12-4
Gary Howe-Cerritos
Silverio Esparza-W Hills 3-0
Richie Taira-Mt. SAC
Marcos Velesques-Bakfl 13-2
Frank Sandoval-Palomar
Johnny Robles-East LA 8-6
Nick Miller-Cuesta

133
Alberto Garcia-Palomar 10-9
Dustin Kirk-Cerritos
George Sakkas-Cuesta F 1:06
Arik Onsurez-Bakersfield
Ronald Collister-Sant Ana 8-7
Carlos Martinez-Rio Hondo
Jeremy Dizon-Mt. SAC F 1:45
Kevin Valdez-East LA

141
Terrill Sidner-Mt. SAC 9-1
Conner Pollock-Cuesta
Daniel Romero-Rio Hond 4-2
Eric Ambriz-Cerritos
Kevin Kelly-Mt. SAC 10-1
Alex Collazo-Santa Ana
Josh Lawson-Palomar 9-0
Josh Madrigal-Rio Hondo

149
A J McKee Cerritos-Default
Joaquin Collister-Santa Ana
Chris Jones Palomar-Default
Jaime Jimenez-Mt. Sac
Johnny Callas-Cuesta Default
　Jannrugul-Cuesta
Jonathon Mandujana ELA 8-6
David Moran-Rio Hondo

157
Keanu Tom-Cerritos 6-1
Magdaleno-hude-East LA
Richard Miranda-Sa Ana 18-2
John Sinclair-Cuesta
Vincent Gomez-Bakfld 6-2
Bruce Valdez-Palomar
Jorge Madina-Mt. SAC 6-1
Joseph Aguila-East LA

165
Daniel Allen-Rio Hondo 6-1
Erik Collin-Palomar
Adrian Herrera-East LA 6-4
Peter Donchev-Palomar
Joseph Else-Cuesta Default
Zachery Michael-Santa Ana
Eric Roberts-Santa Ana 3-1
Ruben Avila-Cerritos

174
Micah Macias-Santa Ana 7-1
Kolton Martin-Mt. SAC
Cesar Luna-Bakersfield 13-5
Dylan Clarke-Cerritos
Amir Bakhshi-Cuesta 6-4
Juan Soto-East LA
Luis Delaorre-Palomar F 3:36
Nate Mesa-Cuesta

184
Alex Graves-Palomar 10-3
Max Kumashiro-Cerritos
Nath Rodriguez-Mt.SAC 6-2
Raul Hernandez-Santa Ana
Jack Robinett-Cuesta F6:25
Anthony Martinez-Rio Hondo
Micah Avila-Bakersfield F7:41
Jacob Heinschon-Bakersfield

197
Jack Murphy-Bakersfield 3-2
Jeremiah Gerl-Cerritos
Keardf Johnson-Mt. SAC 3-2
Oscar Martinez-Cerritos
Brad Schwarze-Palomar Deft
Clayton Hartwell-Cuesta
Jonathan-Fraser-San Ana
Rudy Conrad-Rio Hondo

285
Robert Chism-Cerritos 8-3
Javier Gonzalez-Rio Hondo
Jesse Gomez-Cerritos 4-1
Maury Lemons East LA
Andrew Cruz Mt, SAC 3-2
Jacob Hall Bakersfield
William Amelong East LA
Jeff Sanchis Cuesta

Coach of the Year
Donny Garriott-Cerritos

Team Scores
1 Cerritos   164
2 Mt. SAC   104
3 Palomar   95
4 Santa Ana   71.5
5 Cuesta   58
6 Rio Hondo   51.5
7 East LA   48.5
8 Bakersfield   46.5
9 West Hills   16

Top 6 wrestlers go to state

2015 North Regional
December 5, 2015 Santa Rosa Junior College

125
Julian Gaytan-Fresno
Adrian Camposano-Fresno
Christian Vasquez-Modesto
Tyler Poalillo-Santa Rosa
Christian Cabajal-Sacramento
Brandon Bond-Sierra
Michael LeFuel-Shasta X

133
Jonas Gaytan-Fresno
Seth Hood-Fresno
Darren Nguyen-Chabot
Issac Pilgrim-Sacramento
Ian Morken-S J Delta
Brady Huang-Skyline

141
Ezra Clark-Skyline
Josh Bennett-Sierra
Isaiah Alva-Fresno
Antonio Jimenez-Sacramento
Robert Smith-Santa Rosa
Miguel Coyt-S J Delta
Gernard Labaco-Chabot X

149
Martine Sandoval-Fresno
Alex Aniciete-Lassen
Mark Taijeron-Modesto
Chris Vaughan-Sacramento
Reese Chew-Sierra
Gabriel Hilares-Chabot
Jimmy Gomez-Sierra X

157
Kaleio Romero-Sacramento
Noor Kathem-Modesto
Josh Annis-Fresno
Trevor Bisagno-Sierra
Kyle Do-Chabot
Drew Smith-Lassen

165
Dylan Forzani-Sacramento
Sebastian Suikowsky-Fresno
Derek Lee Loy-Sacramento
Jamal Halvorson-Shasta
Darian Benge-Chabot
Antonio Jauregui-Lassen

174
Trevor Wright-Sacramento
Mo Naser-Fresno
Isaiah Smith-Sacramento
Stephen Martin Skyline
Taryn Christiansen-Sant Rosa
Javier Contreras-Lassen

184
Jnaylyn Hall-Santa Rosa
Nick Rohrer-Sacramento
Luis Jauregui-Fresno
Tytin Johnson-Lassen
Patrick Penick-Shasta
Bill Robinson-Shasta

197
Luke Brewer-Modesto
Jason Zecchini-Sacramento
Fred Duerr-Santa Rosa
Coleman Maher-Skyline
Jay Johnson-Fresno
Vincent Estus-S J Delta

285
Casey Jones-Fresno
Murrell Anderson-Chabot
D'Juan Ewing-Smalls Sacrome
Rory Anderson-Lassen
Quintton Bowlds-Santa Rosa
Jose Garcia-Modesto

Most Outstanding Wrestler
Trevor Wright-Sacramento

Team Scores
1 Fresno   213
2 Sacramento 184.5
3 Santa Rosa 75
4 Modesto   74
5 Lassen   60.5
6 Skyline   54.5
7 Chabot   53.5
8 Sierra   44
9 Shasta   39.5
10 Delta   20

X = True Sixth
Top 6 wrestlers to state

2015 South Regional
December 5, 2015 Mt. San Antonia College

125
Gio Castillo-Mt. SAC 5-3
Estevan Cabanas-Cerritos
Norman Abas-Bakfld Fall 3:48
Nick Miller-Cuesta
Jose Chona-Santa Ana F 4:52
Luis Perez-Rio Hondo
Pedro Sarabia-Bakfld 12-9 X
Austin Almendarez-V Valley

133
Anthony Vargas-Cerritos 2-1
Jake Schaeffer-Palomar
Chris Kimball-Palomar Deft
Torrey Casper-Bakersfield
Johnny Robles-East LA 9-7
Preston Gannon-Rio Hondo
Mike Rodriguez-W Hills Deft
Issac Jones-West Hills

141
Mario Lopez-Mt. SAC 3-1
Daniel Romero-Rio Hondo
Andrew Gomez-Sant Ana 7-3
Elias Mercado-Rio Hondo
Richard Pocock-Cerritos 2-0
Jesse Jaime-Mt. SAC -
Silvester Alfaro-Bakfld 11-3
Ernie Chambers-Palomar

149
Terrill Sidner-M SAC 18-2
Danny Lopez-Bakersfield
Brock Dias-West Hills F 5:57
Cody Davis-Cerritos
Tristan Steinman-San Ana 6-5
Landon Kim-Cuesta
James Schmidt-R Hon 15-2 X
Dom Fratangelo-Cuesta

157
Aaron Negrete-Cerritos 8-4
Jose Regama-Mt. SAC
Luis Quintero-Cuesta 11-8
Dylan Moreno-Cerritos
Josh Cortes-Cuesta Fall 4:02
Kirk Kaliszewski-Palomar
Landon Myers-Sa Ana 13-3 X
Romero Monserrat-West Hills

165
Erik Collin-Palomar 4-2
Roger Arce-Rio Hondo
Eric Roberts-Santa Ana 11-6
Louie De La Torre-Palomar
Arman Fayazzi-Santa Ana 7-1
Deshawn Boyd-West Hills
Geo Hagan Victor-Valley
Deft Jacob Maas-Bakersfield

174
Lukas Basham-W Hills F 2:00
Joel Villa-Cerritos
Alex Gallo-Palomar Default
Hector Vargas-Mt. SAC
Victor Bryson-Cuesta 11-7
Juan Soto-East LA 7-4
Andrew Binger-Bakfld 4-2
Jonathan Virk-Rio Hondo

184
Alex Graves-Palomar 11-3
Kolton Martin-Mt. SAC
John Robles-Cerritos 3-0
Zack Mitchell-Bakersfield
Will Thorton-Cuesta 5-3
Ty Freeman-Santa Ana
Jorge Guerrero-East La 5-3
Maurise Stephens-West Hills

197
Oscar Martinez-Cerrito F 2:57
Nathan Arogon-Mt. SAC
Jose Robledo-Bakersfield 5-1
Raul Briseno-Palomar
Josh Escobedo-Rio Hondo 8-4
Ned Estrada-East LA
Matt Sutte-West Hills F1:27 X
Anthony Stenschke-Cuesta

285
Jesse Gomez-Cerritos F 6:56
Andrew Cruz-Mt. SAC
Kyle Lincoln-West Hills 9-3
Seville Hayes-Palomar
Josh Davis-Bakersfield Default
Clayton Hartwell-Cuesta
Anthony Florido-East LA 3-1
Brandon Ramos-Rio Hondo

Champs of Champs
Jesse Gomez-Cerritos
MVP Upper Weight
Lukas Basham-West Hills
MVP Lower Weight
Terrill Sidner-Mt. SAC
Coach of the Year
Donny Garriot-Cerritos
Assistant Coach of the Year
Don Barrios-Palomar

X = True Sixth
Top 6 wrestlers to state

Team Scores
1 Cerritos 173
2 Mt. SAC 161
3 Palomar 152
4 Bakersfield 104
5 Cuesta 93.5
6 West Hills 89.5
7 Rio Hondo 89
8 Santa Ana 82.5
9 East LA 40.5
10 Victor Valley 16

2016 North Regional
December 4, 2016 San Joaquin College

125
Julian Gaytan-Fresno
Landon McBride-Sierra
Morgan Sausedo-Sacramento
Gilbert Martinez-Chabot
Raymond Monela-Chabot
A J Rosas-Fresno
Cody Tauzon-Chabot
Nathaniel Screni-Skyline

133
Aaron Mora-Fresno
Devon Lyle-Chabot
Ian Morken-Delta
Ray Angeles-Sacramento
Tanner Robson-Skyline
Anson Morales-Santa Rosa
Anthony Adrdrighetto-Skyli X

141
Clinton McAlester-Fresno
Hunter Minton-Sacramento
Carsen Paynter-Chabot
Carlos Vasquez-S J Delta
Isaac Warf-Chabot
Quinn Hall-Shasta
Juan Aquilar-Modesto
Devon Silver-Sacramento

149
Dylan Martinez-Fresno
Dean Esquilbel-Fresno
Alexander Lopez-Sacramento
Alex Anicete-Lassen
Blake Boswell-Santa Ana
Jose Ruelas-Modesto
Modesto Silvestre-S J Delta
Sean Tiner-Chabot

157
Noor Kathem-Modesto
Joshua Annis-Fresno
Daniel Larman-Sacramento
Garrett Heath-Santa Rosa
Brady Green-Skyline
Kevin Garcia-Chabot
Antonio Jeuregui-Lassen
Stephen Watten-S J Delta

165
Derek Lee Loy-Sacramento
Ricardo Bribiescas-Skyline
Joel Anguiano-Santa Rosa
Andrew Brodland-Sierra
Justin Nievas-Modesto
C J Sanchez-Fresno
Elijah Johnson-Chabot
Drew Engbersan-Sierra

174
Zach Wally-Chabot
Niko Chapman-Sacramento
Jerrin Dean-Fresno
Dupra Goodman-Skyline
Jesus Quintanas-Sierra
Stephen Dixon-S J Delta
Brian Rivas-Santa Rosa

184
Trevor Wright-Sacramento
Kalan Hasley-Sacramento
Don Freesha-Fresno
Frank Sabala-Modesto
Jon Good-Sierra
Hugo Plancarte-Skyline
Ricco Vazquez-Santa Rosa

197
Kalvin Stuckey-Fresno
Wes Ruffer-Lassen
Ben Sira-Chabot
Tavian Del Rosario-Sacrament
Paris Henry-Santa Rosa
Matt Ayla-Skyline
Vincent Estus-S J Delta

285
Tristan Smith-Modesto
Angel Mariscal-Fresno
Gabriel Cardona-Chabot
Jerrad Kirk-Sacramento
Colton Farley-Santa Rosa
David Corona-Skyline
Nate Foisaqa-Lassen
Aliahrga Wardog-S J Delta

Team Scores
1 Fresno   210.5
2 Sacramento 189
3 Chabot   138.5
4 Modesto   76
5 Skyline   68.5
6 Santa Rosa 65.5
7 Sierra   65
8 S J Delta   54
9 Lassen   37
10 Shasta   13

X = True Sixth
Top 6 wrestlers to state

2016 South Regional
December 4, 2016 Cuesta College

125
Norberto Buenrostro-Cer 2-1
Pedro Saraba-Bakersfield
John Whisner-Mt. SAC Forfeit
Elijah Diaz-Mt. SAC
Robert Garcia-Palomar 13-10
Elesio Medina-Santa Ana
Gustavo MiramontesW H 3-1
Isaac Galaviz-Cuesta

133
Alberto Garcia-Palomar 12-6
Adrian Marrufo-West Hills
Pedro Corona-Bakfld 15-0
Julian Meleeio-Mt. SAC Forf
Leif Dominguez-Cuesta
Alex Contreras-East LA Forfeit
Ross Arve-Cuesta

141
Richard Pocock-Cerritos 7-2
Andrew Gomez-Santa Ana
Asper Sherow Mt. SAC Forfeit
Kevin Kelly-Mt. SAC
Eric Reyes-Palomar 4-0
Arik Onsurez-Bakersfield
Esteban Corona Bakf F 1:00 X
Aaron Watts-West Valley

149
Joseph Dominguez M SAC 3-1
Wyatt Gerl-Cerritos
Chris Kimball-Palomar 12-11
Tristan Steinmon-Santa Ana
Josh Caro-Rio Hondo 10-1
Andrew Alvarez-West Hills
Marvin Apreza-Cuesta 6-2
Luis Cervantes-Santa Ana

157
Dylan Moreno-Cerritos Forf
Kevin James-Cerritos
Nathan Pimentel-W Hills 15-6
Brandon Tierney-Santa Ana
Apollo Santos-Mt. SAC 8-3
Jessy Diaz-Palomar
Axel Molina Rio Hondo 11-3
Elijah Hernandes-Santa Ana

165
Ryan Soto-Victor Valley 3-2
Blake Vasquez-Cerritos
Kennith Kirk-Cerritos F 6:50
Kevin Hope-Mt. SAC
Arman Eayyazi-Santa Ana 4-3
Jacob Alcobendas-Rio Hondo
Sean McDannold-Palo F 2:30
J R Trevino- Bakersfield

174
Alex Garcia-Cuesta 7-2
Reed South-Mt. SAC
Isaiah Leyva-Cerritos 9-1
Reuben Arreola-West Hills
Gabriel Rodriguez-East LA For
Braucio Banuelos-Palomar
Jacob Mattson-Bakfl F 1:52 X
Lorenzo Fajardo-Victor Valley

184
Bruce Valdez-Palomar Forfeit
Bryant Vasquez-Cerritos
Ivan Sevilla-West Hills 9-4
Isaac De La Cruz-Cuesta
Barnabus Yi-Mt. SAC 20-14
Raphael Madrigal-Rio Hondo
Rodolfo Castulo-Bakfld X

197
David Van Weems-Cerrit 15-7
Andrew Ramos-Rio Hondo
Alex Gomez-Palomar Fall
Zavion Roberson-Bakersfield
Zack Mitchell-Bakersfield Fall
Angel Alcantar-Mt. SAC
Oscar Martinez-East LA 5-1
Michael Perez-West Hills

285
Chance Eskam-Palomar 3-2
Brandon Sotomayor-East LA
David Zavala-Cerritos Forfeit
Ramiro Macias-Bakersfield
Marco Valdivia-Ri Hondo Forf
Seville Hayes-Palomar
Jon Peterson-V Valley F :40 X
Eddie Salgado-Santa Ana

Team Scores
1	Cerritos	205
2	Palomar	171
3	Mt. SAC	148.5
4	Bakersfield	104.5
5	West Hills	81.5
6	Santa Ana	74.5
7	Rio Hondo	60.5
8	Cuesta	57
9	East LA	46.5
10	Victor Valley	31

X = True Sixth
Top 6 wrestlers to state

2017 North Regional
December 2, 2017 San Joaquin Delta

125
Branden Bettencourt Fresno
Morgan Sauseda Sacrament
Danny Borrego Skyline
Brandon Mendoza Modesto
Gregg Viloria S J Delta
Brandon Julien Chabot
Raj Walker Santa Rosa
133
Isiah Perez Fresno
Tyler Poalilo Santa Rosa
Jeremy Newman Sierra
Trever Mattox Sacramento
Nick Paoletti Shasta
Elijah Blake Shasta
141
Aaron Mora Fresno
Abraham Del Torro Fresno
Branden Rullian S J Delta
Kobe Woltz Sierra
Brennan Gilligan Shasta
Sal Pochiero Sacramento
David Ortega Skyline X
149
Dylan Martinez Fresno
Blake Boswell Santa Ana
Josh Aceves Skyline
Carlos Vazquez S J Delta
Jason Stokkeland Sacramento
Dylan Adams Sierra
157
Josh McMillian Fresno
Conrad Lopez Fresno
William Schwertscharf Mode
Ryan Peterson Chabot
Muhammad Lafeet S J Delta
Modesto Silvestre S J Delta
Zack Franco Skyline
165
Victor Vargas Fresno
Issac Bertalotto Sacramento
Rafael Vega Chabot
Ian Black Santa Rosa
Brian Horn Sacramento
Alonzo Cadenas Modesto
Marc Chamberlain Chabot X

174
Anthony Cress Chabot
Abel Garcia Sacramento
Cameron Casey Santa Rosa
Miguel Ruiz Fresno
Michael Passaglin Sierra
Jonathon Campos Lassen
Thomas Monserrat Skyline
184
Tevin Bailey Lassen
Dylan Kranich S J Delta
Isaac Sillas Sacramento
Jay Johnson Fresno
Jackson Blankenship Shasta
Hugo Plancarte Skyline
Kyle Thorton Chabot
197
Rob Nickerson Sacramento
Marcus Macias Fresno
Joseph Salt Skyline
Tristan Bogovic Shasta
Daniel Warden Sacramento
Lazaro Caversaco Chabot X
Diego Lopez Santa Rosa
285
Romon Guzman Skyline
Casey Jones Fresno
Cola Mair Lassen
Jesse Flores Modesto
Chumkaur Dhaliwal Chabot
Robby Kaempfer Shasta
Beau Medicne-Crow Sac

Team Scores
1 Fresno   260.5
2 Sacramento   167
3 Skyline   102.5
4 Chabot   91.5
5 Santa Rosa   80
6 S J Delta   70
7 Sierra   62
8 Shasta   54
9 Lassen   50
10 Modesto   44

X = True Sixth
Top 6 wrestlers to state

2017 South Regionals
December 2, 2017 Bakersfield College

125
Isaac Guerrero-Palomar
Ejijah Diaz-Mt. SAC
John Whisner-Mt. SAC
Richard Vaillancourt-Moorpa
Messiah Owens-Cerritos
Adrian Guevara-Rio Hondo

133
Pedro Corona-Bakfld Default
Josh Brown-Cerritos
Adam Valdez-Mt. SAC
Josh Fuentes-Santa Ana
Zackary Moistner-Palomar
Marco Velaszquez- Bakfld
Lucas Howes-Palomar

141
Joseph-Dominguez-Mt. SAC
Adrian Marrufo-West Hills
Jeremy Huang-Santa Ana
Nick Camacho-Cerritos
Arturo Osorio-Palomar
Jacob Jimenez-Palomar

149
Emmitt Kuntz-Bakfld Default
Nathan Navida-Palomar
Wolgang Bernal-Mt. SAC
Manuel Salcedo-Mt. SAC
Khalil Howard-Rio Hondo
Jace Heryford-Cuesta

157
Wyatt Gerl-Cerritos
James Schmidt-Rio Hondo
Joseph Valdez-Mt. SAC
Brayden Riley-Bakersfield
Sean McDanold-Palomar
Jose Paez-West Hills

165
Blake Vasquez-Cerritos
Matthew Mejia-Mt. SAC
Apollo Santos-Mt. SAC
Anthony Espinoza-Rio Hondo
Josh Koning-Moorpark
Brandon Tierney-Santa Ana

174
Hector Vargas-Mt. SAC
Brraylis Banuelos-Palomar
Zach Gonzales-Cerritos
Robert Flores-Moorpark
Christian Rouleau-Cuesta
Jeronimo Cardoso-West Hills

184
Jeremy Mass-Bak Coin Toss
Adrian Godinez-Bakersfield
Luis Melecio-Mt. SAC
Angel Verduzco-Cerritos
Leo Perez-Santa Ana
Merceles Velasquez-Palomar

197
David Van Weems-Cerrit Deft
Zavion Roberson-Bakersfield
Kobe Rosas-West Hills
Robert Ramirez-Rio Hondo
David Chavaria-Mt. SAC
Noah Lossing-Cerritos

285
Chance Eskam-Palomar
Brandon Sotomayer-East LA
Ricky Garcia-West Hills
Ramiro Macias-Bakersfield
Gabrial Herrera-Mt. SAC
Marco Valdivia-Rio Hondo

Team Scores
1 Mt. SAC   193.5
2 Cerritos   149
3 Bakersfield   148.5
4 Palomar   140
5 Rio Hondo   80.5

Others
Moorpark
Santa Ana
West Hills
East LA

2018 North Regional
December 1, 2018 Sierra College

125
Greg Villor-S J Delta 3-2
Mario Moreno-Fresno
Owen Jones-Santa Rosa 1-0
Trevor Bagan-Santa Rosa
Houston Scibek-Modesto 5-3
Jacob Hiller-Shasta
Ryan Ortiz-Sacramento F3:50
Seth Chaney-SJ Delta

133
Isaiah Perez-Fresno 1-0
Kyle Jimenez-Fresno
Ivan Gomez-Modesto F 2:07
Tanner Robson-Skyline
Ryan Harlow-Sacrament F:54
Murtaza-Nabaada Sierra
Jacob Laughlin-Lassen Deft
Felipe Duenas-Chabot

141
Luis Ramos-Fresno Fall 1:14
Logan Garcia-Lassen
Ezra Clark-Skyline 14-6
Michael Mello-Sacramento
Branden-S J Delta 1-0
Trenton Edalgo-S J Delta
Tucker Ellis-Shasta 10-9
Eli Clark-Skyline

149
Daniel Ruiz-Fresno 8-0
Daniel Cota-Modesto
Josh Aceves-Skyline F 1:41
Dylan Crawford-Sacramento
Chase Peterson-Sierra 1-0
Christopher-Valencia Sierra
Steven Watson-S J Delta Forft
Travis Maynard-Modesto

157
Ruben Garcia-Fresno 1-0
Conrad Lopez-Fresno
Conrad Trevino-Sac Forf
Ryan Perterson-Chabot
Manny Curry-Sac Forf
Eric Murdock-Chabot
Greg Ewert-Santa Rosa 12-10
Temistocle Politi-Shasta

165
Augestine-Garcia Fresno
Abel Garcia-Sacramento
Jackson Blankenship-ShF6:02
Kawena Esperas-Lassen
Joshua Wright-San Rosa 10-8
Aaron Robinson-S J Delta
Kevin Garcia-Chabot Fall :45
Alexander Wong-Skyline

174
Abner Romero-Fresno F 3:59
Hunter Gonzalez-Sierra
Cameron Casey-San Rosa 1-0
Isaac Bertolotto-Sacramento
Evan Kitchen-Lassen 4-1
Juan Rosales-Modesto
Rafael Vega-Chabot 8-6
Michael Barajas-Chabot

184
Bronson Harmon-Sacram 3-2
Jhaylyn Hall-Santa Rosa
Tevin Bailey Lassen-Fall 6:55
Steven Abbott-Sacramento
Victor Cruz-Modesto 2-1
Jerrin Dean-Fresno
Michael Carse-Chabot F :26
Devin Andrade-Skyline

197
Anthony Cress-Chabot 5-1
Brian Horn-Sacramento
Matthew Martinez-Fresn 4-2
Karin Shakur-Santa Rosa
Tony Rodgers-Lassen Fall 4:31
Tristan Begovic-Shasta
Joe Bynum-Lassen Default
Travis Carpenter-Sierra

285
Cole Mair-Lassen 4-2
Ramon Guzman-Skyline
Angel Mariscal-Fresno F 1:47
Robert Kaempfer-Shasta
Jordan Denny-Sacramet 14-7
Torribio Larios-Modesto
Jacob Bernstein-S RosTB I 2-1
Jacob Gehret-Skyline

Team Scores
1 Fresno   238.5
2 Sacramento   168.5
3 Lassen   109
4 Santa Rosa   96.5
5 Skyline   75
6 Modesto   75
7 Chabot   73
8 S J Delta   60.5
9 Shasta   57.5
10 Sierra   50.5

2018 South Regional
December 1, 2018

125
Marcus-Hutcherson Bak 10-5
Isaac Guerrero-Palomar
John Sosa-West Hills 4-2
Keithen Estrada-Bakersfield
Josh Mendoza-Cerritos Deft
Richard Vaillancort-Moorpark
Zac Cunningham-MS 15-5
Victor Atherton-Rio Hondo

133
Raul Ortiz-Palomar 2-1
Eric Martinez-Palomar
Oliver Rivero-Santa Ana Deft
Ethan Diaz-Mt. SAC
Jose Espinoza-Cerritos 7-2
Jared Callison-Bakersfield
Andy Rodriguez-Morp F 2:00
Salvador Velascdo-West Hills

141
Josh Brown-Cerritos 13-6
Eric Reyes-Palomar
Aaron Diaz-Mt. SAC 10-5
Josh Fuentes-Norikiyo-S Ana
Analzaiah Ozuna-Bakfld Deft
Nick Camacho-Cerritos
Alexis Becerra-Bakfld 20-5
Rudy Borquez-Rio Hondo

149
Adam Valdez-Mt. SAC Deft
Devin Daugherty- Cerritos
Larry Rodriguez-Cerritos Deft
Humphry Quirie-Cuesta
Emmett Kuntz-Bakfld Deft
Nathan Navida-Palomar
Andrew Saucedo-Mt. SAC
Jose Perez-West Hills

157
Luis Vargas-Santa Ana F 2:15
Miguel Gallardo-Mt. SAC
Joe Romero-West Hills F 1:34
Emmanuel Zepeda-East LA
Jesse Pacheco-Cerritos 5-4
Jessy Diaz-Palomar
Rodrigo Magallon-E LA 12-3
Sergio Camacho-Moorpark

165
Mace Anderson-Palom F 6:20
Kennith Kirk-Cerritos
Devin Top-Moorpark 21-7
Ian Vasquez-Mt. SAC
Luis Cervantes-Santa Ana 6-3
Kevin Mello-Bakersfield
Pablo Gonzalez-W Hills f 4:11
Daniel Brisena-East LA

174
Zack Gonzalez-Cerritos 13-4
Cameron Cox-Palomar
Gabriel Rodriguez-E LA 15-7
Noah Collazo-West Hills
Robert Flores-Moorpark 11-2
Colby Huynh-Mt. SAC
Chris Montoya-R Hondo Deft
Jacob Matison-Bakersfield

184
Nick Kimball-Palomar 13-4
Jarrod Nunez-Cerritos
Layce Barmaki-Palomar Deft
Luis Melecio-Mt. SAC
Victor Bryson-Cuesta Default
Jeremy Maas-Bakersfield
Ricky Cortez-East LA 13-8
Wilfredo Choto-Victor Valley

197
Anthony Stenschke-Cue 12-5
Adrian Godinez-Bakersfield
Andy Voong-Rio Hondo 17-3
Kalani Sorensen-Palomar
Efren Velez-East LA 11-7
Luis Garcia-Mt. SAC
Josh Bustamante-Cerrito Deft
Ricky Garcia-West Hills

285
Cristian Ayala-Mt SAC 6-2
Jacob Hall-Bakersfield
Diego Sanchez-R Hond F 1:30
Randy Gonzalez-Cerritos
Koby Rosas-West Hills 10-2
Christopher Alvizures-Mt SAC
Patrick Slatic-West Hills 2-0
Doniel Garcia-Victor Valley

Team Scores

1	Palomar	152
2	Cerritos	133
3	Mt. SAC	116
4	Bakersfield	94.5
5	West Hills	61.5
6	Santa Ana	58
7	East LA	50.5
8	Cuesta	40
9	Rio Hondo	35
10	Moorpark	34.5
11	Victor Valley	8

2019 North Regional
December 7, 2019 San Joaquin Delta

125
Mario Moreno-Fresno
Gavin Sweeny-Sierra
Brandon Mendoza-Modesto
Ramiro Castillo-Fresno
John Sosa-West Hills
Nick Foster-Lassen
Danny Borrego-Skyline
Trey Watters-Lassen

133
Louie Bravo-Fresno
Cole Kachmar-Sacramento
Owen Jones-Santa Rosa
Houston Scibek-Modesto
Salvador Velasco-West Hills
Jude Miranda-West Hills
Jacob Hiller-Sacramento
Rainier Colina-Modesto

141
Raul Ortiz-Sacramento
Anthony Chavez-Fresno
Ivan Gomez-Modesto
Devin Holman-Modesto
Logan Blocher-Lassen
Jeomar Banda-Santa Rosa
Trenton Edalgo-S J Delta X
Nick Mascardo S J Delta

149
Daniel Ruiz-Fresno
Chris Gaxiola-Fresno
Logan Garcia-Lassen
Greg Ewert-Santa Rosa
Joe Kachmar-Sacramento
Nico Cappabianca-Skyline
Grant Anderson-Sierra
Anthony Molina-West Hills

157
Hunter LaRue-Sacramento
Ryan Ojeda-Sierra
Josh McMillan-Fresno
William Schertscharf-Modes
Gabriel De Haro-Lassen
Lance Brazet-West Hills
Hunter Avila-West Hills
Vincent Blensdorf-Skyline

165
Augustine-Garcia Fresno
Manny Curry-Sacramento
Darin Chick-S J Delta
Alex Thornburg-Sacramento
Joseph Valdez-Sierra
Jeronimo Cardoso-West Hills
Anthony Martinez-Santa Ros
Christian Richer-Lassen

177
Chase Miles-Sacramento
Davyn Kreb-Sierra
Arturo Rivas-Fresno
Noah Collazo-West Hills
Kevin Fernandez-Modesto
Jamal Starks-S J Delta
Tyler Moore-Lassen
David Fowler-Sierra

184
Stephen Martin-Skyline
Russell Rucklos-Lassen
Daniel Long-Fresno
Bobby Mello-Sacramento
Auston May-Sierra
Ricky Mello-Sacramento
Johnathon Vale-West Hills X
Gurbir Dhaliwal-Chabot

197
Jack Kilner-Fresno
Hunter Gonzalez-Sierra
Lazaro Carrasco-Chabot
Patrick Slatic-West Hills
Steven Karas-Sierra
Jordan Monroe-Santa Rosa
Brock Piombo-McCarthy Delt
Randy Nemendez-Lassen

285
Armando Barcenas-Fresno
Victor Yakshin-Sierra
Alex Mosquada-Sierra
David Padilla-West Hills
Javante Gregoire-Santa Rosa
Hayden Elias-Sacramento
Ron Mendosa-S J Delta
Henry Espinal-Chabot

Team Scores
1 Fresno   237
2 Sacramento   164
3 Sierra   134.5
4 West Hills   112
5 Lassen   98
6 Modesto   96
7 Santa Rosa   85.5
8 S J Delta   58
9 Skyline   42.5
10 Chabot   28.5

X = True sixth

2019 South Regional
December 7, 2019 Santa Ana College

125
Jonathan Prata-Cerritos
Conner Diamond-Mt. SAC
Keithen Estrada-Bakersfield
Adrian Guevara-Rio Hondo
Salvador Alvarez-East LA
Juan Diaz-Palomar
Nick Gonzalez-Cuesta
Ryan Lucero-Moorpark

133
Andres Gonzalez-Cerritos
Kahill Tucker-Rio Hondo
Stefano McKinney-Cerritos
Jose Mata-Santa Ana
Angel Rosales-Bakersfield
Nic Weissinger-Mt. SAC
Donaven Medina Moorpark X
Khrystoph Victor-Valley

141
Isaiah Mora-Cerritos
David Ortega-Victor Valley
Chris Espinoza-Rio Honda
Bradley Chirino-Mt. SAC
Ali Kaveh-Santa Ana
Jesus Langarica-Rio Honda
Isaih Calderon-Santa Ana
Alexis Becerra-Bakersfield

149
Adrian Gonzales-Bakersfield
V'ante Moore-Cerritos
Josue Aguilar-East LA
Ismarl Cruz-Rio Hondo
Lance McNatt Palomar
James Adams-Mt. SAC
Justin Jerricoff-Cuesta X
Anthony Galvez-Moorpark

157
Larry Rodriguez-Cerritos
Emmanuel Zepeda-East LA
Doroteo Lopez-East LA
Ian Vasquez-Mt. SAC
Issac Escareno-Rio Hondo
Taro Harman-Palomar
Kai Schaefer-Cuesta X
Gabe Salcedo-Bakersfield

165
Jacob Hansen-Moorpark
Wetzel Hill-Mt. SAC
Scott Hokit-Bakersfield
Drake De La Cruz-Cerritos
Nicolas Lopez-East LA
Eric Carrillo-Mt. SAC
Frank Sanchez-Palomar X
Aaron Noon-Moorpark

174
Jonathan Hunter-Bakersfield
Kevin Hope-Mt. SAC
Bryan Samayoa-Cerritos
Jacob Annis-Bakersfield
Kevin Ayala-Mt. SAC
Daniel Serrano-Cerritos
James Rodriguez-Palomar
Carlos Durazo-East LA

184
Joey Conroy-Palomar
Breck Jeffus-Cuesta
Jordan Annis-Bakersfield
Angel Verduzco-Cerritos
Juan Zapien-East LA
Melad Ayyoub-Mt. SAC
Armando Varelas-Bakersfield
Zach Ortiz-Moorpark

197
Hamza Al-Saudi-Cerritos
Andy Voong-Rio Hoondo
Colby Huynh-Mt. SAC
Ricardo Gonzalez-Bakersfield
Joseph Nava-Santa Ana
Jesus Hernandez-Palomar
Jacob Duran-East LA

285
Enrique Galicia-Palomar
Juan Camacho-Cuesta
Behnam Hodiabkenar-Moopa
David Aranda-East LA
Randy Arriaga-Cerritos
Jackson Clark-Mt. SAC
Donald Oliver-Bakersfield
Diego Sanchez-Rio Hondo

Team Scores

1	Cerritos	216.5
2	Bakersfield	188.5
3	Mt. SAC	168
4	East LA	126
5	Rio Hondo	119.5
6	Palomar	94
7	Moorpark	85.5
8	Santa Ana	58
9	Cuesta	54.5
10	Victor Valley	25

X = True Sixth
Top 6 wrestlers to state

2021 North Regional
December 4, 2021 Sierra College

125
Salahdin Farukh-Sie 18-10
Austin Pimentel-Fresno
Lesner Velasquez-Shas F 1:56
Sadiri Andoya-S J Delta
Armando Martinez-WH F1:16
Damon Looper-Modesto

133
Adrian Chavez-Fresno 5-1
Trevor Bagan-Santa Rosa
Vince Olivera Sacrament 10-4
Preston Bagan-Santa Rosa
Dylan Duncan-Sacram F 3:14
Ferando Diaz-Marquez Skylin
Rainier Colina-Modest F 2:16
Sterlandjy Metayer-Lassen

141
Kendall Frank-Sacrament 6-0
Antonio Davis-Yuke Sierra
Wayne Joint-West Hills Deft
Wyatt Carter-Modesto
S Lundquist-Brewer Sie Deft
Will Torres-West Hills
D Shaharuddin-Sky F 4:03 X
Josiah Torculas-Shasta

149
Lupe Ayon-West Hills 9-0
Alfredo Mendoza-Sacrament
Mikael Melaku-Chabot 6-2
Joaquin Mosqueda-Sierra
Luis Rios Fresno 11-2
Leem Kue-Modesto

157
Noah Cortez-Fresno 5-1
Conrad Trevino-Oceguera Sac
Temistocle Politi-Shast F 5:40
Travis Maynard -Modesto
Scott Coleman-Lassen Fall :22
Lunden Cabeje-West Hills
Dustin Hayes-Sierra Fall 2:58
Jordan Fields-Santa Rosa

165
Hassan Khan-Sacramento 6-5
Willy LaMacchia-Skyline
Diego Cruz-Fresno 12-8
Bryan Thorne-Skyline
Marcos Gamez-Fresno F :44
Aaron Lucatero-Modesto
Alex Thornburg-Sacrom 19-3

174
Reymundo Raiz-Fresno 16-3
Gabe Guzman-Sierra
Liam Leckie-Sacramento 6-4
Jacob Turner-Modesto
Juan Diaz-Marquez-Sky F 6:28
Diego Lopez-San Rosa F 5:50
Caleb Byrd-S J Delta

184
ERIC Karas-Sacramento 8-1
Justin Tripp-West Hills
Melvin Naranjo-Fresno 3-1
David Fowler Sierra
Logan Colbert-Modesto 11-6
Max Voelkel-Lassen
Robert Aguilar- S J Delta

197
Angel Solis West-Hills 3-1
Steven Karas-Sacramento
Nicholas Edheveste-Fre F5:35
Joel Lopez-Shasta
Grant Hicks-Modesto Forfeit
Gilbert Solorio-Modesto
Edgar Tolentino-Chabot F2:01
Alex Argel-S J Delta

285
Rudy Garcia-Fresno Fall 1 :50
Taven Avila -West Hills
Jacob Larsen-San Rosa F 1:36
Joseph Alaniz-Fresno
Brandon Reed-Skyline 4-3
David Stewart-Modesto
Dalton Paine-S J Delta 17-2
Fritz McIntosh-Shasta

Team Scores
1	Fresno	199.5
2	Sacramento	172.5
3	West Hills	128
4	Modesto	116
5	Sierra	105
6	Skyline	73.5
7	Shasta	63
8	Santa Rosa	57.5
9	Chabot	31.5
10	S J Delta	30.5
11	Lassen	24.5

X = True Sixth
Top 6 wrestlers to state

2021 South Regional
December 4, 2021 Cuesta College

125
Jonathan-Prata-Cerritos
Alexis Tellez-Rio Hondo
Conner Diamond-Mt. SAC
Christopher-Betancourt-MS
Victor Atherton-Rio Hondo
Eathon Rider-Bakersfield
Alex Cardoza-Victor Valley
Juan Diaz-Palomar

133
Davis Seans-Mt. SAC
Jason Mendoza-Cerritos
Roland Dominguez-Cerritos
Owen Wilson-Palomar
Hector Camarena-Santa Ana
Luis Perez-Rio Hondo
Lucas Jeetan-Palomar

141
Thomas Chapman-Mt. SAC
Jose Cisneros-Victor Valley
Zayn Patel-Santa Ana
Hector Ramirez-East LA
Kimo Servino-Cerritos
Randall Lockwood-Palomar
Miguel Cabrera-Rio Hondo
Albert Mechamal-Moorpark

149
Juan Lopez-Mt. SAC
Felix Osorio-Cerritos
Caoilte Drury-Cerritos
Josue Aguilar-East La
Donovan Sanin-Rio Hondo
Everardo Rueda-Bakersfield
Zach Jensen-Moorpark
Chris Codoy-Victor Valley

157
Daniel Bracamonte-Cerritos
Jerry Rubio-Mt. SAC
Gavin Kaminski-Palomar
Adrian Rios-Rio Hondo
Sami Barakai-Cuesta
Josiah Quiroz-Bakersfield
Nickolas Poma-Santa Ana
Isreal Manriquez-Vict Valley

165
Armondo Murillo-Cerritos
Isaiah Vasquez-Mt. SAC
Saeed Perez-Santa Ana
Humphery Quire-Cuesta
Gabe Carrillo-Cuesta
Gracen Hayes-Bakersfield
Joseph Estrada-Rio Hondo
J P Raygoza-Moorpark

174
Wetzel Hill-Mt. SAC
Stone Robledo-Cerritos
Joseph Fernandez-Moorpark
Nick Lopez-East LA
Nick Banas-Cuesta
Uriel Vasquez-Bakersfield
Deniz Ari-Santa Ana

184
Jonathan Hunter-Bakersfield
Troy Garza-East LA
Luke Hansen-Moorpark
Joseph Rodriguez-Cerritos
Ahmed Khattab-Mt. SAC
Armando Rodriguez-Palomar
Quinn Patrick-Cuesta
Brayan Macias Morales-Palo

197
Nate Kendricks-Mt. SAC
Anthonie Banuelos-Bakfld
Chente Trujilo-Bakersfield
Devin Peries-East LA
Lue Le Vasseur-Moorpark
Ricardo Cardona-Rio Hondo
Justin Sawai-Cerritos
Oscar De La Cruz-Palomar

285
Jonovan Smith-Cerritos
Borys Peresadko-Moorpark
Jesse Garcia-Mt. SAC
Nathan Ramos-East LA
Corbin Hayes-Bakersfield
Owen Firm-Victor Valley
Ivan Posadas-Bakersfield
Allen Salgado-Palomar

Team Scores
1 Mt. SAC   186.5
2 Cerritos   95.5
3 Bakersfield   95.5
4 East LA   93.5
5 Rio Hondo   75.5
6 Moorpark   73.5
7 Palomar   54.5
8 Santa Ana   51
9 Victor Valley 45.5
10 Cuesta   37

2022 North Regional
December 3, 2022 Sacramento City College

125
Arius Leven-Sacrame SV 1 6-4
Eczequiel Jaurieta-Fresno
Xander Romero-W Hills 5-1
Ivan Torres-Lassen
Sadiri Andaya-S J Delta 5-1
Jeomar Banda-S Rosa SV 8-6
Andrew Aquino-Chabot
Andre Afague-Shasta 10-6
Josue Guzman-Modesto

133
Devin Murphy-Fresno 16-0
Joaquin Mosqueda-Sierra
Liam Nelson-Sierra Fall 2:03
Julian Lizardo Sacramento
Cesar Guzman-W Hills F 1:47
Weston Coble-Chabot
Jacob Joseph-Modesto

141
Wayne Joint-West Hills 5-2
Wyatt Carter-Modesto
Abraham Cerda-Fresn F 3:54
Salaham Farukh-Sierra
Nik Oba Santa-Rosa Default
Talon Niim- Sacramento
Victor Alonso-Gil-S Ros F 2:43
Andrew Edwards-Skyline
Will Torres-West Hills

149
Anthony Nunes-Modest 10-2
Nathan Vasquez-Skyline
Matthew Arias-Fresno DQ
Chase Mirelez-Modesto
Phillip Arroyo-West Hills 8-2
Jacob Benson-Shasta
Adrian Rangel-Chabot 19-4
Joseph Insalaco-Sierra
Gabriel Fialho-Sac 12-2
Hamzeh Bakir-Skyline

157
Jackson Morgan-Fresno Deft
Noha Cortez-Fresno
Kendall Frank Sacram Deft
Ethan Boyd-Sacramento
Willy Lamacchia-Skyline Forfe
Carlos Mesa-Sierra
Devonya Kee-West Hills 8-6
Thomas Venezia-Skyline
Horeb Francisco-Modesto

165
Roman Mendez-Fresno 3-2
Jon Hernandez-Sacramento
Hector Alatorre-W Hill F 2:09
Isaiah Castro-Sierra
Jake Grover-Sierra Fall :24
Elias McAtee-Santa Rosa
Ezekiel Lara-Skyline Defalt
Alex Olivia-S J Delta

174
Jake Prudek-Fresno Default
Reymundo Raiz-Fresno
Gabriel Guzman-Sierra F 2:36
Benicio Martinez-Sacrament
Jacob Turner-Modesto 20-7
Bryant Bartlett-Shasta
Mojo Sarsour-Skyline Defalt
Francisco Espinoza-Chabot

184
Justin Tripp-W Hills SV 1 5-3
Luke Myer- Fresno
Justin Sierra Sacramento 11-1
Logan Colbert-Modesto
Andrew Hamant Sac T B 1 5-2
Michael Negrete-Sierra
Caden Noha-Shasta Default
Alan Marquez-Shasta

197
Keven Fernandez-Modest 7-2
Joel Lopez-Shasta
Rudy Garcia-Fresno Fall 1:18
Denzel Mabry-Sacramento
Maximo Fernandez-Lass Deft
Frankie Pomilia-Santa Rosa
Gabriel Hindman-Sierra 9-2
Diego Hernandez-Skyline
Javante Gregoire-S Ros F 1:34
Gabriel Ortega-S J Delta

285
Carson Hatch-Modesto 5-3
Javier Martinez-Fresno
Brandon Reed-Skyline 3-0
Felipe Dematos-S J Delta
Garret Hicks Modesto-Forfeit
Daniel Jacuinde-West Hills
Eli Mandujano-Shasta 8-3
Jonathan Hider-Chabot
Luke Christensen-Sac F 5:55
Jose Flores Flores-Shasta

Team Scores
1 Fresno 311
2 Modesto 195.5
3 Sacramento 190
4 West Hills 144
5 Sierra 133
6 Skyline 83.5
7 Shasta 59
8 Santa Rosa 49
9 S J Delta 46.5
10 Lassen 42.5
11 Chabot 19.5

141-Wayne Joint-West Hills, Lemoore
Most Outstanding Wrestler

2022 South Regional
December 3, 2022 East Los Angeles College

125
Christopher Calderon-MS 8-0
Christopher Betancourt-Mt S
Alexis Tellez-Rio Hondo Forf
Blade Owens-Victor Valley
Dylan Atherton-R Hon F 6:37
Damien Lopez-Santa Ana
Gabe Rivera-Cuesta 9-6
Diego Jasso-Cerritos
Ethan Rider-Bakfld F 2:00
Denzel Ayala-Palomar

133
David Sanchez-Mt. SAC 13-7
Anthony Pererya-Cerritos
Jose Cisneros-Vic Valley 7-6
Devin Martinez-Rio Hondo
Derrek Alcantar Bakfld Forfeit
Raul Jimenez-Cerritos
Owen Wilson-Palomar F 1:09
Trevor Wilson-Victor Valley
Nathan Ramirez-San Ana 8-2
C J Howard-Palomar

141
Mario De La Torres-Cerrit 7-0
Riley Fitzsimmons-Mt. SAC
Jason Valencia Mt. SAC F 1:29
Zack Zernk-Moorpark
Howard Tieu-Rio Hondo 6-0
Ethan Irizarry-East LA
Dustin Riquelme Palomar For
Cael Cooper-Cuesta
Richard Martinez-Bak F 2:52
Anthony Diaz-East LA

149
Billt Looney-Mt. SAC 5-3
Felix Osorio-Cerritos
Aidan Hansen-Moorpark TF
Zeke Hueter-Santa Ana
Dorian Parker-Palomar 6-5
Caleb Blasius-Victor Valley
James Juarez-Bakersfield 7-6
Joshua Padilla-East LA
Erinn Jackson-Moorpa F 1:57
Nati Morales-De La Vega Cue

157
J J Gutierrez-Paloma SV 11-10
Marcus Lobato-Mt. SAC
Trevor Thompson-Cerrit 11-5
Jonathan Aldana-Santa Ana
Cael Garriott-Cerritos 10-5
James O'Neal Jr.-Victor Valley
Derrick Meza-Rio Hondo Forf
Devin Saldana-Bakersfield
Carlos Martinez-Bakfld 6-0
Randy Lockwood-Palomar

165
Armando Murillo Cerri SV 5-3
Jesus Gutierrez-Victor Valley
Gracen Hayes-Bakfld F 4:21
Caidence Turne- Mt. SAC
Armando Renteria Moor 11-3
Hassan Alexander-Palomar
Quinn Patrick-Cuesta F 5:34
Anthony Yerena-Rio Hondo

174
Luke Combs-Bakersfield 11-4
Stone Robledo-Cerritos
Daniel Hernandez-Palo F 4:15
Riley Lowery-Cuesta
Sergio Gutierrez-San Ana Deft
Steven Ceja-East LA
Anthony Hidalgo-R Ho SV 3-1
Landen DeGennaro-Moorpar
Jesse Herrera-Mt. SAC 14-5
Edward Saldana-Victor Valley

184
Jakob Hand-Mt. SAC 3-2
Celso Silva-Palomar
Rafeal Guerra-Cerritos F 2:14
Leon Tippett-Cuesta
Jeremiah Juarez-R Hon F 1:58
Troy Garza-East LA
Joseph Robles-V Valley F 1:44
Herberth Challapa-East LA

197
Malachi Lyles Cerritos-2-1 OT
Nate Kendricks-Mt. SAC
Armando Medrano-BaTB 5-4
Devin Peries-East LA
Izcali Rub Morfin-S A F 2:07
Jesus Rodrigue-Palomar
Ricardo Cardona-Rio Hondo

285
Corbin Hayes-Bakersfield 9-3
Kobe Pablo-Cerritos
Jesse Garcia-Mt. SAC 5-3
Angelo Franco-Victor Valley
Emitt Mercado-R Hondo Forf
Frank Herrera-Victor Valley
Javier Montoya-Palomar 10-2
Sherman Barney-Cuesta
Thomas Phillips-Rio Hondo

Team Scores
1 Mt. SAC   295
2 Cerritos   268
3 Palomar   133.5
4 Bakersfield   128.5
5 Victor Valley   125.5
6 Rio Hondo   119
7 Santa Ana   69
8 Moorpark   57.5
9 East LA   57
10 Cuesta   51

2023 North Regional
December 2, 2023 Modesto Junior College

125
Tallon Chambers-Fresno 10-2
Dakota Sanders-Redwoods
Abram Granados-Fresno Def
Scotty Moore-Skyline
Danny Arellano-Sierra 12-6
Joseph Mills-Modesto
Jesus Juarez-Sierra F 4:48
Fernando Becerra-S J Delta
Isaac Weaver Redwoods F :46
Brandon Esparza-Santa Rosa

133
Adrian Chavez-Fresno 15-5
Ben Quilpa-Sacramento
Dustin Merlos-Lassen F 1:56
Marcus Mirelos-S J Delta
Nick Jimenez-Sierra F 4:02
Klay Browning-Sierra
Jordan Robinson-Chabot 10-7
William Smith-Redwoods
Omar Green-Redwoods F :45
Rigo Sosa-Santa Rosa

141
Matthew Terrence-Fre F 6:04
Ahmaad Lewis-Sacramento
Kymani Capri-Redwoods 11-1
Emmanuel Plascencia-Fresno
Azim Azimy-Chabot 16-15
Zane Kowalkowski-Shasta
Aceyn Myer-Shasta 19-3
Jake Butler-Santa Rosa
Noah Abel-Sierra F 2:04
Hashir Arif-S J Delta

149
Anthony Nunes-Modesto 5-2
Matthew Arias-Fresno
Ammar Khan-Sacrame F 1:08
Jason Belleji-S J Delta
Kevin Goodman Chabot 9-8
Tobias Robert Lasron-Lassen
Joseph Insalaco-Sierra F :47
David Sypnicki-Santa Rosa
Jacob Benson-Shasta TF 17-0
Neil Jefferson-Redwoods

157
Chase Mirelez-Modesto 12-2
Nicholas Dehart-Fresno
Nathan Vasquez-Skyline 10-6
Alfredo Trejo-Mendoza Sacra
Caden Diamond-Sacra F 6:22
Talan Lomeli-Shasta
Bryan Fraser-Chabot F 2:30
Fernando O'Brien-Modesto
Zackary Morgan-S Rosa Forfei
Not Given

165
Joshua Thomas-Sierra Defaul
Ethan Boyd-Sacramento
Isaac Romero Martinez M 4-2
Jamison McNight-Shasta
Ben Montez-Fresno Forfeit
Thomas Venezia-Skyline
Anthony Smith-Redwd F 1:30
Will Smith-Skyline
Robin Oxlaj-Santa Ro F 3:18
Richard Torrez-Modesto

174
Andrew Hamant-Sacram 10-4
Efrain Duenas-Modesto
Marcos Gamez-Fresno 9-8
Jeffery Skyrud-Redwoods
Luke Peasley Skyline 8-6
Michael Negrete-Sierra
Caden Noha-Shasta TF 15-0
William Westbrock-Sant Rosa
Jesus Anguiano-Sa Rosa 12-3
Diego Hernandez-Skyline

184
Adrain C-Morales-Sacr F 1:29
Bryan Thorne-Skyline
Adrian Garcia-Fresno F 1:27
Juan Magallon-Redwoods
Feroze Azimy-Chabot 6-4
Robert De La Torre-S J Delta
Ricky McCulloch-Sierra 11-10
Andrew Zarate-Lassen
Andres Rodrigues-Sacra F :31
Riddoc Collins-Modesto

197
Etan Birch-Sacramento F 1:29
Rayhan Jaleel-Santa Rosa
Callan Ivy-Chabot F 2:13
Frankie Pomilia IV-Santa Rosa
Prince Gainous-Lassen 13-10
Gilbert Solorio-Modesto
Marco Silva-Fresno F 5 :16
Kale Krellar-Lassen
Benn Rieder-Redwood F 7:00
Malik Lugar-Sierra

285
Isaiah Perez-Chabot 6-0
Evan Glines-Sacramento
Cody Ruiz-Modesto F 2:41
Gerard Marshall-Redwoods
Chris Bayne-Fresno F 1:33
Haizi Mikbell-S J Delta
Jorge Quintero-S J Delt F 2:56
Mahamed Mukoma-Shasta
Fritz McIntosh-Shasta F 1:44
Tully Meyer-Santa Rosa

Team Scores
1	Fresno	226
2	Sacramento	224.5
3	Modesto	128
4	Redwoods	111.5
5	Sierra	96.5
6	Chabot	82
7	Skyline	72
8	S J Delta	54
9	Shasta	47
10	Santa Rosa	45.5
11	Lassen	42

2023 South Regional
December 2, 2023 Palomar College

125
Christopher-Calderon M.SA F
Adrian Limon-Mt. SAC
Dylan Atherton R Hondo 19-1
Cameron Fernando-Morpark
Jacob Benavidez-Rio Ho 10-4
Carlos Garcia-Cerritos
Andres Cervantes-Cuest 19-3
Logan Rubio-Santa Ana
Richard Martinez-Bakfld 21-3
Tayari Tye Victor-Valley 21-5

133
Devin Martinez-Rio Hon 10-4
Derreck Alcantar-Bakfled
Pedro Lacerda-Mt, SAC Forf
Emilio Medino-Mt. SAC
Gio Urbieta-West-Hills Defaul
Elijah Martinez-West Hills
Makoa Shefte-Santa Ana 9-0
Artemis Shmuel-Santa Ana
John Islas East-LA MD 17-7
Matthew Alarcon-Vic Valley

141
Evan Roy Victor Valley-Defaul
Zachary Parker-Mt SAC
Finnegan Long Rio-Hondo 6-1
Michael Padilla-East LA
Elijah Nero-Palomar 17-10
Jake Topartzer-Cerritos
Kimo Servino-Cerritos F 2:25
Howard Tieu-Rio Hondo
Albert Mechama-MP 13-1
Markis Gonzales-Bakerfld

149
Mario DeLaTorre-Cerrito 10-7
Brandon Bollinger-Vict Valley
Brian Gieger-Mt. SAC 6-5
Jasper Centeno-Cerritos
Dorian Parker Palomar Defaul
Hector Ramirez-East LA
Luciano EsoldoVict Valley 8-6
Jose Lira-Santa Ana
Ian Rodriguez Cuesta F 2:58
Estanislao Arevalo-Bakfld

157
Alex Ramirez-Mt. SAC F :57
Caolite Drury-Cerritos
Anthony Perez-Cerritos 20-4
Gabe Carrillo-Moorpark
Joshua Paddilla-Eas LA F 2:23
Zeke Hueter-Santa Ana
Jesus Navarrete Bakfld Defaul
Devonya Kee-West Hills
Silas Brailey-Cuesta TF 18-3
Brady Svetich-Cuesta

165
Edward Ramirez-Sant Ana 7-4
Adrian Juarez-Bakersfield
Armando-Renteria-MP F 2:07
Cael Garriott-Cerritos
Caidence Turner-Mt. SAC 7-2
Joseph Estrada-Rio Hondo
Armando Vega-Bakfld 5-2
Israel Manriquez-Victo Valley
Degan Morlan-Mrpark F 2:16
Alan Marquez-West Hills

174
Nathan Cruz-Mt SAC MD 8-0
Jazziel Perez-Moorpark
D J Weimer-Palomar TF 18-1
Joshua Shepard-Bakersfield
Juan Nuno-West Hills SV 4-1
Sergio Gutierrez-Santa And
Anthony Hidalgo-Rio Hon Def
Zach Harkey-Cerritos
Reily Lowry-Cuesta F :30
Joseph Castro-Victor Valley

184
R Roman-Amador Bakfld 19-4
Ben Setum-Cerritos
Isaac Villalobos-Bakfld F 7:00
Rabih Badrani-Palomar
Anthony Incantalupo-R H FF
Jesse Herrera-Mt. SAC
Danny Cox-Palomar
Andres Carrillo-Santa Ana
Carson Brander-Cuesta F 2:51
Zackery Leon-Victor Valley

197
Christian Davidson-Cu F 2:33
Armando Sandoval-Cerritos
Uriel Vasquez-Bakersfield 5-3
Isaac Lopez-Mt. SAC
Miles Kline-Moorpark F 1:34
David Calix-Santa Ana
Liam Clark-Palomar F 5:16
Anthony Deleon-Victor Valley
Brandon Garduno-R H F 2:38
Pedro Valdez-East LA

285
Kobe Pablo-Cerritos 7-2
Dib Sawaya-Mt. SAC
Taven Avila-West Hills F 5:58
Angelo Franco Victor Valley
Mustafa Farha Palomar 4-1
Dylan Avila Santa Ana
Joseph Nava Santa Ana 7-0
Brayan Macias Palomar
Joseph R Gonzalez M P F :53
Alonzo Cardona Victor Valley

Team Scores
1 Mt. SAC   223.5
2 Cerritos   170
3 Bakersfield   135.5
4 Rio Hondo   111.5
5 Palomar   109
6 Santa Ana   91.5
7 Moorpark   87.5
8 Victor Valley 86.5
9 West Hills   55.5
10 Cuesta   49.5
11 East LA   34

2024 North Regional
December 7, 2024 Santa Rosa Junior College

125
Zane Cerda-Fresno F 6:28
Billy Thornton-Sacramento
Dakota Sanders-Redwd F:45
Daniel Arellano Sacramento
Eczequiel Jaurrieta-Fres F:56
Derek Ruffin-Santa Rosa
Jesus Juarez-Sierra SV 1:56
Shevy Landis-ku-Lassen
Abdullah Noori-Chabot 15-0
Cristian Cruz-Skyline

133
Dustin Merlos-Lassen 15-1
Marcus Mireles-S J Delta
Ben Jones-Sacramento 15-10
Zeth Cerda-Fresno
Erickson Edpao-S Rosa F 1:26
Rylan Mitchell-S J Delta
Eben Jones-Sierra F:51
Aaron Ly-Chabot
Omar Green Redwood F 1:14
Marcus Mullin-Thomas Skylie

141
Abraham Cerda-Fresno 8-0
Talon Niimi-Sacramento
Azim Azimy-Chabot 7-2
Karmine Berndt-Santa Rosa
Ali Hamzia-Sana Rosa Forfeit
Abriel Padilla-Modesto
Noah Abel-Shasta MD 11-2
Aceyn Meyer-Shasta
Owen Willis-Serra Injury
Alex Davidson-Lassen

149
James Wright-Fresno 13-2
Demarcus Turner-Modesto
Phu Le-Sacramento F 1:28
Tobias Robert-Larson -Lassen
Vicente Robarte-S Rosa 9-4
Brock Birkett-Sierra
Angel Anya-Lassen Injury
Zane Kowalkowski-Skylin 8-5
Esmatullah Sultani-Chabot

157
Islam Abdullaeu-Sierra 10-3
Noah Reynolds-Fresno
Quinten Maldanado-Del F:28
Talan Lomeli-Shasta
Caden Diamond Sacra F2:23
Ayden Marshall-Modesto
Ikaika Madayag-S Rosa Forf
Abdul Meskienyar-Chabot
Leo Rubino-Iobue-Sky F 2:33
Frank Valente-Redwoods

165
Max McWilliams-Fresn TB2-1
Isaac Romero-Martinez-Mod
Khalid Ghani-Modesto 13-4
Munther Saleh Sacramento
Sawyer Casarez-Shasta 11-4
Luke Peasley-Skyline
Conor Boyle-Lassen 18-3
Kyle Hayes-Sierra
Amrit Cheema-S Rosa 19-3
Julian Hernandez-Chabot

174
Jake Prudek-Fresno 3-2
Fazal Mohammad-Chabot
Maksim Sherstney-Sier F2:49
Rosalio Leal-Modesto
Zack Morgan-Santa Rosa 13-6
Kelly Little-Sacramento
Justin Barillas-S J Delta F 2:03
Brian Mills-Lassen

184
Logan Leckie-Sacramento 7-4
Adrian Perez-Pulido-Modesto
Andrew Zarate-Lassen 4-2
Ricardo Ugalde-Fresno
Francisco Espinoza-Cha F6:03
Jesus Anguiano-Santa Rosa
Luke Harrison-Sacramen 15-2
Vince Marin S J Delta
Mathew Casado-Sierra F 1:40
Brian Campana Skyline

197
Rayhan Jaleel Santa Rosa Inj
Almazbekov Abodym-Chabot
Vaea salt-Sacramento MD 8-0
Prince Gainoue-Lassen
Juan Luquin-Fresno Forfeit
Joe Ellis-Santa Rosa
Chris Wells-Lassen F 2:28
Erick Lopez alecio Modesto
Garrison Palmer-Shasta Injur
James Bonton Sierra

285
Joseph Alaniz-Fresno Forfeit
Javier Martinez-Fresno
Cody Ruiz-Modesto F 1:45
Kenrick Salcido-Sacramento
Bryce Meggers-Sierra Forfeit
Sepehr Hojati-Sierra
Cesar Lopez-Lassen F 2:28
Aiden Riddleberger-S Rosa
Angel Blanco-Skyline 17-5
Jacob Aho-Skyline

Team Scores
1 Fresno   257.5
2 Sacramento   192.5
3 Modesto   140
4 Santa Rosa   128
5 Sierra   106
6 Lassen   106
7 Chabot   84
8 S J Delta   59.5
9 Shasta   48.5
10 Redwoods   30
11 Skyline   11

Coaches
Fresno-Paul Keysaw
Sacramento-Marques Gales
Modesto-Jesse Vasquez
Santa Rosa-Fred Duerr
Sierra-Don Martinez
Lassen-Lonnie Nalls
Chabot-Michael Grijalba
S J Delta-Nike Sander
Shasta-Erin Raza
Redwoods-Brandon Benvenuti
Skyline-James Haddon

2024 South Regional
December 7, 2024 East Los Angeles College

125
Jimmy Reyes-Lemoore 9-4
Jesse Hernandez-Cerritos
Caden Hanover-Palomar 18-4
Dominic Marquez-Cuesta
Rylan Madrid-Mt. SAC 16-0
Isaac Antunez-Santa Ana
Blade Owens-Vic Valley F2:53
Joshuah Valdivia-Lemoore
Isaiah Cruz-Cerritos 4-1
Devan Guiterrez-Bakersfield

133
Jason Saenz-Mt. SAC 7-4
Mason Carrillo-Moorpark
Ricardo Solorio-S Ana F 2:31
Andrew Diaz-Victor Valley
Gio Urbieta-Lemoore 13-4
Makai Ito-Palomar
Daiman Rodriguez-Cue Med
David Govea-East LA
Elijah Flores-Cerritos F 1:36
Aaron Lopez-Santa Ana

141
Diego Peraza-Palomar 13-7
Yoshia Funakoshi-Cerritos
Chris Guerrero Vic Valley 3-2
Aldo Quintero-Mt. SAC
Shawn Torres-R Hondo Med
Angel Salgado-Victor Valley
Brendon Ko-Bakersfield 14-9
Adam Duong-Rio Hondo
Trevor Wagstaff-S Ana 6-1
Casar Guzman-Lemoore

149
Alireza Kaveh-Santa Ana 23-6
Brian Geiger-Mt. SAC
Michael Williams-M SAC 12-1
Nicholas Rodrigues-Palomar
Isaia Tuimavave-Bakfld Forf
Larry Cruz-Rio Hondo
Mattias Valdez-V Valley F2:45
Izaac Olivas-Lemoore
Luke VanBrabant-Cue F 3:41
Imanuel Flores-Cerritos

157
Maxximus Martinez-M S 12-1
Joe Anthony Perez-Palomar
Grant Eklund-Cuesta TF 16-0
Nicolas Pham-Cerritos
James Juarez-Bakersfield Forf
Giovanni Ruiz Bakersfield
Jacob Moreo-Rio Hondo Forf
Cory Flores-Santa Ana
Andrew Longoria-R Ho F 6:01
Luciano Esoldo Victor Valley

165
Jack Estevez Mt. SAC 3-1
Preston Scharf-Cuesta
Philip Arroyo-Lemoore
Marshall Beecham-Cuesta
Ricardo Valdez-Vic Valley Forf
Matthew York-Rio Hondo
D J Weimer-Palomar TF 15-0
Armando Vega Bakersfield
Kevin Casillas Santa Ana 9-3
Mario Rodas-Portillo Bakfld

174
Tyler Hanna-Cerritos 6-2
Jakob Hand Mt. SAC
Javier Montes-Mt. SAC 10-1
Steven Ceja-Rio Hondo
Aiden Valencia-Vic Valley Inj
Adrian Juarez-Bakersfield
Danny Cox-Palomar F 2:47
Joey Clark-Lemoore
Edward Saldana-V Valley 9-8
Caden Terry-Moorpark

184
Roman Loya Mt. SAC F2:28
Ivan Natceli Palomar
Farzad Hashimi-Cerritos 14-5
Robert Felipe-Lemoore
Miguel Montano-Bakfld Med
Frankie Stevenson-Vic Valley
Ben Stum-Cerritos Injury
Bobby Ramirez-Rio Hondo
Rabih Badrani-Palomar 8-1
Benjamin Green-Cuesta

197
Mo Talebi-Mt. SAC TF 19-4
Dylan Henry-Palomar
Chance Evans-Cuesta F 3:51
Angel Cervantes-Bakersfield
Jaremiah Juarez-R Hond 15-4
Nelson Ramirez-Cerritos
Jakar Carter-Palomar F 1:57
Joseph Robles Victor Valley
Wolfgang Wimmer-MP F 1:09
Juan Pablo-Lemoore

285
Julian Bilezikjian-Ri H SV 6-3
Jonathan Garcia-Bakersfield
Xavier Moran-Lemoore F :43
Mustafa Farha-Palomar
Isaac Lopez-Mt. SAC F 2:58
Diego Flores-Cerritos
Daniel Jacuinde-Lemoore 4-0
Alonzo Cardona-Victor Valley
Emiliano Flores-East LA SV4-1
Raymond Gonzalez-East LA

Team Scores
1 Mt. SAC   245.5
2 Palomar   169
3 Cerritos   120.5
4 Victor Valley   109
5 Cuesta   104
5 Lemoore   104
7 Bakersfield   93.5
8 Rio Hondo   93
9 Santa Ana   60
10 Moorpark   25
11 East LA   5

Coaches
Mt, SAC-David Rivera
Palomar-Timothy Box
Cerritos-Donny Garriott
Victor Valley-Randy Humphrey
Cuesta-Joe Dansby
Lemoore-Marcio Botellio
Bakersfield-Marcos Austin
Rio Hondo-Mike Tellez
Santa Ans-Vince Silva
Moorpark-Lindley Kistler
East LA-Miguel Soto

8-Time CCCAA Coach of the Year-Head Coach Paul Keysaw and Assistant Coach of the Year- George Moreno being Honored Both of Fresno City College

Coach Pfutzenreuter with State Championship trophy

HARRY KANE
Bakersfield College First Wrestling Coach

GARY deBEAUBIEN
Head Coach Santa Ana College

BILL MUSICK - Fresno
Coach of the Year
Bill Musick in 18 years has guided his FCC wrestling teams to three state championships. 2 second place finishes and 3 third place finishes. FCC has won 10 regional titles. 14 conference titles. Overall reccord 202-48-4.

THE HISTORY OF
CALIFORNIA COMMUNITY COLLEGE WRESTLING
1957 - 2024

CREDITS:

John Sachs	Moorpark Wrestling
Nick Ellis	Redwoods Wrestling
Bill Kalivas	San Joaquin Delta Wrestling
George Moreno	Tom Hazell
Amateur Wrestling News	Ken Bos
Bakersfield California	Gary deBeaubien
USA Wrestling	Jeff Smith
Wrestling International News	Mark Austin
California Wrestler	Al Fontes
Newspapers.com	Dennis Bardsley
CCCAA Wrestling	John Van Gaston
Lassen Wrestling	

Special thanks to the people who took the time to get back to me with some type of help.

Please send corrections and/or additions to:
Mike Stricker
5417 Brigadoon Lane
Bakersfield, CA. 93312-1954
mstricker1945@gmail.com

DISCLAIMER: The accuracy of the information here is limited to the accuracy of the sources and the recording of the sources.

Other books by Mike Stricker

The History of Central Section Wrestling (and more) 1952-2007
The History of Central Section Wrestling (and more) 2007-2020

To order:
Email: orders@janawaypublishing.com
Website: www.janawaypublishing.com
Phone: (805) 925-1952